Book of Origins
Creation Stories From Around the World

edited by W.B. Vogt

Front Cover and Spine Art Credits:
Oil Painting Frame
Credit: Wellcome Collection. CC BY 4.0
https://wellcomecollection.org/works/p9q7v3y7
https://creativecommons.org/licenses/by/4.0
God creates man in the Garden of Eden. Coloured etching, 17
Credit: Wellcome Collection. CC BY 4.0
https://wellcomecollection.org/works/khww8x63
https://creativecommons.org/licenses/by/4.0

Back Cover Art Credits:
God creating the starring firmament, Sun and Moon.
Credit: Wellcome Collection. CC BY 4.0
https://wellcomecollection.org/works/vcsmx3s2
https://creativecommons.org/licenses/by/4.0

 Flower Leaf Books

Copyright Notice
The source texts on which this work is based
are in the public domain in the United States.
This derived work, compilation,
edits, updated translations, accompanying text and cover design
© copyright 2019 by Cyrus Media Inc. All rights reserved.

ISBN: 978-1-7343000-0-0

Contents

1	Out of Chaos	9
2	Divine Evolutions	35
3	Sons of God	43
4	Generations of Creation	73
5	Mysteries of Reason	107
6	Sacred Lotus	163
7	Eastern Star	187
8	Northern Heroes	215
9	Glimmering Waters	233
10	Nature's Spirit	255
11	Of Anahuac	293
12	Land Without Cold	313

Introduction

The following pages span several thousand years of human history and represent the hard work of numerous authors, scribes, and translators. At no other time in history has such a vast expanse of cultural knowledge and wisdom been available to a single reader. We live in an exciting time.

The goal of this book is to present, in readable English text, some of the greatest stories ever told—stories that, to the cultures in which they were originally shared, were important enough to pass on for generations, to write down, and in some cases to literally *set in stone*. To this end, each work presented herein has been updated and edited with great care. The intent in editing these texts was to achieve higher *readability*, and to create a book composed of some of the most valuable and cherished public domain translations that is consistent and readable, with updated language. Most translators from the times the translations were produced used archaic words and an older style of English. Here we present these groundbreaking works in what we hope the reader will find to be an approachable, accessible form. Some key features include:

- A narrow topical focus, including only texts relating to the origins of humanity and the universe.

- Updated, easier to understand English translations, edited for clarity and readability.

- More consistent punctuation than the original texts collectively provided.

- Elimination of copious footnotes and front-matter, allowing the texts to stand on their own.

- References to all original texts *where the text is used* for easy comparison and access to the original works.

- Two indexes: An index of sources texts, and a separate comprehensive index, giving the reader full freedom to study and cross reference topics across all sources.

Another key aim in compiling this book was to *respect the stories and those cultures from which they originated*. Care was taken to avoid inserting new interpretations or meanings, and comments of translators or writers relating the stories of these cultures that were contemptuous towards their subjects have been carefully eliminated so as to leave the story intact, but eliminate the negative biases and attitudes of the person communicating it. (There was in actuality little need for such changes, as largely the translators and/or those relaying the information held in high regard the works and cultures that they dedicated their time to.)

This work would not have been possible without the existence of modern computers and the Internet, and the valuable treasure-troves of public domain texts that have been placed on the web by numerous hardworking and passionate people. Projects like the Internet Archive (archive.org), Project Gutenberg (gutenberg.org), and the Sacred Texts Archive (sacred-texts.com) are a gift to humanity that we should cherish, promote, support, and defend. The original works on which this derivative work is based can be obtained from the above websites for comparison or further research.

We hope that this book will pick up where these and many other sources leave off—not stopping at just presenting a text, but attempting to present it in the best possible way so that you as the reader can get the maximum possible benefit from each work.

Chapter 1

Out of Chaos

Marduk 1

Enuma Elish. Compilation. Updated and edited version based on the translations by Leonard William King and E.A. Wallis Budge.

Tablet 1

1 When the heavens above were yet unnamed, 2 And the earth beneath did not yet have a name, 3 And Apsu, the oldest of beings, who created them, 4 And chaos, Tiamat, the mother of them both, 5 Their waters were mingled together, 6 And no field had been formed—no marsh could be seen;

7 When of the gods, none had been called into being, 8 No name had been recorded, and no destinies had been ordained. 9 Then the gods were created in the midst of heaven. 10 Lahmu and Lahamu were called into being [or "made to shine"]. 11 They increased in stature together. 12 Then Anshar and Kishar were created, and others besides them.

13 Long were the days, the years increased. 14 Then Anu, their son, came into being. 15 The god Anshar made his eldest son Anu in his own image. 16 And the god Anu created Nudimmud (Ea) in the image of himself. 17 Nudimmud was the first among his fathers, 18 Abounding in all wisdom, the deep thinker, the orator. 19 He excelled in strength above his father, 20 and was unrivaled among the gods. 21 Thus the gods were established.

22 But Tiamat was still troubled, 23 Her belly was stirred up to its uttermost depths. 24 In disorder [...] 25 Apsu could not diminish their conflict. 26 And Tiamat roared [...] 27 She conquered, and their deeds [...] 28 Their way was evil [...]

29 Then Apsu, the father of the great gods, 30 Shouted out and summoned Mummu, his minister, and said: 31 "Oh Mummu, my minister who

makes my spirit rejoice, 32 "Come, to Tiamat we will go!"

33 So they went, and laid down facing Tiamat, 34 They consulted on a plan with regard to the gods—their children. 35 Apsu opened his mouth, 36 And to Tiamat, the glistening one, he said: 37 "[...] their way [...], 38 By day I find no peace, by night I have no rest. 39 But I will put an end to their ways, I will sweep them away, 40 There will be lamentation, and then we will rest again in peace."

41 When Tiamat heard these words, 42 she was stirred up to wrath and shrieked to her husband, 43 ...grievously, she raged all alone. 44 She uttered a curse, and to Apsu she said: 45 "What we have made, we will destroy. 46 Their way will be made difficult, and then we will rest again in peace."

47 Mummu answered, and counseled Apsu, 48 and hostile to the gods was the counsel Mummu gave: 49 "Come, their way is strong, but you will destroy it; 50 Then by day you will find peace, and by night you will have rest."

51 When Apsu heard him, his face grew bright, 52 Since they were planning evil against the gods, his children. 53 Mummu embraced his neck... 54 He took him on his knee, he kissed him, 55 They planned the cursing in the assembly, 56 They repeated the curses to the gods their eldest sons. 57 The gods made answer [...] 58 They began a lamentation...

59 Endowed with understanding, the prudent god, the exalted one, 60 Ea, who knows everything that is, searched out their plan. 61 He brought it to a stop, he made the form of everything to stand still. 62 He recited a cunning incantation, very powerful and holy.

[63 to 108 are fragments: [...] misery [...] the god Anu, [...] an avenger [...] and he will confound Tiamat. [...] he [...] for ever. [...] the evil, [...] he spoke: "[...] your [...] he has conquered and [...] he weeps and sits in tribulation [...] of fear, [...] we will not rest in peace."[...] Apsu is laid waste(?), [...] and Mummu, who were taken captive, in [...] you did, [...] let us rest in peace [...] they will strike [...] let us rest in peace [...] you will take vengeance for them, [...] into the storm you will [...] And Tiamat heard the word of the bright god, and said: "[...] you will entrust! let us wage war!" [...] the gods in the midst of [...] for the gods did she create.]

109 They banded themselves together and at the side of Tiamat they advanced; 110 They were furious, they devised plots without resting night and day. 111 They prepared for battle, fuming and raging; 112 They set the battle in array, they uttered cries of hostility,

113 Ummu-Khubur, who formed all things, 114 Set up the unrivaled weapon, she spawned giant serpents, 115 Sharp of tooth, and merciless of fang; 116 She filled their bodies with venom instead of blood. 117 Grim,

monstrous serpents, she clothed with terror, 118 With splendor she decked them, she crafted them of lofty stature, 119 so that fright and horror might overcome him that looked upon them. 120 Their bodies reared up and none could withstand their attack.

121 She set up vipers, and dragons, and the god Lakhamu, 122 the Whirlwind, the ravening Dog, the Scorpion-man, 123 the mighty Storm-wind, the Fish-man, the horned Beast. 124 They bore cruel weapons, and did not flinch from battle. 125 Most mighty were Tiamat's commands, they could not be resisted, 126 Thus she created eleven monsters of this kind.

127 Among the gods, her first-born son who had collected her company, 128 That is to say, Kingu, she set on high, she made him greatest among them, 129 Leader of the hosts in battle, disposer of the troops, 130 To give the battle-signal, to advance to the attack. 131 He who in the battle is the master of the weapon, 132 To him she entrusted; in costly apparel she made him sit, saying: 133 "I have uttered the spell for you, in the assembly of the gods I have raised you to power. 134 I have filled your hand with the sovereignty of the whole company of the gods. 135 May you be magnified, you who are my chosen spouse, 136 May the Anunnaki make great your renown over all of them."

137 She gave him the Tablet of Destinies, on his breast she fastened it, saying: 138 "As for you, your command will not fall empty, whatever goes forth from your mouth will be established."

139 Now Kingu, having been exalted, having received the power of Anu, 140 Decreed the destinies for the gods his sons, saying: 141 "Let the opening of your mouth quench the Fire god; 142 He who is glorious in battle and is most mighty, will do great deeds."

Tablet 2

1 Tiamat made solid that which she had crafted, 2 She bound the gods her children with evil. 3 To avenge Apsu, Tiamat planned evil, 4 But how she had collected her forces, the god [...] to Ea divulged.

5 As Ea listened to the story, 6 He was deeply afflicted and he sat in sorrow.

7 The days went by, and his anger was softened, 8 And to the dwelling of Anshar his father he went his way. 9 He went and standing before Anshar, the father who begat him, 10 All that Tiamat had plotted he repeated to him, 11 Saying, "Tiamat our mother has conceived a hatred for us, 12 With all her force she raged, full of wrath. 13 All the gods have turned to her, 14 All those, whom you created, they go at her side. 15 They have joined forces and at the side of Tiamat they advance; 16 "They are furious, they devise plots without resting night and day. 17 They prepare for battle, fuming and raging; 18 They have joined their forces and are making war.

19 "Ummu-Khubur, who formed all things, 20 has set up the unrivaled weapon, she has spawned giant serpents, 21 Sharp of tooth, and merciless of fang; 22 She has filled their bodies with venom instead of blood. 23 Grim, monstrous serpents, she has clothed with terror, 24 With splendor she has decked them, she has crafted them of lofty stature, 25 so that fright and horror might overcome him that looked upon them, 26 so that their bodies rear up, and none can withstand their attack.

27 "She set up vipers, and dragons, and the god Lakhamu, 28 the Whirlwind, the ravening Dog, the Scorpion-man, 29 the mighty Storm-wind, the Fish-man, the horned Beast. 30 They bore cruel weapons, and did not flinch from battle. 31 Most mighty were Tiamat's commands, they could not be resisted, 32 Thus she created eleven monsters of this kind.

33 "Among the gods, her first-born son who had collected her company, 34 That is to say, Kingu, she set on high, she made him greatest among them, 35 Leader of the hosts in battle, disposer of the troops, 36 To give the battle-signal, to advance to the attack. 37 He who in the battle is the master of the weapon, 38 To him she entrusted; in costly apparel she made him sit, saying: 39 'I have uttered the spell for you, in the assembly of the gods I have raised you to power. 40 I have filled your hand with the sovereignty of the whole company of the gods. 41 May you be magnified, you who are my chosen spouse, 42 May the Anunnaki make great your renown over all of them.'

43 She gave him the Tablet of Destinies, on his breast she fastened it, saying: 44 "As for you, your command will not fall empty, whatever goes forth from your mouth will be established."

45 Now Kingu, having been exalted, having received the power of Anu, 46 Decreed the destinies for the gods his sons, saying: 47 "Let the opening of your mouth quench the Fire god; 48 He who is glorious in battle and is most mighty, will do great deeds."

49 When Anshar heard how Tiamat was fiercely in revolt, 50 [...] he bit his lips, 51 [...], his mind was not at peace, 52 His [...], he made a bitter lamentation: 53 [...] battle, 54 [...] you [...]

55 And Anshar said to Ea, "You have defeated Mummu and Apsu, 56 but Tiamat has exalted Kingu, and where is one who can oppose her?"

[57 - 71 are lost]

72 Anshar then addressed his son Anu: 73 "... this is a difficulty, my warrior, whose strength is great and whose attack cannot be withstood, 75 Go and stand in the presence of Tiamat, 76 that her spirit may be quieted and her heart may be softened. 77 But if she will not listen to you, 78 speak our words to her so that she might be pacified."

79 Anu heard the order of his father Anshar. 80 He took the straight road to her, and hurried on the way

to her. 81 He came close to her, and searched out the plan of Tiamat. 82 But he could not prevail against her, so he turned back.

83 He (Anu) went to his father Anshar who created him, 84 and he spoke to him concerning Tiamat, saying: 85 "She laid hands upon me that withered me up."

86 Anshar was distressed, he looked down at the ground. 87 He turned pale; towards Ea he lifted up his head. 88 All the Anunnaki assembled at their posts. 89 They shut their mouths, they sat in lamentation, 90 saying, "Nowhere is there a god who can attack Tiamat. 91 He would not escape from Tiamat's presence with his life!"

92 The Lord Anshar, the Father of the gods, spoke majestically. 93 He lifted up his heart, and he addressed the Anunnaki, saying 94 "He whose strength is mighty will be our avenger. The [...] in the strife, Marduk the Hero."

96 Ea called Marduk to the place where he gave oracles. 97 Marduk came, and according to his heart he addressed him, 98 saying, "Oh Marduk, listen to the counsel and advice of your father. 99 You are the son who refreshes his heart. 100 Draw near and enter the presence of Anshar. 101 Stand there with joy, for when he looks upon you he will be at rest."

[104-109 are fragments: [...] an avenger [...] valiant [...] in the place of his decision [...] he spoke to him: [...] your father.]

110 "You are my son, who makes merciful his heart. 111 [...] to the battle you will draw near, 112 [...] whoever beholds you will have peace." 113 And the lord Marduk rejoiced at the word of his father, 114 and he drew near and stood before Anshar. 115 Anshar beheld him and his heart was filled with joy.

116 Anshar kissed Marduk's lips, and Anshar's fear was gone. Then Marduk said: 117 "My father, I will not let your words be overcome. 118 Let me go, that I may accomplish all that is in your heart. 119 Anshar, let not the word of your lips be overcome, 120 Let me go, that I may accomplish all that is in your heart.

121 Anshar replied: "What man is it, who has brought you forth to battle? 122 [...] Tiamat, who is a woman, pursues you with weapons. 123 Rejoice our hearts and make us glad. 124 You yourself will soon trample on the neck of Tiamat. 125 Rejoice our hearts and make us glad. 126 You yourself will soon trample on the neck of Tiamat."

127 "My son, who knows all things, 128 Pacify Tiamat with your holy incantation. 129 Set out on your way with have, 130 For your blood will not be poured out. You will return again."

131 The lord Marduk rejoiced at the words of his father, 132 His heart was lifted up, and to his father he spoke, saying: 133 "Oh Lord of the gods, Leader of the great gods, 134 should I, as your avenger, 135 conquer Tiamat and give you life, 136

Appoint an assembly, proclaim and magnify my position, 137 Sit down with Upshukkinaku joyfully, 138 Let me issue decrees by my word, even as you do. 139 Whatever I bring to pass, let it remain unaltered. 140 May the words of my mouth never be changed or made to fail."

Tablet 3

1 Anshar opened his mouth, and 2 to Gaga, his envoy, spoke the word: 3 "Gaga, who makes my spirit glad, 4 I am sending you to the gods Lakhmu and Lakhamu. 5 You must understand the intention of my heart. 6 [...] you will cause to be brought before you. 7 [...] all the gods.

8 "Let them make a council, let them sit down to a feast, 9 let them eat bread, let them mix wine, 10 that to Marduk, their avenger, they may issue decrees. 11 Go Gaga, and stand before them, 12 and repeat to them everything I am about to tell you, saying:

13 "Your son Anshar has sent me, 14 he has made known to me the intention of his heart.

15 "Tiamat our mother has conceived a hatred for us, 16 With all her force she raged, full of wrath. 17 All the gods have turned to her, 18 All those, whom you created, they go at her side. 19 They have joined forces and at the side of Tiamat they advance; 20 They are furious, they devise plots without resting night and day. 21 They prepare for battle, fuming and raging; 22 They have joined their forces and are making war.

23 "Ummu-Khubur, who formed all things, 24 has set up the unrivaled weapon, she has spawned giant serpents, 25 Sharp of tooth, and merciless of fang; 26 She has filled their bodies with venom instead of blood. 27 Grim, monstrous serpents, she has clothed with terror, 28 With splendor she has decked them, she has crafted them of lofty stature, 29 so that fright and horror might overcome him that looked upon them, 30 so that their bodies rear up, and none can withstand their attack.

31 "She set up vipers, and dragons, and the god Lakhamu, 32 the Whirlwind, the ravening Dog, the Scorpion-man, 33 the mighty Storm-wind, the Fish-man, the horned Beast. 34 They bore cruel weapons, and did not flinch from battle. 35 Most mighty were Tiamat's commands, they could not be resisted, 36 Thus she created eleven monsters of this kind.

37 "Among the gods, her first-born son who had collected her company, 38 That is to say, Kingu, she set on high, she made him greatest among them, 39 Leader of the hosts in battle, disposer of the troops, 40 To give the battle-signal, to advance to the attack. 41 He who in the battle is the master of the weapon, 42 To him she entrusted; in costly apparel she made him sit, saying: 43 'I have uttered the spell for you, in the assembly of the gods I have raised you to power. 44 I have filled your hand with the sovereignty

of the whole company of the gods. 45 May you be magnified, you who are my chosen spouse, 46 May the Anunnaki make great your renown over all of them.'

47 "She gave him the Tablet of Destinies, on his breast she fastened it, saying: 48 'As for you, your command will not fall empty, whatever goes forth from your mouth will be established.'

49 "Now Kingu, having been exalted, having received the power of Anu, 50 Decreed the destinies for the gods his sons, saying: 51 'Let the opening of your mouth quench the Fire god; 52 He who is glorious in battle and is most mighty, will do great deeds.'

53 "I sent Anu, but he could not prevail against her; 54 Ea was afraid and turned back. 55 But Marduk, your son, the envoy of the gods, has set out. 56 His heart has been stirred to oppose Tiamat. 57 He opened his mouth and spoke to me, saying: 58 'Should I, as your avenger, 59 conquer Tiamat and give you life, 60 Appoint an assembly, proclaim and magnify my position, 61 Sit down with Upshukkinaku joyfully, 62 Let me issue decrees by my word, even as you do. 63 Whatever I bring to pass, let it remain unaltered. 64 May the words of my mouth never be changed or made to fail.'

65 "Hurry, therefore, and swiftly decree for him the fate which you bestow, 66 that he may go and fight your strong enemy!"

67 Gaga left and hurried on his way 68 to the god Lakhmu and the goddess Lakhamu, the gods his fathers. Reverently, 69 He paid homage, and he kissed the ground at their feet. 70 He humbled himself; then he stood up and spoke to them, saying:

71 "Your son Anshar has sent me, 72 he has made known to me the intention of his heart.

73 "Tiamat our mother has conceived a hatred for us, 74 With all her force she raged, full of wrath. 75 All the gods have turned to her, 76 All those, whom you created, they go at her side. 77 They have joined forces and at the side of Tiamat they advance; 78 They are furious, they devise plots without resting night and day. 79 They prepare for battle, fuming and raging; 80 They have joined their forces and are making war.

81 "Ummu-Khubur, who formed all things, 82 has set up the unrivaled weapon, she has spawned giant serpents, 83 Sharp of tooth, and merciless of fang; 84 She has filled their bodies with venom instead of blood. 85 Grim, monstrous serpents, she has clothed with terror, 86 With splendor she has decked them, she has crafted them of lofty stature, 87 so that fright and horror might overcome him that looked upon them, 88 so that their bodies rear up, and none can withstand their attack.

89 "She set up vipers, and dragons, and the god Lakhamu, 90 the Whirlwind, the ravening Dog, the Scorpion-man, 91 the mighty Storm-wind, the Fish-man, the horned Beast. 92 They bore cruel weapons, and did not flinch

from battle. 93 Most mighty were Tiamat's commands, they could not be resisted, 94 Thus she created eleven monsters of this kind.

95 "Among the gods, her first-born son who had collected her company, 96 That is to say, Kingu, she set on high, she made him greatest among them, 97 Leader of the hosts in battle, disposer of the troops, 98 To give the battle-signal, to advance to the attack. 99 He who in the battle is the master of the weapon, 100 To him she entrusted; in costly apparel she made him sit, saying: 101 'I have uttered the spell for you, in the assembly of the gods I have raised you to power. 102 I have filled your hand with the sovereignty of the whole company of the gods. 103 May you be magnified, you who are my chosen spouse, 104 May the Anunnaki make great your renown over all of them.'

105 "She gave him the Tablet of Destinies, on his breast she fastened it, saying: 106 'As for you, your command will not fall empty, whatever goes forth from your mouth will be established.'

107 "Now Kingu, having been exalted, having received the power of Anu, 108 Decreed the destinies for the gods his sons, saying: 109 'Let the opening of your mouth quench the Fire god; 110 He who is glorious in battle and is most mighty, will do great deeds.'

111 "I sent Anu, but he could not prevail against her; 112 Ea was afraid and turned back. 113 But Marduk, your son, the envoy of the gods, has set out. 114 His heart has been stirred to oppose Tiamat. 115 He opened his mouth and spoke to me, saying: 116 'Should I, as your avenger, 117 conquer Tiamat and give you life, 118 Appoint an assembly, proclaim and magnify my position, 119 Sit down with Upshukkinaku joyfully, 120 Let me issue decrees by my word, even as you do. 121 Whatever I bring to pass, let it remain unaltered. 122 May the words of my mouth never be changed or made to fail.'

123 "Hurry, therefore, and swiftly decree for him the fate which you bestow, 124 that he may go and fight your strong enemy!"

125 The gods Lahmu and Lahamu heard and cried aloud, 126 All of the Igigi gods wept bitterly, saying: 127 "Who were our enemies before the gods were posted in heaven? 128 We cannot comprehend the work of Tiamat."

129 Then they gathered themselves together and went, 130 The great gods, all of them, who decree fate. 131 They entered in, they filled the court before Anshar. 132 Gods kissed one another in the divine assembly. 133 They held a meeting, they sat down to a feast, 134 They ate bread, they mixed wine. 135 The sweet drink, the mead, confused their [...], 136 They drank themselves drunk, their bodies were filled to overflowing, 137 They were wholly at ease, their spirit was exalted; 138 Then for Marduk, their avenger, did they decree his fate.

Tablet 4

1 They prepared for him a majestic chamber, 2 Marduk sat in the seat of kingship in the presence of his fathers, who said to him: 3 "You are chiefest among the great gods, 4 your position is unequaled, your words are as fixed as the sky. 5 Oh Marduk, you are the chiefest of the great gods, 6 your position is unequaled, your words are as fixed as the sky. 7 From this day onward your command will not be overturned. 8 The power to lift up and to bring down will be in your hand. 9 The words that go forth from your mouth will be established. Against your command there will be no resistance. 10 No other god will overstep your boundaries. 11 When worship is lacking if the shrines of the gods, 12 it will be found in abundance in your sanctuary.

13 "Oh Marduk, you are our avenger! 14 We give you sovereignty over all creation. 15 You will sit down in the council and your word will be exalted. 16 Your weapon will never lose its power. It will crush your enemies. 17 Oh Lord, spare the life of the one who puts his trust in you, 18 but pour out the life of the God who devises evil."

19 Then a cloak was set in their midst, 20 and to Marduk their firstborn they said: 21 "May you, Oh Lord, hold the foremost position amongst the gods. 22 To build up and to tear down, speak the word, and it will come to pass. 23 Speak the word and the cloak will vanish. 24 Speak a second time and the cloak will reappear undamaged."

25 Then Marduk spoke the word, and the garment vanished; 26 Again he spoke, and the garment reappeared. 27 When the gods his fathers saw the fulfillment of his word, 28 They rejoiced, and paid homage to him saying "Marduk is king!"

29 They bestowed upon him the scepter, and the throne, and the ring, 30 They give him the unrivaled weapon, the destroyer of the enemy, saying: 31 "Go, and cut off the life of Tiamat, 32 And let the wind carry her blood into the depths."

33 After the gods his fathers had decreed for the lord his fate, 34 They set him down the path that leads to prosperity and success. He strung his bow, making ready his weapon, 36 He slung a spear on himself and attached it to his belly. 37 He raised his club, grasping it in his right hand. 38 The bow and the quiver he hung at his side. 39 He set the lightning in front of him, 40 With burning flame he filled his body.

41 He made a net with which to enclose Tiamat, 42 He ordered the four winds to take their position so that no part of her might escape. 43 The South wind and the North wind and the East wind and the West wind 44 He brought near to the net, the gift of his father Anu. 45 He created the evil wind, and the tempest, and the hurricane, 46 And the fourfold wind, and the sevenfold wind, and the whirlwind, and the wind which had no

equal;

47 He sent forth the seven winds which he had created, 48 to disturb the inward parts of Tiamat. They followed after him. 49 Then the Lord raised up the tempest, his mighty weapon. 50 He went up in his chariot, the storm unequaled in terror. 51 He equipped it, yoking it to a team of four horses. 52 Destructive, ferocious, overwhelming, and swift of pace; 53 [...] were their teeth, they were dotted with foam; 54 They were skilled in biting, they were trained to trample under foot. [Lines 55-57 are fragments: 55 [...], mighty in battle, 56 Left and right [...] 57 His garment was [...], he was clothed with terror,]

58 With streams of brightness his head was crowned. 59 Then he set out, and hurried on his way, 60 And towards the raging Tiamat he set his face. 61 On his lips he held [...], 62 [...] he grasped in his hand.

63 At that moment the gods were looking upon him with fixed intensity, 64 The gods his fathers looked upon him, they beheld him.

65 And the Lord drew near, looking upon the inward parts of Tiamat, 66 He perceived the plan of Kingu, her husband.

67 As Marduk looked, Kingu staggered in his gait, 68 His will was destroyed, his motion was paralyzed 69 And the gods his helpers who were marching by his side 70 saw the collapse of their leader and their sight was troubled.

71 Tiamat shrieked but did not turn her head. 72 With lips full of rebellion she maintained her stubbornness, saying: 73 "You have come as the Lord of the gods, 74 They have appointed you in the place that should be theirs."

75 Then the Lord raised the tempest, his mighty weapon, 76 and against Tiamat, who was raging, thus he spoke the word: 77 "You have made yourself mighty, you have exalted yourself on high. 78 Your heart has stirred in you to invoke war. 79 [...] their fathers [...], 80"[...] their [...] you hate [...] 81 You have raised up Kingu to be your husband. 82 You have made him to usurp the attributes of Anu, that he should issue decrees. 83 You have plotted evil. 84 Against the gods, my fathers, you have contrived your wicked plan. 85 Let your troops ready themselves, let them equip their weapons. 86 Stand! You and I, let us fight!"

87 On hearing these words Tiamat 88 Was possessed with rage; she lost her reason. 89 Tiamat uttered loud, piercing cries. 90 She trembled and shook to her very foundations. 91 She recited an incantation, she pronounced her spell, 92 And the gods of the battle demanded their weapons.

93 Tiamat and Marduk, the envoy of the gods, roused themselves, 94 They advanced to fight each other, they drew near in battle. 95 The Lord spread out his net and caught her, 96 and the evil wind that was behind him, he let loose in her face. 97 As Tiamat opened her mouth to its full extent,

98 He made the evil wind to enter it, while her lips were still open. 99 The raging winds filled her belly, 100 and her courage was taken from her, and her mouth was opened wide.

101 Marduk seized the spear and burst her belly, 102 He severed her inward parts, he pierced her heart. 103 He overcame her and cut off her life; 104 He cast down her body and stood upon it.

105 After Marduk had slain the leader Tiamat, 106 Her might was broken and her troops her scattered. 107 And the gods, her allies, who marched by her side, 108 Trembled in fear, and turned back. 109 They took to flight to save their lives; 110 But they were surrounded, so that they could not escape. 111 He took them captive, he destroyed their weapons; 112 They were cast into the net, and they were caught in the snare. 113 The world was filled with their cries of grief. 114 They received punishment from Marduk, they were held in restraint.

115 And on the eleven creatures which she had filled with the power of striking terror, 116 Upon the troop of devils, who marched at her side, 117 He brought affliction, their strength he [diminished]; 118 He trampled them and their rebellion under his feet.

119 Moreover, Kingu, who had been exalted over them, 120 He conquered, and counted him of little worth, as the god Dugga. 121 Marduk took from him the Tablets of Destiny that were not rightly his, 122 He sealed them with a seal and on his own breast he fastened them.

123 Now after the hero Marduk had conquered and cast down his enemies, 124 And made the arrogant enemy to be like the dust underfoot, 125 And had established Anshar's triumph over the enemy, 126 And had attained the purpose of Nudimmud (Ea), 127 He imposed strict restraint on the gods whom he had made captive.

128 And to Tiamat, whom he had conquered, he returned. 129 The Lord stood upon Tiamat's hinder parts, 130 And with his merciless club he smashed her skull. 131 He cut through the channels of her blood, 132 And he made the North wind carry it away into the depths.

133 The gods his fathers saw, and they rejoiced and were glad; 134 They brought to him gifts of triumph and peace,

135 Then the Lord Marduk paused, looking upon her dead body, 136 He separated flesh from hair, he devised a cunning plan. 137 He split her up like a flat fish into two halves; 138 One half of her he established as a covering for the heavens. 139 He fixed a bolt, he stationed a watchman, 140 And ordered them not to let her waters escape.

141 He passed through the heavens, contemplating the regions thereof. 142 He took himself to the dwelling of Nudimmud (Ea) that is opposite to the Deep (Apsu), 143 And the lord measured the structure of the Deep, 144 And he founded E-Shara, a place similar to it. 145 In the place E-shara

which he created as heaven, 146 He made the gods Anu, Bel and Ea to inhabit their own cities.

Tablet 5

1 Marduk appointed the Stations for the great gods 2 And set in heaven the Stars of the Zodiac which are their likenesses. 3 He fixed the year, and appointed the limits thereof. 4 For each of the twelve months he fixed three stars. 5 According to the day of the year he [...] images. 6 He founded the Station of Nibir (Jupiter) to settle their boundaries, 7 That none might go astray. 8 He set the Station of Bel and Ea nearby.

9 He opened great gates on both sides, 10 He made strong the bolt on the left and on the right. 11 In the midst thereof he fixed the zenith.

12 He gave the god Nannar (the Moon-god) his brightness and committed the night to his care. 13 He appointed him, a being of the night, to determine the days; 14 Every month without ceasing, he set him in a disk, saying: 15 "At the beginning of the month when you rise over the land, 16 Make your horns to project to limit six days of the month. 17 On the seventh day make yourself like a crown. 18 On the fourteenth day [...] [Lines 19-74 lost or mostly fragments]

75 The gods his fathers looked on the net which he had made, 76 Observing how craftily the bow had been constructed, 77 They praised the work which Marduk had done.

78 Then the god Anu lifted up the bow in the company of the gods, 79 He kissed the bow, saying: "That [...]" 80 He proclaimed the names of the bow to be as follows: 81 "Truly, the first is 'Long Wood,' the second is [...] 82 "Its third name is 'Bow Star in heaven' [...] 83 He fixed a station for it [...] [Remaining lines lost or fragments]

Tablet 6

1 On hearing the words of the gods, the heart of Marduk moved him to carry out the works of a craftsman. 2 He opened his mouth and told Ea that which he had planned in his heart, he gave counsel saying: 3 "I will solidify blood, I will form bone. 4 I will set up man, he will be called 'Man'. 5 I will create the being 'Man'. 6 The service of the gods will be established, and I will set them free. 7 I will make twofold the ways of the gods, and I will beautify them. 8 They are now together in one place, but they will be split in two."

9 Ea answered and spoke to him. 10 For the consolation of the gods he repeated a word of counsel to him, saying: 11 "Let one brother god be given from among them, let him suffer destruction that men may be fashioned. 12 Let the great gods be assembled, and let the chosen one be given so that the other gods may be established."

13 Marduk assembled the great gods, and approaching graciously, he issued a decree. 14 Opening his mouth,

he addressed the gods; the King spoke to Anunnaki saying: 15 "Certainly, that which I spoke to you previously was true. 16 This time I also speak the truth. There were some who opposed me. 17 Who was it that created the strife? 18 Who caused Tiamat to revolt and to battle against me? 19 Let him who created the strife be given as a sacrifice. 20 I will cause the axe, in the act of sinking, to do away with his sin."

21 The great gods, the Igigi, answered him. 22 To the King of the gods of heaven and earth, the Prince of the gods, their Lord, they said: 23 "It was Kingu who created the strife, 24 Who made Tiamat to revolt and to battle against you."

25 They bound him in chains and brought him before Ea, they inflicted punishment on him, they drained his blood. 26 From his blood Ea fashioned mankind for the service of the gods, and he set the gods free. 27 After Ea had fashioned man he [...] put responsibilities on him. 28 For the work which was not pleasing, Man was chosen. 29 Marduk, the King of the gods, divided [gods and men]. He set the Anunnaki on high. 30 He laid down for Anu a law that protected his heart [acting] as a guard. 31 He made twofold the ways on earth and in the heavens. 32 By decrees [...] 33 The Annunaki who [...]

34 The Annunaki [...] 35 They spoke to their Lord Marduk, saying: 36 "Oh Moon-god Nannaru, who has established our splendor, 37 What benefit have we conferred on you? 38 Come, let us make a temple whose name will be celebrated. 39 Come at night, our time of festival, and let us take our ease therein. 40 Come, the staff shall rule [...] 41 On the day that we reach, we will take our ease therein." 42 On hearing this Marduk [...] 43 And his face shone bright like the day. 44 He said 45 "Similar to [...] Babylon, the construction of which you desire, 45 I will make [...] a city. I will fashion a splendid altar."

46 The Anunnaki worked the mold for making bricks, their bricks were [...] 47 In the second year the temple was as high as a hill, and the summit of E-Sagila reached the celestial ocean. 48 They made the tower to reach the celestial ocean, dedicating altars to Marduk, Enlil, and Ea. 49 The tower stood before them majestically. At the bottom and the top they observed its two horns. 50 After the Annunaki had finished the construction of E-Sagila, and had completed the building of their temples, 51 They gathered together from the [...] of the ocean (Apsu). In Barh-Mah, the home which they had made, 52 Marduk made the gods his fathers take their places, saying "This Babylon will be your home. No mighty one will destroy his house. The great gods will dwell therein."

[Source Note: After line 52 the middle portions of several lines of text are obliterated, but from what remains of it, it is clear that the gods partook of a meal of consecration of the shrine of E-Sagila, and then proceeded to issue decrees. Next Marduk assigns seats to the Seven Gods of Fate and to Enlil and Anu, and then he lays up in E-Sagila the famous bow which he bore during his fight against Tiamat. When the text again becomes connected we find the gods singing a hymn of praise to Marduk.]

94 "Whatever is [...] those gods and goddesses shall bear. 95 They will never forget, they will cleave to gods. 96 [...] they will make bright. They will make shrines. 97 Certainly, the decision concerning the black-headed belongs to the gods. 98 Of all our names they have called, Marduk is most holy. 99 [...] they proclaimed and venerated his names. 100 His countenance is exceedingly bright, his work is [...] 101 Marduk, whose father Anu proclaimed his name from birth, 102 Who has set the day at his door [...] his going, 103 by whose help the storm wind was bound... 104 Delivered the gods his fathers in the time of trouble. 105 Certainly the gods have proclaimed his sonship. 106 In his bright light, let them walk forever. 107 On men who he formed and fashioned with his fingers, 108 Has he imposed the service of the gods, having set the gods free. [...]

110 [...] they looked at him, 111 "He is the far-seeing god, truthfully... 112 Who has made glad the hearts of the Anunnaki, who has made them to [rejoice]. 113 The god Maruddukku, most certainly, he is the object of trust of his country. 114 Let men praise him [...] 115 The King of the Protecting Heart, has risen and has bound the Serpent. 116 Broad is his heart, mighty is his belly. 117 King of the gods of heaven and of earth, whose name our company has proclaimed, 118 We will fulfill the words of his mouth. Over his fathers the gods, 119 Indeed, over the gods of heaven and earth—all of them, 120 We will exalt his kingship. 121 We will look to the king of all heaven and earth at night, when the place of all the gods is in sadness. 112 He has assigned our dwelling in heaven and in earth in the time of trouble. 123 He has allotted stations to the Igigi and the Anunnaki. 124 The gods themselves are magnified by his name. May he lead their sanctuaries. 125 Asar-Lu-Dug [...] is his name by which his father Anu has named him. 126 Certainly, he is the light of the gods, the mighty [...] 127 Who [...] all the parts of heaven and of land 128 By a mighty battle he saved our home in the time of trouble. 129 Asar-Lu-Dug, the god who made man to live, did the god [...] call him in the second place. 130 And the gods who had been formed, whom he fashioned as though they were his offspring. 131 He is the Lord who has made all the gods to live by his holy word.

[Source Note: Lines 132-139 are too fragmentary to translate, but it is clear from the text that remains that Lakhmu, and Lakhamu, and Anshar all proclaimed the names of Marduk. When the text again becomes connected Marduk has just been addressing the gods.]

140 In Up-shukkinaku he appointed their council for them. 141 They said: "Of our son, the Hero, our Avenger, 142 We will exalt his name by our speech." 143 They sat down and in their group they proclaimed his status. 144 Every one of them proclaimed his name in the sanctuary.

Tablet 7

1 "Oh Asari, Founder of planting, 2 Creator of grain and plants, who caused the green plants to spring up!"

3 "Oh Asaru-alim, who is revered in the house of counsel, who abounds in counsel,"

4 The gods paid homage, and fear took hold of them.

5 "Oh Asaru-alim-nuna, the mighty one, the Light of the father who brought him about, 6 Who directs the decrees of Anu, Bel, and Ea!"

7 "He was their patron, he ordained their [destinies]; 8 He, whose provision is abundance, goes forth [...]! 9 Tutu is he who created them anew."

10 "Should their wants be pure, then are they satisfied; 11 Should he make an incantation, then the gods are appeased; 12 Should they attack him in anger, he withstands their onslaught!"

13 "Let him therefore be exalted in the assembly of the gods; 14 None among the gods can rival him!"

15 "Tutu is Zi-ukkina, the Life of the host of the gods, 16 Who established for the gods the bright heavens. 17 He set them on their way, and ordained their destiny. 18 Never will his [...] deeds be forgotten among men."

19 "Tutu is Zi-azag thirdly they named, the Bringer of Purification, 20 The God of the Favoring Breeze, the Lord of Hearing and Mercy, 21 The Creator of Fullness and Abundance, the Founder of Bountifulness, 22 Who increases all that is small."

23 "'In sore distress we felt his favoring breeze', 24 Let them say, let them pay reverence, let them bow in humility before him!"

25 "Tutu is Aga-azag, may mankind fourthly magnify! 26 The Lord of the Pure Incantation, who makes the dead to live, 27 Who had mercy on the gods in captivity, 28 Who riveted on the gods his enemies the yoke which had been resting on them. 29 For their forgiveness did he create mankind, 30 The Merciful One in whose power it is to give life. 31 His deeds will endure forever, they will never be forgotten 32 In the mouth of mankind, whom his hands have made."

31 "Tutu is Mu-azag, fifthly, his Pure Incantation may their mouths proclaim, 34 Who through his Pure Incantation has destroyed all the evil ones!"

35 "Shag-zu, who knows the heart of the gods, who sees through the innermost part! 36 The evil-doer he has not allowed to go forth with him! 37 Founder of the assembly of the gods, who [...] their hearts! 38 Subduer of the disobedient, [...]! 39 Who rebel-

lion and [...]!"

41 "Tutu is Zi-si, the [...], 42 Who put an end to anger, who [...]!"

43 Tutu is Suh-kur, "the Destroyer of the enemy, 44 Who put their plans to confusion, [...], 45 Who destroyed all the wicked, [...] 46 [...] let them [...]! [47 missing/omitted]"

[Lines 48-106 are mostly fragments and possibly misplaced: "He named the four quarters (of the world)], mankind [he created], [And upon] him understanding [...] Tiamat [...] distant [...] may [...] The mighty one [...]! [...] Agi [...] The Creator of the earth [...] Zulummu [...] The Giver of counsel and of whatsoever [...]! Mummu, the Creator of [...]! Mulil, the heavens [...], Who for [...]! Gishkul, let [...] Lugal-ab-[...], who in [...] the chief of all lords, [...] supreme is his might! Lugal-durmah, the King of the band of gods, the Lord of rulers, Who is exalted in a royal habitation, who among the gods is gloriously supreme! Adu-nuna, the Counselor of Ea, who created the gods his fathers, to the path of whose majesty no god can ever attain! [...] Dul-azag he made it known, [...] pure is his dwelling! [...] of those without understanding is Lugal-dul-azaga! [...] supreme is his might! [...] in the midst of Tiamat, [...] of the battle! [...] him [...] the star, which shines in the heavens."]

107 "May he hold the Beginning and the End , may they pay homage to him, 108 Saying, 'He who forced his way through the midst of Tiamat without resting, 109 Let his name be Nibiru, the Seizer of the middle!'"

110 "For he set the courses of the stars of the heavens, 111 And the gods he led like sheep. 112 He conquered Tiamat, he ended her life."

113 "In the future of mankind, when the days grow old, 114 May these words be heard without ceasing, may they reign for all eternity. 115 Since he created the heavens and fashioned the firm earth, 116 Father Bel proclaimed his name to be 'Lord of the World'."

117 All the Igigi repeated the title. 118 Ea heard and his spirit rejoiced, saying 119 "He whose name his fathers have made glorious, 120 Shall be even as I, his name shall be Ea! 121 The binding of all my decrees shall he control, 122 All my commands shall he make known!"

123 By the name of "Fifty" did the great gods 124 Proclaim his fifty names, they made his path pre-eminent."

Epilogue

125 Let them be held in remembrance, and let the first man proclaim them; 126 Let the wise and the learned meditate on all of them. 127 Let the father repeat them and teach them to his son. 128 Let them be in the ears of the shepherd. 129 Let a man rejoice in Marduk, the Lord of the gods, 130 That his land may be fertile and he himself may have prosperity. 131 His word is true. His command changes not. 132 No god can undo the words

Out of Chaos

of his mouth. 133 The gods treated him with contempt, but he turned not his back in retreat. 134 When he is angry, no god can withstand him. 135 His heart is large, and his compassion is great. 136 Of sin and wickedness before him [...] 137 The first man confesses in humility before him.

138 [...] to [...] 139 [...] of Marduk may the gods [...] 140 [May] they [...] his name [...]! 141 [...] they took and [...]; 142 [...]!

Marduk 2

Merodach the Dragon Slayer. Updated and edited version of the text from Myths of Babylonia and Assyria by Donald A. MacKenzie

In the beginning the whole universe was a sea. Heaven on high had not been named, nor the earth beneath. Their father was Apsu, the father of the primordial Deep, and their mother was Tiamat, the spirit of Chaos. No plain was yet formed, no marsh could be seen; the gods had no existence, nor had their fates been determined. Then there was a movement in the waters, and the deities issued forth. The first who had being were the god Lachmu and the goddess Lachamu. Long ages went past. Then were created the god Anshar and the goddess Kishar. When the days of these deities had increased and extended, they were followed by Anu, god of the sky, whose consort was Anatu; and Ea, most wise and all-powerful, who was without an equal. Now Ea, god of the deep, was also Enki, "lord of earth", and his eternal spouse, Damkina, was Gashan-ki, "lady of earth". The son of Ea and Damkina was Bel, the lord, who in time created mankind. Thus were the high gods established in power and in glory.

Now Apsu and Tiamat remained amidst confusion in the deeps of chaos. They were troubled because their offspring, the high gods, aspired to control the universe and set it in order. Apsu was still powerful and fierce, and Tiamat snarled and raised tempests, smiting herself. Their purpose was to work evil amidst eternal confusion.

Then Apsu called upon Mummu, his counselor, the son who shared his desires, and said, "Oh Mummu, you who are pleasing to me, let us go forth together to Tiamat and speak with her."

So the two went forth and prostrated themselves before the Chaos Mother to consult with her as to what should be done to prevent the accomplishment of the purpose of the high gods.

Apsu opened his mouth and spoke, saying, "Oh Tiamat, you gleaming one, the purpose of the gods troubles me. I cannot rest by day nor can I repose by night. I will confound them and destroy their purpose. I will bring sorrow and mourning so that we may lie down undisturbed by them."

Tiamat heard these words and

snarled. She raised angry and roaring tempests; in her furious grief she uttered a curse, and then spoke to Apsu, saying, "What shall we do so that their purpose may be confounded and we may lie down undisturbed again?"

Mummu, the counselor, addressing Apsu, made answer, and said, "Although the gods are powerful, you can overcome them; although their purpose is strong, you can confound it. Then you will have rest by day and peace by night to lie down."

The face of Apsu grew bright when he heard these words spoken by Mummu, yet he trembled to think of the purpose of the high gods, to whom he was hostile. With Tiamat he lamented because the gods had changed all things; the plans of the gods filled their hearts with dread; they sorrowed and spoke with Mummu, plotting evil.

Then Ea, who knows all, drew near; he beheld the evil ones conspiring and muttering together. He uttered a pure incantation and accomplished the downfall of Apsu and Mummu, who were taken captive.

Kingu, who shared the desires of Tiamat, spoke to her words of counsel, saying, "Apsu and Mummu have been overcome and we cannot repose. You will be their Avenger, Oh Tempestuous One."

Tiamat heard the words of this bright and evil god, and made answer, saying, "On my strength you can trust. So let war be waged."

Then were the hosts of chaos and the deep gathered together. By day and by night they plotted against the high gods, raging furiously, making ready for battle, fuming and storming and taking no rest.

Mother Chuber, the creator of all, provided irresistible weapons. She also brought into being eleven kinds of fierce monsters—giant serpents, sharp of tooth with unsparing fangs, whose bodies were filled with poison instead of blood; snarling dragons, clad with terror, and of such lofty stature that whoever saw them was overwhelmed with fear, nor could any escape their attack when they lifted themselves up; vipers and pythons, and the Lachamu, hurricane monsters, raging hounds, scorpion men, tempest furies, fish men, and mountain rams. These she armed with fierce weapons and they had no fear of war.

Then Tiamat, whose commands are unchangeable and mighty, exalted Kingu, who had come to her aid, above all the evil gods; she made him the leader to direct the army in battle, to go in front, to open the attack. Robing Kingu in splendor, she seated him on high and spoke, saying:

"I have established your command over all the gods. You will rule over them. Be mighty, you my chosen husband, and let your name be exalted over all the spirits of heaven and spirits of earth."

To Kingu did Tiamat deliver the tablets of fate; she laid them in his bosom, and said, "your commands cannot be changed; your words shall remain firm."

Thus was Kingu exalted; he was vested with the divine power of Anu to decree the fate of the gods, saying, "Let your mouth open to confound the fire god; be mighty in battle nor brook resistance."

Then had Ea knowledge of Tiamat's doings, how she had gathered her forces together, and how she had prepared to work evil against the high gods with purpose to avenge Apsu. The wise god was stricken with grief, and he moaned for many days. Thereafter he went and stood before his father, Anshar, and spoke, saying, "Our mother, Tiamat, has turned against us in her wrath. She has gathered the gods about her, and those you did create are with her also."

When Anshar heard all that Ea revealed regarding the preparations made by Tiamat, he smote his loins and clenched his teeth, and was ill at ease. In sorrow and anger he spoke and said, "You did go forth before to battle; you did bind Mummu and smite Apsu. Now Kingu is exalted, and there is none who can oppose Tiamat."

Anshar called his son, Anu, before him, and spoke, saying: "Oh mighty one without fear, whose attack is irresistible, go now before Tiamat and speak so that her anger may subside and her heart be made merciful. But if she will not hearken to you, speak you for me, so that she may be reconciled."

Anu was obedient to the commands of Anshar. He departed, and descended by the path of Tiamat until he beheld her fuming and snarling, but he feared to approach her, and turned back.

Then Ea was sent forth, but he was stricken with terror and turned back also.

Anshar then called upon Marduk, son of Ea, and addressed him, saying, "My son, who softens my heart, you will go forth to battle and none shall stand against you."

The heart of Marduk was made glad at these words. He stood before Anshar, who kissed him, because he banished fear. Marduk spoke, saying: "Oh lord of the gods, withdraw not your words; let me go forth to do as is your desire. What man has challenged you to battle?"

Anshar made answer and said: "No man has challenged me. It is Tiamat, the woman, who has resolved to wage war against us. But fear not and make merry, for you will bruise the head of Tiamat. Oh wise god, you will overcome her with your pure incantation. Hurry and do not wait; she cannot wound you; you will come back again." The words of Anshar delighted the heart of Marduk, who spoke, saying: "Oh lord of the gods, Oh fate of the high gods, if I, the avenger, am to subdue Tiamat and save all, then proclaim my greatness among the gods. Let all the high gods gather together joyfully in Upshukinaku (the Council Hall), so that my words like yours may remain unchanged, and what I do may never be altered. Instead of you I will decree the fates of the gods."

Then Anshar called to his counselor, Gaga, and addressing him, said: "Oh you, the one who shares my desires, the one who understands the purpose of my heart, go to Lachmu and Lachamu and summon all the high gods to come before me to eat bread and drink wine. Repeat to them all I tell you of Tiamat's preparations for war, of my commands to Anu and Ea, who turned back, fearing the dragon, of my choice of Marduk to be our avenger, and his desire to be equipped with my power to decree fate, so that he may be made strong to combat against our enemy."

As Anshar commanded so did Gaga do. He went to Lachmu and Lachamu and prostrated himself humbly before them. Then he rose and delivered the message of Anshar, their son, adding: "Hurry and speedily decide for Marduk your fate. Permit him to depart to meet your powerful foe."

When Lachmu and Lachamu heard all that Gaga revealed to them they uttered lamentations, while the Igigi (heavenly spirits) sorrowed bitterly, and said: "What change has happened that Tiamat has become hostile to her own offspring? We cannot understand her deeds."

All the high gods then arose and went to Anshar. They filled his council chamber and kissed one another. Then they sat down to eat bread and drink sesame wine. And when they were made drunk and were merry and at their ease, they decreed the fate for Marduk.

In the chamber of Anshar they honored the Avenger. He was exalted as a prince over them all, and they said: "Among the high gods you are the highest; your command is the command of Anu. Henceforth you wilt have power to raise up and to cast down. None of the gods will dispute your authority. Oh Marduk, our avenger, we give you sovereignty over the entire Universe. your weapon will ever be irresistible. Smite down the gods who have raised revolt, but spare the lives of those who repose their trust in you."

Then the gods laid down a garment before Marduk, saying: "Open your mouth and speak words of command, so that the garment may be destroyed; speak again and it will be brought back."

Marduk spoke with his mouth and the garment vanished; he spoke again and the garment was reproduced.

All the gods rejoiced, and they prostrated themselves and cried out, "Marduk is King!"

Thereafter they gave him the scepter and the throne and the insignia of royalty, and also an irresistible weapon with which to overcome his enemies, saying: "Now, Oh Marduk, hurry and slay Tiamat. Let the winds carry her blood to hidden places."

So was the fate of Marduk decreed by the gods; so was a path of prosperity and peace prepared for him. He made ready for battle; he strung his bow and hung his quiver; he slung a dart over his shoulder, and he grasped a club in his right hand; before him he set lightning, and with flaming fire he filled his body. Anu gave to him a great net with which to snare his enemies and prevent their escape. Then Marduk created seven winds—the wind of evil, the uncontrollable wind, the sandstorm, and the whirlwind, the fourfold wind, the sevenfold wind, and the wind that has no equal—and they went after him. Next he seized his mighty weapon, the thunder stone, and leapt into his storm chariot, to which were yoked four rushing and destructive steeds of rapid flight, with foam-flecked mouths and teeth full of venom, trained for battle, to overthrow enemies and trample them underfoot. A light burned on the head of Marduk, and he was clad in a robe of terror. He drove forth, and the gods, his fathers, followed after him: the high gods clustered around and followed him, hurrying to battle.

Marduk drove on, and at length he drew nigh to the secret lair of Tiamat, and he beheld her muttering with Kingu, her consort. For a moment he faltered, and when the gods who followed him beheld this, their eyes were troubled.

Tiamat snarled and turned her head. She uttered curses, and said: "Oh Marduk, I fear not your advance as chief of the gods. My allies are assembled here, and are more powerful than you are."

Marduk uplifted his arm, grasping the dreaded thunder stone, and spoke to Tiamat, the rebellious one, saying: "You have exalted yourself, and with a wrathful heart has prepared for war against the high gods and their fathers, whom you hate in your heart of evil. To Kingu you have given the power of Anu to decree fate, because you are hostile to what is good and loves what is sinful. Gather your forces together, and arm yourself and come forth to battle."

When Tiamat heard these mighty words she raved and cried aloud like one who is possessed; all her limbs shook, and she muttered a spell. The gods seized their weapons.

Tiamat and Marduk advanced to combat against one another. They made ready for battle. The lord of the high gods spread out the net which Anu had given him. He snared the dragon and she could not escape. Tiamat opened her mouth which was seven miles wide, and Marduk called upon the evil wind to smite her; he caused the wind to keep her mouth agape so that she could not close it. All the tempests and the hurricanes entered in, filling her body, and her heart grew weak; she gasped, overpowered. Then the lord of the high gods seized his dart and cast it through the lower part of her body; it tore her inward parts and severed her heart. So was Tiamat slain.

Marduk overturned the body of the dead dragon and stood upon it. All the evil gods who had followed her were stricken with terror and broke into flight. But they were unable to escape. Marduk caught them in his great net, and they stumbled and fell uttering cries of distress, and the whole world resounded with their wailing and lamentations. The lord of the high gods broke the weapons of the evil gods and put them in bondage. Then he fell upon the monsters which Tiamat had created; he subdued them, divested them of their powers, and trampled them under his feet. Kingu he seized with the others. From this god great Marduk took the tablets of fate, and impressing upon them his own seal, placed them in his bosom.

So were the enemies of the high gods overthrown by the Avenger. Ansar's commands were fulfilled and the desires of Ea fully accomplished.

Marduk strengthened the bonds which he had laid upon the evil gods and then returned to Tiamat. He leapt upon the dragon's body; he clove her skull with his great club; he opened the channels of her blood which streamed forth, and caused the north to carry her blood to hidden places. The high gods, his fathers, clustered around; they raised shouts of triumph and made merry. Then they brought gifts and offerings to the great Avenger.

Marduk rested a while, gazing upon the dead body of the dragon. He divided the flesh of Ku-pu, and devised a cunning plan.

Then the lord of the high gods split the body of the dragon like that of a fish cut into two halves. With one half he enveloped the firmament; he fixed it there and set a watchman to prevent the waters falling down. With the other half he made the earth. Then he made the abode of Ea in the deep, and the abode of Anu in high heaven. The abode of Enlil was in the air.

Marduk set all the great gods in their several stations. He also created their images, the stars of the Zodiac, and fixed them all. He measured the year and divided it into months; for twelve months he made three stars each. After he had given starry images of the gods separate control of each day of the year, he founded the station of Nibiru (Jupiter), his own star, to determine the limits of all stars, so that none might err or go astray. He placed beside his own the stations of Enlil and Ea, and on each side he opened mighty gates, fixing bolts on the left and on the right. He set the zenith in the center

Marduk decreed that the moon god should rule the night and measure the days, and each month he was given a crown. Its various phases the great lord determined, and he commanded that on the evening of its fullest brilliancy it should stand opposite the sun.

He placed his bow in heaven (as a constellation) and his net also.

Marduk 3

From Ancient Babylon. Updated and edited version of the translation by Leonard William King

Tablet 1

1 The holy house, the house of the gods, in the holy place had not yet been made; 2 No reed had sprung up, no tree had been created. 3 No brick had been laid, no building had been set up; 4 No house had been erected, no city had been built; 5 No city had been made, no creature had been created. 6 Nippur had not been made, E-kur had not been built; 7 Erech had not been created, E-ana had not been built; 8 The Deep had not been created, Eridu had not been built; 9 Of the holy house, the house of the gods, the habitation had not been made. 10 All lands were sea.

11 At that time there was a movement in the sea; 12 Then was Eridu made, and E-sagil was built, 13 E-sagil, where in the midst of the Deep the god Lugal-dul-azaga dwells; 14 The city of Babylon was built, and E-sagil was finished. 15 The gods, the Anunnaki, he created at one time; 16 The holy city, the dwelling, of their hearts' desire, they proclaimed supreme.

17 Marduk laid a reed upon the face of the waters, 18 He formed dust and poured it out beside the reed. 19 That he might cause the gods to dwell in the habitation of their hearts' desire, 20 He formed mankind. 21 The goddess Aruru together with him created the seed of mankind.

22 The beasts of the field and living creatures in the field he formed. 23 He created the Tigris and the Euphrates, and he set them in their place; 24 Their names he declared in proper fashion. 25 The grass, the rush of the marsh, the reed, and the forest he created, 26 The green herb of the field he created, 27 The lands, the marshes, and the swamps; 28 The wild cow and her young, the wild calf; the ewe and her young, the lamb of the fold; 29 Plantations and forests; 30 The he-goat and the mountain-goat [...] him.

31 The Lord Marduk laid in a dam by the side of the sea, 32 He [...] a swamp, he made a marsh, 33 [...] he brought into existence. 34 Reeds he formed, trees he created; 35 [...] he made in their place. 36 Bricks he laid, buildings he set up; 37 Houses he made, cities he built; 38 Cities he made, creatures he created. 39 Nippur he made, E-kur he built; 40 Erech he made, E-ana he built. [Remaining lines lost]

Tablet 2

1 [...] the decree [...] 2 [...] 3 Your exalted minister is Papsukal, the wise counselor of the gods. 5 May Nin-aha-kudû, the daughter of Ea, 6 Purify you with the pure censer, 7 And may she cleanse you with cleansing fire! 8 With a cup of pure water from the Deep will you purify your way!

10 By the incantation of Marduk, the king of the hosts of heaven and earth, 11 May the abundance of the land enter into you, 12 And may your decree be accomplished for ever!

13 Oh Ezida, you glorious dwelling, you are dear to the hearts of Anu and Ishtar! 15 May Ezida shine like

the heavens, may it be bright like the earth, may it be glorious like the heart of heaven, 16 And may [...] be firmly established!

Creation of The Gods

Excerpt. Chaldean Legend of Creation. Updated and edited version from The Chaldean Account of Genesis, by George Smith, from the writings of Lucius Cornelius Alexander Polyhistor, 1st Century BC ("Ancient Fragments" by I.P. Cory)

[...] 2 His word is the command of the gods... 3 His gleaming-white instrument is the gleaming-white instrument of the gods. 4 He is lord of that which is above and that which is below, the lord of the spirits of earth, 5 Who drinks turbid waters and drinks not clear waters; 6 In whose field that warrior's weapon all that rests there 7 Has captured and destroyed. 8 On a tablet he wrote not, he opened not the mouth, and bodies and produce 9 He caused not to come forth in the land, and I approached him not. 10 Warriors with the body of a bird of the valley, men 11 With the faces of ravens, 12 Did the great gods create. 13 In the ground the gods created his city. 14 Tiamat suckled them. 15 Their offspring the mistress of the gods created. 16 In the midst of the mountains they grew up and became heroes and 17 Increased in number. 18 Seven kings, brethren, appeared as fathers; 19 Six thousand in number were their armies. 20 The god Ba-nini their father was king; their mother 21 The queen was Melili; 22 Their eldest brother who went before them, Me-mangab was his name; 23 Their second brother, Me-dudu was his name; 24 Their third brother, Me-man-pakh was his name; 25 Their fourth brother, Me-da-da was his name; 26 Their fifth brother, Me-man-takh was his name; 27 Their sixth brother, Me-ru-ru was his name; 28 Their seventh brother, Me-rara was his name.

The River of Creation

Excerpt. Updated and edited version of the translation by Leonard William King

1 Oh, you River, who did create all things, 2 When the great gods dug you out, 3 They set prosperity upon your banks, 4 Within you Ea, the King of the Deep, created his dwelling, 5 The deluge they sent not before you existed! 6 Fire, and wrath, and splendor, and terror 7 Have Ea and Marduk presented to you! 8 You judge the cause of mankind! 9 Oh, River, you are mighty! Oh River, you are supreme! Oh River, you are righteous!

From Chaos

The Cosmology of the Phoenicians. From Sanchoniatho. Updated and edited version from the writings of Lucius Cornelius Alexander Polyhistor,

Out of Chaos

1st Century BC, from Ancient Fragments, by I.P. Cory

The beginning of all things was a dark and condensed windy air, or a breeze of thick air and a Chaos as turbid and black as Erebus: and that these were unbounded, and for a long series of ages destitute of form. But when this wind became enamored of its own first principles, and an intimate union took place, that connection was called Pothos: and it was the beginning of the creation of all things. And Chaos knew not its own production; but from its embrace with the wind was generated Môt; which some call Ilus (Mud), but others the putrefaction of a watery mixture. And from this sprung all the seed of creation, and the generation of the universe.

And there were certain animals without sensation, from which intelligent animals were produced, and these were called Zophasemin, that is, the overseers of the heavens; and they were formed in the shape of an egg: and from Môt shone forth the sun, and the moon, the lesser and the greater stars.

And when the air began to send forth light, by its fiery influence on the sea and earth, winds were produced, and clouds, and very great defluxions and torrents of the heavenly waters. And when they were thus separated, and carried out of their proper places by the heat of the sun, and all met again in the air, and were dashed against each other, thunder and lightnings were the result: and at the sound of the thunder, the before-mentioned intelligent animals were aroused, and startled by the noise, and moved upon the earth and in the sea, male and female.

The Necessity of Chaos

Various Fragments. Updated and edited version from the writings of Lucius Cornelius Alexander Polyhistor, 1st Century BC, from Ancient Fragments, by I.P. Cory

From Orpheus. First I sung the obscurity of ancient Chaos, How the Elements were ordered, and the Heaven reduced to bound; And the generation of the wide-bosomed Earth, and the depth of the Sea, And Eros the most ancient, self-perfecting, and of manifold design; How he generated all things, and parted them from one another. And I have sung of Cronus so miserably undone, and how the kingdom of the blessed Immortals descended to the thunder-loving Zeus.

From Orpheus. First I have sung the vast necessity of ancient Chaos, And Cronus, who in the boundless tracts brought forth The Ether, and the splendid and glorious Eros of a two-fold nature, the illustrious father of night, existing from eternity. Whom men call Phanes, for he first appeared. I have sung the birth of powerful Brimo (Hecate), and the unhallowed deeds of the earth-born giants, who showered down from heaven their blood, the lamentable seed of generation, from which sprung the race of mortals, who inhabit the boundless earth forever.

From Aristophanes. First was Chaos and Night, and black Erebus and vast Tartarus; And there was neither Earth, nor Air, nor Heaven: but in the boundless bosoms of Erebus, Night, with her black wings, first produced an aerial egg, from which, at the completed time, sprang forth the lovely Eros, glittering with golden wings upon his back, like the swift whirlwinds. Embracing the dark-winged Chaos in the vast Tartarus, he begot our race (the birds), and first brought us to light. The race of the Immortals did not exist until Eros mingled all things together; But when the elements were mixed one with another, Heaven was produced—along with Ocean, Earth, and the imperishable race of all the blessed Gods.

Divine Nature in Chaos

From The Ancient Hermetic Books. The glory of all things is God, and Deity, and divine Nature. The principle of all things existing is God, and the Intellect, and Nature, and Matter, and Energy, and Fate, and Conclusion, and Renovation. For there existed boundless Darkness in the abyss, and water, and a subtle spirit, intellectual in power, existing in Chaos. But the holy Light broke forth, and the elements were produced from among the sand of a watery essence.

Chapter 2

Divine Evolutions

Book of Knowing 1

Updated and edited version from Legends of the Gods by E.A. Wallis Budge

The Book of Knowing the Evolutions of Ra, and of Overthrowing Apep.

These are the words which the god Neb-er-tcher spoke after he had, come into being: "I am he who came into being in the form of the god Khepera, and I am the creator of that which came into being, that is to say, I am the creator of everything which came into being: now the things which I created, and which came forth out of my mouth after that I had come into being myself were exceedingly many.

"The sky had not come into being, the earth did not exist, and the children of the earth, and the creeping things, had not been made at that time. I myself raised them up from out of Nu, from a state of helpless inertness. I found no place on which I could stand. I worked a charm upon my own heart, I laid the foundation of things by Maat, and I made everything which had form. I was then one by myself, for I had not emitted from myself the god Shu, and I had not spit out from myself the goddess Tefnut; and there existed no other who could work with me. I laid the foundations of things in my own heart, and there came into being multitudes of created things, which came into being from the created things which were born from the created things which arose from what they brought forth. I had union with my closed hand, and I embraced my shadow as a wife, and I poured seed into my own mouth, and I sent forth from myself issue in the form of the gods Shu and Tefnut. Said my father Nu: My Eye was covered up behind them (Shu. and Tefnut), but after two hen periods had passed from the time when they departed from me, from being one god I became three gods, and I came into being in the earth.

"Then Shu and Tefnut rejoiced from out of the inert watery mass in which I was, and they brought to me my Eye (the Sun). Now after these things I gathered together my members, and I wept over them, and men and women sprang into being from the tears which came forth from my Eye. And when my Eye came to me, and found that I had made another Eye (the Moon) in place where it was, it was angry with me, after which I endowed it with some of the splendor which I had made for the first Eye, and I made it to occupy its place in my Face, and henceforth it ruled throughout all this earth.

"When there fell on them their moment through plant-like clouds, I restored what had been taken away from them, and I appeared from out of the plant-like clouds. I created creeping things of every kind, and everything which came into being from them. Shu and Tefnut brought forth Seb and Nut; and Seb and Nut brought forth Osiris, and Heru-khent-an-maati, and Set, and Isis, and Nephthys at one birth, one after the other, and they produced their multitudes of offspring in this earth."

Book of Knowing 2

Updated and edited version from Legends of the Gods by E.A. Wallis Budge

The Book of Knowing the Evolutions of Ra, and of Overthrowing Apep. These are the words of the god Neb-er-tcher, who said:

"I am the creator of what has come into being, and I myself came into being under the form of the god Khepera, and I came into being in primeval time. I came into being in the form of Khepera, and I am the creator of what did come into being, that is to say, I formed myself out of the primeval matter, and I made and formed myself out of the substance which existed in primeval time.

"My name is Osiris, who is the primeval matter of primeval matter. I have done my will in everything in this earth. I have spread myself abroad, and I have made strong my hand. I was One by myself, for the gods had not been brought forth, and I had emitted from myself neither Shu nor Tefnut. I brought my own name into my mouth as a word of power, and with it I immediately came into being under the form of things which are and under the form of Khepera.

"I came into being from out of primeval matter, and from the beginning I appeared under the form of the multitude of things which exist; nothing existed at that time in this earth, and it was I who made everything that was made. I was One: by myself, and there was no other being who worked with me in that place. I made all the things under the forms of which I appeared then by means of the Soul-God which I raised into firmness

Divine Evolutions

at that time from out of Nu, from a state of inactivity. I found no place on which I could stand, I worked by the power of a spell by means of my heart. I laid a foundation for things before me, and everything that was made, I made. I was One by myself, and I laid the foundation of things by means of my heart, and I made the other things which came into being, and the things of Khepera which were made were manifold, and their offspring came into existence from the things to which they gave birth.

"It was I who emitted Shu, and it was I who emitted Tefnut, and from being the One god I became three gods; the two other gods who came into being on this earth sprang from me, and Shu and Tefnut were raised up from out of Nu in which they were. Now behold, they brought my Eye to me after two hen periods since the time when they went forth from me. I gathered together my members and afterwards I had union with my hand, and my heart came to me from out of my hand, and the seed fell into my mouth, and I emitted from myself the gods Shu and Tefnut, and so from being the One god I became three gods; thus the two other gods who came into being on this earth sprang from me, and Shu and Tefnut were raised up from out of Nu in which they were.

"My father Nu says that they covered up my Eye with the plant-like clouds which were behind them for very many hen periods. Plants and creeping things sprang up from the god Rem, through the tears which I let fall. I cried out to my Eye, and men and women came into existence. Then I bestowed upon my Eye the uraeus of fire, and it was angry with me when another Eye came and grew up in its place; its vigorous power fell on the plants, on the plants which I had placed there, and it set order among them, and it took up its place in my face, and it does rule the whole earth. Then Shu and Tefnut brought forth Osiris, and Heru-khenti-an-maa, and Set, and Isis, and Nephthys and behold, they have produced offspring, and have created a multitude of children in this earth, by means of the beings which came into existence from the creatures which they produced. They invoke my name, and they overthrow their enemies, and they make words of power for the overthrowing of Apep, over whose hands and arms Aker keeps ward. His hands and arms shall not exist, his feet and legs shall not exist, and he is chained in one place while Ra inflicts upon him the blows which are decreed for him. He is thrown upon his accursed back, his face is slit open because of the evil which he has done, and he shall remain upon his accursed back."

The Legend of Ra and Isis

Updated and edited version from Legends of the Gods by E.A. Wallis Budge

The chapter of the divine god, who created himself, who made the heavens and the earth, and the breath of life, and fire, and the gods, and men, and beasts, and cattle, and reptiles, and the fowl of the air, and the fish, who is the king of men and gods, who exists in one form, to whom periods of one hundred and twenty years act as single years, whose names by reason of their multitude are unknowable, for even the gods know them not. Behold, the goddess Isis lived in the form, of a woman, who had the knowledge of words of power. Her heart turned away in disgust from the millions of men, and she chose for herself the millions of the gods, but esteemed more highly the millions of the spirits. Was it not possible to become even as was Ra in heaven and upon earth, and to make herself mistress of the earth, and a mighty goddess–thus she meditated in her heart–by the knowledge of the Name of the holy god? Behold, Ra entered heaven each day at the head of his mariners, establishing himself upon the double throne of the two horizons. Now the divine one had become old, he dribbled at the mouth, and he let his emissions go forth from him upon the earth, and his spittle fell upon the ground. This Isis kneaded in her hand, with some dust, and she fashioned it in the form of a sacred serpent, and made it to have the form of a dart, so that none might be able to escape alive from it, and she left it lying upon the road on which the great god traveled, according to his desire, about the two lands. Then the holy god rose up in the tabernacle of the gods in the great double house among those who were in his train, and as he journeyed on his way according to his daily desire, the holy serpent shot its fang into him, and the living fire was departing from the god's own body, and the reptile destroyed the dweller among the cedars. And the mighty god opened his mouth, and the cry of His Majesty (life, strength, health!) reached to the heavens, and the company of the gods said, "What is it?" and his gods said, "What is the matter?" And the god found no words with which to answer concerning himself. His jaws shook, his lips trembled, and the poison took possession of all his flesh just as Hapi (the Nile) takes possession of the land through which he flows.

Then the great god made firm his heart and he cried out to those who were in his following: "Come to me, Oh you who have come into being from my members, you gods who have proceeded from me, for I would make you to know what has happened. I have been smitten by some deadly thing, of which my heart has no knowledge, and which I have neither seen with my eyes nor made with my hand; and I have no knowledge at all who has done this to me. I have never before felt any pain like it, and no pain can be worse than this is. I am a Prince, the son of a Prince, and the divine emanation which was produced from a god. I am a Great One, the son of a Great

One, and my father has determined for me my name. I have multitudes of names, and I have multitudes of forms, and my being exists in every god. I have been invoked by Temu and Heru-Hekennu. My father and my mother uttered my name, and they hid it in my body at my birth so that none of those who would use against me words of power might succeed in making their enchantments have dominion over me. I had come forth from my tabernacle to look upon that which I had made, and was making my way through the two lands which I had made, when a blow was aimed at me, but I know not of what kind. Behold, is it fire? Behold, is it water? My heart is full of burning fire, my limbs are shivering, and my members have darting pains in them. Let there be brought to me my children the gods, who possess words of magic, whose mouths are cunning in uttering them, and whose powers reach up to heaven."

Then his children came to him, and every god was there with his cry of lamentation. Isis came with her words of magic, and her mouth was filled with the breath of life, for the words which she puts together destroy diseases, and her words make to live those who are dead. And she said, "What is this, Oh divine father? What is it? Has a serpent shot his venom into you? Has a thing which you have fashioned lifted up its head against you? Certainly it shall be overthrown by beneficent words of power, and I will make it retreat in the sight of your rays." The holy god opened his mouth, saying, I was going along the road and passing through the two lands of my country, for my heart wished to look upon what I had made, when I was bitten by a serpent which I did not see; behold, is it fire? Behold, is it water? I am colder than water, I am hotter than fire, all my members sweat, I myself quake, mine eye is unsteady. I cannot look at the heavens, and water forces itself on my face as in the time of the Inundation." And Isis said to Ra, "Oh my divine father, tell me your name, for he who is able to pronounce his name lives." And Ra said, "I am the maker of the heavens and the earth, I have knit together the mountains, and I have created everything which exists upon them. I am the maker of the Waters, and I have made Meht-ur to come into being; I have made the Bull of his Mother, and I have caused the joys of love to exist. I am the maker of heaven, and I have caused to be hidden the two gods of the horizon, and I have placed the souls of the gods within them. I am the Being who opens his eyes and the light comes; I am the Being who shuts his eyes and there is darkness. I am the Being who gives the command, and the waters of Hapi (the Nile) burst forth, I am the Being whose name the gods know not. I am the maker of hours and the creator of days. I am the opener of the festivals, and the maker of the floods of water. I am the creator of the fire of life whereby the works of the houses are caused to come into being. I am

Khepera in the morning, and Ra at the time of his culmination, and Temu in the evening." Nevertheless the poison was not driven from its course, and the great god felt no better. Then Isis said to Ra, "Among the things which you have said to me your name has not been mentioned. Declare it to me, and the poison shall come forth; for the person who has declared his name shall live." Meanwhile the poison burned with blazing fire and the heat thereof was stronger than that of a blazing flame. Then the Majesty of Ra said, "I will allow myself to be searched through by Isis, and my name shall come forth from my body and go into hers." Then the divine one hid himself from the gods, and the throne in the Boat of Millions of Years was empty. And it came to pass that when it was the time for the heart to come forth from the god, she said to her son Horus, "The great god shall bind himself by an oath to give his two eyes." Thus was the great god made to yield up his name, and Isis, the great lady of enchantments, said, "Flow on, poison, and come forth from Ra; let the Eye of Horus come forth from the god and shine outside his mouth. I have worked, and I make the poison to fall on the ground, for the venom has been mastered. Truly the name has been taken away from the great god. Let Ra live, and let the poison die; and if the poison live then Ra shall die. And similarly, a certain man, the son of a certain man, shall live and the poison shall die." These were the words which spoke Isis, the great lady, the mistress of the gods, and she had knowledge of Ra in his own name. The above words shall be said over an image of Temu and an image of Heru-Hekennu, and over an image of Isis and an image of Horus.

The Origin of Horus

Updated and edited version from Legends of the Gods by E.A. Wallis Budge

Homage to you, Osiris, Lord of eternity, King of the gods, whose names are manifold, whose transformations are sublime, whose form is hidden in the temples whose Ka is holy, the Governor of Tetut, the mighty one of possessions in the shrine, the Lord of praises in the home of Anetch, President of the tchefa food in Anu, Lord who are commemorated in the town of Maati, the hidden Soul, the Lord of Qerret, the sublime one in White Wall, the Soul of Ra and his very body, who have your dwelling in Henensu, the beneficent one, who are praised in Nart, who makes to rise up your Soul, Lord of the Great House in the city of the Eight Gods, who inspires great terror in Shas-hetep, Lord of eternity, Governor of Abtu (Abydos).

Your domain reaches far into Ta-tchesert, and your name is firmly established in the mouths of men. You are the two-fold substance of the Two Lands everywhere, and the divine food of the KAU, the Governor of the Companies of the Gods, and the perfect Spirit-soul among Spirit-souls. The god Nu draws his waters from you, and you bring forth the north wind at evening, and wind from your nostrils to the satisfaction of your heart.

Your heart flourishes, and you bring forth the splendor of tchef food. The height of heaven and the stars thereof are obedient to you, and you cause to be opened the great gates of the sky. You are the lord to whom praises are sung in the southern heaven, you are he to whom thanks are given in the northern heaven. The stars which never diminish are under the place of your face, and your seats are the stars which never rest. Offerings appear before you by the command of Keb. The Companies of the Gods ascribe praise to you, the Star-gods of the Tuat smell the earth before you, the domains make bowings before you, and the ends of the earth make supplication to you when they see you.

Those who are among the holy ones are in terror of him, and the Two Lands, all of them, make acclamations to him when they meet His Majesty. You are a shining Noble at the head of the nobles, permanent in your high rank, established in your sovereignty, the beneficent Power of the Company of the Gods. Well-pleasing is your face, and you are beloved by him that sees you. You set the fear of you in all lands, and because of their love for you men hold your name to be preeminent. Every man makes offerings to you, and you are the Lord who is commemorated in heaven and on earth. Manifold are the cries of acclamation to you in the Uak festival, and the Two Lands shout joyously to you with one accord. You are the eldest, the first of your brothers, the Prince of the Company of the Gods, and the establisher of Truth throughout the Two Lands. You set your son upon the great throne of his father Keb. You are the beloved one of your mother Nut, whose valor is most mighty when you overthrow the Seba Fiend.

You have slaughtered your enemy, and have installed fear in your Adversary. You are the bringer-in of the farthest boundaries, and are stable of heart, and your two feet are lifted up; you are the heir of Keb and of the sovereignty of the Two Lands, and he has seen your splendid qualities, and has commanded you to guide the lands by your hand so long as times and seasons endure.

You have made this earth with your hand, the waters thereof, the winds thereof, the trees and herbs thereof, the cattle thereof of every kind, the birds thereof of every kind, the fish thereof of every kind, the creeping things thereof, and the four-footed beasts thereof. The land of the desert belongs by right to the son of Nut, and the Two Lands have contentment in making him to rise upon the throne of his father like Ra.

You roll up into the horizon, you set the light above the darkness, you illuminate the Two Lands with the light from your two plumes, you flood the Two Lands like the Disk at the beginning of the dawn. Your White Crown pierces the height of heaven saluting the stars, you are the guide of every god. You are perfect in command and word. You are the favored one of the Great Company of the Gods, and you are the beloved one of the Little Company of the Gods.

Your sister Isis acted as a protector to you. She drove your enemies away, she averted seasons of calamity from you, she recited the word with the magical power of her mouth, being skilled of tongue and never halting for a word, being perfect in command and word. Isis the magician avenged her brother. She went about seeking for him untiringly.

She flew round and round over this earth uttering wailing cries of grief, and she did not alight on the ground until she had found him. She made light to come forth from her feathers, she made air to come into being by means of her two wings, and she cried out the death cries for her brother.

She made to rise up the helpless members of him whose heart was at rest, she drew from him his essence, and she made from him an heir. She suckled the child in solitude and none knew where his place was, and he grew in strength. His hand is mighty within the house of Keb, and the Company of the Gods rejoice greatly at the coming of Horus, the son of Osiris, whose heart is firmly established, the triumphant one, the son of Isis, the flesh and bone of Osiris. The Tchatcha of Truth, and the Company of the Gods, and Neb-ertcher himself, and the Lords of Truth, gather together to him, and assemble therein.

Truly those who defeat iniquity rejoice in the House of Keb to bestow the divine rank and dignity upon him to whom it belongs, and the sovereignty upon him whose it is by right.

Chapter 3

Sons of God

One God

Of Hermetic Origins. Updated and edited version from the writings of Lucius Cornelius Alexander Polyhistor, 1st Century BC, from Ancient Fragments, by I.P. Cory

The Self-Created God

From The Ancient Hermetic Books. Before all things that essentially exist, and before the total principles, there is one God, prior to the first God and King, remaining immovable in the solitude of his unity; for neither is the Intelligible intermingled with him, nor any other thing. He is established, the exemplar of the God who is the father of himself, self-begotten, the only father, and who is truly good. For he is something greater, and the first; the fountain of all things, and the root of all primary Intelligible existing forms. But out of this one, the self-ruling God made himself shine forth; for this reason he is the father of himself, and self-ruling: for he is the first principle and God of Gods. He is the monad from the one; before essence, yet the first principle of essence, for from him is entity and essence; on which account he is celebrated as the chief of the Intelligible beings. These are the most ancient principles of all things, which Hermes places first in order, before the ethereal and empyrean gods and the celestial.

From Chaos to Man

Updated and edited version from the writings of Lucius Cornelius Alexander Polyhistor, 1st Century BC, from Ancient Fragments, by I.P. Cory

What Orpheus has asserted on the subject is as follows: "From the beginning the Ether was manifested in time," evidently having been fabricated by

God: "and on every side of the Ether was the Chaos; and gloomy Night enveloped and obscured all things which were under the Ether." By attributing to Night a priority, he intimates the explanation to be, that there existed an incomprehensible nature, and a being supreme above all others, and preexisting, the demiurgus of all things, as well of the Ether itself (and of the night) as of all the creation which existed and was concealed under the Ether. Moreover he says, "Earth was invisible on account of the darkness: but the Light broke through the Ether, and illuminated the Earth and all the material of the creation:" signifying by this Light, which burst forth through the Ether, the before-mentioned being who was supreme above all things: "and its name," which Orpheus learned from the oracle, is "Metis, Phanes, Ericepæus," which in the common Greek language may be translated will (or counsel), light, life-giver; signifying, when explained, that these three powers of the three names are the one power and strength of the only God, whom no one ever beheld, and of whose power no one can have an idea or comprehend the nature. "By this power all things were produced, as well incorporeal principles as the sun and moon, and their influences, and all the stars, and the earth and the sea, and all things that are visible and invisible in them. And man," says he, "was formed by this God out of the earth, and endued with a reasonable soul," in like manner as Moses has revealed.

Creation to Babel

Excerpt. From Holy Bible, WEB Version, Genesis Chapters 1-11

Genesis 1

The Creation of the World

1 In the beginning, God created the heavens and the earth. 2 The earth was formless and empty. Darkness was on the surface of the deep and God's Spirit was hovering over the surface of the waters. 3 God said, "Let there be light," and there was light. 4 God saw the light, and saw that it was good. God divided the light from the darkness. 5 God called the light "day", and the darkness he called "night". There was evening and there was morning, the first day. 6 God said, "Let there be an expanse in the middle of the waters, and let it divide the waters from the waters." 7 God made the expanse, and divided the waters which were under the expanse from the waters which were above the expanse; and it was so. 8 God called the expanse "sky". There was evening and there was morning, a second day. 9 God said, "Let the waters under the sky be gathered together to one place, and let the dry land appear;" and it was so. 10 God called the dry land "earth", and the gathering together of the waters he called "seas". God saw that it was good. 11 God

said, "Let the earth yield grass, herbs yielding seeds, and fruit trees bearing fruit after their kind, with their seeds in it, on the earth;" and it was so. 12 The earth yielded grass, herbs yielding seed after their kind, and trees bearing fruit, with their seeds in it, after their kind; and God saw that it was good. 13 There was evening and there was morning, a third day. 14 God said, "Let there be lights in the expanse of the sky to divide the day from the night; and let them be for signs to mark seasons, days, and years; 15 and let them be for lights in the expanse of the sky to give light on the earth;" and it was so. 16 God made the two great lights: the greater light to rule the day, and the lesser light to rule the night. He also made the stars. 17 God set them in the expanse of the sky to give light to the earth, 18 and to rule over the day and over the night, and to divide the light from the darkness. God saw that it was good. 19 There was evening and there was morning, a fourth day. 20 God said, "Let the waters abound with living creatures, and let birds fly above the earth in the open expanse of the sky." 21 God created the large sea creatures and every living creature that moves, with which the waters swarmed, after their kind, and every winged bird after its kind. God saw that it was good. 22 God blessed them, saying, "Be fruitful, and multiply, and fill the waters in the seas, and let birds multiply on the earth." 23 There was evening and there was morning, a fifth day. 24 God said, "Let the earth produce living creatures after their kind, livestock, creeping things, and animals of the earth after their kind;" and it was so. 25 God made the animals of the earth after their kind, and the livestock after their kind, and everything that creeps on the ground after its kind. God saw that it was good. 26 God said, "Let's make man in our image, after our likeness. Let them have dominion over the fish of the sea, and over the birds of the sky, and over the livestock, and over all the earth, and over every creeping thing that creeps on the earth." 27 God created man in his own image. In God's image he created him; male and female he created them. 28 God blessed them. God said to them, "Be fruitful, multiply, fill the earth, and subdue it. Have dominion over the fish of the sea, over the birds of the sky, and over every living thing that moves on the earth." 29 God said, "Behold, I have given you every herb yielding seed, which is on the surface of all the earth, and every tree, which bears fruit yielding seed. It will be your food. 30 To every animal of the earth, and to every bird of the sky, and to everything that creeps on the earth, in which there is life, I have given every green herb for food;" and it was so. 31 God saw everything that he had made, and, behold, it was very good. There was evening and there was morning, a sixth day.

Genesis 2

The Seventh Day, God Rests

1 The heavens, the earth, and all their vast array were finished. 2 On the seventh day God finished his work which he had done; and he rested on the seventh day from all his work which he had done. 3 God blessed the seventh day, and made it holy, because he rested in it from all his work of creation which he had done.

The Creation of Man and Woman

4 This is the history of the generations of the heavens and of the earth when they were created, in the day that Yahweh God made the earth and the heavens. 5 No plant of the field was yet in the earth, and no herb of the field had yet sprung up; for Yahweh God had not caused it to rain on the earth. There was not a man to till the ground, 6 but a mist went up from the earth, and watered the whole surface of the ground. 7 Yahweh God formed man from the dust of the ground, and breathed into his nostrils the breath of life; and man became a living soul. 8 Yahweh God planted a garden eastward, in Eden, and there he put the man whom he had formed. 9 Out of the ground Yahweh God made every tree to grow that is pleasant to the sight, and good for food, including the tree of life in the middle of the garden and the tree of the knowledge of good and evil. 10 A river went out of Eden to water the garden; and from there it was parted, and became the source of four rivers. 11 The name of the first is Pishon: it flows through the whole land of Havilah, where there is gold; 12 and the gold of that land is good. Bdellium and onyx stone are also there. 13 The name of the second river is Gihon. It is the same river that flows through the whole land of Cush. 14 The name of the third river is Hiddekel. This is the one which flows in front of Assyria. The fourth river is the Euphrates. 15 Yahweh God took the man, and put him into the garden of Eden to cultivate and keep it. 16 Yahweh God commanded the man, saying, "You may freely eat of every tree of the garden; 17 but you shall not eat of the tree of the knowledge of good and evil; for in the day that you eat of it, you will surely die." 18 Yahweh God said, "It is not good for the man to be alone. I will make him a helper comparable to him." 19 Out of the ground Yahweh God formed every animal of the field, and every bird of the sky, and brought them to the man to see what he would call them. Whatever the man called every living creature became its name. 20 The man gave names to all livestock, and to the birds of the sky, and to every animal of the field; but for man there was not found a helper comparable to him. 21 Yahweh God caused the man to fall into a deep sleep. As the man slept, he took one of his ribs, and closed up the flesh in its place. 22 Yahweh God made a woman from

the rib which he had taken from the man, and brought her to the man. 23 The man said, "This is now bone of my bones, and flesh of my flesh. She will be called 'woman,' because she was taken out of Man." 24 Therefore a man will leave his father and his mother, and will join with his wife, and they will be one flesh. 25 The man and his wife were both naked, and they were not ashamed.

Genesis 3

The Fall

1 Now the serpent was more subtle than any animal of the field which Yahweh God had made. He said to the woman, "Has God really said, 'You shall not eat of any tree of the garden'?" 2 The woman said to the serpent, "We may eat fruit from the trees of the garden, 3 but not the fruit of the tree which is in the middle of the garden. God has said, 'You shall not eat of it. You shall not touch it, lest you die.'" 4 The serpent said to the woman, "You won't really die, 5 for God knows that in the day you eat it, your eyes will be opened, and you will be like God, knowing good and evil." 6 When the woman saw that the tree was good for food, and that it was a delight to the eyes, and that the tree was to be desired to make one wise, she took some of its fruit, and ate; and she gave some to her husband with her, and he ate it, too. 7 Their eyes were opened, and they both knew that they were naked. They sewed fig leaves together, and made coverings for themselves. 8 They heard Yahweh God's voice walking in the garden in the cool of the day, and the man and his wife hid themselves from the presence of Yahweh God among the trees of the garden. 9 Yahweh God called to the man, and said to him, "Where are you?" 10 The man said, "I heard your voice in the garden, and I was afraid, because I was naked; and I hid myself." 11 God said, "Who told you that you were naked? Have you eaten from the tree that I commanded you not to eat from?" 12 The man said, "The woman whom you gave to be with me, she gave me fruit from the tree, and I ate it." 13 Yahweh God said to the woman, "What have you done?" The woman said, "The serpent deceived me, and I ate." 14 Yahweh God said to the serpent, "Because you have done this, you are cursed above all livestock, and above every animal of the field. You shall go on your belly and you shall eat dust all the days of your life. 15 I will put hostility between you and the woman, and between your offspring and her offspring. He will bruise your head, and you will bruise his heel." 16 To the woman he said, "I will greatly multiply your pain in childbirth. In pain you will bear children. Your desire will be for your husband, and he will rule over you." 17 To Adam he said, "Because you have listened to your wife's voice, and ate from the tree, about which I commanded you, saying, 'You shall not eat of it,' the ground is cursed for your sake. You

will eat from it with much labor all the days of your life. 18 It will yield thorns and thistles to you; and you will eat the herb of the field. 19 By the sweat of your face will you eat bread until you return to the ground, for out of it you were taken. For you are dust, and to dust you shall return." 20 The man called his wife Eve because she would be the mother of all the living. 21 Yahweh God made garments of animal skins for Adam and for his wife, and clothed them. 22 Yahweh God said, "Behold, the man has become like one of us, knowing good and evil. Now, lest he reach out his hand, and also take of the tree of life, and eat, and live forever—" 23 Therefore Yahweh God sent him out from the garden of Eden, to till the ground from which he was taken. 24 So he drove out the man; and he placed cherubim at the east of the garden of Eden, and a flaming sword which turned every way, to guard the way to the tree of life.

Genesis 4

Cain and Abel

1 The man knew Eve his wife. She conceived, and gave birth to Cain, and said, "I have gotten a man with Yahweh's help." 2 Again she gave birth, to Cain's brother Abel. Abel was a keeper of sheep, but Cain was a tiller of the ground. 3 As time passed, Cain brought an offering to Yahweh from the fruit of the ground. 4 Abel also brought some of the firstborn of his flock and of its fat. Yahweh respected Abel and his offering, 5 but he didn't respect Cain and his offering. Cain was very angry, and the expression on his face fell. 6 Yahweh said to Cain, "Why are you angry? Why has the expression of your face fallen? 7 If you do well, won't it be lifted up? If you don't do well, sin crouches at the door. Its desire is for you, but you are to rule over it." 8 Cain said to Abel, his brother, "Let's go into the field." While they were in the field, Cain rose up against Abel, his brother, and killed him. 9 Yahweh said to Cain, "Where is Abel, your brother?" He said, "I don't know. Am I my brother's keeper?" 10 Yahweh said, "What have you done? The voice of your brother's blood cries to me from the ground. 11 Now you are cursed because of the ground, which has opened its mouth to receive your brother's blood from your hand. 12 From now on, when you till the ground, it won't yield its strength to you. You will be a fugitive and a wanderer in the earth." 13 Cain said to Yahweh, "My punishment is greater than I can bear. 14 Behold, you have driven me out today from the surface of the ground. I will be hidden from your face, and I will be a fugitive and a wanderer in the earth. Whoever finds me will kill me." 15 Yahweh said to him, "Therefore whoever slays Cain, vengeance will be taken on him sevenfold." Yahweh appointed a sign for Cain, so that anyone finding him would not strike him. 16 Cain left Yahweh's presence, and lived in the land of

Nod, east of Eden. 17 Cain knew his wife. She conceived, and gave birth to Enoch. He built a city, and called the name of the city, after the name of his son, Enoch. 18 To Enoch was born Irad. Irad became the father of Mehujael. Mehujael became the father of Methushael. Methushael became the father of Lamech. 19 Lamech took two wives: the name of the first one was Adah, and the name of the second one was Zillah. 20 Adah gave birth to Jabal, who was the father of those who dwell in tents and have livestock. 21 His brother's name was Jubal, who was the father of all who handle the harp and pipe. 22 Zillah also gave birth to Tubal Cain, the forger of every cutting instrument of brass and iron. Tubal Cain's sister was Naamah. 23 Lamech said to his wives, "Adah and Zillah, hear my voice. You wives of Lamech, listen to my speech, for I have slain a man for wounding me, a young man for bruising me. 24 If Cain will be avenged seven times, truly Lamech seventy-seven times." 25 Adam knew his wife again. She gave birth to a son, and named him Seth, saying, "for God has given me another child instead of Abel, for Cain killed him." 26 A son was also born to Seth, and he named him Enosh. At that time men began to call on Yahweh's name.

Genesis 5

Adam's Descendants to Noah

1 This is the book of the generations of Adam. In the day that God created man, he made him in God's likeness. 2 He created them male and female, and blessed them. On the day they were created, he named them Adam. 3 Adam lived one hundred thirty years, and became the father of a son in his own likeness, after his image, and named him Seth. 4 The days of Adam after he became the father of Seth were eight hundred years, and he became the father of other sons and daughters. 5 All the days that Adam lived were nine hundred thirty years, then he died. 6 Seth lived one hundred five years, then became the father of Enosh. 7 Seth lived after he became the father of Enosh eight hundred seven years, and became the father of other sons and daughters. 8 All of the days of Seth were nine hundred twelve years, then he died. 9 Enosh lived ninety years, and became the father of Kenan. 10 Enosh lived after he became the father of Kenan eight hundred fifteen years, and became the father of other sons and daughters. 11 All of the days of Enosh were nine hundred five years, then he died. 12 Kenan lived seventy years, then became the father of Mahalalel. 13 Kenan lived after he became the father of Mahalalel eight hundred forty years, and became the father of other sons and daughters 14 and all of the days of Kenan were nine hundred ten years, then he died. 15 Mahalalel lived sixty-five years, then became the father of Jared. 16 Mahalalel lived after he became the father of Jared eight hundred thirty years, and became the father of other sons and

daughters. 17 All of the days of Mahalalel were eight hundred ninety-five years, then he died. 18 Jared lived one hundred sixty-two years, then became the father of Enoch. 19 Jared lived after he became the father of Enoch eight hundred years, and became the father of other sons and daughters. 20 All of the days of Jared were nine hundred sixty-two years, then he died. 21 Enoch lived sixty-five years, then became the father of Methuselah. 22 After Methuselah's birth, Enoch walked with God for three hundred years, and became the father of more sons and daughters. 23 All the days of Enoch were three hundred sixty-five years. 24 Enoch walked with God, and he was not found, for God took him. 25 Methuselah lived one hundred eighty-seven years, then became the father of Lamech. 26 Methuselah lived after he became the father of Lamech seven hundred eighty-two years, and became the father of other sons and daughters. 27 All the days of Methuselah were nine hundred sixty-nine years, then he died. 28 Lamech lived one hundred eighty-two years, then became the father of a son. 29 He named him Noah, saying, "This one will comfort us in our work and in the toil of our hands, caused by the ground which Yahweh has cursed." 30 Lamech lived after he became the father of Noah five hundred ninety-five years, and became the father of other sons and daughters. 31 All the days of Lamech were seven hundred seventy-seven years, then he died. 32 Noah was five hundred years old, then Noah became the father of Shem, Ham, and Japheth.

Genesis 6

Increasing Corruption on Earth

1 When men began to multiply on the surface of the ground, and daughters were born to them, 2 God's sons saw that men's daughters were beautiful, and they took any that they wanted for themselves as wives. 3 Yahweh said, "My Spirit will not strive with man forever, because he also is flesh; so his days will be one hundred twenty years." 4 The Nephilim were in the earth in those days, and also after that, when God's sons came in to men's daughters and had children with them. Those were the mighty men who were of old, men of renown. 5 Yahweh saw that the wickedness of man was great in the earth, and that every imagination of the thoughts of man's heart was continually only evil. 6 Yahweh was sorry that he had made man on the earth, and it grieved him in his heart. 7 Yahweh said, "I will destroy man whom I have created from the surface of the ground—man, along with animals, creeping things, and birds of the sky—for I am sorry that I have made them." 8 But Noah found favor in Yahweh's eyes.

Noah and the Flood

9 This is the history of the generations of Noah: Noah was a righteous man, blameless among the people of his time.

Noah walked with God. 10 Noah became the father of three sons: Shem, Ham, and Japheth. 11 The earth was corrupt before God, and the earth was filled with violence. 12 God saw the earth, and saw that it was corrupt, for all flesh had corrupted their way on the earth. 13 God said to Noah, "I will bring an end to all flesh, for the earth is filled with violence through them. Behold, I will destroy them and the earth. 14 Make a ship of gopher wood. You shall make rooms in the ship, and shall seal it inside and outside with pitch. 15 This is how you shall make it. The length of the ship shall be three hundred cubits, its width fifty cubits, and its height thirty cubits. 16 You shall make a roof in the ship, and you shall finish it to a cubit upward. You shall set the door of the ship in its side. You shall make it with lower, second, and third levels. 17 I, even I, will bring the flood of waters on this earth, to destroy all flesh having the breath of life from under the sky. Everything that is in the earth will die. 18 But I will establish my covenant with you. You shall come into the ship, you, your sons, your wife, and your sons' wives with you. 19 Of every living thing of all flesh, you shall bring two of every sort into the ship, to keep them alive with you. They shall be male and female. 20 Of the birds after their kind, of the livestock after their kind, of every creeping thing of the ground after its kind, two of every sort will come to you, to keep them alive. 21 Take with you some of all food that is eaten, and gather it to yourself; and it will be for food for you, and for them." 22 Thus Noah did. He did all that God commanded him.

Genesis 7

1 Yahweh said to Noah, "Come with all of your household into the ship, for I have seen your righteousness before me in this generation. 2 You shall take seven pairs of every clean animal with you, the male and his female. Of the animals that are not clean, take two, the male and his female. 3 Also of the birds of the sky, seven and seven, male and female, to keep seed alive on the surface of all the earth. 4 In seven days, I will cause it to rain on the earth for forty days and forty nights. I will destroy every living thing that I have made from the surface of the ground." 5 Noah did everything that Yahweh commanded him. 6 Noah was six hundred years old when the flood of waters came on the earth. 7 Noah went into the ship with his sons, his wife, and his sons' wives, because of the floodwaters. 8 Clean animals, unclean animals, birds, and everything that creeps on the ground 9 went by pairs to Noah into the ship, male and female, as God commanded Noah. 10 After the seven days, the floodwaters came on the earth. 11 In the six hundredth year of Noah's life, in the second month, on the seventeenth day of the month, on that day all the fountains of the great deep burst open, and the sky's windows opened. 12 It rained on

the earth forty days and forty nights. 13 In the same day Noah, and Shem, Ham, and Japheth—the sons of Noah—and Noah's wife and the three wives of his sons with them, entered into the ship— 14 they, and every animal after its kind, all the livestock after their kind, every creeping thing that creeps on the earth after its kind, and every bird after its kind, every bird of every sort. 15 Pairs from all flesh with the breath of life in them went into the ship to Noah. 16 Those who went in, went in male and female of all flesh, as God commanded him; then Yahweh shut him in. 17 The flood was forty days on the earth. The waters increased, and lifted up the ship, and it was lifted up above the earth. 18 The waters rose, and increased greatly on the earth; and the ship floated on the surface of the waters. 19 The waters rose very high on the earth. All the high mountains that were under the whole sky were covered. 20 The waters rose fifteen cubits higher, and the mountains were covered. 21 All flesh died that moved on the earth, including birds, livestock, animals, every creeping thing that creeps on the earth, and every man. 22 All on the dry land, in whose nostrils was the breath of the spirit of life, died. 23 Every living thing was destroyed that was on the surface of the ground, including man, livestock, creeping things, and birds of the sky. They were destroyed from the earth. Only Noah was left, and those who were with him in the ship. 24 The waters flooded the earth one hundred fifty days.

Genesis 8

The Flood Subsides

1 God remembered Noah, all the animals, and all the livestock that were with him in the ship; and God made a wind to pass over the earth. The waters subsided. 2 The deep's fountains and the sky's windows were also stopped, and the rain from the sky was restrained. 3 The waters continually receded from the earth. After the end of one hundred fifty days the waters receded. 4 The ship rested in the seventh month, on the seventeenth day of the month, on Ararat's mountains. 5 The waters receded continually until the tenth month. In the tenth month, on the first day of the month, the tops of the mountains were visible. 6 At the end of forty days, Noah opened the window of the ship which he had made, 7 and he sent out a raven. It went back and forth, until the waters were dried up from the earth. 8 He himself sent out a dove to see if the waters were abated from the surface of the ground, 9 but the dove found no place to rest her foot, and she returned into the ship to him, for the waters were on the surface of the whole earth. He put out his hand, and took her, and brought her to him into the ship. 10 He waited yet another seven days; and again he sent the dove out of the ship. 11 The dove came back to him at evening and, behold, in her mouth was a freshly plucked olive leaf. So Noah knew that

the waters were abated from the earth. 12 He waited yet another seven days, and sent out the dove; and she didn't return to him anymore. 13 In the six hundred first year, in the first month, the first day of the month, the waters were dried up from the earth. Noah removed the covering of the ship, and looked. He saw that the surface of the ground was dry. 14 In the second month, on the twenty-seventh day of the month, the earth was dry. 15 God spoke to Noah, saying, 16 "Go out of the ship, you, your wife, your sons, and your sons' wives with you. 17 Bring out with you every living thing that is with you of all flesh, including birds, livestock, and every creeping thing that creeps on the earth, that they may breed abundantly in the earth, and be fruitful, and multiply on the earth." 18 Noah went out, with his sons, his wife, and his sons' wives with him. 19 Every animal, every creeping thing, and every bird, whatever moves on the earth, after their families, went out of the ship. God's Covenant with Noah 20 Noah built an altar to Yahweh, and took of every clean animal, and of every clean bird, and offered burnt offerings on the altar. 21 Yahweh smelled the pleasant aroma. Yahweh said in his heart, "I will not again curse the ground any more for man's sake because the imagination of man's heart is evil from his youth. I will never again strike every living thing, as I have done. 22 While the earth remains, seed time and harvest, and cold and heat, and summer and winter, and day and night will not cease."

Genesis 9

1 God blessed Noah and his sons, and said to them, "Be fruitful, multiply, and replenish the earth. 2 The fear of you and the dread of you will be on every animal of the earth, and on every bird of the sky. Everything that moves along the ground, and all the fish of the sea, are delivered into your hand. 3 Every moving thing that lives will be food for you. As I gave you the green herb, I have given everything to you. 4 But flesh with its life, that is, its blood, you shall not eat. 5 I will surely require accounting for your life's blood. At the hand of every animal I will require it. At the hand of man, even at the hand of every man's brother, I will require the life of man. 6 Whoever sheds man's blood, his blood will be shed by man, for God made man in his own image. 7 Be fruitful and multiply. Increase abundantly in the earth, and multiply in it." 8 God spoke to Noah and to his sons with him, saying, 9 "As for me, behold, I establish my covenant with you, and with your offspring after you, 10 and with every living creature that is with you: the birds, the livestock, and every animal of the earth with you, of all that go out of the ship, even every animal of the earth. 11 I will establish my covenant with you: All flesh will not be cut off any more by the waters of the flood. There will never again be

a flood to destroy the earth." 12 God said, "This is the token of the covenant which I make between me and you and every living creature that is with you, for perpetual generations: 13 I set my rainbow in the cloud, and it will be a sign of a covenant between me and the earth. 14 When I bring a cloud over the earth, that the rainbow will be seen in the cloud, 15 I will remember my covenant, which is between me and you and every living creature of all flesh, and the waters will no more become a flood to destroy all flesh. 16 The rainbow will be in the cloud. I will look at it, that I may remember the everlasting covenant between God and every living creature of all flesh that is on the earth." 17 God said to Noah, "This is the token of the covenant which I have established between me and all flesh that is on the earth."

Noah's Descendants

18 The sons of Noah who went out from the ship were Shem, Ham, and Japheth. Ham is the father of Canaan. 19 These three were the sons of Noah, and from these the whole earth was populated. 20 Noah began to be a farmer, and planted a vineyard. 21 He drank of the wine and got drunk. He was uncovered within his tent. 22 Ham, the father of Canaan, saw the nakedness of his father, and told his two brothers outside. 23 Shem and Japheth took a garment, and laid it on both their shoulders, went in backwards, and covered the nakedness of their father. Their faces were backwards, and they didn't see their father's nakedness. 24 Noah awoke from his wine, and knew what his youngest son had done to him. 25 He said, "Canaan is cursed. He will be a servant of servants to his brothers." 26 He said, "Blessed be Yahweh, the God of Shem. Let Canaan be his servant. 27 May God enlarge Japheth. Let him dwell in the tents of Shem. Let Canaan be his servant." 28 Noah lived three hundred fifty years after the flood. 29 All the days of Noah were nine hundred fifty years, and then he died.

Genesis 10

Nations Descended from Noah

1 Now this is the history of the generations of the sons of Noah and of Shem, Ham, and Japheth. Sons were born to them after the flood. 2 The sons of Japheth were: Gomer, Magog, Madai, Javan, Tubal, Meshech, and Tiras. 3 The sons of Gomer were: Ashkenaz, Riphath, and Togarmah. 4 The sons of Javan were: Elishah, Tarshish, Kittim, and Dodanim. 5 Of these were the islands of the nations divided in their lands, everyone after his language, after their families, in their nations. 6 The sons of Ham were: Cush, Mizraim, Put, and Canaan. 7 The sons of Cush were: Seba, Havilah, Sabtah, Raamah, and Sabteca. The sons of Raamah were: Sheba and Dedan. 8 Cush became the father of Nimrod. He began to be a mighty one in the earth. 9 He was a mighty

hunter before Yahweh. Therefore it is said, "like Nimrod, a mighty hunter before Yahweh". 10 The beginning of his kingdom was Babel, Erech, Accad, and Calneh, in the land of Shinar. 11 Out of that land he went into Assyria, and built Nineveh, Rehoboth Ir, Calah, 12 and Resen between Nineveh and the great city Calah. 13 Mizraim became the father of Ludim, Anamim, Lehabim, Naphtuhim, 14 Pathrusim, Casluhim (which the Philistines descended from), and Caphtorim. 15 Canaan became the father of Sidon (his firstborn), Heth, 16 the Jebusites, the Amorites, the Girgashites, 17 the Hivites, the Arkites, the Sinites, 18 the Arvadites, the Zemarites, and the Hamathites. Afterward the families of the Canaanites were spread abroad. 19 The border of the Canaanites was from Sidon—as you go toward Gerar—to Gaza—as you go toward Sodom, Gomorrah, Admah, and Zeboiim—to Lasha. 20 These are the sons of Ham, after their families, according to their languages, in their lands and their nations. 21 Children were also born to Shem (the elder brother of Japheth), the father of all the children of Eber. 22 The sons of Shem were: Elam, Asshur, Arpachshad, Lud, and Aram. 23 The sons of Aram were: Uz, Hul, Gether, and Mash. 24 Arpachshad became the father of Shelah. Shelah became the father of Eber. 25 To Eber were born two sons. The name of the one was Peleg, for in his days the earth was divided. His brother's name was Joktan. 26 Joktan became the father of Almodad, Sheleph, Hazarmaveth, Jerah, 27 Hadoram, Uzal, Diklah, 28 Obal, Abimael, Sheba, 29 Ophir, Havilah, and Jobab. All these were the sons of Joktan. 30 Their dwelling extended from Mesha, as you go toward Sephar, the mountain of the east. 31 These are the sons of Shem, by their families, according to their languages, lands, and nations. 32 These are the families of the sons of Noah, by their generations, according to their nations. The nations divided from these in the earth after the flood.

Genesis 11

The Tower of Babel

1 The whole earth was of one language and of one speech. 2 As they traveled from the east, they found a plain in the land of Shinar, and they lived there. 3 They said to one another, "Come, let's make bricks, and burn them thoroughly." They had brick for stone, and they used tar for mortar. 4 They said, "Come, let's build ourselves a city, and a tower whose top reaches to the sky, and let's make a name for ourselves, lest we be scattered abroad on the surface of the whole earth." 5 Yahweh came down to see the city and the tower, which the children of men built. 6 Yahweh said, "Behold, they are one people, and they all have one language, and this is what they begin to do. Now nothing will be withheld from them, which they intend to do. 7 Come, let's go down, and there confuse their language, that they may

not understand one another's speech." 8 So Yahweh scattered them abroad from there on the surface of all the earth. They stopped building the city. 9 Therefore its name was called Babel, because there Yahweh confused the language of all the earth. From there, Yahweh scattered them abroad on the surface of all the earth.

Shem's Descendants

10 This is the history of the generations of Shem: Shem was one hundred years old when he became the father of Arpachshad two years after the flood. 11 Shem lived five hundred years after he became the father of Arpachshad, and became the father of more sons and daughters. 12 Arpachshad lived thirty-five years and became the father of Shelah. 13 Arpachshad lived four hundred three years after he became the father of Shelah, and became the father of more sons and daughters. 14 Shelah lived thirty years, and became the father of Eber. 15 Shelah lived four hundred three years after he became the father of Eber, and became the father of more sons and daughters. 16 Eber lived thirty-four years, and became the father of Peleg. 17 Eber lived four hundred thirty years after he became the father of Peleg, and became the father of more sons and daughters. 18 Peleg lived thirty years, and became the father of Reu. 19 Peleg lived two hundred nine years after he became the father of Reu, and became the father of more sons and daughters. 20 Reu lived thirty-two years, and became the father of Serug. 21 Reu lived two hundred seven years after he became the father of Serug, and became the father of more sons and daughters. 22 Serug lived thirty years, and became the father of Nahor. 23 Serug lived two hundred years after he became the father of Nahor, and became the father of more sons and daughters. 24 Nahor lived twenty-nine years, and became the father of Terah. 25 Nahor lived one hundred nineteen years after he became the father of Terah, and became the father of more sons and daughters. 26 Terah lived seventy years, and became the father of Abram, Nahor, and Haran.

Terah's Descendants

27 Now this is the history of the generations of Terah. Terah became the father of Abram, Nahor, and Haran. Haran became the father of Lot. 28 Haran died in the land of his birth, in Ur of the Chaldees, while his father Terah was still alive. 29 Abram and Nahor married wives. The name of Abram's wife was Sarai, and the name of Nahor's wife was Milcah, the daughter of Haran, who was also the father of Iscah. 30 Sarai was barren. She had no child. 31 Terah took Abram his son, Lot the son of Haran, his son's son, and Sarai his daughter-in-law, his son Abram's wife. They went from Ur of the Chaldees, to go into the land of Canaan. They came to Haran and lived there. 32 The days of Terah were two hundred five years. Terah died in Haran.

The Ark

Updated and edited version from the writings of Lucius Cornelius Alexander Polyhistor, 1st Century BC, from Ancient Fragments, by I.P. Cory

There is above Minyas in the land of Armenia a very great mountain which is called Baris; to which, it is said, that many people retreated at the time of the deluge, and were saved; and that one in particular was carried there in an ark, and landed on its summit, and that the remains of the vessel were long preserved upon the mountain. Perhaps this was the same individual of whom Moses the legislator of the Jews has made mention.

Gilgamesh

Gilgamesh Learns of the Flood. Updated and edited version from Myths of Babylonia and Assyria, Donald A. Mackenzie)

The story of the Deluge which was related to Gilgamesh by Pirnapishtim.

"Hear me, Oh Gilgamesh, and I will make revelation regarding the hidden actions of the high gods. As you know, the city of Shurippak is situated upon the bank of the Euphrates. The gods were within it: there they assembled together in council. Anu, the father, was there, and Bel the counselor and warrior, Ninip the messenger, and Ennugi the governor. Ea, the wise lord, sat also with them. In their hearts the gods agreed together to send a great deluge.

"Thereafter Ea made known the purpose of the divine rulers in the hut of reeds, saying: 'Oh hut of reeds, hear; Oh wall, understand... Oh man of Shurippak, son of Umbara Tutu, tear down your house and build a ship; leave all that you possess and save your life, and preserve in the ship the living seed of every kind. The ship that you will build must be of great proportions in length and height. It must be made to float on the great deep.'

"I heard the command of Ea and understood, and I made answer, saying, 'Oh wise lord, as you have said so will I do, for your counsel is most excellent. But how shall I give reason for my actions to the young men and the elders?'

"Ea opened his mouth and said to me, his servant: 'What you will say to them is this—It has been revealed to me that Bel does hate me, therefore I cannot remain any longer in his domain, this city of Shurippak, so I must depart to the domain of Ea and dwell with him [...] to you will Bel send an abundance of rain, so that you may obtain birds and fishes in plenty and have a rich harvest. But Shamash has appointed a time for Ramman to pour down destruction from the heavens.'"

"I gathered together all that I possessed, my silver and gold and seeds of every kind, and my goods also. These I placed in the ship. Then I sent aboard all my family and house servants, the animals of the field and the beasts of the field and the workers–every one of them I sent up.

"The god Shamash appointed the time, saying: 'I will cause the Night Lord to send much rain and bring destruction. Then enter you the ship and shut your door.'

"At the appointed time the Night Lord sent much rain. I saw the beginning of the deluge and I was afraid to look up. I entered the ship and shut the door. I appointed Buzur-Kurgala, the sailor, to be captain, and put under his command the great vessel and all that it contained.

"At the dawn of day I saw rising towards the heavens a dark cloud, and in the midst of it Ramman thundered. Nebo and Marduk went in front, speeding like emissaries over hills and plains. The cables of the ship were let loose.

"Then Ninip, the tempest god, came near, and the storm broke in fury before him. All the earth spirits leapt up with flaming torches and the whole land was afire. The thunder god swept over the heavens, blotting out the sunlight and bringing thick darkness. Rain poured down the whole day long, and the earth was covered with water; the rivers were swollen; the land was in confusion; men stumbled about in the darkness, battling with the elements. Brothers were unable to see brothers; no man could recognize his friends. The spirits above looked down and beheld the rising flood and were afraid: they fled, and in the heaven of Anu they crouched as hounds do in protecting enclosures.

"In time Ishtar, the lady of the gods, cried out in distress, saying: 'The elder race has perished and turned to clay because that I have consented to evil counsel in the assembly of the gods. Alas! I have allowed my people to be destroyed. I gave being to man, but where is he? Like the offspring of fish he cumbers the deep.'

"The earth spirits were weeping with Ishtar: they sat down cowering with tightened lips and spoke not; they mourned in silence.

"Six days and six nights went past, and the tempest raged over the waters which gradually covered the land. But when the seventh day came, the wind fell, the whirling waters grew peaceful, and the sea retreated. The storm was over and the rain of destruction had ceased. I looked forth. I called aloud over the waters. But all mankind had perished and turned to clay. Where fields had been I saw marshes only.

"Then I opened wide the window of the ship, and the sunlight suffused my countenance. I was dazzled and sank down weeping and the tears streamed over my face. Everywhere I looked I saw water.

"At length, land began to appear. The ship drifted towards the country of Nitsir, and then it was held fast by the mountain of Nitsir. Six days went past and the ship remained steadfast. On the seventh day I sent forth a dove, and she flew away and searched this way and that, but found no resting place, so she returned. I then sent forth a swallow, and she returned likewise. Next I sent forth a raven, and she flew away. She saw that the waters were shrinking, and gorged and croaked and waded, but did not come back. Then I brought forth all the animals into the air of heaven.

"An offering I made on the mountain. I poured out a libation. I set up incense vessels seven by seven on heaped-up reeds and used cedar wood with incense. The gods smelt the sweet savor, and they clustered like flies about the sacrificer.

"Thereafter Ishtar came near. Lifting up the jewels, which the god Anu had fashioned for her according to her desire, she spoke, saying: 'Oh! These gods! I vow by the lapis lazuli gems upon my neck that I will never forget! I will remember these days for ever and ever. Let all the gods come here to the offering, save Bel Enlil alone, since he ignored my counsel, and sent a great deluge which destroyed my people.'

"But Bel Enlil came also, and when he beheld the ship he paused. His heart was filled with wrath against the gods and the spirits of heaven. Angrily he spoke and said: 'Has one escaped? It was decreed that no human being should survive the deluge.'

"Ninip, son of Bel, spoke, saying: 'Who has done this save Ea alone? He knows all things.'

"Ea, god of the deep, opened his mouth and said to the warrior Bel: 'you are the lord of the gods, Oh warrior. But you would not listen to my counsel and caused the deluge to be. Now punish the sinner for his sins and the evil doer for his evil deed, but be merciful and do not destroy all mankind. May there never again be a flood. Let the lion come and men will decrease. May there never again be a flood. Let the leopard come and men will decrease. May there never again be a flood. Let famine come upon the land; let Ura, god of pestilence, come and snatch off mankind. [...] I did not reveal the secret purpose of the mighty gods, but I caused Atra-chasis (Pir-napishtim) to dream a dream in which he had knowledge of what the gods had decreed.'

"Having pondered for a time over these words, Bel entered the ship alone. He grasped my hand land led me forth, even me, and he led forth my wife also, and caused her to kneel down beside me. Then he stood between us and gave his blessing. He spoke, saying: 'In time past Pir-napishtim was a man. Henceforth Pir-napishtim and his wife will be like to deities, even us. Let them dwell apart beyond the river mouths.'

"Thereafter Bel carried me here beyond the mouths of rivers."

Oannes

Of Creation and the Flood. From Berossus. Updated and edited version from the writings of Lucius Cornelius Alexander Polyhistor, 1st Century BC, from Ancient Fragments, by I.P. Cory

Berossus, in the first book of his history of Babylonia, informs us that he lived in the age of Alexander the son of Philip. And he mentions that there were written accounts, preserved at Babylon with the greatest care, comprehending a period of above fifteen myriads of years: and that these writings contained histories of the heavens and of the sea; of the birth of mankind; and of the kings, and of the memorable actions which they had achieved.

He describes Babylonia as a country situated between the Tigris and the Euphrates: that it abounded with wheat, and barley, and ocrus, and sesame; and that in the lakes were produced the roots called gongre, which are fit for food, and in respect to nutriment similar to barley. There were also palm trees and apples, and a variety of fruits; fish and also, birds—both those which are merely of flight, and those which frequent the lakes. He adds that those parts of the country which bordered upon Arabia were without water, and barren; but that the parts which lay on the other side were both hilly and fertile.

At Babylon there were—in those times—a great many of people of various nations, who inhabited Chaldea, and lived in a lawless manner like the beasts of the field. In the first year there appeared, from that part of the Erythrean sea which borders upon Babylonia, an animal destitute of reason, named Oannes, whose whole body (according to the account of Apollodorus) was that of a fish; that under the fish's head he had another head, with feet also below, similar to those of a man, subjoined to the fish's tail. His voice too, and language, was articulate and human; a representation of him is preserved even to this day.

This Being was accustomed to pass the day among men; but took no food at that season; and he gave them an insight into letters and sciences, and arts of every kind. He taught them to construct cities, to found temples, to compile laws, and explained to them the principles of geometrical knowledge. He made them distinguish the seeds of the earth, and showed them how to collect the fruits. In short, he instructed them in everything which could tend to soften manners and humanize their lives. From that time, nothing material has been added by way of improvement to his instructions. And when the sun had set, this Being Oannes, retired again into the sea, and passed the night in the deep; for he was amphibious. After this there appeared other animals like Oannes, of which Berossus proposes to give an account when he comes to the history of the kings. Moreover Oannes wrote concerning the generation of mankind; and of their civil society; and the following is the substance of what he said:

"There was a time in which there existed nothing but darkness and an abyss of waters, in which resided most hideous beings, which were produced of a two-fold principle. There ap-

Sons of God

peared men, some of whom were furnished with two wings, others with four, and with two faces. They had one body but two heads: the one that of a man, the other of a woman: and likewise in their several organs both male and female. Other human figures were to be seen with the legs and horns of goats: some had horses' feet: while others united the hind quarters of a horse with the body of a man, resembling in shape the hippocentaurs. Bulls likewise were bred there with the heads of men; and dogs with fourfold bodies, terminated in their extremities with the tails of fishes: horses also with the heads of dogs: men too and other animals, with the heads and bodies of horses and the tails of fishes. In short, there were creatures in which were combined the limbs of every species of animals. In addition to these, fishes, reptiles, serpents, with other monstrous animals, which assumed each other's shape and countenance. Of all which were preserved delineations in the temple of Belus at Babylon.

The person, who presided over them, was a woman named Omoroca; which in the Chaldean language is Thalatth; in Greek Thalassa, the sea; but which might equally be interpreted the Moon. All things being in this situation, Belus came, and cut the woman asunder: and of one half of her he formed the earth, and of the other half the heavens; and at the same time destroyed the animals within her. All this, he said, was an allegorical description of nature. For, the whole universe consisting of moisture, and animals being continually generated therein, the deity above-mentioned took off his own head: upon which the other gods mixed the blood, as it gushed out, with the earth; and from these were formed men. On this account it is that they are rational, and partake of divine knowledge. This Belus, by whom they signify Jupiter, divided the darkness, and separated the Heavens from the Earth, and reduced universe to order. But the animals, not being able to bear the prevalence of light, died. Belus, upon this, seeing a vast space unoccupied, though by nature fruitful, commanded one of the gods to take off his head, and to mix the blood with the earth; and from these to form other men and animals, which should be capable of bearing the air. Belus formed also the stars, and the sun, and the moon, and the five planets.

Xisuthrus

Of Creation and the Flood. From Berossus. Updated and edited version from the writings of Lucius Cornelius Alexander Polyhistor, 1st Century BC, from Ancient Fragments, by I.P. Cory

After the death of Ardates, his son Xisuthrus reigned eighteen sari. In his time happened a great deluge; the history of which is here described. The Deity, Cronus, appeared to him in a vision, and warned him that upon the fifteenth day of the month Daesius there would be a flood, by which mankind would be destroyed. He therefore urged him to write a history of the beginning, procedure, and conclusion of all things; and to bury it in the city of the Sun at Sippara; and to build a vessel, and take with him into it his friends and relations; and to convey on board everything necessary to sustain life, together with all the different animals; both birds and quadrupeds, and trust himself fearlessly to the deep. Having asked the Deity to where he was to sail, he was told, "To the Gods," upon which he offered up a prayer for the good of mankind. He then obeyed the divine admonition: and built a vessel five stadia in length, and two in breadth. Into this he put every thing which he had prepared; and last of all conveyed into it his wife, his children, and his friends.

After the flood had been upon the earth, and was in time abated, Xisuthrus sent out birds from the vessel; which, not finding any food, nor any place on which they might rest their feet, returned to him again. After an interval of some days, he sent them forth a second time; and they now returned with their feet tinged with mud. He made a trial a third time with these birds; but they returned to him no more: from this he judged that the surface of the earth had appeared above the waters. He therefore made an opening in the vessel, and upon looking out found that it was stranded upon the side of some mountain; upon which he immediately exited it with his wife, his daughter, and the pilot. Xisuthrus then paid his adoration to the earth: and having constructed an altar, offered sacrifices to the gods, and, with those who had come out of the vessel with him, disappeared.

Those who remained within, finding that their companions did not return, exited the vessel with many lamentations, and called continually on the name of Xisuthrus. They saw him no more; but they could distinguish his voice in the air, and could hear him admonish them to pay due regard to religion; and likewise informed them that it was upon account of his piety that he was translated to live with the gods; that his wife and daughter, and the pilot, had obtained the same honor. To this he added, that they should return to Babylonia; and, as it was ordained, search for the writings at Sippara, which they were to make known to all mankind: moreover that the place in which they then were was the land of Armenia. The rest having heard these words, offered sacrifices to the gods; and taking a circuit, journeyed towards Babylonia.

The vessel being thus stranded in Armenia, some part of it yet remains in the Corcyrean mountains of Armenia; and the people scrape off the bitumen, with which it had been outwardly coated, and make use of it by way of an antidote and amulet. When they returned to Babylon, and had found the writings at Sippara, they built cities, and erected temples: Babylon was thus inhabited again.

Sisithrus

Of the Chaldean Kings and the Flood. Updated and edited version from the writings of Lucius Cornelius Alexander Polyhistor, 1st Century BC, from Ancient Fragments, by I.P. Cory

It is said that the first king of the country was Alorus, and that he gave out a report that God had appointed him to be the Shepherd of the people: he reigned ten sari: now a sarus is esteemed to be three thousand six hundred years; a neros six hundred; and a sossus sixty.

After him Alaparus reigned three sari: to him succeeded Amillarus from the city of Pantibiblon, who reigned thirteen sari; in his time came up from the sea a second Annedotus, a semi-daemon very similar in his form to Oannes: after Amillarus reigned Ammenon twelve sari, who was of the city of Pantibiblon: then Megalarus of the same place reigned eighteen sari: then Daos, the shepherd, governed for the space of ten sari; he was of Pantibiblon; in his time four double-shaped personages came up out of the sea to land, whose names were Euedocus, Eneugamus, Eneuboulus, and Anementus: afterwards in the time of Euedoreschus appeared another Anodaphus. After these reigned other kings, and last of all Sisithrus: so that in the whole, the number amounted to ten kings, and the term of their reigns to an hundred and twenty sari.

After Euedoreschus some others reigned, and then Sisithrus. To him the deity Cronus foretold that on the fifteenth day of the month Desius there would be a deluge of rain: and he commanded him to deposit all the writings whatever which were in his possession, in the city of the Sun in Sippara.

Sisithrus, when he had complied with commands, sailed immediately to Armenia, and was presently inspired by God. Upon the third day after the cessation of the rain Sisithrus sent out birds, by way of experiment, that he might judge whether the flood had subsided. But the birds passing over an unbounded sea, without finding any place of rest, returned again to Sisithrus. This he repeated with other birds. And when upon the third trial he succeeded, for the birds then returned with their feet stained with mud, the gods translated him from among men.

With respect to the vessel, which yet remains in Armenia, it is a custom of the inhabitants to form bracelets and amulets of its wood.

The Tower of Babel

Of the Tower of Babel, Of the Tower and the Titan War. Updated and edited version from the writings of Lucius Cornelius Alexander Polyhistor, 1st Century BC, from Ancient Fragments, by I.P. Cory

Despising the Gods

From Abydenus. They say that the first inhabitants of the earth, glorying in their own strength and size, and despising the gods, undertook to raise a tower whose top should reach the sky, in the place in which Babylon now stands; but when it approached the heavens, the winds assisted the gods, and overthrew the work upon its contrivers: and its ruins are said to be still at Babylon; and the gods introduced a diversity of tongues among men, who till that time had all spoken the same language and a war arose between Cronus and Titan. The place in which they built the tower is now called Babylon, on account of the confusion of the tongues; for confusion is by the Hebrews called Babel.

The Division of Language

From Alexander Polyhistor. The Sibyl says that when all men formerly spoke the same language; some among them undertook to erect a large and lofty tower, that they might climb up into heaven. But God, sending forth a whirlwind, confounded their design, and gave to each tribe a particular language of its own; which is the reason that the name of that city is Babylon. After the deluge lived Titan and Prometheus, when Titan undertook a war against Cronus.

Dispersion

From Hestiaeus. The priests who escaped took with them the implements of the worship of the Enyalian Jove, and came to Senaar in Babylonia. But they were again driven from there by the introduction of a diversity of tongues after which they founded colonies in various parts, each settling in such situations as chance or the direction of God led them to occupy.

Scattered Giants

From Eupolemus. The city of Babylon owes its foundation to those who were saved from the catastrophe of the deluge: they were the Giants, and they built the tower which is noticed in history.

But the tower being overthrown by the interposition of God, the Giants were scattered over all the earth.

The Rise of Kingdoms

From the Sibylline Oracles. When the judgments of the Almighty God Were ripe for execution; when the Tower rose to the skies upon Assyria's plain, And all mankind one language only knew...

A dread commission from on high was given to the fell whirlwinds, which with dire alarms beat on the Tower, and to its lowest base it shook and convulsed.

And now all intercourse, by some occult and overruling power, ceased among men: by utterance they strove perplexed and anxious to disclose their mind; but their lips failed them; and in lieu of words they produced a painful babbling sound: the place was from then on called Babel; by the apostate crew named from the event.

Then severed far away, they sped uncertain into the realms unknown: thus kingdoms rose; and the glad world was filled. She then mentions Cronus, Titan and Jäpetus, and the three sons of the patriarch governing the world in the tenth generation after the deluge, thus, the triple division of the earth is afterwards mentioned, over which each of the patriarchs ruled in peace. Then is mentioned the death of Noah, and lastly the war between Cronus and Titan.

On Abraham

Of Abraham. Updated and edited version from the writings of Lucius Cornelius Alexander Polyhistor, 1st Century BC, from Ancient Fragments, by I.P. Cory

Berossus: From Josephus. After the deluge, in the tenth generation, was a certain man among the Chaldeans renowned for his justice and great exploits, and for his skill in the celestial sciences.

From Nicolaus Damascenus. Abram was king of Damascus, and he came there as a stranger with an army from that part of the country which is situated above Babylon of the Chaldeans: but after a short time he again emigrated from this region with his people and transferred his habitation to the land, which was then called Cananea, but now Judea, together with all the multitude which had increased with him; of whose history I shall give an account in another book. The name of Abram is well known even to this day in Damascus: and a village is pointed out which is still called the House of Abram.

From Eupolemus. In the tenth generation in the city Camarina of Babylonia, which some call the city Urie, and which signifies a city of the Chaldeans, the thirteenth in descent lived Abraham, of a noble race, and superior to all others in wisdom; of whom they relate that he was the inventor of astrology and the Chaldean magic, and that on account of his eminent piety he was esteemed by God. It is further said, that under the directions of God he removed and lived in Phoenicia, and there taught the Phoenicians the motions of the sun and moon and all other things; for which reason he was held in great reverence by their King.

Abraham

Excerpt. From Holy Bible, WEB Version, Genesis Chapters 12-17.

Genesis 12

The Call of Abram

1 Now Yahweh said to Abram, "Leave your country, and your relatives, and your father's house, and go to the land that I will show you. 2 I will make of you a great nation. I will bless you and make your name great. You will be a blessing. 3 I will bless those who bless

you, and I will curse him who treats you with contempt. All the families of the earth will be blessed through you." 4 So Abram went, as Yahweh had told him. Lot went with him. Abram was seventy-five years old when he departed from Haran. 5 Abram took Sarai his wife, Lot his brother's son, all their possessions that they had gathered, and the people whom they had acquired in Haran, and they went to go into the land of Canaan. They entered into the land of Canaan. 6 Abram passed through the land to the place of Shechem, to the oak of Moreh. At that time, Canaanites were in the land. 7 Yahweh appeared to Abram and said, "I will give this land to your offspring." He built an altar there to Yahweh, who had appeared to him. 8 He left from there to go to the mountain on the east of Bethel and pitched his tent, having Bethel on the west, and Ai on the east. There he built an altar to Yahweh and called on Yahweh's name. 9 Abram traveled, still going on toward the South.

Abram and Sarai in Egypt

10 There was a famine in the land. Abram went down into Egypt to live as a foreigner there, for the famine was severe in the land. 11 When he had come near to enter Egypt, he said to Sarai his wife, "See now, I know that you are a beautiful woman to look at. 12 It will happen, when the Egyptians see you, that they will say, 'This is his wife.' They will kill me, but they will save you alive. 13 Please say that you are my sister, that it may be well with me for your sake, and that my soul may live because of you." 14 When Abram had come into Egypt, Egyptians saw that the woman was very beautiful. 15 The princes of Pharaoh saw her, and praised her to Pharaoh; and the woman was taken into Pharaoh's house. 16 He dealt well with Abram for her sake. He had sheep, cattle, male donkeys, male servants, female servants, female donkeys, and camels. 17 Yahweh afflicted Pharaoh and his house with great plagues because of Sarai, Abram's wife. 18 Pharaoh called Abram and said, "What is this that you have done to me? Why didn't you tell me that she was your wife? 19 Why did you say, 'She is my sister,' so that I took her to be my wife? Now therefore, see your wife, take her, and go your way." 20 Pharaoh commanded men concerning him, and they escorted him away with his wife and all that he had.

Genesis 13

Abram and Lot Separate

1 Abram went up out of Egypt—he, his wife, all that he had, and Lot with him—into the South. 2 Abram was very rich in livestock, in silver, and in gold. 3 He went on his journeys from the South as far as Bethel, to the place where his tent had been at the beginning, between Bethel and Ai, 4 to the place of the altar, which he had made there at the first. There Abram called on Yahweh's name. 5 Lot also, who

went with Abram, had flocks, herds, and tents. 6 The land was not able to bear them, that they might live together; for their possessions were so great that they couldn't live together. 7 There was strife between the herdsmen of Abram's livestock and the herdsmen of Lot's livestock. The Canaanites and the Perizzites lived in the land at that time. 8 Abram said to Lot, "Please, let there be no strife between you and me, and between your herdsmen and my herdsmen; for we are relatives. 9 Isn't the whole land before you? Please separate yourself from me. If you go to the left hand, then I will go to the right. Or if you go to the right hand, then I will go to the left." 10 Lot lifted up his eyes, and saw all the plain of the Jordan, that it was well-watered everywhere, before Yahweh destroyed Sodom and Gomorrah, like the garden of Yahweh, like the land of Egypt, as you go to Zoar. 11 So Lot chose the Plain of the Jordan for himself. Lot traveled east, and they separated themselves the one from the other. 12 Abram lived in the land of Canaan, and Lot lived in the cities of the plain, and moved his tent as far as Sodom. 13 Now the men of Sodom were exceedingly wicked and sinners against Yahweh. 14 Yahweh said to Abram, after Lot was separated from him, "Now, lift up your eyes, and look from the place where you are, northward and southward and eastward and westward, 15 for I will give all the land which you see to you and to your offspring forever. 16 I will make your offspring as the dust of the earth, so that if a man can count the dust of the earth, then your offspring may also be counted. 17 Arise, walk through the land in its length and in its width; for I will give it to you." 18 Abram moved his tent, and came and lived by the oaks of Mamre, which are in Hebron, and built an altar there to Yahweh.

Genesis 14

Abram Rescues Lot

1 In the days of Amraphel, king of Shinar; Arioch, king of Ellasar; Chedorlaomer, king of Elam; and Tidal, king of Goiim, 2 they made war with Bera, king of Sodom; Birsha, king of Gomorrah; Shinab, king of Admah; Shemeber, king of Zeboiim; and the king of Bela (also called Zoar). 3 All these joined together in the valley of Siddim (also called the Salt Sea). 4 They served Chedorlaomer for twelve years, and in the thirteenth year they rebelled. 5 In the fourteenth year Chedorlaomer came, and the kings who were with him, and struck the Rephaim in Ashteroth Karnaim, the Zuzim in Ham, the Emim in Shaveh Kiriathaim, 6 and the Horites in their Mount Seir, to El Paran, which is by the wilderness. 7 They returned, and came to En Mishpat (also called Kadesh), and struck all the country of the Amalekites, and also the Amorites, that lived in Hazazon Tamar. 8 The king of Sodom, and the king of Gomorrah, the king of Admah, the king

of Zeboiim, and the king of Bela (also called Zoar) went out; and they set the battle in array against them in the valley of Siddim 9 against Chedorlaomer king of Elam, Tidal king of Goiim, Amraphel king of Shinar, and Arioch king of Ellasar; four kings against the five. 10 Now the valley of Siddim was full of tar pits; and the kings of Sodom and Gomorrah fled, and some fell there. Those who remained fled to the hills. 11 They took all the goods of Sodom and Gomorrah, and all their food, and went their way. 12 They took Lot, Abram's brother's son, who lived in Sodom, and his goods, and departed. 13 One who had escaped came and told Abram, the Hebrew. At that time, he lived by the oaks of Mamre, the Amorite, brother of Eshcol and brother of Aner. They were allies of Abram. 14 When Abram heard that his relative was taken captive, he led out his three hundred eighteen trained men, born in his house, and pursued as far as Dan. 15 He divided himself against them by night, he and his servants, and struck them, and pursued them to Hobah, which is on the left hand of Damascus. 16 He brought back all the goods, and also brought back his relative Lot and his goods, and the women also, and the other people.

Abram Blessed by Melchizedek

17 The king of Sodom went out to meet him after his return from the slaughter of Chedorlaomer and the kings who were with him, at the valley of Shaveh (that is, the King's Valley). 18 Melchizedek king of Salem brought out bread and wine. He was priest of God Most High. 19 He blessed him, and said, "Blessed be Abram of God Most High, possessor of heaven and earth. 20 Blessed be God Most High, who has delivered your enemies into your hand." Abram gave him a tenth of all. 21 The king of Sodom said to Abram, "Give me the people, and take the goods for yourself." 22 Abram said to the king of Sodom, "I have lifted up my hand to Yahweh, God Most High, possessor of heaven and earth, 23 that I will not take a thread nor a sandal strap nor anything that is yours, lest you should say, 'I have made Abram rich.' 24 I will accept nothing from you except that which the young men have eaten, and the portion of the men who went with me: Aner, Eshcol, and Mamre. Let them take their portion."

Genesis 15

God's Covenant with Abram

1 After these things Yahweh's word came to Abram in a vision, saying, "Don't be afraid, Abram. I am your shield, your exceedingly great reward." 2 Abram said, "Lord Yahweh, what will you give me, since I go childless, and he who will inherit my estate is Eliezer of Damascus?" 3 Abram said, "Behold, you have given no children to me: and, behold, one born in my house is my heir." 4 Behold, Yahweh's word came to him, saying, "This man will not be your heir, but he who will

come out of your own body will be your heir." 5 Yahweh brought him outside, and said, "Look now toward the sky, and count the stars, if you are able to count them." He said to Abram, "So will your offspring be." 6 He believed in Yahweh, who credited it to him for righteousness. 7 He said to Abram, "I am Yahweh who brought you out of Ur of the Chaldees, to give you this land to inherit it." 8 He said, "Lord Yahweh, how will I know that I will inherit it?" 9 He said to him, "Bring me a heifer three years old, a female goat three years old, a ram three years old, a turtledove, and a young pigeon." 10 He brought him all these, and divided them in the middle, and laid each half opposite the other; but he didn't divide the birds. 11 The birds of prey came down on the carcasses, and Abram drove them away. 12 When the sun was going down, a deep sleep fell on Abram. Now terror and great darkness fell on him. 13 He said to Abram, "Know for sure that your offspring will live as foreigners in a land that is not theirs, and will serve them. They will afflict them four hundred years. 14 I will also judge that nation, whom they will serve. Afterward they will come out with great wealth; 15 but you will go to your fathers in peace. You will be buried at a good old age. 16 In the fourth generation they will come here again, for the iniquity of the Amorite is not yet full." 17 It came to pass that, when the sun went down, and it was dark, behold, a smoking furnace and a flaming torch passed between these pieces. 18 In that day Yahweh made a covenant with Abram, saying, "I have given this land to your offspring, from the river of Egypt to the great river, the river Euphrates: 19 the land of the Kenites, the Kenizzites, the Kadmonites, 20 the Hittites, the Perizzites, the Rephaim, 21 the Amorites, the Canaanites, the Girgashites, and the Jebusites.

Genesis 16

Sarai and Hagar

1 Now Sarai, Abram's wife, bore him no children. She had a servant, an Egyptian, whose name was Hagar. 2 Sarai said to Abram, "See now, Yahweh has restrained me from bearing. Please go in to my servant. It may be that I will obtain children by her." Abram listened to the voice of Sarai. 3 Sarai, Abram's wife, took Hagar the Egyptian, her servant, after Abram had lived ten years in the land of Canaan, and gave her to Abram her husband to be his wife. 4 He went in to Hagar, and she conceived. When she saw that she had conceived, her mistress was despised in her eyes. 5 Sarai said to Abram, "This wrong is your fault. I gave my servant into your bosom, and when she saw that she had conceived, she despised me. May Yahweh judge between me and you." 6 But Abram said to Sarai, "Behold, your maid is in your hand. Do to her whatever is good in your eyes." Sarai dealt harshly with her,

and she fled from her face. 7 Yahweh's angel found her by a fountain of water in the wilderness, by the fountain on the way to Shur. 8 He said, "Hagar, Sarai's servant, where did you come from? Where are you going?" She said, "I am fleeing from the face of my mistress Sarai." 9 Yahweh's angel said to her, "Return to your mistress, and submit yourself under her hands." 10 Yahweh's angel said to her, "I will greatly multiply your offspring, that they will not be counted for multitude." 11 Yahweh's angel said to her, "Behold, you are with child, and will bear a son. You shall call his name Ishmael, because Yahweh has heard your affliction. 12 He will be like a wild donkey among men. His hand will be against every man, and every man's hand against him. He will live opposed to all of his brothers." 13 She called the name of Yahweh who spoke to her, "You are a God who sees," for she said, "Have I even stayed alive after seeing him?" 14 Therefore the well was called Beer Lahai Roi. Behold, it is between Kadesh and Bered. 15 Hagar bore a son for Abram. Abram called the name of his son, whom Hagar bore, Ishmael. 16 Abram was eighty-six years old when Hagar bore Ishmael to Abram.

Genesis 17

God's Covenant with Abraham

1 When Abram was ninety-nine years old, Yahweh appeared to Abram and said to him, "I am God Almighty. Walk before me, and be blameless. 2 I will make my covenant between me and you, and will multiply you exceedingly." 3 Abram fell on his face. God talked with him, saying, 4 "As for me, behold, my covenant is with you. You will be the father of a multitude of nations. 5 Your name will no more be called Abram, but your name will be Abraham; for I have made you the father of a multitude of nations. 6 I will make you exceedingly fruitful, and I will make nations of you. Kings will come out of you. 7 I will establish my covenant between me and you and your offspring after you throughout their generations for an everlasting covenant, to be a God to you and to your offspring after you. 8 I will give to you, and to your offspring after you, the land where you are traveling, all the land of Canaan, for an everlasting possession. I will be their God." 9 God said to Abraham, "As for you, you will keep my covenant, you and your offspring after you throughout their generations. 10 This is my covenant, which you shall keep, between me and you and your offspring after you. Every male among you shall be circumcised. 11 You shall be circumcised in the flesh of your foreskin. It will be a token of the covenant between me and you. 12 He who is eight days old will be circumcised among you, every male throughout your generations, he who is born in the house, or bought with money from any foreigner who is not of your offspring. 13 He who is born in your house, and

he who is bought with your money, must be circumcised. My covenant will be in your flesh for an everlasting covenant. 14 The uncircumcised male who is not circumcised in the flesh of his foreskin, that soul shall be cut off from his people. He has broken my covenant."

Chapter 4

Generations of Creation

Of the Wind

The Generations of the Phoenicians. From Sanchoniatho. Updated and edited version from the writings of Lucius Cornelius Alexander Polyhistor, 1st Century BC, from Ancient Fragments, by I.P. Cory

Of the wind Colpias, and his wife Baau, which is interpreted Night, were begotten two mortal men, Aeon and Protogonus so called: and Aeon discovered food from trees.

The immediate descendants of these were called Genus and Genea, and they dwelt in Phoenicia: and when there were great droughts they stretched forth their hands to heaven towards the Sun, which they supposed to be God—the only lord of heaven, calling him Beelsamin, which in the Phoenician dialect signifies Lord of Heaven, but among the Greeks is equivalent to Zeus.

Afterwards by Genus the son of Aeon and Protogonus were begotten mortal children, whose names were Phôs, Pûr, and Phlox. These found out the method of producing fire by rubbing pieces of wood against each other, and taught men the use thereof.

These gave rise to sons of vast bulk and height, whose names were conferred upon the mountains which they occupied: thus from them Cassius, and Libanus, and Antilibanus, and Brathu received their names.

Memrumus and Hypsuranius were the issue of these men by connection with their mothers; the women of those times, without shame, having intercourse with any men whom they might chance to meet. Hypsuranius inhabited Tyre: and he invented huts constructed of reeds and rushes, and the papyrus. And he fell into enmity with his brother Usous, who was the inventor of clothing for the body which he made of the skins of the wild beasts which he could catch. And when there were violent storms of rain and wind, the trees about Tyre being rubbed against each other, took fire, and all the forest in the neighborhood was consumed. And Usous having taken a tree, and broken off its boughs, was the first who dared to venture on the sea. And he consecrated two pillars to Fire and Wind, and worshiped them, and poured out upon them the blood of the wild beasts he took in hunting: and when these men were dead, those that remained consecrated to them rods, and worshiped the pillars, and held anniversary feasts in honor of them.

And in times long subsequent to these; were born of the race of Hypsuranius, Agreus and Halieus, the inventors of the arts of hunting and fishing, from whom huntsmen and fishermen derive their names.

Of these were begotten two brothers who discovered iron, and the forging thereof. One of these called Chrysor, who is the same with Hephaestus, exercised himself in words, and charms and divinations; and he invented the hook, and the bait, and the fishing-line, and boats of a light construction; he was the first of all men that sailed. For this reason he was worshiped after his death as a God, under the name of Diamichius. And it is said that his brothers invented the art of building walls with bricks.

Afterwards, of this race were born two youths, one of whom was called Technites, and the other was called Geinus Autochthôn. These discovered the method of mingling stubble with the loam of bricks, and of baking them in the sun; they were also the inventors of tiling.

By these were begotten others, of whom one was named Agrus, the other Agrouerus or Agrotes, of whom in Phoenicia there was a statue held in the highest veneration, and a temple drawn by yokes of oxen: and at Byblus he is called, by way of eminence, the greatest of the Gods. These added to the houses, courts and porticos and crypts: husbandmen, and such as hunt with dogs, derive their origin from these: they are called also Aletae, and Titans.

From these were descended Amynus and Magus, who taught men to construct villages and tend flocks.

By these men were begotten Misor and Sydyc, that is, Well-freed and Just: and they found out the use of salt.

From Misor descended Taautus, who invented the writing of the first letters: him the Egyptians called Thoor, the Alexandrians Thoyth, and the Greeks Hermes. But from Sydyc descended the Dioscuri, or Cabiri, or Corybantes, or Samothraces: these first built a ship complete.

From these descended others; who were the discoverers of medicinal herbs, and of the cure of poisons and of charms.

Contemporary with these was one Elioun, called Hypsistus, (the most high); and his wife named Beruth, and they dwelt about Byblus.

By these was begotten Epigeus or

Generations of Creation

Autochthon, whom they afterwards called Ouranus (Heaven); so that from him that element, which is over us, by reason of its excellent beauty is named heaven: and he had a sister of the same parents, and she was called Ge (Earth), and by reason of her beauty the earth was called by the same name.

Hypsistus, the father of these, having been killed in a conflict with wild beasts, was consecrated, and his children offered libations and sacrifices to him.

But Ouranus, succeeding to the kingdom of his father, contracted a marriage with his sister Ge, and had by her four sons, Ilus who is called Cronus, and Betylus, and Dagon, which signifies Siton (bread-corn), and Atlas.

But by other wives Ouranus had much issue; at which Ge, being vexed and jealous of Ouranus, reproached him so that they parted from each other: nevertheless Ouranus returned to her, again by force whenever he thought proper, and having laid with her, again departed: he attempted also to kill the children whom he had by her; but Ge often defended herself with the assistance of auxiliary powers.

But when Cronus arrived at man's estate, acting by the advice and with the assistance of Hermes Trismegistus, who was his secretary, he opposed himself to his father Ouranus, that he might avenge the indignities which had been offered to his mother.

And to Cronus were born children, Persephone and Athena; the former of whom died a virgin; but, by the advice of Athena and Hermes, Cronus made a scimitar and a spear of iron. Then Hermes addressed the allies of Cronus with magic words, and wrought in them a keen desire to make war against Ouranus on behalf of Ge. And Cronus having thus overcome Ouranus in battle, drove him from his kingdom, and succeeded him in the imperial power. In the battle was taken a well-beloved concubine of Ouranus who was pregnant; and Cronus bestowed her in marriage upon Dagon, and, while she was with him, she was delivered of the child which she had conceived by Ouranus, and called his name Demarous.

After these events Cronus surrounded his habitation with a wall, and founded Byblus, the first city of Phoenicia. Afterwards Cronus having conceived a suspicion of his own brother Atlas, by the advice of Hermes, threw him into a deep cavern in the earth, and buried him.

At this time the descendants of the Dioscuri, having built some light and other more complete ships, put to sea; and being cast away over against Mount Cassius, there consecrated a temple.

But the auxiliaries of Ilus, who is Cronus, were called Eloeim, as it were, the allies of Cronus; being so called after Cronus. And Cronus, having a son called Sadidus, dispatched him with his own sword, because he held him in suspicion, and with his own hand deprived his child of life. And in like manner he cut off the head of his own daughter, so that all the gods were astonished at the disposition of Cronus.

But in process of time, while Ouranus was still in banishment, he sent his daughter Astarte, being a virgin, with two other of her sisters, Rhea and Dione, to cut off Cronus by treachery; but Cronus took the damsels, and married them notwithstanding they were his own sisters. When Ouranus understood this, he sent Eimarmene and Mora with other auxiliaries to make war against Cronus: but Cronus gained the affections of these also, and detained them with himself. Moreover, the god Ouranus devised Baetulia, contriving stones that moved as having life.

And by Astarte Cronus had seven daughters called Titanides, or Artemides; by Rhea also he had seven sons, the youngest of whom was consecrated from his birth; also by Dione he had daughters; and by Astarte again he had two other sons, Pothos and Eros.

And Dagon, after he had found out bread-corn, and the plow, was called Zeus Arotrius.

To Sydyc, who was called the just, one of the Titanides bare Asclepius: and to Cronus there were born also in Peraea three sons, Cronus bearing the same name with his father, and Zeus Belus, and Apollo.

Contemporary with these were Pontus, and Typhon, and Nereus the father of Pontus: from Pontus descended Sidon, who by the excellence of her singing first invented the hymns of odes or praises: and Poseidon.

But to Demarous was born Melicarthus, who is also called Heracles.

Ouranus then made war against Pontus, but afterwards relinquishing the attack he attached himself to Demarous, when Demarous invaded Pontus: but Pontus put him to flight, and Demarous vowed a sacrifice for his escape.

In the thirty-second year of his power and reign, Ilus, who is Cronus, having laid an ambuscade for his father Ouranus in a certain place situated in the middle of the earth, when he had got him into his hands dismembered him over against the fountains and rivers.

There Ouranus was consecrated, and his spirit was separated, and the blood of his parts flowed into the fountains and the waters of the rivers; and the place, which was the scene of this transaction, is shown even to this day.

[...]

But Astarte called the greatest, and Demarous named Zeus, and Adodus who is entitled the king of gods, reigned over the country by the consent of Cronus: and Astarte put upon her head, as the mark of her sovereignty, a bull's head: and traveling about the habitable world, she found a star falling through the air, which she took up, and consecrated in the holy island of Tyre: and the Phoenicians say that Astarte is the same as Aphrodite.

Moreover, Cronus visiting the dif-

Generations of Creation

ferent regions of the habitable world, gave to his daughter Athena the kingdom of Attica: and when there happened a plague with a great mortality, Cronus offered up his only begotten son as a sacrifice to his father Ouranus, and circumcised himself, and compelled his allies to do the same: and not long afterwards he consecrated after his death another of his sons, called Muth, whom he had by Rhea; this Muth the Phoenicians esteem the same as Death and Pluto.

After these things, Cronus gave the city of Byblus to the goddess Baaltis, which is Dione, and Berytus to Poseidon, and to the Caberi who were husbandmen and fishermen: and they consecrated the remains of Pontus at Berytus.

But before these things the god Taautus, having portrayed Ouranus, represented also the countenances of the gods Cronus, and Dagon, and the sacred characters of the elements. He contrived also for Cronus the ensign of his royal power, having four eyes in the parts before and in the parts behind, two of them closing as in sleep; and upon the shoulders four wings, two in the act of flying, and two reposing as at rest. And the symbol was, that Cronus while he slept was watching, and reposed while he was awake. And in like manner with respect to the wings, that he was flying while he rested, yet rested while he flew.

But for the other gods there were two wings only to each upon his shoulders, to intimate that they flew under the control of Cronus; and there were also two wings upon the head, the one as a symbol of the intellectual part, the mind, and the other for the senses.

And Cronus visiting the country of the south, gave all Egypt to the god Taautus, that it might be his kingdom.

These things, the Caberi, the seven sons of Sydyc, and their eighth brother Asclepius, first of all set down in the records in obedience to the commands of the god Taautus.

All these things the son of Thabion, the first Hierophant of all among the Phoenicians, allegorized and mixed up with the occurrences and accidents of nature and the world, and delivered to the priests and prophets, the superintendents of the mysteries: and they, perceiving the rage for these allegories increase, delivered them to their successors, and to foreigners: of whom one was Isiris, the inventor of the three letters, the brother of Chna who; is called the first Phoenician.

Zeus

Fragment. Updated and edited version from the writings of Lucius Cornelius Alexander Polyhistor, 1st Century BC, from Ancient Fragments, by I.P. Cory

From Orpheus. Zeus is the first. Zeus the thunderer, is the last. Zeus is the head. Zeus is the middle, and by Zeus all things were fabricated. Zeus is male, Immortal Zeus is female. Zeus is the foundation of the earth and of the starry heaven. Zeus is the breath of all things. Zeus is the rushing of indefatigable fire. Zeus is the root of the sea: He is the Sun and Moon. Zeus is the king; He is the author of universal life; One Power, one Dæmon, the mighty prince of all things: One kingly frame, in which this universe revolves, Fire and water, earth and ether, night and day, and Metis (Counsel) the primeval father, and all-delightful Eros (Love). All these things are united in the vast body of Zeus.

Would you behold his head and his fair face, It is the resplendent heaven, round which his golden locks of glittering stars are beautifully exalted in the air. On each side are the two golden taurine horns, The risings and settings, the tracks of the celestial gods; His eyes the sun and the Opposing moon; His unfallacious Mind the royal incorruptible Ether.

Works and Days

Excerpt. From Hesiod's Works and Days. Updated and edited version from the translation by Hugh G. Evelyn-White

Beginning of Toil

(ll.1-10) Muses of Pieria who give glory through song, come here, tell of Zeus your father and chant his praise. Through him mortal men are famed or un-famed, sung or unsung alike, as great Zeus wills. For easily he makes strong, and easily he brings the strong man low; easily he humbles the proud and raises the obscure, and easily he straightens the crooked and blasts the proud—Zeus who thunders aloft and has his dwelling most high. Attend with eye and ear, and make judgments straight with righteousness. And I, Perses, would tell of true things.

(ll.11-24) So, after all, there was not one kind of Strife alone, but all over the earth there were two. As for the one, a man would praise her when he came to understand her; but the other is blameworthy: and they are wholly different in nature. For one fosters evil war and battle, being cruel: her no man loves; but inevitably, through the will of the deathless gods, men pay harsh Strife her honor due. But the other is the elder daughter of dark Night, and the son of Cronos who sits above and dwells in the ether, set her in the roots of the earth: and she is far kinder to men. She stirs up even the shiftless to toil; for a man grows eager to work when he considers his neighbor, a rich man who hastens to plow and plant and put his house in good order; and neighbor vies with is neighbor as he hurries after wealth. This Strife is wholesome for men. And potter is angry with potter, and craftsman with craftsman, and beggar is jealous of beggar, and minstrel of minstrel.

(ll.25-41) Perses, lay up these things in your heart, and do not let that Strife who delights in mischief hold your heart back from work, while you peep and peer and listen to the

Generations of Creation

wrangles of the courthouse. Little concern has he with quarrels and courts who has not a year's provisions laid up early, even that which the earth bears, Demeter's grain. When you have got plenty of that, you can raise disputes and strive to get another's goods. But you shall have no second chance to deal so again: no, let us settle our dispute here with true judgment which is of Zeus and is perfect. For we had already divided our inheritance, but you seized the greater share and carried it off, greatly swelling the glory of our bribe—swallowing lords who love to judge such a cause as this. Fools! They know not how much more the half is than the whole, nor what great advantage there is in mallow and asphodel.

(ll.42-53) For the gods keep hidden from men the means of life. Else you would easily do work enough in a day to supply you for a full year even without working; soon would you put away your rudder over the smoke, and the fields worked by ox and sturdy mule would run to waste. But Zeus in the anger of his heart hid it, because Prometheus the crafty deceived him; therefore he planned sorrow and mischief against men. He hid fire; but that the noble son of Iapetus stole again for men from Zeus the counselor in a hollow fennel-stalk, so that Zeus who delights in thunder did not see it. But afterwards Zeus who gathers the clouds said to him in anger:

(ll.54-59) 'Son of Iapetus, surpassing all in cunning, you are glad that you have outwitted me and stolen fire—a great plague to you yourself and to men that shall be. But I will give men as the price for fire an evil thing in which they may all be glad of heart while they embrace their own destruction.'

(ll.60-68) So said the father of men and gods, and laughed aloud. And he told famous Hephaestus to make haste and mix earth with water and to put in it the voice and strength of human kind, and fashion a sweet, lovely maiden-shape, like to the immortal goddesses in face; and Athene to teach her needlework and the weaving of the varied web; and golden Aphrodite to shed grace upon her head, along with cruel longing and cares that weary the limbs. And he charged Hermes the guide, the Slayer of Argus, to put in her a shameless mind and a deceitful nature.

(ll.69-82) So he ordered. And they obeyed the lord Zeus the son of Cronos. Immediately the famous Lame God molded clay in the likeness of a modest maid, as the son of Cronos purposed. And the goddess bright-eyed Athene girded and clothed her, and the divine Graces and queenly Persuasion put necklaces of gold upon her, and the rich-haired Hours crowned her head with spring flowers. And Pallas Athene decorated her form with all manners of finery. Also the Guide, the Slayer of Argus, contrived within her lies and crafty words and a deceitful nature at the will of loud thundering Zeus, and the Herald of the gods put

speech in her. And he called this woman Pandora , because all they who dwelt on Olympus gave each a gift, a plague to men who eat bread.

(ll.83-89) But when he had finished the sheer, hopeless snare, the Father sent glorious Argus-Slayer, the swift messenger of the gods, to take it to Epimetheus as a gift. And Epimetheus did not think on what Prometheus had said to him, bidding him never take a gift of Olympian Zeus, but to send it back for fear it might prove to be something harmful to men. But he took the gift, and afterwards, when the evil thing was already his, he understood.

(ll.90-105) For before this the tribes of men lived on earth remote and free from ills and hard toil and heavy sickness which bring the Fates upon men; for in misery men grow old quickly. But the woman took off the great lid of the jar with her hands and scattered all these and her thought caused sorrow and mischief to men. Only Hope remained there, in an unbreakable home within, under the rim of the great jar, and did not fly out at the door; for before that, the lid of the jar stopped her, by the will of Aegis-holding Zeus who gathers the clouds. But the rest, countless plagues, wander amongst men; for earth is full of evils and the sea is full. Of themselves diseases come upon men continually by day and by night, bringing mischief to mortals silently; for wise Zeus took away speech from them. So is there no way to escape the will of Zeus.

(ll.106-108) Or if you desire, I will summarize for you another tale well and skilfully—and you should lay it up in your heart—how the gods and mortal men sprang from one source.

The First Generation

(ll.109-120) First of all the deathless gods who dwell on Olympus made a golden race of mortal men who lived in the time of Cronos when he was reigning in heaven. And they lived like gods without sorrow of heart, remote and free from toil and grief: miserable age rested not on them; but with legs and arms never failing they made merry with feasting beyond the reach of all evils. When they died, it was as though they were overcome with sleep, and they had all good things; for the fruitful earth unforced gave them fruit abundantly and without limitation. They dwelt in ease and peace upon their lands with many good things, rich in flocks, and loved by the blessed gods.

The Second Generation

(ll.121-139) But after earth had covered this generation—they are called pure spirits dwelling on the earth, and are kind, delivering from harm, and guardians of mortal men; for they roam everywhere over the earth, clothed in mist and keep watch on judgments and cruel deeds, givers of wealth; for this royal right also they received; then they who dwell on Olympus made a second generation which

was of silver and less noble by far. It was like the golden race neither in body nor in spirit. A child was brought up at his good mother's side one hundred years, an utter simpleton, playing childishly in his own home. But when they were full grown and were come to the full measure of their prime, they lived only a little time in sorrow because of their foolishness, for they could not keep from sinning and from wronging one another, nor would they serve the immortals, nor sacrifice on the holy altars of the blessed ones as it is right for men to do wherever they dwell. Then Zeus the son of Cronos was angry and put them away, because they would not give honor to the blessed gods who live on Olympus.

The Third Generation

(ll.140-155) But when earth had covered this generation also—they are called blessed spirits of the underworld by men, and, though they are of second order, yet honor attends them also—Zeus the Father made a third generation of mortal men, a brazen race, sprung from ash-trees; and it was in no way equal to the silver age, but was terrible and strong. They loved the lamentable works of Ares and deeds of violence; they ate no bread, but were hard of heart like adamant, fearful men. Great was their strength and unconquerable the arms, which grew from their shoulders on their strong limbs. Their armor was of bronze, and their houses of bronze, and of bronze were their implements: there was no black iron. These were destroyed by their own hands and passed to the dank house of chill Hades, and left no name: terrible though they were, black Death seized them, and they left the bright light of the sun.

The Fourth Generation

(ll.156-169b) But when earth had covered this generation also, Zeus the son of Cronos made yet another, the fourth, upon the fruitful earth, which was nobler and more righteous, a godlike race of hero-men who are called demigods, the race before our own, throughout the boundless earth. Grim war and dread battle destroyed a part of them, some in the land of Cadmus at seven-gated Thebe when they fought for the flocks of Oedipus, and some, when it had brought them in ships over the great sea gulf to Troy for rich-haired Helen's sake: there death's end enshrouded a part of them. But to the others father Zeus the son of Cronos gave a living and an abode apart from men, and made them dwell at the ends of earth. And they live untouched by sorrow in the islands of the blessed along the shore of deep swirling Ocean, happy heroes for whom the grain-giving earth bears honey-sweet fruit flourishing thrice a year, far from the deathless gods, and Cronos rules over them; for the father of men and gods released him from his bonds. And these last equally have honor and glory.

The Fifth Generation

(ll.169c-169d) And again far-seeing Zeus made yet another generation, the fifth, of men who are upon the bountiful earth.

(ll.170-201) Thereafter, would that I were not among the men of the fifth generation, but either had died before or been born afterwards. For now truly is a race of iron, and men never rest from labor and sorrow by day, and from perishing by night; and the gods shall lay sore trouble upon them. But, notwithstanding, even these shall have some good mingled with their evils. And Zeus will destroy this race of mortal men also when they come to have gray hair on the temples at their birth. The father will not agree with his children, nor the children with their father, nor guest with his host, nor comrade with comrade; nor will brother be dear to brother as before. Men will dishonor their parents as they grow quickly old, and will carp at them, chiding them with bitter words, being hard-hearted, not knowing the fear of the gods. They will not repay their aged parents the cost of their nurture, for might shall be their right: and one man will sack another's city. There will be no favor for the man who keeps his oath or for the just or for the good; but rather men will praise the evildoer and his violent dealings. Strength will be right and reverence will cease to be; and the wicked will hurt the worthy man, speaking false words against him, and will swear an oath upon them. Envy, foul-mouthed, delighting in evil, with scowling face, will go along with wretched men one and all. And then Aidos and Nemesis, with their sweet forms wrapped in white robes, will go from the wide-pathed earth and forsake mankind to join the company of the deathless gods; and bitter sorrows will be left for mortal men, and there will be no help against evil.

A Fable

(ll.202-211) And now I will tell a fable for princes who themselves understand. Thus said the hawk to the nightingale with speckled neck, while he carried her high up among the clouds, gripped fast in his talons, and she, pierced by his crooked talons, cried pitifully. To her he spoke disdainfully: 'Miserable thing, why do you cry out? One far stronger than you now holds you fast, and you must go wherever I take you, songstress as you are. And if I please I will make my meal of you, or let you go. He is a fool who tries to withstand the stronger, for he does not get the mastery and suffers pain besides his shame.' So said the swiftly flying hawk, the long-winged bird.

The Right

(ll.212-237) But you, Perses, listen to right and do not foster violence; for violence is bad for a poor man. Even the prosperous cannot easily bear its burden, but is weighed down under it when he has fallen into delusion. The better path is to go by on the other

side towards justice; for Justice beats Outrage when she comes at length to the end of the race. But only when he has suffered does the fool learn this. For Oath keeps pace with wrong judgments There is a noise when Justice is being dragged in the way where those who devour bribes and give sentence with crooked judgments, take her. And she, wrapped in mist, follows to the city and homes of the people, weeping, and bringing mischief to men, even to such as have driven her forth in that they did not deal straightly with her. But they who give straight judgments to strangers and to the men of the land, and go not aside from what is just, their city flourishes, and the people prosper in it: Peace, the nurse of children, is abroad in their land, and all-seeing Zeus never decrees cruel war against them. Neither famine nor disaster ever haunt men who do true justice; but light-heartedly they tend the fields which are all their care. The earth bears them food in plenty, and on the mountains the oak bears acorns upon the top and bees in the midst. Their woolly sheep are laden with fleeces; their women bear children like their parents. They flourish continually with good things, and do not travel on ships, for the grain-giving earth bears them fruit.

Punishment for Evil

(ll.238-247) But for those who practice violence and cruel deeds... far-seeing Zeus, the son of Cronos, ordains a punishment. Often even a whole city suffers for a bad man who sins and devises presumptuous deeds, and the son of Cronos lays great trouble upon the people, famine and plague together, so that the men perish away, and their women do not bear children, and their houses become few, through the contriving of Olympian Zeus. And again, at another time, the son of Cronos either destroys their wide army, or their walls, or else makes an end of their ships on the sea.

(ll.248-264) You princes, mark well this punishment you also; for the deathless gods are near among men and mark all those who oppress their fellows with crooked judgments, and heed not the anger of the gods. For upon the bountiful earth Zeus has thirty thousand spirits, watchers of mortal men, and these keep watch on judgments and deeds of wrong as they roam, clothed in mist, all over the earth. And there is virgin Justice, the daughter of Zeus, who is honored and reverenced among the gods who dwell on Olympus, and whenever anyone hurts her with lying slander, she sits beside her father, Zeus the son of Cronos, and tells him of men's wicked heart, until the people pay for the mad folly of their princes who, being evil minded, pervert judgment and give sentence crookedly. Keep watch against this, you princes, and make straight your judgments, you who devour bribes; put crooked judgments altogether from your thoughts.

(ll.265-266) He does mischief to

himself who does mischief to another, and evil planned harms the plotter most.

(ll.267-273) The eye of Zeus, seeing all and understanding all, beholds these things too, if he so wills, and fails not to mark what sort of justice is this that the city keeps within it. Now, therefore, may neither I myself be righteous among men, nor my son—for then it is a bad thing to be righteous—if indeed the unrighteous shall have the greater right. But I think that all-wise Zeus will not yet bring that to pass.

(ll.274-285) But you, Perses, lay up these things within you heart and listen now to right, ceasing altogether to think of violence. For the son of Cronos has ordained this law for men, that fishes and beasts and winged fowls should devour one another, for right is not in them; but to mankind he gave right which proves far the best. For whoever knows the right and is ready to speak it, far-seeing Zeus gives him prosperity; but whoever deliberately lies in his witness and forswears himself, and so hurts Justice and sins beyond repair, that man's generation is left obscure thereafter. But the generation of the man who swears truthfully is better from then on.

Effort Towards Good

(ll.286-292) To you, foolish Perses, I will speak good sense. Evil can be had easily and in abundance: the road to her is smooth, and she lives very near us. But between us and Goodness the gods have placed the sweat of our brows: long and steep is the path that leads to her, and it is rough at the first; but when a man has reached the top, then she is easy to reach, even if before that she was hard.

Theogony

The Theogony of Hesiod. Updated and edited version from the translation by Hugh G. Evelyn-White

(ll.1-25) From the Heliconian Muses let us begin to sing, who hold the great and holy mount of Helicon, and dance on soft feet about the deep blue spring and the altar of the almighty son of Cronos, and, when they have washed their tender bodies in Permessus or in the Horse's Spring or Olmeius, make their fair, lovely dances upon highest Helicon and move with vigorous feet. From there they arise and go abroad by night, veiled in thick mist, and utter their song with lovely voice, praising Zeus the aegis-holder and queenly Hera of Argos who walks on golden sandals and the daughter of Zeus the aegis-holder bright-eyed Athene, and Phoebus Apollo, and Artemis who delights in arrows, and Poseidon the earth-holder who shakes the earth, and revered Themis and quick-glancing Aphrodite, and Hebe with the crown of gold, and fair Dione, Leto, Iapetus, and Cronos the crafty counselor, Eos and great Helius and

Generations of Creation

bright Selene, Earth too, and great Oceanus, and dark Night, and the holy race of all the other deathless ones that are eternal. And one day they taught Hesiod a glorious song while he was shepherding his lambs under holy Helicon, and this word first the goddesses said to me—the Muses of Olympus, daughters of Zeus who holds the aegis:

(ll.26-28) "Shepherds of the wilderness, wretched things of shame, mere bellies, we know how to speak many false things as though they were true; but we know how, when we will, to utter true things."

(ll.29-35) So said the ready-voiced daughters of great Zeus, and they plucked and gave me a rod, a shoot of sturdy laurel, a marvelous thing, and breathed into me a divine voice to celebrate things that shall be and things there were before; and they told me to sing of the race of the blessed gods that are eternally, but ever to sing of themselves both first and last. But why all this about oak or stone?

A Race of Gods

(ll.36-52) Come, let us begin with the Muses who gladden the great spirit of their father Zeus in Olympus with their songs, telling of things that are and that shall be and that were before with consenting voice. Untiringly flows the sweet sound from their lips, and the house of their father Zeus the loud-thunderer is glad at the lily-like voice of the goddesses as it spreads abroad, and the peaks of snowy Olympus resound, and do the homes of the immortals. And they uttering their immortal voice, celebrate in song first of all the revered race of the gods from the beginning, those whom Earth and wide Heaven gave rise to, and the gods sprung of these, givers of good things. Then, next, the goddesses sing of Zeus, the father of gods and men, as they begin and end their strain, how much he is the most excellent among the gods and supreme in power. And again, they chant the race of men and strong giants, and gladden the heart of Zeus within Olympus—the Olympian Muses, daughters of Zeus the aegis-holder.

(ll.53-74) Them in Pieria did Mnemosyne (Memory), who reigns over the hill of Eleuther, bear of union with the father, the son of Cronos, a forgetting of ill and a rest from sorrow. For nine nights did wise Zeus lie with her, entering her holy bed remote from the immortals. And when a year was passed and the seasons came round as the months waned, and many days were accomplished, she gave birth to nine daughters, all of one mind, whose hearts are set upon song and their spirit free from care, a little way from the topmost peak of snowy Olympus. There are their bright dancing-places and beautiful homes, and beside them the Graces and Himerus (Desire) live in delight. And they, uttering through their lips a lovely voice, sing the laws of all and the excellent ways of the immortals, uttering their lovely voice.

Then they went to Olympus, delighting in their sweet voice, with heavenly song, and the dark earth resounded about them as they chanted, and a lovely sound rose up beneath their feet as they went to their father. And he was reigning in heaven, himself holding the lightning and glowing thunderbolt, when he had overcome by might his father Cronos; and he distributed fairly to the immortals their portions and declared their privileges.

(ll. 75-103) These things, then, the Muses sang who dwell on Olympus, nine daughters begotten by great Zeus, Cleio and Euterpe, Thaleia, Melpomene and Terpsichore, and Erato and Polyhymnia and Urania and Calliope, who is the chiefest of them all, for she attends on worshipful princes: whomsoever of heaven-nourished princes the daughters of great Zeus honor, and behold him at his birth, they pour sweet dew upon his tongue, and from his lips flow gracious words. All the people look towards him while he settles causes with true judgments: and he, speaking surely, would soon make wise end even of a great quarrel; for therefore are there princes wise in heart, because when the people are being misguided in their assembly, they set right the matter again with ease, persuading them with gentle words. And when he passes through a gathering, they greet him as a god with gentle reverence, and he is conspicuous amongst the assembled: such is the holy gift of the Muses to men. For it is through the Muses and far-shooting Apollo that there are singers and harpers upon the earth; but princes are of Zeus, and happy is he whom the Muses love: sweet flows speech from his mouth. For though a man have sorrow and grief in his newly-troubled soul and live in dread because his heart is distressed, when a singer, the servant of the Muses, chants the glorious deeds of men of old and the blessed gods who inhabit Olympus, at once he forgets his heaviness and remembers not his sorrows at all but the gifts of the goddesses soon turn him away from these.

(ll. 104-115) Hail, children of Zeus! Grant lovely song and celebrate the holy race of the deathless gods who are eternal, those that were born of Earth and starry Heaven and gloomy Night and them that briny Sea did rear. Tell how at the first gods and earth came to be, and rivers, and the boundless sea with its raging swell and the gleaming stars, and the wide heaven above, and the gods who were born of them, givers of good things, and how they divided their wealth, and how they shared their honors amongst them, and also how at the first they took many-folded Olympus. These things declare to me from the beginning, you Muses who dwell in the house of Olympus, and tell me which of them first came to be.

(ll. 116-138) Truly at the first Chaos came to be, but next wide-bosomed Earth, the ever sure foundations of all the deathless ones who hold the peaks of snowy Olympus, and

dim Tartarus in the depth of the wide-pathed Earth, and Eros (Love), fairest among the deathless gods, who unnerves the limbs and overcomes the mind and wise counsels of all gods and all men within them. From Chaos came forth Erebus and black Night; but of Night were born Aether and Day, whom she conceived and bore from union in love with Erebus. And Earth first bore starry Heaven, equal to herself, to cover her on every side, and to be an ever sure abiding-place for the blessed gods. And she brought forth long Hills, graceful haunts of the goddess-nymphs who dwell amongst the glens of the hills. She bore also the fruitless deep with his raging swells, Pontus, without sweet union of love. But afterwards she lay with Heaven and bore deep-swirling Oceanus, Coeus and Crius and Hyperion and Iapetus, Theia and Rhea, Themis and Mnemosyne and gold-crowned Phoebe and lovely Tethys. After them was born Cronos the wily, youngest, and most terrible of her children, and he hated his lusty sire.

The Titans

(ll.139-146) And again, she bore the Cyclopes, overbearing in spirit, Brontes, and Steropes and stubborn-hearted Arges, who gave Zeus the thunder and made the thunderbolt. In all else they were like the gods, but one eye only was set in the midst of their foreheads. And they were surnamed Cyclopes *(Orb-eyed)* because one orbed eye was set in their foreheads. Strength and might and craft were in their works.

(ll.147-163) And again, three other sons were born of Earth and Heaven, great and doughty beyond telling, Cottus and Briareos and Gyes, presumptuous children. From their shoulders sprang a hundred arms, not to be approached, and each had fifty heads upon his shoulders on their strong limbs, and irresistible was the stubborn strength that was in their great forms. For of all the children that were born of Earth and Heaven, these were the most terrible, and they were hated by their own father from the first.

And he used to hide them all away in a secret place of Earth as soon as each was born, and would not tolerate them coming up into the light: and Heaven rejoiced in his evil doing. But vast Earth groaned within, being straightened, and she made the element of gray flint and shaped a great sickle, and told her plan to her dear sons. And she spoke, cheering them, while she was vexed in her dear heart:

(ll.164-166) "My children, gotten of a sinful father, if you will obey me, we should punish the vile outrage of your father; for he first thought of doing shameful things."

(ll.167-169) So she said; but fear seized them all and none of them uttered a word. But great Cronos the wily took courage and answered his dear mother:

(ll.170-172) "Mother, I will undertake to do this deed, for I reverence

not our father of evil name, for he first thought of doing shameful things."

(ll.173-175) So he said: and vast Earth rejoiced greatly in spirit, and set and hid him in an ambush, and put in his hands a jagged sickle, and revealed to him the whole plot.

(ll.176-206) And Heaven came, bringing on night and longing for love, and he lay about Earth spreading himself full upon her.

Then the son from his ambush stretched forth his left hand and in his right took the great long sickle with jagged teeth, and swiftly lopped off his own father's members and cast them away to fall behind him. And not vainly did they fall from his hand; for all the bloody drops that gushed forth Earth received, and as the seasons moved round she bore the strong Erinyes and the great Giants with gleaming armor, holding long spears in their hands and the Nymphs whom they call Meliae all over the boundless earth. And so soon as he had cut off the members with flint and cast them from the land into the surging sea, they were swept away over the main a long time: and a white foam spread around them from the immortal flesh, and in it there grew a maiden. First she drew near holy Cythera, and from there, afterwards, she came to sea-surrounded Cyprus, and came forth an awful and lovely goddess, and grass grew up around her beneath her shapely feet. Her gods and men call Aphrodite, and the foam-born goddess and rich-crowned Cytherea, because she grew amid the foam, and Cytherea because she reached Cythera, and Cyprogenes because she was born in billowy Cyprus, and Philommedes because she sprang from the members. And with her went Eros, and comely Desire followed her at her birth at the first and as she went into the assembly of the gods. This honor she has from the beginning, and this is the portion allotted to her amongst men and undying gods—the whisperings of maidens and smiles and deceits with sweet delight and love and graciousness.

(ll.207-210) But these sons whom he gave rise to himself, great Heaven used to call Titans (Strainers) in reproach, for he said that they strained and did presumptuously a fearful deed, and that vengeance for it would come afterwards.

(ll.211-225) And Night bore hateful Doom and black Fate and Death, and she bore Sleep and the tribe of Dreams. And again the goddess murky Night, though she lay with none, bore Blame and painful Woe, and the Hesperides who guard the rich, golden apples and the trees bearing fruit beyond glorious Ocean. Also she bore the Destinies and ruthless avenging Fates, Clotho and Lachesis and Atropos, who give men at their birth both evil and good to have, and they pursue the transgressions of men and of gods: and these goddesses never cease from their dread anger until they punish the sinner with a sore penalty. Also deadly Night bore Nemesis (Indignation) to afflict mortal men, and

after her, Deceit and Friendship and hateful Age and hard-hearted Strife.

(ll.226-232) But abhorred Strife bore painful Toil and Forgetfulness and Famine and tearful Sorrows, Fightings also, Battles, Murders, Manslaughters, Quarrels, Lying Words, Disputes, Lawlessness and Ruin, all of one nature, and Oath who most troubles men upon earth when anyone willfully swears a false oath.

(ll.233-239) And Sea gave rise to Nereus, the eldest of his children, who is true and lies not: and men call him the Old Man because he is trusty and gentle and does not forget the laws of righteousness, but thinks just and kind thoughts. And yet again he got great Thaumas and proud Phoreys, being mated with Earth, and fair-cheeked Ceto and Eurybia who has a heart of flint within her.

(ll.240-264) And of Nereus and rich-haired Doris, daughter of Ocean the perfect river, were born children, passing lovely amongst goddesses, Ploto, Eucrante, Sao, and Amphitrite, and Eudora, and Thetis, Galene and Glauce, Cymothoe, Speo, Thoe and lovely Halie, and Pasithea, and Erato, and rosy-armed Eunice, and gracious Melite, and Eulimene, and Agaue, Doto, Proto, Pherusa, and Dynamene, and Nisaea, and Actaea, and Protomedea, Doris, Panopea, and comely Galatea, and lovely Hippothoe, and rosy-armed Hipponoe, and Cymodoce who with Cymatolege and Amphitrite easily calms the waves upon the misty sea and the blasts of raging winds, and Cymo, and Eione, and rich-crowned Alimede, and Glauconome, fond of laughter, and Pontoporea, Leagore, Euagore, and Laomedea, and Polynoe, and Autonoe, and Lysianassa, and Euarne, lovely of shape and without blemish of form, and Psamathe of charming figure and divine Menippe, Neso, Eupompe, Themisto, Pronoe, and Nemertes who has the nature of her deathless father. These fifty daughters sprang from blameless Nereus, skilled in excellent crafts.

(ll.265-269) And Thaumas wedded Electra the daughter of deep-flowing Ocean, and she bore him swift Iris and the long-haired Harpies, Aello *(storm-swift)* and Ocypetes *(Swift-flier)* who on their swift wings keep pace with the blasts of the winds and the birds; for quick as time they dart along.

(ll 270-294) And again, Ceto bore to Phoreys the fair-cheeked Graiae, sisters gray from their birth: and both deathless gods and men who walk on earth call them Graiae, Pemphredo well-clad, and saffron-robed Enyo, and the Gorgons who dwell beyond glorious Ocean in the frontier land towards Night where are the clear-voiced Hesperides, Sthenno, and Euryale, and Medusa who suffered a woeful fate: she was mortal, but the two were undying and grew not old. With her lay the Dark-haired One in a soft meadow amid spring flowers. And when Perseus cut off her head, there sprang forth great Chrysaor and the horse Pegasus who is so called because he was born near the springs (pegae)

of Ocean; and that other, because he held a golden blade in his hands. Now Pegasus flew away and left the earth, the mother of flocks, and came to the deathless gods: and he dwell in the house of Zeus and brings to wise Zeus the thunder and lightning. But Chrysaor was joined in love to Callirrhoe, the daughter of glorious Ocean, and begot three-headed Geryones. Him mighty Heracles slew in sea-surrounded Erythea by his shambling oxen on that day when he drove the wide-browed oxen to holy Tiryns, and had crossed the ford of Ocean and killed Orthus and Eurytion the herdsman in the dim stead out beyond glorious Ocean.

(ll.295-305) And in a hollow cave she bore another monster, irresistible, in no way similar either to mortal men or to the undying gods, even the goddess fierce Echidna who is half a nymph with glancing eyes and fair cheeks, and half again a huge snake, great and awful, with speckled skin, eating raw flesh beneath the secret parts of the holy earth. And there she has a cave deep down under a hollow rock far from the deathless gods and mortal men. There, then, did the gods appoint her a glorious house to dwell in: and she keeps guard in Arima beneath the earth, grim Echidna, a nymph who dies not nor grows old all her days.

(ll.306-332) Men say that Typhaon the terrible, outrageous and lawless, was joined in love to her, the maid with glancing eyes. So she conceived and brought forth fierce offspring; first she bore Orthus the hound of Geryones, and then again she bore a second, a monster not to be overcome and that may not be described, Cerberus who eats raw flesh, the brazen-voiced hound of Hades, fifty-headed, relentless and strong. And again she bore a third, the evil-minded Hydra of Lerna, whom the goddess, white-armed Hera nourished, being angry beyond measure with the mighty Heracles. And her Heracles, the son of Zeus, of the house of Amphitryon, together with warlike Iolaus, destroyed with the unpitying sword through the plans of Athene the spoil-driver. She was the mother of Chimaera who breathed raging fire, a creature fearful, great, swift-footed and strong, who had three heads, one of a grim-eyed lion; in her hinderpart, a dragon; and in her middle, a goat, breathing forth a fearful blast of blazing fire. It was she that Pegasus and noble Bellerophon did slay; but Echidna was subject in love to Orthus and brought forth the deadly Sphinx which destroyed the Cadmeans, and the Nemean lion, which Hera, the good wife of Zeus, brought up and made to haunt the hills of Nemea, a plague to men. There he preyed upon the tribes of her own people and had power over Tretus of Nemea and Apesas: yet the strength of stout Heracles overcame him.

(ll.333-336) And Ceto was joined in love to Phorcys and bore her youngest, the awful snake who guards the apples all of gold in the secret

Generations of Creation

places of the dark earth at its great bounds. This is the offspring of Ceto and Phoreys.

(ll.334-345) And Tethys bore to Ocean eddying rivers, Nilus, and Alpheus, and deep-swirling Eridanus, Strymon, and Meander, and the fair stream of Ister, and Phasis, and Rhesus, and the silver eddies of Achelous, Nessus, and Rhodius, Haliacmon, and Heptaporus, Granicus, and Aesepus, and holy Simois, and Peneus, and Hermus, and Caicus fair stream, and great Sangarius, Ladon, Parthenius, Euenus, Ardescus, and divine Scamander.

(ll.346-370) Also she brought forth a holy company of daughters who with the lord Apollo and the Rivers have youths in their keeping—to this charge Zeus appointed them—Peitho, and Admete, and Ianthe, and Electra, and Doris, and Prymno, and Urania divine in form, Hippo, Clymene, Rhodea, and Callirrhoe, Zeuxo and Clytie, and Idyia, and Pasithoe, Plexaura, and Galaxaura, and lovely Dione, Melobosis and Thoe and handsome Polydora, Cerceis lovely of form, and soft eyed Pluto, Perseis, Ianeira, Acaste, Xanthe, Petraea the fair, Menestho, and Europa, Metis, and Eurynome, and Telesto saffron-clad, Chryseis and Asia and charming Calypso, Eudora, and Tyche, Amphirho, and Ocyrrhoe, and Styx who is the chiefest of them all. These are the eldest daughters that sprang from Ocean and Tethys; but there are many besides. For there are three thousand neat-ankled daughters of Ocean who are dispersed far and wide, and in every place alike serve the earth and the deep waters, children who are glorious among goddesses. And as many other rivers are there, babbling as they flow, sons of Ocean, whom queenly Tethys bore, but their names it is hard for a mortal man to tell, but people know those by which they separately dwell.

(ll.371-374) And Theia was subject in love to Hyperion and bore great Helius (Sun) and clear Selene (Moon) and Eos (Dawn) who shines upon all that are on earth and upon the deathless Gods who live in the wide heaven.

(ll.375-377) And Eurybia, bright goddess, was joined in love to Crius and bore great Astraeus, and Pallas, and Perses who also was eminent among all men in wisdom.

(ll.378-382) And Eos bore to Astraeus the strong-hearted winds, brightening Zephyrus, and Boreas, headlong in his course, and Notus—a goddess mating in love with a god. And after these Erigenia bore the star Eosphorus *(Dawn-bringer)*, and the gleaming stars with which heaven is crowned.

(ll.383-403) And Styx the daughter of Ocean was joined to Pallas and bore Zelus (Emulation) and trim-ankled Nike (Victory) in the house. Also she brought forth Cratos (Strength) and Bia (Force), wonderful children. These have no house apart from Zeus, nor any dwelling nor path except that wherein God leads them, but they dwell always with Zeus the loud-thunderer. For so did Styx the

deathless daughter of Ocean plan on that day when the Olympian Lightener called all the deathless gods to great Olympus, and said that whosoever of the gods would fight with him against the Titans, he would not cast him out from his rights, but each should have the office which he had before amongst the deathless gods. And he declared that he who was without office and rights as was just. So deathless Styx came first to Olympus with her children through the wit of her dear father. And Zeus honored her, and gave her very great gifts, for her he appointed to be the great oath of the gods, and her children to live with him always. And as he promised, so he performed fully to them all.

But he himself mightily reigns and rules.

(ll.404-452) Again, Phoebe came to the desired embrace of Coeus.

Then the goddess through the love of the god conceived and brought forth dark-gowned Leto, always mild, kind to men and to the deathless gods, mild from the beginning, gentlest in all Olympus. Also she bore Asteria of happy name, whom Perses once led to his great house to be called his dear wife. And she conceived and bore Hecate whom Zeus the son of Cronos honored above all. He gave her splendid gifts, to have a share of the earth and the unfruitful sea. She received honor also in starry heaven, and is honored exceedingly by the deathless gods. For to this day, whenever any one of men on earth offers rich sacrifices and prays for favor according to custom, he calls upon Hecate. Great honor comes full easily to him whose prayers the goddess receives favorably, and she bestows wealth upon him; for the power surely is with her. For as many as were born of Earth and Ocean amongst all these she has her due portion. The son of Cronos did her no wrong nor took anything away of all that was her portion among the former Titan gods: but she holds, as the division was at the first from the beginning, privilege both in earth, and in heaven, and in sea. Also, because she is an only child, the goddess receives not less honor, but much more still, for Zeus honors her. Whom she wills she greatly aids and advances: she sits by worshipful kings in judgment, and in the assembly whom she wills is distinguished among the people. And when men arm themselves for the battle that destroys men, then the goddess is at hand to give victory and grant glory readily to whom she wills. Good is she also when men contend at the games, for there too the goddess is with them and benefits them: and he who by might and strength gets the victory wins the rich prize easily with joy, and brings glory to his parents. And she is good to stand by horsemen, whom she wills, and to those whose business is in the gray uneasy sea, and who pray to Hecate and the loud-crashing Earth-Shaker, easily the glorious goddess gives great catch, and easily she takes it away as soon as seen, if she so wills. She is good in the byre with Hermes

Generations of Creation

to increase the stock. The droves of cattle and wide herds of goats and flocks of fleecy sheep, if she wills she increases from a few, or makes many to be less. So then, albeit her mother's only child, she is honored amongst all the deathless gods. And the son of Cronos made her a nurse of the young who after that day saw with their eyes the light of all-seeing Dawn. So from the beginning she is a nurse of the young, and these are her honors.

The Olympians

(ll.453-491) But Rhea was subject in love to Cronos and bore splendid children, Hestia, Demeter, and gold-shod Hera and strong Hades, pitiless in heart, who dwells under the earth, and the loud-crashing Earth-Shaker, and wise Zeus, father of gods and men, by whose thunder the wide earth is shaken. These great Cronos swallowed as each came forth from the womb to his mother's knees with this intent, that no other of the proud sons of Heaven should hold the kingly office amongst the deathless gods. For he learned from Earth and starry Heaven that he was destined to be overcome by his own son, strong though he was, through the contriving of great Zeus. Therefore he kept no blind outlook, but watched and swallowed down his children: and unceasing grief seized Rhea. But when she was about to bear Zeus, the father of gods and men, then she besought her own dear parents, Earth and starry Heaven, to devise some plan with her that the birth of her dear child might be concealed, and that retribution might overtake great, crafty Cronos for his own father and also for the children whom he had swallowed down. And they readily heard and obeyed their dear daughter, and told her all that was destined to happen touching Cronos the king and his stout-hearted son. So they sent her to Lyetus, to the rich land of Crete, when she was ready to bear great Zeus, the youngest of her children. Vast Earth received him from Rhea in wide Crete to nourish and to bring up. There came Earth carrying him swiftly through the black night to Lyctus first, and took him in her arms and hid him in a remote cave beneath the secret places of the holy earth on thick-wooded Mount Aegeum; but to the mightily ruling son of Heaven, the earlier king of the gods, she gave a great stone wrapped in swaddling clothes. Then he took it in his hands and thrust it down into his belly: wretch! He knew not in his heart that in place of the stone his son was left behind, unconquered and untroubled, and that he was soon to overcome him by force and might and drive him from his honors, himself to reign over the deathless gods.

(ll.492-506) After that, the strength and glorious limbs of the prince increased quickly, and as the years rolled on, great Cronos the wily was beguiled by the deep suggestions of Earth, and brought up again his offspring, vanquished by the arts

and might of his own son, and he vomited up first the stone which he had swallowed last. And Zeus set it fast in the wide-pathed earth at excellent Pytho under the glens of Parnassus, to be a sign from then on and a marvel to mortal men. And he set free from their deadly bonds the brothers of his father, sons of Heaven whom his father in his foolishness had bound. And they remembered to be grateful to him for his kindness, and gave him thunder and the glowing thunderbolt and lightening: for before that, huge Earth had hidden these. In them he trusts and rules over mortals and immortals.

(ll.507-543) Now Iapetus took as a wife the neat-ankled mad Clymene, daughter of Ocean, and went up with her into one bed. And she bore him a stout-hearted son, Atlas: also she bore very glorious Menoetius and clever Prometheus, full of various wiles, and scatter-brained Epimetheus who from the first was a mischief to men who eat bread; for it was he who first took of Zeus the woman, the maiden whom he had formed. But Menoetius was outrageous, and far-seeing Zeus struck him with a lurid thunderbolt and sent him down to Erebus because of his mad presumption and exceeding pride. And Atlas through hard constraint upholds the wide heaven with untiring head and arms, standing at the borders of the earth before the clear-voiced Hesperides; for this lot wise Zeus assigned to him. And ready-witted Prometheus he bound with inextricable bonds, cruel chains, and drove a shaft through his middle, and set on him a long-winged eagle, which used to eat his immortal liver; but by night the liver grew as much again each way as the long-winged bird devoured in the whole day. That bird Heracles, the valiant son of shapely-ankled Alcmene, slew; and delivered the son of Iapetus from the cruel plague, and released him from his affliction—not without the will of Olympian Zeus who reigns on high, that the glory of Heracles the Theban-born might be yet greater than it was before over the plentiful earth. This, then, he regarded, and honored his famous son; though he was angry, he ceased from the wrath which he had before because Prometheus matched himself in wit with the almighty son of Cronos. For when the gods and mortal men had a dispute at Mecone, even then Prometheus was forward to cut up a great ox and set portions before them, trying to trick the mind of Zeus. Before the rest he set flesh and inner parts thick with fat upon the hide, covering them with an ox paunch; but for Zeus he put the white bones dressed up with cunning art and covered with shining fat. Then the father of men and of gods said to him:

(ll.543-544) "Son of Iapetus, most glorious of all lords, good sir, how unfairly you have divided the portions!"

(ll.545-547) So said Zeus whose wisdom is everlasting, rebuking him. But wily Prometheus answered him, smiling softly and not forgetting his

Generations of Creation

cunning trick:

(ll.548-558) "Zeus, most glorious and greatest of the eternal gods, take which ever of these portions your heart within you bids." So he said, thinking trickery. But Zeus, whose wisdom is everlasting, saw and failed not to perceive the trick, and in his heart he thought mischief against mortal men which also was to be fulfilled. With both hands he took up the white fat and was angry at heart, and wrath came to his spirit when he saw the white ox-bones craftily tricked out; and because of this the tribes of men upon earth burn white bones to the deathless gods upon fragrant altars. But Zeus who drives the clouds was greatly vexed and said to him:

(ll.559-560) "Son of Iapetus, clever above all. So, sir, you have not yet forgotten your cunning arts!"

(ll.561-584) So spoke Zeus in anger, whose wisdom is everlasting; and from that time he was always mindful of the trick, and would not give the power of unrelenting fire to the Melian race of mortal men who live on the earth. But the noble son of Iapetus outwitted him and stole the far-seen gleam of unrelenting fire in a hollow fennel stalk. And Zeus who thunders on high was stung in spirit, and his dear heart was angered when he saw amongst men the far-seen ray of fire. Forthwith he made an evil thing for men as the price of fire; for the very famous Limping God formed of earth the likeness of a shy maiden as the son of Cronos willed. And the goddess bright-eyed Athene girded and clothed her with silvery raiment, and down from her head she spread with her hands an embroidered veil, a wonder to see; and she, Pallas Athene, put about her head lovely garlands, flowers of new-grown herbs. Also she put upon her head a crown of gold which the very famous Limping God made himself and worked with his own hands as a favor to Zeus his father. On it was much curious work, wonderful to see; for of the many creatures which the land and sea rear up, he put most upon it, wonderful things, like living beings with voices: and great beauty shone out from it.

(ll.585-589) But when he had made the beautiful evil to be the price for the blessing, he brought her out, delighting in the finery which the bright-eyed daughter of a mighty father had given her, to the place where the other gods and men were. And wonder took hold of the deathless gods and mortal men when they saw that which was sheer guile, not to be withstood by men.

(ll.590-612) For from her is the race of women and female kind: of her is the deadly race and tribe of women who live amongst mortal men to their great trouble, no helpmates in hateful poverty, but only in wealth. And as in thatched hives bees feed the drones whose nature is to do mischief—by day and throughout the day until the sun goes down the bees are busy and lay the white combs, while the drones stay at home in the covered hives and reap

the toil of others into their own bellies—even so Zeus who thunders on high made women to be an evil to mortal men, with a nature to do evil. And he gave them a second evil to be the price for the good they had: whoever avoids marriage and the sorrows that women cause, and will not wed, reaches deadly old age without anyone to tend his years, and though he at least has no lack of livelihood while he lives, yet, when he is dead, his kinsfolk divide his possessions amongst them. And as for the man who chooses the lot of marriage and takes a good wife suited to his mind, evil continually contends with good; for whoever happens to have mischievous children, lives always with unceasing grief in his spirit and heart within him; and this evil cannot be healed.

(ll.613-616) So it is not possible to deceive or go beyond the will of Zeus; for not even the son of Iapetus, kind Prometheus, escaped his heavy anger, but of necessity strong bands confined him, although he knew many a wile.

Battle With the Titans

(ll.617-643) But when their father was vexed in his heart with Obriareus and Cottus and Gyes, he bound them in cruel bonds, because he was jealous of their exceeding manhood and comeliness and great size: and he made them live beneath the wide-pathed earth, where they were afflicted, being set to dwell under the ground, at the end of the earth, at its great borders, in bitter anguish for a long time and with great grief at heart. But the son of Cronos and the other deathless gods whom rich-haired Rhea bore from union with Cronos, brought them up again to the light at Earth's advising. For she herself recounted all things to the gods fully, how that with these they would gain victory and a glorious cause to boast about themselves. For the Titan gods and as many as sprang from Cronos had long been fighting together in stubborn war with heart-grieving toil, the lordly Titans from high Othrys—and the gods, givers of good, whom rich-haired Rhea bore in union with Cronos, from Olympus. So they, with bitter wrath, were fighting continually with one another for ten full years, and the hard strife had no close or end for either side, and the issue of the war hung evenly balanced. But when he had provided those three with all things fitting, nectar and ambrosia which the gods themselves eat, and when their proud spirit revived within them all after they had fed on nectar and delicious ambrosia, then it was that the father of men and gods spoke amongst them:

(ll.644-653) "Hear me, bright children of Earth and Heaven, that I may say what my heart within me bids. A long while now have we, who are sprung from Cronos and the Titan gods, fought with each other every day to get victory and to prevail. For this reason do you show your great might and unconquerable strength, and face the Titans in bitter strife; remember

our friendly kindness, and from what sufferings you have come back to the light from your cruel bondage under misty gloom through our counsels."

(ll.654-663) So he said. And blameless Cottus answered him again: "Divine one, you speak that which we know well. No, we know that your wisdom and understanding exceeds even that of ourselves, and that you became a defender of the deathless ones from chilling doom. And through your devising we have come back again from the murky gloom and from our merciless bonds, enjoying what we looked not for, oh lord, son of Cronos. And so now with fixed purpose and deliberate counsel we will aid your power in dreadful strife and will fight against the Titans in hard battle."

(ll.664-686) So he said: and the gods, givers of good things, applauded when they heard his word, and their spirit longed for war even more than before, and they all, both male and female, stirred up hated battle that day, the Titan gods, and all that were born of Cronos together with those dread, mighty ones of overwhelming strength whom Zeus brought up to the light from Erebus beneath the earth. A hundred arms sprang from the shoulders of all alike, and each had fifty heads growing upon his shoulders upon stout limbs. These, then, stood against the Titans in grim strife, holding huge rocks in their strong hands. And on the other part the Titans eagerly strengthened their ranks, and both sides at one time showed the work of their hands and their might. The boundless sea rang terribly around, and the earth crashed loudly: wide Heaven was shaken and groaned, and high Olympus reeled from its foundation under the charge of the undying gods, and a heavy quaking reached dim Tartarus and the deep sound of their feet in the fearful onset and of their hard missiles. So, then, they launched their grievous shafts upon one another, and the cry of both armies as they shouted reached to starry heaven; and they met together with a great battle cry.

(ll.687-712) Then Zeus no longer held back his might; but his heart was filled with fury and he showed forth all his strength. From Heaven and from Olympus he came forth, hurling his lightning: the bolt flew thick and fast from his strong hand together with thunder and lightning, whirling an awesome flame. The life-giving earth crashed around in burning, and the vast wood crackled loud with fire all about. All the land seethed, and Ocean's streams and the unfruitful sea. The hot vapor lapped round the earth-born Titans: flame unspeakable rose to the bright upper air: the flashing glare of the thunder-stone and lightning blinded their eyes for all that there were strong. Astounding heat seized Chaos: and to see with eyes and to hear the sound with ears it seemed even as if Earth and wide Heaven above came together; for such a mighty crash would have arisen if Earth were being hurled to ruin, and

Heaven from on high were hurling her down; so great a crash was there while the gods were meeting together in strife. Also the winds brought a rumbling earthquake and dust storm, thunder and lightning and the lurid thunderbolt, which are the shafts of great Zeus, and carried the clangor and the war cry into the midst of the two hosts. A horrible uproar of terrible strife arose: mighty deeds were shown and the battle inclined. But until then, they kept at one another and fought continually in cruel war.

(ll. 713-735) And amongst the foremost Cottus and Briareos and Gyes insatiate for war raised fierce fighting: three hundred rocks, one upon another, they launched from their strong hands and overshadowed the Titans with their missiles, and buried them beneath the wide-pathed earth, and bound them in bitter chains when they had conquered them by their strength for all their great spirit, as far beneath the earth to Tartarus. For a brazen anvil falling down from heaven nine nights and days would reach the earth upon the tenth: and again, a brazen anvil falling from earth nine nights and days would reach Tartarus upon the tenth. Round it runs a fence of bronze, and night spreads in triple line all about it like a neck-circlet, while above grow the roots of the earth and unfruitful sea. There by the counsel of Zeus who drives the clouds the Titan gods are hidden under misty gloom, in a dank place where exist the ends of the huge earth. And they may not go out; for Poseidon fixed gates of bronze upon it, and a wall runs all round it on every side. There Gyes and Cottus and great-souled Obriareus live, trusty warders of Zeus who holds the aegis.

(ll. 736-744) And there, all in their order, are the sources and ends of gloomy earth and misty Tartarus and the unfruitful sea and starry heaven, loathsome and dank, which even the gods abhor.

It is a great gulf, and if once a man were within the gates, he would not reach the floor until a whole year had reached its end, but cruel blast upon blast would carry him this way and that. And this marvel is awful even to the deathless gods.

(ll. 744-757) There stands the awful home of murky Night wrapped in dark clouds. In front of it the son of Iapetus stands immovably upholding the wide heaven upon his head and untiring hands, where Night and Day draw near and greet one another as they pass the great threshold of bronze: and while the one is about to go down into the house, the other comes out at the door.

And the house never holds them both within; but always one is out of the house passing over the earth, while the other stays at home and waits until the time for her journeying come; and the one holds all-seeing light for them on earth, but the other holds in her arms Sleep the brother of Death, even evil Night, wrapped in a vaporous cloud.

(ll. 758-766) And there the children

of dark Night have their dwellings, Sleep and Death, awful gods. The glowing Sun never looks upon them with his beams, neither as he goes up into heaven, nor as he comes down from heaven. And the former of them roams peacefully over the earth and the sea's broad back and is kind to men; but the other has a heart of iron, and his spirit within him is pitiless as bronze: whomsoever among men he has once seized he holds fast: and he is hateful even to the deathless gods.

(ll. 767-774) There, in front, stand the echoing halls of the god of the lower world, strong Hades, and of awful Persephone. A fearful hound guards the house in front, pitiless, and he has a cruel trick. On those who go in he fawns with his tail and both is ears, but suffers them not to go out back again, but keeps watch and devours whomsoever he catches going out of the gates of strong Hades and awful Persephone.

(ll. 775-806) And there dwells the goddess loathed by the deathless gods, terrible Styx, eldest daughter of back-flowing Ocean. She lives apart from the gods in her glorious house vaulted over with great rocks and propped up to heaven all round with silver pillars. Rarely does the daughter of Thaumas, swift-footed Iris, come to her with a message over the sea's wide back.

But when strife and quarrel arise among the deathless gods, and when any of them who live in the house of Olympus lies, then Zeus sends Iris to bring in a golden jug the great oath of the gods from far away, the famous cold water which trickles down from a high and menacing rock. Far under the wide-pathed earth a branch of Oceanus flows through the dark night out of the holy stream, and a tenth part of his water is allotted to her. With nine silver-swirling streams he winds about the earth and the sea's wide back, and then falls into the main; but the tenth flows out from a rock, a sore trouble to the gods. For whosoever of the deathless gods that hold the peaks of snowy Olympus pours a libation of her water is renounced, lies breathless until a full year is completed, and never comes near to taste ambrosia and nectar, but lies spiritless and voiceless on a strewn bed: and a heavy trance overshadows him. But when he has spent a long year in his sickness, another more difficult penance follows after the first. For nine years he is cut off from the eternal gods and never joins their councils or their feasts, nine full years. But in the tenth year he comes again to join the assemblies of the deathless gods who live in the house of Olympus. Such an oath, then, did the gods appoint the eternal and primeval water of Styx to be: and it spouts through a rugged place.

(ll. 807-819) And there, all in their order, are the sources and ends of the dark earth and misty Tartarus and the unfruitful sea and starry heaven, loathsome and dank, which even the gods abhor.

And there are shining gates and an

immovable threshold of bronze having unending roots and grown of itself. And beyond, away from all the gods, live the Titans, beyond gloomy Chaos. But the glorious allies of loud-crashing Zeus have their dwelling upon Ocean's foundations, even Cottus and Gyes; but Briareos, being admirable, the deep-roaring Earth-Shaker made his son-in-law, giving him Cymopolea his daughter to wed.

(ll.820-868) But when Zeus had driven the Titans from heaven, huge Earth bore her youngest child Typhoeus of the love of Tartarus, by the aid of golden Aphrodite. Strength was with his hands in all that he did and the feet of the strong god were untiring. From his shoulders grew a hundred heads of a snake, a fearful dragon, with dark, flickering tongues, and from under the brows of his eyes in his marvelous heads flashed fire, and fire burned from his heads as he glared. And there were voices in all his dreadful heads which uttered every kind of sound unspeakable; for at one time they made sounds such that the gods understood, but at another, the noise of a bull bellowing aloud in proud ungovernable fury; and at another, the sound of a lion, relentless of heart; and at another, sounds like whelps, wonderful to hear; and again, at another, he would hiss, so that the high mountains echoed. And truly a thing past help would have happened on that day, and he would have come to reign over mortals and immortals, had not the father of men and gods been quick to perceive it. But he thundered hard and mightily: and the earth around resounded terribly and the wide heaven above, and the sea and Ocean's streams and the nether parts of the earth. Great Olympus reeled beneath the divine feet of the king; as he arose the earth groaned. And through the two of them heat took hold on the dark-blue sea, through the thunder and lightning, and through the fire from the monster, and the scorching winds and blazing thunderbolt. The whole earth seethed, and sky and sea: and the long waves raged along the beaches round and about, at the rush of the deathless gods: and there arose an endless shaking. Hades trembled where he rules over the dead below, and the Titans under Tartarus who live with Cronos, because of the unending clamor and the fearful strife. So when Zeus had raised up his might and seized his arms, thunder and lightning and lurid thunderbolt, he leaped from Olympus and struck him, and burned all the marvelous heads of the monster about him. But when Zeus had conquered him and lashed him with strokes, Typhoeus was hurled down, a maimed wreck, so that the huge earth groaned. And flame shot forth from the thunder-stricken lord in the dim rugged glens of the mount, when he was smitten. A great part of huge earth was scorched by the terrible vapor and melted as tin melts when heated by men's art in channeled crucibles; or as iron, which is hardest of all things, is softened

by glowing fire in mountain glens and melts in the divine earth through the strength of Hephaestus. Even so, then, the earth melted in the glow of the blazing fire. And in the bitterness of his anger Zeus cast him into wide Tartarus.

(ll.869-880) And from Typhoeus come boisterous winds which blow damply, except Notus and Boreas and clear Zephyr. These are a god-sent kind, and a great blessing to men; but the others blow fitfully upon the seas. Some rush upon the misty sea and work great havoc among men with their evil, raging blasts; for varying with the season they blow, scattering ships and destroying sailors. And men who meet these upon the sea have no help against the mischief. Others again over the boundless, flowering earth spoil the fair fields of men who dwell below, filling them with dust and cruel uproar.

(ll.881-885) But when the blessed gods had finished their toil, and settled by force their struggle for honors with the Titans, they pressed far-seeing Olympian Zeus to reign and to rule over them, by Earth's prompting. So he divided their dignities amongst them.

Delegation of Powers

(ll.886-900) Now Zeus, king of the gods, made Metis his wife first, and she was wisest among gods and mortal men. But when she was about to bring forth the goddess, bright-eyed Athene, Zeus craftily deceived her with cunning words and put her in his own belly, as Earth and starry Heaven advised. For they advised him so, to the end that no other should hold royal sway over the eternal gods in place of Zeus; for very wise children were destined to be born of her, first the maiden bright-eyed Tritogeneia, equal to her father in strength and in wise understanding; but afterwards she was to bear a son of overbearing spirit, king of gods and men. But Zeus put her into his own belly first, that the goddess might devise for him both good and evil.

(ll.901-906) Next he married bright Themis who bore the Horae (Hours), and Eunomia (Order), Dike (Justice), and blooming Eirene (Peace), who mind the works of mortal men, and the Moerae (Fates) to whom wise Zeus gave the greatest honor, Clotho, and Lachesis, and Atropos who give mortal men evil and good to have.

(ll.907-911) And Eurynome, the daughter of Ocean, beautiful in form, bore him three fair-cheeked Charites (Graces), Aglaea, and Euphrosyne, and lovely Thaleia, from whose eyes as they glanced flowed love that unnerves the limbs: and beautiful is their glance beneath their brows.

(ll.912-914) Also he came to the bed of all-nourishing Demeter, and she bore white-armed Persephone whom Aidoneus carried off from her mother; but wise Zeus gave her to him.

(ll.915-917) And again, he loved

Mnemosyne with the beautiful hair: and of her the nine gold-crowned Muses were born who delight in feasts and the pleasures of song.

(ll.918-920) And Leto was joined in love with Zeus who holds the aegis, and bore Apollo and Artemis delighting in arrows, children lovely above all the sons of Heaven.

(ll.921-923) Lastly, he made Hera his blooming wife: and she was joined in love with the king of gods and men, and brought forth Hebe and Ares and Eileithyia.

Divine Offspring

(ll.924-929) But Zeus himself gave birth from his own head to bright-eyed Tritogeneia, the awful, the strife-stirring, the host-leader, the untiring, the queen, who delights in tumults and wars and battles. But Hera without union with Zeus—for she was very angry and quarreled with her mate—bore famous Hephaestus, who is skilled in crafts more than all the sons of Heaven.

(ll.929a-929t) But Hera was very angry and quarreled with her mate. And because of this strife she bore without union with Zeus who holds the aegis a glorious son, Hephaestus, who excelled all the sons of Heaven in crafts. But Zeus lay with the fair-cheeked daughter of Ocean and Tethys apart from Hera... *[Missing Portion of Text]* ...deceiving Metis (Thought) although she was full wise. But he seized her with his hands and put her in his belly, for fear that she might bring forth something stronger than his thunderbolt: therefore did Zeus, who sits on high and dwells in the aether, swallow her down suddenly. But she straightway conceived Pallas Athene: and the father of men and gods gave her birth by way of his head on the banks of the river Trito. And she remained hidden beneath the inward parts of Zeus, even Metis, Athena's mother, worker of righteousness, who was wiser than gods and mortal men. There the goddess (Athena) received that whereby she excelled in strength all the deathless ones who dwell in Olympus, she who made the host-scaring weapon of Athena. And with it Zeus gave her birth, arrayed in arms of war.

(ll.930-933) And of Amphitrite and the loud-roaring Earth-Shaker was born great, wide-ruling Triton, and he owns the depths of the sea, living with his dear mother and the lord his father in their golden house, an awful god.

(ll.933-937) Also Cytherea bore to Ares the shield-piercer Panic and Fear, terrible gods who drive in disorder the close ranks of men in numbing war, with the help of Ares, sacker of towns: and Harmonia whom high-spirited Cadmus made his wife.

(ll.938-939) And Maia, the daughter of Atlas, bore to Zeus glorious Hermes, the herald of the deathless gods, for she went up into his holy bed.

(ll.940-942) And Semele, daughter of Cadmus was joined with him

Generations of Creation

in love and bore him a splendid son, joyous Dionysus—a mortal woman, an immortal son. And now they both are gods.

(ll.943-944) And Alemena was joined in love with Zeus who drives the clouds and bore mighty Heracles.

(ll.945-946) And Hephaestus, the famous Lame One, made Aglaea, youngest of the Graces, his buxom wife.

(ll.947-949) And golden-haired Dionysus made brown-haired Ariadne, the daughter of Minos, his buxom wife: and the son of Cronos made her deathless and ageless for him.

(ll.950-955) And mighty Heracles, the valiant son of neat-ankled Alemena, when he had finished his grievous toils, made Hebe the child of great Zeus and gold-shod Hera his shy wife in snowy Olympus. Happy is he! For he has finished his great works and lives amongst the dying gods, untroubled and ageless all his days.

(ll.956-962) And Perseis, the daughter of Ocean, bore to untiring Helios Circe and Aeetes the king. And Aeetes, the son of Helios who shows light to men, took to wife fair-cheeked Idyia, daughter of Ocean the perfect stream, by the will of the gods: and she was subject to him in love through golden Aphrodite and bore him neat-ankled Medea.

(ll.963-968) And now farewell, you dwellers on Olympus and you islands and continents and briny sea within. Now sing the company of goddesses, sweet-voiced Muses of Olympus, daughter of Zeus who holds the aegis—even those deathless ones who lay with mortal men and bare children resembling gods.

(ll.969-974) Demeter, bright goddess, was joined in sweet love with the hero Iasion in a thrice-plowed fallow in the rich land of Crete, and bore Plutus, a kind god who goes everywhere over land and the sea's wide back, and he who finds him and into whose hands he comes he makes rich, bestowing great wealth upon him.

Children Resembling Gods

(ll.975-978) And Harmonia, the daughter of golden Aphrodite, bore to Cadmus Ino and Semele and fair-cheeked Agave and Autonoe whom long haired Aristaeus wedded, and Polydorus also in rich- crowned Thebe.

(ll.979-983) And the daughter of Ocean, Callirrhoe was joined in the love of rich Aphrodite with stout hearted Chrysaor and bore a son who was the strongest of all men, Geryones, whom mighty Heracles killed in sea-surrounded Erythea for the sake of his shambling oxen.

(ll.984-991) And Eos bore to Tithonus brazen-crested Memnon, king of the Ethiopians, and the Lord Emathion. And to Cephalus she bore a splendid son, strong Phaethon, a man like the gods, whom, when he was a young boy in the tender flower of glorious youth with childish thoughts, laughter-loving Aphrodite seized and

caught up and made a keeper of her shrine by night, a divine spirit.

(ll.993-1002) And the son of Aeson by the will of the gods led away from Aeetes the daughter of Aeetes the heaven-nurtured king, when he had finished the many grievous labors which the great king, overbearing Pelias, that outrageous and presumptuous doer of violence, put upon him. But when the son of Aeson had finished them, he came to Iolcus after long toil bringing the coy-eyed girl with him on his swift ship, and made her his voluptuous wife. And she was subject to Iason, shepherd of the people, and bore a son Medeus whom Cheiron the son of Philyra brought up in the mountains. And the will of great Zeus was fulfilled.

(ll.1003-1007) But of the daughters of Nereus, the Old Man of the Sea, Psamathe the fair goddess, was loved by Aeacus through golden Aphrodite and bore Phocus. And the silver-shod goddess Thetis was subject to Peleus and brought forth lion-hearted Achilles, the destroyer of men.

(ll.1008-1010) And Cytherea with the beautiful crown was joined in sweet love with the hero Anchises and bore Aeneas on the peaks of Ida with its many wooded glens.

(ll.1011-1016) And Circe the daughter of Helius, Hyperion's son, loved steadfast Odysseus and bore Agrius and Latinus who was faultless and strong: also she brought forth Telegonus by the will of golden Aphrodite. And they ruled over the famous Tyrenians, very far off in a recess of the holy islands.

(ll.1017-1018) And the bright goddess Calypso was joined to Odysseus in sweet love, and bore him Nausithous and Nausinous.

(ll.1019-1020) These are the immortal goddesses who laid with mortal men and bore them children resembling gods.

(ll.1021-1022) But now, sweet-voiced Muses of Olympus, daughters of Zeus who holds the aegis, sing of the company of women.

Belus

Various Fragments. Updated and edited version from the writings of Lucius Cornelius Alexander Polyhistor, 1st Century BC, from Ancient Fragments, by I.P. Cory

From Eupolemus. The Babylonians say that the first was Belus, who is the same as Cronus. And from him descended Belus and Chanaan; and this Chanaan was the father of the Phoenicians. Another of his sons was Chum, who is called by the Greeks Asbolus, father of the Ethiopians, and the father of Mestraim, the father of the Egyptians. The Greeks say, moreover, that Atlas was the discoverer of astrology.

From Thallus. Thallus makes mention of Belus, the king of the Assyrians, and Cronus the Titan; and says that Belus, with the Titans, made war against Zeus and his companions, who are called Gods. He says, moreover, that Gygus was defeated, and fled to Tartessus.

According to the history of Thallus, Belus preceded the Trojan war 322 years.

From Castor. Belus was king of the Assyrians; and under him the Cyclops assisted Jupiter with thunderbolts and lightning in his contest with the Titans. At that time there were kings of the Titans, one of whom was Ogygus. And the Giants, in their attempted inroad upon the Gods, were slain by the assistance of Hercules and Dionysus, who were themselves of the Titan race.

Belus, after his death was esteemed a God.

After him, Ninus reigned over the Assyrians fifty-two years. He married Semiramis, who, after his death, reigned over the Assyrians forty-two years. Then reigned Zames, who is Ninyas.

Chapter 5

Mysteries of Reason

A Strange Tale

Excerpt. From Timaeus, by Plato. Updated and edited version from the translation by Benjamin Jowett.

Critias: Then listen, Socrates, to a tale which, though strange, is certainly true, having been attested by Solon, who was the wisest of the seven sages. He was a relative and a dear friend of my great-grandfather, Dropides, as he himself says in many passages of his poems; and he told the story to Critias, my grandfather, who remembered and repeated it to us. There were of old, he said, great and marvelous actions of the Athenian city, which have passed into oblivion through lapse of time and the destruction of mankind, and one in particular, greater than all the rest. This we will now rehearse. It will be a fitting monument of our gratitude to you, and a hymn of praise true and worthy of the goddess, on this her day of festival.

Socrates: Very good. And what is this ancient famous action of the Athenians, which Critias declared, on the authority of Solon, to be not a mere legend, but an actual fact?

Critias: I will tell an old-world story which I heard from an aged man; for Critias, at the time of telling it, was as he said, nearly ninety years of age, and I was about ten. Now the day was that day of the Apaturia which is called the Registration of Youth, at which, according to custom, our parents gave prizes for recitations, and the poems of several poets were recited by us boys, and many of us sang the poems of Solon, which at that time had not gone out of fashion. One of our tribe, either because he thought so or to please Critias, said that in his judgment Solon was not only the wisest of men, but also the noblest of poets. The old man, as I very well remember, brightened up at hearing this and said, smiling: Yes, Amynander, if Solon had only, like other poets, made poetry the business of his life, and had completed the tale which he brought with him from Egypt, and had not been compelled, by reason of the factions and troubles which he found stirring in his own country when he came home, to attend to other matters, in my opinion he would have been as famous as Homer or Hesiod, or any poet.

And what was the tale about, Critias? said Amynander.

About the greatest action which the Athenians ever did, and which ought to have been the most famous, but, through the lapse of time and the destruction of the actors, it has not come down to us.

Tell us, said the other, the whole story, and how and from whom Solon heard this veritable tradition.

He replied: In the Egyptian Delta, at the head of which the river Nile divides, there is a certain district which is called the district of Sais, and the great city of the district is also called Sais, and is the city from which King Amasis came. The citizens have a deity for their founder; she is called in the Egyptian tongue Neith, and is asserted by them to be the same whom the Hellenes call Athene; they are great lovers of the Athenians, and say that they are in some way related to them. To this city came Solon, and was received there with great honor; he asked the priests who were most skillful in such matters, about antiquity, and made the discovery that neither he nor any other Hellene knew anything worth mentioning about the times of old. On one occasion, wishing to draw them on to speak of antiquity, he began to tell about the most ancient things in our part of the world—about Phoroneus, who is called "the first man," and about Niobe; and after the Deluge, of the survival of Deucalion and Pyrrha; and he traced the genealogy of their descendants, and reckoning up the dates, tried to compute how many years ago the events of which he was speaking happened. Shortly after one of the priests, who was of a very great age, said: Oh Solon, Solon, you Hellenes are never anything but children, and there is not an old man among you. Solon in return asked him what he meant. I mean to say, he replied, that in mind you are all young; there is no old opinion handed down among you by ancient tradition, nor any science which is aged. And I will tell you why. There have been, and will be again, many destructions of mankind arising out of many causes; the greatest have been brought about by the agencies of fire and water, and other lesser ones by innumerable other causes. There is a story, which even you have preserved, that once upon a time Paethon, the son of Helios, having yoked the steeds in his father's chariot, because he was not able to drive them in the path of his father, burnt up all that was upon the earth, and was himself destroyed by a thunderbolt. Now this has the form of a myth, but really signifies a declination of the bodies moving in the heavens around the earth, and a great conflagration of things upon the earth, which recurs after long intervals; at such times those who live upon the mountains and in dry and lofty places are more liable to destruction than those who dwell by rivers or on the seashore. And from this calamity the Nile, who is our never-failing honor, delivers and preserves us. When, on the other hand, the gods purge the earth with a deluge of water, the survivors in your country are herdsmen and shepherds who dwell on the mountains, but those who, like you, live in cities are carried by the rivers into the sea. As in this land, neither then nor at any other time, does the water come down from above on the fields, having always a tendency to come up from below; for which reason the traditions preserved here are the most ancient.

The fact is, that wherever the extremity of winter frost or of summer does not prevent, mankind exist, sometimes in greater, sometimes in lesser numbers. And whatever happened either in your country or in ours, or in any other region of which we are informed—if there were any actions noble or great or in any other way remarkable, they have all been written down by us of old, and are preserved in our temples. Whereas just when you and other nations are beginning to be provided with letters and the other requisites of civilized life, after the usual interval, the stream from heaven, like a pestilence, comes pouring down, and leaves only those of you who are destitute of letters and education; and so you have to begin all over again like children, and know nothing of what happened in ancient times, either among us or among yourselves. As for those genealogies of yours which you just now recounted to us, Solon, they are no better than the tales of children. In the first place you remember a single deluge only, but there were many previous ones; in the next place, you do not know that there formerly dwelt in your land the fairest and noblest race of men which ever lived, and that you and your whole city are descended from a small seed or remnant of them which survived. And this was unknown to you, because, for many generations, the survivors of that destruction died, leaving no written word. For there was a time, Solon, before the great deluge of all, when the city which now is Athens was first in war and in every way the best governed of all cities, is said to have performed the noblest deeds and to have had the fairest constitution of any of which tradition tells, under the face of heaven.

Solon marveled at his words, and earnestly requested the priests to inform him exactly and in order about these former citizens. You are welcome to hear about them, Solon, said the priest, both for your own sake and for that of your city, and above all, for the sake of the goddess who is the common patron and parent and educator of both our cities. She founded your city a thousand years before ours, receiving from the Earth and Hephaestus the seed of your race, and afterwards she founded ours, of which the constitution is recorded in our sacred registers to be eight thousand years old. As touching your citizens of nine thousand years ago, I will briefly inform you of their laws and of their most famous action; the exact particulars of the whole we will hereafter go through at our leisure in the sacred registers themselves. If you compare these very laws with ours you will find that many of ours are the counterpart of yours as they were in the olden time. In the first place, there is the caste of priests, which is separated from all the others; next, there are the artificers, who ply their several crafts by themselves and do not intermix; and also there is the class of shepherds and of hunters, as well as that of husbandmen; and you will observe, too, that the warriors in Egypt are distinct from all the other classes, and are commanded by the law to devote themselves solely to military pursuits; moreover, the weapons which they carry are shields and spears, a style of equipment which the goddess taught of Asiatics first to us, as in your part of the world first to you. Then as to wisdom, do you observe how our law from the very first made a study of the whole order of things, extending even to prophecy and medicine which gives health, out of these divine elements deriving what was needful for human life, and adding every sort of knowledge which was akin to them.

All this order and arrangement the goddess first imparted to you when establishing your city; and she chose the spot of earth in which you were born, because she saw that the happy temperament of the seasons in that land would produce the wisest of men. For this reason the goddess, who was a lover both of war and of wisdom, selected and first of all settled that spot which was the most likely to produce men likest herself. And there you dwelt, having such laws as these and still better ones, and excelled all mankind in all virtue, as became the children and disciples of the gods.

Many great and wonderful deeds are recorded of your state in our histories. But one of them exceeds all the rest in greatness and valor For these histories tell of a mighty power which unprovoked made an expedition against the whole of Europe and Asia, and to which your city put an end. This power came forth out of the Atlantic Ocean, for in those days the Atlantic was navigable; and there was an island situated in front of the straits which are by you called the Pillars of Heracles; the island was larger than Libya and Asia put together, and was the way to other islands, and from these you might pass to the whole of the opposite continent which surrounded the true ocean; for this sea which is within the Straits of Heracles is only a harbor, having a narrow entrance, but that other is a real sea, and the surrounding land may be most truly called a boundless continent. Now in this island of Atlantis there was a great and wonderful empire which had rule over the whole island and several others, and over parts of the continent, and, furthermore, the men of Atlantis had subjected the parts of Libya within the columns of Heracles as far as Egypt, and of Europe as far as Tyrrhenia. This vast power, gathered into one, endeavored to subdue at a blow our country and yours and the whole of the region within the straits; and then, Solon, your country shone forth, in the excellence of her virtue and strength, among all mankind. She was preeminent in courage and military skill, and was the leader of the Hellenes. And when the rest fell off from her, being compelled to stand alone, after having undergone the very extremity of danger, she defeated and triumphed over the invaders, and preserved from slavery those who were not yet subjugated, and generously liberated all the rest of us who dwell within the pillars. But afterwards there occurred violent earthquakes and floods; and in a single day and night of misfortune all your warlike men in a body sank into the earth, and the island of Atlantis in like manner disappeared in the depths of the sea. For which reason the sea in those parts is impassable and impenetrable, because there is a shoal of mud in the way; and this was caused by the subsidence of the island.

I have told you briefly, Socrates, what the aged Critias heard from Solon and related to us. And when you were speaking yesterday about your city and citizens, the tale which I have just been repeating to you came into my mind, and I remarked with astonishment how, by some mysterious coincidence, you agreed in almost every particular with the narrative of Solon; but I did not like to speak at the moment. For a long time had elapsed, and I had forgotten too much; I thought that I must first of all run over the narrative in my own mind, and then I would speak. And so I readily assented to your request yesterday, considering that in all such cases the chief difficulty is to find a tale suitable to our purpose, and that with such a tale we should be fairly well provided.

And therefore, as Hermocrates has told you, on my way home yesterday I at once communicated the tale to my companions as I remembered it; and after I left them, during the night by thinking I recovered nearly the whole it. Truly, as is often said, the lessons of our childhood make wonderful impression on our memories; for I am not sure that I could remember all the discourse of yesterday, but I should be much surprised if I forgot any of these things which I have heard very long ago. I listened at the time with childlike interest to the old man's narrative; he was very ready to teach me, and I asked him again and again to repeat his words, so that like an indelible picture they were branded into my mind. As soon as the day broke, I rehearsed them as he spoke them to my companions, that they, as well as myself, might have something to say. And now, Socrates, to make an end to my preface, I am ready to tell you the whole tale. I will give you not only the general heads, but the particulars, as they were told to me. The city and citizens, which you yesterday described to us in fiction, we will now transfer to the world of reality. It shall be the ancient city of Athens, and we will suppose that the citizens whom you imagined, were our veritable ancestors, of whom the priest spoke; they will perfectly harmonize, and there will be no inconsistency in saying that the citizens of your republic are these ancient Athenians. Let us divide the subject among us, and all endeavor according to our ability gracefully to execute the task which you have imposed upon us. Consider then, Socrates, if this narrative is suited to the purpose, or whether we should seek for some other instead.

Socrates: And what other, Critias, can we find that will be better than this, which is natural and suitable to the festival of the goddess, and has the very great advantage of being a fact and not a fiction? How or where shall we find another if we abandon this? We cannot, and therefore you must tell the tale, and good luck to you; and I in return for my yesterday's discourse will now rest and be a listener.

Critias: Let me proceed to explain to you, Socrates, the order in which we have arranged our entertainment. Our intention is, that Timaeus, who is the most of an astronomer amongst us, and has made the nature of the universe his special study, should speak first, beginning with the generation of the world and going down to the creation of man; next, I am to receive the men whom he has created of whom some will have profited by the excellent education which you have given them; and then, in accordance with the tale of Solon, and equally with his law, we will bring them into court and make them citizens, as if they were those very Athenians whom the sacred Egyptian record has recovered from oblivion, and from that time forward we will speak of them as Athenians and fellow citizens.

Socrates: I see that I shall receive in my turn a perfect and splendid feast of reason. And now, Timaeus, you, I suppose, should speak next, after duly calling upon the Gods.

Timaeus: All men, Socrates, who have any degree of right feeling, at the beginning of every enterprise, whether small or great, always call upon God. And we, too, who are going to discourse of the nature of the universe, how created or how existing without creation, if we be not altogether out of our wits, must invoke the aid of Gods and Goddesses and pray that our words may be acceptable to them and consistent with themselves. Let this, then, be our invocation of the Gods, to which I add an exhortation of myself to speak in such a manner as will be most intelligible to you, and will most accord with my own intent.

First then, in my judgment, we

must make a distinction and ask, What is that which always is and has no becoming; and what is that which is always becoming and never is? That which is apprehended by intelligence and reason is always in the same state; but that which is conceived by opinion with the help of sensation and without reason, is always in a process of becoming and perishing and never really is. Now everything that becomes or is created must of necessity be created by some cause, for without a cause nothing can be created. The work of the creator, whenever he looks to the unchangeable and fashions the form and nature of his work after an unchangeable pattern, must necessarily be made fair and perfect; but when he looks to the created only, and uses a created pattern, it is not fair or perfect. Was the heaven then or the world, whether called by this or by any other more appropriate name—assuming the name, I am asking a question which has to be asked at the beginning of an inquiry about anything—was the world, I say, always in existence and without beginning? or created, and had it a beginning? Created, I reply, being visible and tangible and having a body, and therefore sensible; and all sensible things are apprehended by opinion and sense and are in a process of creation and created. Now that which is created must, as we affirm, of necessity be created by a cause. But the father and maker of all this universe is past finding out; and even if we found him, to tell of him to all men would be impossible. And there is still a question to be asked about him: Which of the patterns had the artificer in view when he made the world—the pattern of the unchangeable, or of that which is created? If the world be indeed fair and the artificer good, it is manifest that he must have looked to that which is eternal; but if what cannot be said without blasphemy is true, then to the created pattern. Everyone will see that he must have looked to, the eternal; for the world is the fairest of creations and he is the best of causes. And having been created in this way, the world has been framed in the likeness of that which is apprehended by reason and mind and is unchangeable, and must therefore of necessity, if this is admitted, be a copy of something. Now it is all-important that the beginning of everything should be according to nature. And in speaking of the copy and the original we may assume that words are akin to the matter which they describe; when they relate to the lasting and permanent and intelligible, they ought to be lasting and unalterable, and, as far as their nature allows, irrefutable and immovable—nothing less. But when they express only the copy or likeness and not the eternal things themselves, they need only be likely and analogous to the real words. As being is to becoming, so is truth to belief. If then, Socrates, amid the many opinions about the gods and the generation of the universe, we are not able to give notions which are altogether and in every respect exact and consistent with one another, do not be surprised. Enough, if we adduce probabilities as likely as any others; for we must remember that I who am the speaker, and you who are the judges, are only mortal men, and we ought to accept the tale which is probable and inquire no further.

Socrates: Excellent, Timaeus; and we will do precisely as you bid us. The prelude is charming, and is already accepted by us—may we beg of you to proceed to the strain?

Timaeus: Let me tell you then why the creator made this world of generation. He was good, and the good can never have any jealousy of anything. And being free from jealousy, he desired that all things should be as like himself as they could be. This is in the truest sense the origin of creation and of the world, as we shall do well in believing on the testimony of wise men: God desired that all things should be good and nothing bad, so far as this was attainable. For this reason, also finding the whole visible sphere not at rest, but moving in an irregular and disorderly fashion, out of disorder he brought order, considering that this was in every way better than the other. Now the deeds of the best could never be or have been other than the fairest; and the creator, reflecting on the things which are by nature visible, found that no unintelligent creature taken as a whole was fairer than the intelligent taken as a whole; and that intelligence could not be present in anything which was devoid of soul. For which reason, when he was framing the universe, he put intelligence in soul, and soul in body, that he might be the creator of a work which was by nature fairest and best. Consequently, using the language of probability, we may say that the world became a living creature truly endowed with soul and intelligence by the providence of God.

This being supposed, let us proceed to the next stage: In the likeness of what animal did the Creator make the world? It would be an unworthy thing to liken it to any nature which exists as a part only; for nothing can be beautiful which is like any imperfect thing; but let us suppose the world to be the very image of that whole of which all other animals both individually and in their tribes are portions. For the original of the universe contains in itself all intelligible beings, just as this world comprehends us and all other visible creatures. For the Deity, intending to make this world like the fairest and most perfect of intelligible beings, framed one visible animal comprehending within itself all other animals of a kindred nature. Are we right in saying that there is one world, or that they are many and infinite? There must be one only, if the created copy is to accord with the original. For that which includes all other intelligible creatures cannot have a second or companion; in that case there would be need of another living being which would include both, and of which they would be parts, and the likeness would be more truly said to resemble not them, but that other which included them. In order then that the world might be solitary, like the perfect animal, the creator made not two worlds or an infinite number of them; but there is and ever will be one only-begotten and created heaven.

Now that which is created is of necessity corporeal, and also visible and tangible. And nothing is visible where there is no fire, or tangible which has no solidity, and nothing is solid without earth. For this reason also God in the beginning of creation made the body of the universe to consist of fire and earth. But two things cannot be rightly put together without a third; there must be some bond of union between them. And the fairest bond is that which makes the most complete fusion of itself and the things which it combines; and proportion is best adapted to effect such a union. For whenever in any three numbers, whether cube or square, there is a mean, which is to the last term what the first term is to it; and again, when the mean is to the first term as the last term is to the mean—then the mean becoming first and last, and the first and last both becoming means, they will all of them of necessity come to be the same, and having become the same with one another will be all one. If the universal frame had been created a surface only and having no depth, a single mean would have sufficed to bind together itself and the other terms; but now, as the world must be solid, and solid bodies are always compacted not by one mean but by two, God placed water and air in the mean between fire and earth, and made them to have the same proportion so far as was possible (as fire is to air so is air to water, and as air is to water so is water to earth); and thus he bound and put together a visible and tangible heaven. And for these reasons, and out of such elements which are in number four, the body of the world was created, and it was harmonized by proportion, and therefore has the spirit of friendship; and having been reconciled to itself, it was indissoluble by the hand of any other than the framer.

Now the creation took up the whole of each of the four elements; for the Creator compounded the world out of all the fire and all the water and all the air and all the earth, leaving no part of any of them nor any power of them outside. His intention was, in the first place, that the animal should be as far as possible a perfect whole and of perfect parts: secondly, that it should be one, leaving no remnants out of which another such world might be created: and also that it should be free from old age and unaffected by disease. Considering that if heat and cold and other powerful forces which unite bodies surround and attack them from without when they are unprepared, they decompose them, and by bringing diseases and old age upon them, make them waste away—for this cause and on these grounds he made the world one whole, having every part entire, and being therefore perfect and not liable to old age and disease. And he gave to the world the figure which was suitable and also natural. Now to the animal which was to comprehend all animals, that figure was suitable which comprehends within itself all other figures. This is why he made the world in the form of a globe, round as from a lathe, having its extremes in every direction equidistant from the center, the most perfect and the most like itself of all figures; for he considered that the like is infinitely fairer than the unlike. This he finished off, making the surface smooth all around for many reasons; in the first place, because the living being had no need of eyes when there was nothing remaining outside him to be seen; nor of ears when there was nothing to be heard; and there was no surrounding atmosphere to be breathed; nor would there have been any use of organs by the help of which he might receive his food or get rid of what he had already digested, since there was nothing which went from him or came into him: for there was nothing beside him. Of design he was created thus, his own waste providing his own food, and all that he did or suffered taking place in and by himself. For the Creator conceived that a being which was self-sufficient would be far more excellent than one which lacked anything; and, as he had no need to take anything or defend himself against any one, the Creator did not think it necessary to bestow upon him hands: nor had he any need of feet, nor of the whole apparatus of walking; but the movement suited to his spherical form was assigned to him, being of all the seven that which is most appropriate to mind and intelligence; and he was made to move in the same manner and on the same spot, within his own limits revolving in a circle. All the other six motions were taken away from him, and he was made not to partake of their deviations. And as this circular movement required no feet, the universe was created without legs and without feet.

Such was the whole plan of the eternal God about the god that was to be, to whom for this reason he gave a body, smooth and even, having a surface in every direction equidistant from the center, a body entire and perfect, and formed out of perfect bodies. And in the center he put the soul, which he diffused throughout the body, making it also to be the exterior environment of it; and he made the universe a circle moving in a circle, one and solitary, yet by reason of its excellence able to converse with itself, and needing no other friendship or acquaintance. Having these purposes in view he created the world a blessed god.

Now God did not make the soul after the body, although we are speaking of them in this order; for having brought them together he would never have allowed that the elder should be ruled by the younger; but this is a random manner of speaking which we have, because somehow we ourselves too are very much under the dominion of chance. Whereas he made the soul in origin and excellence prior to and older than the body, to be the ruler and mistress, of whom the body was to be the subject. And he made her out of the following elements and : Out of the indivisible and unchangeable, and also out of that which is divisible and has to do with material bodies, he compounded a third and intermediate kind of essence, partaking of the nature of the same and of the other, and this compound he placed accordingly in a mean between the indivisible, and the divisible and material. He took the three elements of the same, the other, and the essence, and mingled them into one form, compressing by force the reluctant and unsociable nature of the other into the same. When he had mingled them with the essence and out of three made one, he again divided this whole into as many portions as was fitting, each portion being a compound of the same, the other, and the essence. And he proceeded to divide after this manner: First of all, he took away one part of the whole (1), and then he separated a second part which was double the first (2), and then he took away a third part which was half as much again as the second and three times as much as the first (3), and then he took a fourth part which was twice as much as the second (4), and a fifth part which was three times the third (9), and a sixth part which was eight times the first (8), and a seventh part which was twenty-seven times the first (27). After this he filled up the double intervals (between 1, 2, 4, 8) and the triple (between 1, 3, 9, 27) cutting off yet other portions from the mixture and placing them in the intervals, so that in each interval there were two kinds of means, the one exceeding and exceeded by equal parts of its extremes (as for example 1, 4/3, 2, in which the mean 4/3 is one-third of more than 1, and one-third of less than 2), the other being that kind of mean which exceeds and is exceeded by an equal number. Where there were intervals of 3/2 and of 4/3 and of 9/8, made by the connecting terms in the former intervals, he filled up all the intervals of 4/3 with the interval of 9/8, leaving a fraction over; and the interval which this fraction expressed was in the ratio of 256 to 243. And thus the whole mixture out of which he cut these portions was all exhausted by him. This entire compound he divided length-ways into two parts, which he joined to one another at the center like the letter X, and bent them into a circular form, connecting them with themselves and each other at the point opposite to their original meeting-point; and, comprehending them in a uniform revolution upon the same axis, he made the one outer and the other the inner circle. Now the motion of the outer circle he called the motion of the same, and the motion of the inner circle the motion of the other or diverse. The motion of the same he carried round by the side to the right, and the motion of the diverse diagonally to the left. And he gave dominion to the motion of the same and like, for that he left single and undivided; but the inner motion he divided in six places and made seven unequal circles having their intervals in ratios of two, and three, three of each, and bade the orbits proceed in a direction opposite to one another; and three (Sun, Mercury, Venus) he made to move with equal swiftness, and the remaining four (Moon, Saturn, Mars, Jupiter) to move with unequal swiftness to the three and to one another, but in due proportion.

Now when the Creator had framed the soul according to his will, he formed within her the corporeal universe, and brought the two together, and united them center to center. The soul, joined everywhere from the center to the circumference of heaven, of which also she is the external envelopment, herself turning in herself, began a divine beginning of never ceasing and rational life enduring throughout all time. The body of heaven is visible, but the soul is invisible, and partakes of reason and harmony, and being made by the best of intellectual and everlasting natures, is the best of things created. And because she is composed of the same and of the other and of the essence, these three, and is divided and united in due proportion, and in her revolutions returns upon herself, the soul, when touching anything which has essence, whether dispersed in parts or undivided, is stirred through all her powers, to declare the sameness or difference of that thing and some other; and to what individuals are related, and by what affected, and in what way and how and when, both in the world of generation and in the world of immutable being. And when reason, which works with equal truth, whether she be in the circle of the diverse or of the same—in voiceless silence holding her onward course in the sphere of the self-moved—when reason, I say, is hovering around the sensible world and when the circle of the diverse also moving truly imparts the intimations of sense to the whole soul, then arise opinions and beliefs sure and certain. But when reason is concerned with the rational, and the circle of the same moving smoothly declares it, then intelligence and knowledge are necessarily perfected. And if any one affirms that in which these two are found to be other than the soul, he will say the very opposite of the truth.

When the father creator saw the creature which he had made moving and living, the created image of the eternal gods, he rejoiced, and in his joy determined to make the copy still more like the original; and as this was eternal, he sought to make the universe eternal, so far as might be. Now the nature of the ideal being was everlasting, but to bestow this attribute in its fullness upon a creature was impossible. For this reason he resolved to have a moving image of eternity, and when he set in order the heaven, he made this image eternal but moving according to number, while eternity itself rests in unity; and this image we call time. For there were no days and nights and months and years before the heaven was created, but when he constructed the heaven he created them also. They are all parts of time, and the past and future are created species of time, which we unconsciously but wrongly transfer to the eternal essence; for we say that he "was," he "is," he "will be," but the truth is that "is" alone is properly attributed to him, and that "was" and "will be" only to be spoken of becoming in time, for they are motions, but that which is immovably the same cannot become older or younger by time, nor ever did or has become, or hereafter will be, older or younger, nor is subject at all to any of those states which affect moving and sensible things and of which generation is the cause. These are the forms of time, which imitates eternity and revolves according to a law of number. Moreover, when we say that what has become is become and what becomes is becoming, and that what will become is about to become and that the non-existent is non-existent—all these are inaccurate modes of expression. But perhaps this whole subject will be more suitably discussed on some other occasion.

Time, then, and the heaven came into being at the same instant in order that, having been created together, if ever there was to be a dissolution of them, they might be dissolved together. It was framed after the pattern of the eternal nature, that it might resemble this as far as was possible; for the pattern exists from eternity, and the created heaven has been, and is, and will be, in all time. Such was the mind and thought of God in the creation of time. The sun and moon and five other stars, which are called the planets, were created by him in order to distinguish and preserve the numbers of time; and when he had made—their several bodies, he placed them in the orbits in which the circle of the other was revolving—in seven orbits seven stars. First, there was the moon in the orbit nearest the earth, and next the sun, in the second orbit above the earth; then came the morning star and the star sacred to Hermes, moving in orbits which have an equal swiftness with the sun, but in an opposite direction; and this is the reason why the sun and Hermes and Lucifer overtake and are overtaken by each other. To enumerate the places which he assigned to the other stars, and to give all the reasons why he assigned them, although a secondary matter, would give more trouble than the primary. These things at some future time, when we are at leisure, may have the consideration which they deserve, but not at present.

Now, when all the stars which were necessary to the creation of time had attained a motion suitable to them—and had become living creatures having bodies fastened by vital chains, and learned their appointed task, moving in the motion of the diverse, which is diagonal, and passes through and is governed by the motion of the same, they revolved, some in a larger and some in a lesser orbit—those which had the lesser orbit revolving faster, and those which had the larger more slowly. Now by reason of the motion of the same, those which revolved fastest appeared to be overtaken by those which moved slower although they really overtook them; for the motion of the same made them all turn in a spiral, and, because some went one way and some another, that which receded most slowly from the sphere of the same, which was the swiftest, appeared to follow it most nearly. That there might be some visible measure of their relative swiftness and slowness as they proceeded in their eight courses, God lighted a fire, which we now call the sun, in the second from the earth of these orbits, that it might give light to the whole of heaven, and that the animals, as many as nature intended, might participate in number, learning arithmetic from the revolution of the same and the like. Thus then, and for this reason the night and the day were created, being the period of the one most intelligent revolution. And the month is accomplished when the moon has completed her orbit and overtaken the sun, and the year when the sun has completed his own orbit. Mankind, with hardly an exception, have not remarked the periods of the other stars, and they have no name for them, and do not measure them against one another by the help of number, and hence they can scarcely be said to know that their wanderings, being infinite in number and admirable for their variety, make up time. And yet there is no difficulty in seeing that the perfect number of time fulfills the perfect year when all the eight revolutions, having their relative degrees of swiftness, are accomplished together and attain their completion at the same time, measured by the rotation of the same and equally moving. After this manner, and for these reasons, came into being such of the stars as in their heavenly progress received reversals of motion, to the end that the created heaven might imitate the eternal nature, and be as like as possible to the perfect and intelligible animal.

Thus far and until the birth of time the created universe was made in the likeness of the original, but inasmuch as all animals were not yet comprehended therein, it was still unlike. What remained, the creator then proceeded to fashion after the nature of the pattern. Now as in the ideal animal the mind perceives ideas or species of a certain nature and number, he thought that this created animal ought to have species of a like nature and number. There are four such; one of them is the heavenly race of the gods; another, the race of birds whose way is in the air; the third, the watery species; and the fourth, the pedestrian and land creatures. Of the heavenly and divine, he created the greater part out of fire, that they might be the brightest of all things and fairest to behold, and he fashioned them after the likeness of the universe in the figure of a circle, and made them follow the intelligent motion of the supreme, distributing them over the whole circumference of heaven, which was to be a true cosmos or glorious world spangled with them all over. And he gave to each of them two movements: the first, a movement on the same spot after the same manner, whereby they ever continue to think consistently the same thoughts about the same things; the second, a forward movement, in which they are controlled by the revolution of the same and the like; but by the other five motions they were unaffected, in order that each of them might attain the highest perfection. And for this reason the fixed stars were created, to be divine and eternal animals, ever-abiding and revolving after the same manner and on the same spot; and the other stars which reverse their motion and are subject to deviations of this kind, were created in the manner already described. The earth, which is our nurse, clinging around the pole which is extended through the universe, he framed to be the guardian and artificer of night and day, first and eldest of gods that are in the interior of heaven. Vain would be the attempt to tell all the figures of them circling as in dance, and their juxtapositions, and the return of them in their revolutions upon themselves, and their approximations, and to say which of these deities in their conjunctions meet, and which of them are in opposition, and in what order they get behind and before one another, and when they are severally eclipsed to our sight and again reappear, sending terrors and intimations of the future to those who cannot calculate their movements—to attempt to tell of all this without a visible representation of the heavenly system would be labor in vain. Enough on this head; and now let what we have said about the nature of the created and visible gods have an end.

To know or tell the origin of the other divinities is beyond us, and we must accept the traditions of the men of old time who affirm themselves to be the offspring of the gods—that is what they say—and they must surely have known their own ancestors. How can we doubt the word of the children of the gods? Although they give no probable or certain proofs, still, as they declare that they are speaking of what took place in their own family, we must conform to custom and believe them. In this manner, then, according to them, the genealogy of these gods is to be received and set forth.

Oceanus and Teyers were the children of Earth and Heaven, and from these sprang Phorcys and Cronos and Rhea, and all that generation; and from Cronos and Rhea sprang Zeus and Here, and all those who are said to be their brethren, and others who were the children of these.

Now, when all of them, both those who visibly appear in their revolutions as well as those other gods who are of a more retiring nature, had come into being, the creator of the universe addressed them in these words: "Gods, children of gods, who are my works, and of whom I am the artificer and father, my creations are indissoluble, if so I will. All that is bound may be undone, but only an evil being would wish to undo that which is harmonious and happy. Consequently, since you are but creatures, you are not altogether immortal and indissoluble, but you shall certainly not be dissolved, nor be liable to the fate of death, having in my will a greater and mightier bond than those with which you were bound at the time of your birth. And now listen to my instructions: Three tribes of mortal beings remain to be created—without them the universe will be incomplete, for it will not contain every kind of animal which it ought to contain, if it is to be perfect. On the other hand, if they were created by me and received life at my hands, they would be on an equality with the gods. In order then that they may be mortal, and that this universe may be truly universal, do you, according to your natures, direct yourselves to the formation of animals, imitating the power which was shown by me in creating you. The part of them worthy of the name immortal, which is called divine and is the guiding principle of those who are willing to follow justice and you—of that divine part I will myself sow the seed, and having made a beginning, I will hand the work over to you. And do you then interweave the mortal with the immortal, and make and beget living creatures, and give them food, and make them to grow, and receive them again in death."

Thus he spoke, and once more into the cup in which he had previously mingled the soul of the universe he poured the remains of the elements, and mingled them in much the same manner; they were not, however, pure as before, but diluted to the second and third degree. And having made it he divided the whole mixture into souls equal in number to the stars, and assigned each soul to a star; and having there placed them as in a chariot, he showed them the nature of the universe, and declared to them the laws of destiny, according to which their first birth would be one and the same for all—no one should suffer a disadvantage at his hands; they were to be sown in the instruments of time severally adapted to them, and to come forth the most religious of animals; and as human nature was of two kinds, the superior race would here after be called man. Now, when they should be implanted in bodies by necessity, and be always gaining or losing some part of their bodily substance, then in the first place it would be necessary that they should all have in them one and the same faculty of sensation, arising out of irresistible impressions; in the second place, they must have love, in which pleasure and pain mingle; also fear and anger, and the feelings which are akin or opposite to them; if they conquered these they would live righteously, and if they were conquered by them, unrighteously. He who lived well during his appointed time was to return and dwell in his native star, and there he would have a blessed and congenial existence. But if he failed in attaining this, at the second birth he would pass into a woman, and if, when in that state of being, he did not desist from evil, he would continually be changed into some brute who resembled him in the evil nature which he had acquired, and would not cease from his toils and transformations until he followed the revolution of the same and the like within him, and overcame by the help of reason the turbulent and irrational mob of later accretions, made up of fire and air and water and earth, and returned to the form of his first and better state. Having given all these laws to his creatures, that he might be guiltless of future evil in any of them, the creator sowed some of them in the earth, and some in the moon, and some in the other instruments of time; and when he had sown them he committed to the younger gods the fashioning of their mortal bodies, and desired them to furnish what was still lacking to the human soul, and having made all the suitable additions, to rule over them, and to pilot the mortal animal in the best and wisest manner which they could, and avert from him all but self-inflicted evils.

When the creator had made all these ordinances he remained in his own accustomed nature, and his children heard and were obedient to their father's word, and receiving from him the immortal principle of a mortal creature, in imitation of their own creator they borrowed portions of fire, and earth, and water, and air from the world, which were hereafter to be restored—these they took and welded them together, not with the indissoluble chains by which they were themselves bound, but with little pegs too small to be visible, making up out of all the four elements each separate body, and fastening the courses of the immortal soul in a body which was in a state of perpetual influx and efflux. Now these courses, detained as in a vast river, neither overcame nor were overcome; but were hurrying and hurried to and fro, so that the whole animal was moved and progressed, irregularly however and irrationally and anyhow, in all the six directions of motion, wandering backwards and forwards, and right and left, and up and down, and in all the six directions. For great as was the advancing and retiring flood which provided nourishment, the affections produced by external contact caused still greater tumult—when the body of any one met and came into collision with some external fire, or with the solid earth or the gliding waters, or was caught in the tempest borne on the air, and the motions produced by any of these impulses were carried through the body to the soul. All such motions have consequently received the general name of "sensations," which they still retain. And they did in fact at that time create a very great and mighty movement; uniting with the ever flowing stream in stirring up and violently shaking the courses of the soul, they completely stopped the revolution of the same by their opposing current, and hindered it from predominating and advancing; and they so disturbed the nature of the other or diverse, that the three double intervals (i.e. between 1, 2, 4, 8), and the three triple intervals (i.e. between 1, 3, 9, 27), together with the mean terms and connecting links which are expressed by the ratios of 3 : 2, and : 3, and of : 8—these, although they cannot be wholly undone except by him who united them, were twisted by them in all sorts of ways, and the circles were broken and disordered in every possible manner, so that when they moved they were tumbling to pieces, and moved irrationally, at one time in a reverse direction, and then again obliquely, and then upside down, as you might imagine a person who is upside down and has his head leaning upon the ground and his feet up against something in the air; and when he is in such a position, both he and the spectator fancy that the right of either is his left, and left right. If, when powerfully experiencing these and similar effects, the revolutions of the soul come in contact with some external thing, either of the class of the same or of the other, they speak of the same or of the other in a manner the very opposite of the truth; and they become false and foolish, and there is no course or revolution in them which has a guiding or directing power; and if again any sensations enter in violently from without and drag after them the whole vessel of the soul, then the courses of the soul, though they seem to conquer, are really conquered.

And by reason of all these affections, the soul, when encased in a mortal body, now, as in the beginning, is at first without intelligence; but when the flood of growth and nutriment abates, and the courses of the soul, calming down, go their own way and become steadier as time goes on, then the several circles return to their natural form, and their revolutions are corrected, and they call the same and the other by their right names, and make the possessor of them to become a rational being. And if these combine in him with any true nurture or education, he attains the fullness and health of the perfect man, and escapes the worst disease of all; but if he neglects education he walks lame to the end of his life, and returns imperfect and good for nothing to the world below. This, however, is a later stage; at present we must treat more exactly the subject before us, which involves a preliminary inquiry into the generation of the body and its members, and as to how the soul was created—for what reason and by what providence of the gods; and holding fast to probability, we must pursue our way.

First, then, the gods, imitating the spherical shape of the universe, enclosed the two divine courses in a spherical body, that, namely, which we now term the head, being the most divine part of us and the lord of all that is in us: to this the gods, when they put together the body, gave all the other members to be servants, considering that it partook of every sort of motion. In order then that it might not tumble about among the high and deep places of the earth, but might be able to get over the one and out of the other, they provided the body to be its vehicle and means of locomotion; which consequently had length and was furnished with four limbs extended and flexible; these God contrived to be instruments of locomotion with which it might take hold and find support, and so be able to pass through all places, carrying on high the dwelling place of the most sacred and divine part of us. Such was the origin of legs and hands, which for this reason were attached to every man; and the gods, deeming the front part of man to be more honorable and more fit to command than the hinder part, made us to move mostly in a forward direction. For this reason man must have his front part unlike and distinguished from the rest of his body.

And so in the vessel of the head, they first of all put a face in which they inserted organs to minister in all things to the providence of the soul, and they appointed this part, which has authority, to be by nature the part which is in front. And of the organs they first contrived the eyes to give light, and the principle according to which they were inserted was as follows: So much of fire as would not burn, but gave a gentle light, they formed into a substance akin to the light of everyday life; and the pure fire which is within us and related thereto they made to flow through the eyes in a stream smooth and dense, compressing the whole eye, and especially the center part, so that it kept out everything of a coarser nature, and allowed to pass only this pure element. When the light of day surrounds the stream of vision, then like falls upon like, and they coalesce, and one body is formed by natural affinity in the line of vision, wherever the light that falls from within meets with an external object. And the whole stream of vision, being similarly affected in virtue of similarity, diffuses the motions of what it touches or what touches it over the whole body, until they reach the soul, causing that perception which we call sight. But when night comes on and the external and kindred fire departs, then the stream of vision is cut off; for going forth to an unlike element it is changed and extinguished, being no longer of one nature with the surrounding atmosphere which is now deprived of fire: and so the eye no longer sees, and we feel disposed to sleep. For when the eyelids, which the gods invented for the preservation of sight, are closed, they keep in the internal fire; and the power of the fire diffuses and equalizes the inward motions; when they are equalized, there is rest, and when the rest is profound, sleep comes over us scarce disturbed by dreams; but where the greater motions still remain, of whatever nature and in whatever locality, they engender corresponding visions in dreams, which are remembered by us when we are awake and in the external world. And now there is no longer any difficulty in understanding the creation of images in mirrors and all smooth and bright surfaces. For from the communion of the internal and external fires, and again from the union of them and their numerous transformations when they meet in the mirror, all these appearances of necessity arise, when the fire from the face coalesces with the fire from the eye on the bright and smooth surface. And right appears left and left right, because the visual rays come into contact with the rays emitted by the object in a manner contrary to the usual mode of meeting; but the right appears right, and the left left, when the position of one of the two concurring lights is reversed; and this happens when the mirror is concave and its smooth surface repels the right stream of vision to the left side, and the left to the right. Or if the mirror be turned vertically, then the concavity makes the countenance appear to be all upside down, and the lower rays are driven upwards and the upper downwards.

All these are to be reckoned among the second and cooperative causes which God, carrying into execution the idea of the best as far as possible, uses as his ministers. They are thought by most men not to be the second, but the prime causes of all things, because they freeze and heat, and contract and dilate, and the like. But they are not so, for they are incapable of reason or intellect; the only being which can properly have mind is the invisible soul, whereas fire and water, and earth and air, are all of them visible bodies. The lover of intellect and knowledge ought to explore causes of intelligent nature first of all, and, secondly, of those things which, being moved by others, are compelled to move others. And this is what we too must do. Both kinds of causes should be acknowledged by us, but a distinction should be made between those which are endowed with mind and are the workers of things fair and good, and those which are deprived of intelligence and always produce chance effects without order or design. Of the second or cooperative causes of sight, which help to give to the eyes the power which they now possess, enough has been said. I will therefore now proceed to speak of the higher use and purpose for which God has given them to us. The sight in my opinion is the source of the greatest benefit to us, for had we never seen the stars, and the sun, and the heaven, none of the words which we have spoken about the universe would ever have been uttered. But now the sight of day and night, and the months and the revolutions of the years, have created number, and have given us a conception of time, and the power of inquiring about the nature of the universe; and from this source we have derived philosophy, than which no greater good ever was or will be given by the gods to mortal man. This is the greatest boon of sight: and of the lesser benefits why should I speak? Even the ordinary man if he were deprived of them would bewail his loss, but in vain. Thus much let me say however: God invented and gave us sight to the end that we might behold the courses of intelligence in the heaven, and apply them to the courses of our own intelligence which are akin to them, the unperturbed to the perturbed; and that we, learning them and partaking of the natural truth of reason, might imitate the absolutely unerring courses of God and regulate our own vagaries. The same may be affirmed of speech and hearing: they have been given by the gods to the same end and for a like reason. For this is the principal end of speech, whereto it most contributes. Moreover, so much of music as is adapted to the sound of the voice and to the sense of hearing is granted to us for the sake of harmony; and harmony, which has motions akin to the revolutions of our souls, is not regarded by the intelligent votary of the Muses as given by them with a view to irrational pleasure, which is deemed to be the purpose of it in our day, but as meant to correct any discord which may have arisen in the courses of the soul, and to be our ally in bringing her into harmony and agreement with herself; and rhythm too was given by them for the same reason, on account of the irregular and graceless ways which prevail among mankind generally, and to help us against them.

Thus far in what we have been saying, with small exception, the works of intelligence have been set forth; and now we must place by the side of them in our discourse the things which come into being through necessity—for the creation is mixed, being made up of necessity and mind. Mind, the ruling power, persuaded necessity to bring the greater part of created things to perfection, and thus and after this manner in the beginning, when the influence of reason got the better of necessity, the universe was created. But if a person will truly tell of the way in which the work was accomplished, he must include the other influence of the variable cause as well. For this reason, we must return again and find another suitable beginning, as about the former matters, so also about these. To which end we must consider the nature of fire, and water, and air, and earth, such as they were prior to the creation of the heaven, and what was happening to them in this previous state; for no one has as yet explained the manner of their generation, but we speak of fire and the rest of them, whatever they mean, as though men knew their natures, and we maintain them to be the first principles and letters or elements of the whole, when they cannot reasonably be compared by a man of any sense even to syllables or first compounds. And let me say thus much: I will not now speak of the first principle or principles of all things, or by whatever name they are to be called, for this reason—because it is difficult to set forth my opinion according to the method of discussion which we are at present employing. Do not imagine, any more than I can bring myself to imagine, that I should be right in undertaking so great and difficult a task. Remembering what I said at first about probability, I will do my best to give as probable an explanation as any other—or rather, more probable; and I will first go back to the beginning and try to speak of each thing and of all. Once more, then, at the commencement of my discourse, I call upon God, and beg him to be our honor out of a strange and unusual inquiry, and to bring us to the haven of probability. So now let us begin again.

This new beginning of our discussion of the universe requires a fuller division than the former; for then we made two classes, now a third must be revealed. The two sufficed for the former discussion: one, which we assumed, was a pattern intelligible and always the same; and the second was only the imitation of the pattern, generated and visible. There is also a third kind which we did not distinguish at the time, conceiving that the two would be enough. But now the argument seems to require that we should set forth in words another kind, which is difficult of explanation and dimly seen. What nature are we to attribute to this new kind of being? We reply, that it is the receptacle, and in a manner the nurse, of all generation. I have spoken the truth; but I must express myself in clearer language, and this will be an arduous task for many reasons, and in particular because I must first raise questions concerning fire and the other elements, and determine what each of them is; for to say, with any probability or certitude, which of them should be called water rather than fire, and which should be called any of them rather than all or some one of them, is a difficult matter. How, then, shall we settle this point, and what questions about the elements may be fairly raised?

In the first place, we see that what we just now called water, by condensation, I suppose, becomes stone and earth; and this same element, when melted and dispersed, passes into vapor and air. Air, again, when inflamed, becomes fire; and again fire, when condensed and extinguished, passes once more into the form of air; and once more, air, when collected and condensed, produces cloud and mist; and from these, when still more compressed, comes flowing water, and from water comes earth and stones once more; and thus generation appears to be transmitted from one to the other in a circle. Thus, then, as the several elements never present themselves in the same form, how can any one have the assurance to assert positively that any of them, whatever it may be, is one thing rather than another? No one can. But much the safest plan is to speak of them as follows: Anything which we see to be continually changing, as, for example, fire, we must not call "this" or "that," but rather say that it is "of such a nature"; nor let us speak of water as "this"; but always as "such"; nor must we imply that there is any stability in any of those things which we indicate by the use of the words "this" and "that," supposing ourselves to signify something thereby; for they are too volatile to be detained in any such expressions as "this," or "that," or "relative to this," or any other mode of speaking which represents them as permanent. We ought not to apply "this" to any of them, but rather the word "such"; which expresses the similar principle circulating in each and all of them; for example, that should be called "fire" which is of such a nature always, and so of everything that has generation. That in which the elements severally grow up, and appear, and decay, is alone to be called by the name "this" or "that"; but that which is of a certain nature, hot or white, or anything which admits of opposite equalities, and all things that are compounded of them, ought not to be so denominated. Let me make another attempt to explain my meaning more clearly. Suppose a person to make all kinds of figures of gold and to be always transmuting one form into all the rest—somebody points to one of them and asks what it is. By far the safest and truest answer is, That is gold; and not to call the triangle or any other figures which are formed in the gold "these," as though they had existence, since they are in process of change while he is making the assertion; but if the questioner be willing to take the safe and indefinite expression, "such," we should be satisfied. And the same argument applies to the universal nature which receives all bodies—that must be always called the same; for, while receiving all things, she never departs at all from her own nature, and never in any way, or at any time, assumes a form like that of any of the things which enter into her; she is the natural recipient of all impressions, and is stirred and informed by them, and appears different from time to time by reason of them. But the forms which enter into and go out of her are the likenesses of real existences modeled after their patterns in wonderful and inexplicable manner, which we will hereafter investigate. For the present we have only to conceive of three natures: first, that which is in process of generation; secondly, that in which the generation takes place; and thirdly, that of which the thing generated is a resemblance. And we may liken the receiving principle to a mother, and the source or spring to a father, and the intermediate nature to a child; and may remark further, that if the model is to take every variety of form, then the matter in which the model is fashioned will not be duly prepared, unless it is formless, and free from the impress of any of these shapes which it is hereafter to receive from without. For if the matter were like any of the supervening forms, then whenever any opposite or entirely different nature was stamped upon its surface, it would take the impression badly, because it would intrude its own shape. Consequently, that which is to receive all forms should have no form; as in making perfumes they first contrive that the liquid substance which is to receive the scent shall be as odorless as possible; or as those who wish to impress figures on soft substances do not allow any previous impression to remain, but begin by making the surface as even and smooth as possible. In the same way that which is to receive perpetually and through its whole extent the resemblances of all eternal beings ought to be devoid of any particular form. For this reason, the mother and receptacle of all created and visible and in any way sensible things, is not to be termed earth, or air, or fire, or water, or any of their compounds or any of the elements from which these are derived, but is an invisible and formless being which receives all things and in some mysterious way partakes of the intelligible, and is most incomprehensible. In saying this we shall not be far wrong; as far, however, as we can attain to a knowledge of her from the previous considerations, we may truly say that fire is that part of her nature which from time to time is inflamed, and water that which is moistened, and that the mother substance becomes earth and air, in so far as she receives the impressions of them.

Let us consider this question more precisely. Is there any self-existent fire? And do all those things which we call self-existent exist? Or are only those things which we see, or in some way perceive through the bodily organs, truly existent, and nothing whatever besides them? And is all that which, we call an intelligible essence nothing at all, and only a name? Here is a question which we must not leave unexamined or undetermined, nor must we affirm too confidently that there can be no decision; neither must we interpolate in our present long discourse a digression equally long, but if it is possible to set forth a great principle in a few words, that is just what we want.

Thus I state my view: If mind and true opinion are two distinct classes, then I say that there certainly are these self-existent ideas unperceived by sense, and apprehended only by the mind; if, however, as some say, true opinion differs in no respect from mind, then everything that we perceive through the body is to be regarded as most real and certain. But we must affirm that to be distinct, for they have a distinct origin and are of a different nature; the one is implanted in us by instruction, the other by persuasion; the one is always accompanied by true reason, the other is without reason; the one cannot be overcome by persuasion, but the other can: and lastly, every man may be said to share in true opinion, but mind is the attribute of the gods and of very few men. Consequently also we must acknowledge that there is one kind of being which is always the same, uncreated and indestructible, never receiving anything into itself from without, nor itself going out to any other, but invisible and imperceptible by any sense, and of which the contemplation is granted to intelligence only. And there is another nature of the same name with it, and like to it, perceived by sense, created, always in motion, becoming in place and again vanishing out of place, which is apprehended by opinion and sense. And there is a third nature, which is space, and is eternal, and admits not of destruction and provides a home for all created things, and is apprehended without the help of sense, by a kind of illegitimate reason, and is hardly real; which we beholding as in a dream, say of all existence that it must of necessity be in some place and occupy a space, but that what is neither in heaven nor in earth has no existence. Of these and other things of the same kind, relating to the true and waking reality of nature, we have only this dreamlike sense, and we are unable to cast off sleep and determine the truth about them. For an image, since the reality, after which it is modeled, does not belong to it, and it exists ever as the fleeting shadow of some other, must be inferred to be in another (i.e. in space), grasping existence in some way or other, or it could not be at all. But true and exact reason, vindicating the nature of true being, maintains that while two things (i.e. the image and space) are different they cannot exist one of them in the other and so be one and also two at the same time.

Thus have I concisely given the result of my thoughts; and my verdict is that being and space and generation, these three, existed in their three ways before the heaven; and that the nurse of generation, moistened by water and inflamed by fire, and receiving the forms of earth and air, and experiencing all the affections which accompany these, presented a strange variety of appearances; and being full of powers which were neither similar nor equally balanced, was never in any part in a state of balance, but swaying unevenly hither and thither, was shaken by them, and by its motion again shook them; and the elements when moved were separated and carried continually, some one way, some another; as, when rain is shaken and winnowed by fans and other instruments used in the threshing of corn, the close and heavy particles are borne away and settle in one direction, and the loose and light particles in another. In this manner, the four kinds or elements were then shaken by the receiving vessel, which, moving like a winnowing machine, scattered far away from one another the elements most unlike, and forced the most similar elements into close contact. For this reason also the various elements had different places before they were arranged so as to form the universe. At first, they were all without reason and measure. But when the world began to get into order, fire and water and earth and air had only certain faint traces of themselves, and were altogether such as everything might be expected to be in the absence of God; this, I say, was their nature at that time, and God fashioned them by form and number. Let it be consistently maintained by us in all that we say that God made them as far as possible the fairest and best, out of things which were not fair and good.

Cycles of Creation

Excerpt. From The Statesman, by Plato. Updated and edited version from the translation by Benjamin Jowett

Stranger: There did really happen, and will again happen, like many other events of which ancient tradition has preserved the record, the portent which is traditionally said to have occurred in the quarrel of Atreus and Thyestes. You have heard no doubt, and remember what they say happened at that time?

Young Socrates: I suppose you to mean the token of the birth of the golden lamb.

Stranger: No, not that; but another part of the story, which tells how the sun and the stars once rose in the west, and set in the east, and that the gods reversed their motion, and gave them that which they now have as a testimony to the right of Atreus.

Young Socrates: Yes; there is that legend also.

Stranger: Again, we have been often told of the reign of Cronos.

Young Socrates: Yes, very often.

Stranger: Did you ever hear that the men of former times were earthborn, and not begotten of one another?

Young Socrates: Yes, that is another old tradition.

Stranger: All these stories, and ten thousand others which are still more wonderful, have a common origin; many of them have been lost in the lapse of ages, or are repeated only in a disconnected form; but the origin of them is what no one has told, and may as well be told now; for the tale is suited to throw light on the nature of the king.

Young Socrates: Very good; and I hope that you will give the whole story, and leave out nothing.

Stranger: Listen, then. There is a time when God himself guides and helps to roll the world in its course; and there is a time, on the completion of a certain cycle, when he lets go, and the world being a living creature, and having originally received intelligence from its author and creator turns about and by an inherent necessity revolves in the opposite direction.

Young Socrates: Why is that?

Stranger: Why, because only the most divine things of all remain ever unchanged and the same, and body is not included in this class. Heaven and the universe, as we have termed them, although they have been endowed by the Creator with many glories, partake of a bodily nature, and therefore cannot be entirely free from perturbation. But their motion is, as far as possible, single and in the same place, and of the same kind; and is therefore only subject to a reversal, which is the least alteration possible. For the lord of all moving things is alone able to move of himself; and to think that he moves them at one time in one direction and at another time in another is blasphemy. Hence we must not say that the world is either self-moved always, or all made to go round by God in two opposite courses; or that two Gods, having opposite purposes, make it move round. But as I have already said (and this is the only remaining alternative) the world is guided at one time by an external power which is divine and receives fresh life and immortality from the renewing hand of the Creator, and again, when let go, moves spontaneously, being set free at such a time as to have, during infinite cycles of years, a reverse movement: this is due to its perfect balance, to its vast size, and to the fact that it turns on the smallest pivot.

Young Socrates: Your account of the world seems to be very reasonable indeed.

Stranger: Let us now reflect and try to gather from what has been said the nature of the phenomenon which we affirmed to be the cause of all these wonders. It is this.

Young Socrates: What?

Stranger: The reversal which takes place from time to time of the motion of the universe.

Young Socrates: How is that the cause?

Stranger: Of all changes of the heavenly motions, we may consider this to be the greatest and most complete.

Young Socrates: I should imagine so.

Stranger: And it may be supposed to result in the greatest changes to the human beings who are the inhabitants of the world at the time.

Young Socrates: Such changes would naturally occur.

Stranger: And animals, as we know, survive with difficulty great and serious changes of many different kinds when they come upon them at once.

Young Socrates: Very true.

Stranger: Hence there necessarily occurs a great destruction of them, which extends also to the life of man; few survivors of the race are left, and those who remain become the subjects of several novel and remarkable phenomena, and of one in particular, which takes place at the time when the transition is made to the cycle opposite to that in which we are now living.

Young Socrates: What is it?

Stranger: The life of all animals

first came to a standstill, and the mortal nature ceased to be or look older, and was then reversed and grew young and delicate; the white locks of the aged darkened again, and the cheeks of the bearded man became smooth, and recovered their former bloom; the bodies of youths in their prime grew softer and smaller, continually by day and night returning and becoming assimilated to the nature of a newly-born child in mind as well as body; in the succeeding stage they wasted away and wholly disappeared. And the bodies of those who died by violence at that time quickly passed through the like changes, and in a few days were no more seen.

Young Socrates: Then how, Stranger, were the animals created in those days; and in what way were they begotten of one another?

Stranger: It is evident, Socrates, that there was no such thing in the then order of nature as the procreation of animals from one another; the earth-born race, of which we hear in story, was the one which existed in those days—they rose again from the ground; and of this tradition, which is now days often unduly discredited, our ancestors, who were nearest in point of time to the end of the last period and came into being at the beginning of this, are to us the heralds. And mark how consistent the sequel of the tale is; after the return of age to youth, follows the return of the dead, who are lying in the earth, to life; simultaneously with the reversal of the world the wheel of their generation has been turned back, and they are put together and rise and live in the opposite order, unless God has carried any of them away to some other lot. According to this tradition they of necessity sprang from the earth and have the name of earth-born, and so the above legend clings to them.

Young Socrates: Certainly that is quite consistent with what has preceded; but tell me, was the life which you said existed in the reign of Cronos in that cycle of the world, or in this? For the change in the course of the stars and the sun must have occurred in both.

Stranger: I see that you enter into my meaning—no, that blessed and spontaneous life does not belong to the present cycle of the world, but to the previous one, in which God superintended the whole revolution of the universe; and the several parts the universe were distributed under the rule of certain inferior deities, as is the way in some places still. There were demigods, who were the shepherds of the various species and herds of animals, and each one was in all respects sufficient for those of whom he was the shepherd; neither was there any violence, or devouring of one another or war or quarrel among them; and I might tell of ten thousand other blessings, which belonged to that dispensation. The reason why the life of man was, as tradition says, spontaneous, is as follows: In those days God himself was their shepherd, and ruled over them, just as man, over them, who is by comparison a divine being, still rules over the lower animals. Under him there were no forms of government or separate possession of women and children; for all men rose again from the earth, having no memory, of the past. And although they had nothing of this sort, the earth gave them fruits in abundance, which grew on trees and shrubs unbidden, and were not planted by the hand of man. And they dwelt naked, and mostly in the open air, for the temperature of their seasons, was mild; and they had no beds, but lay on soft couches of grass, which grew plentifully out of the earth. Such was the life of man in the days of Cronos, Socrates; the character of our present life which is said to be under Zeus, you know from your own experience. Can you, and will you, determine which of them you deem the happier?

Young Socrates: Impossible.

Stranger: Then shall I determine for you as well as I can?

Young Socrates: By all means.

Stranger: Suppose that the nurslings of Cronos, having this boundless leisure, and the power of holding intercourse, not only with men, but with the brute creation, had used all these advantages with a view to philosophy, conversing with the brutes as well as with one another, and learning of every nature which was gifted with any special power, and was able to contribute some special experience to the store of wisdom there would be no difficulty in deciding that they would be a thousand times happier than the men of our own day. Or, again, if they had merely eaten and drank until they were full, and told stories to one another and to the animals—such stories as are now attributed to them—in this case also, as I should imagine, the answer would be easy. But until some satisfactory witness can be found of the love of that age for knowledge and discussion, we had better let the matter drop, and give the reason why we have unearthed this tale, and then we shall be able to get on.

In the fullness of time, when the change was to take place, and the earth-born race had all perished, and every soul had completed its proper cycle of births and been sown in the earth her appointed number of times, the pilot of the universe let the helm go, and retired to his place of view; and then Fate and innate desire reversed the motion of the world. Then also all the inferior deities who share the rule of the supreme power, being informed of what was happening, let go the parts of the world which were under their control. And the world turning round with a sudden shock, being impelled in an opposite direction from beginning to end, was shaken by a mighty earthquake, which wrought a new destruction of all manner of animals. Afterwards, when sufficient time had elapsed, the tumult and confusion and earthquake ceased, and the universal creature, once more at peace attained to a calm, and settle down into his own orderly and accustomed course, having the charge and rule of himself and of all the creatures which are contained in him, and executing, as far as he remembered them, the instructions of his Father and Creator, more precisely at first, but afterwards with less exactness. The reason of the falling off was the admixture of matter in him; this was inherent in the primal nature, which was full of disorder, until attaining to the present order. From God, the constructor; the world received all that is good in him, but from a previous state came elements of evil and unrighteousness, which, consequently, first of all passed into the world, and were then transmitted to the animals. While the world was aided by the pilot in nurturing the animals, the evil was small, and great the good which he produced, but after the separation, when the world was let go, at first all proceeded well enough; but, as time went there was more and more forgetting, and the old discord again held sway and burst forth in full glory; and at last small was the good, and great was the admixture of evil, and there was a danger of universal ruin to the world, and the things contained in him. Therefore God, the orderer of all, in his tender care, seeing that the world was in great straits, and fearing that all might be dissolved in the storm and disappear in infinite chaos, again seated himself at the helm; and bringing back the elements which had fallen into dissolution and disorder to the motion which had prevailed under his dispensation, he set them in order and restored them, and made the world imperishable and immortal.

And this is the whole tale, of which the first part will suffice to illustrate the nature of the king. For when the world turned towards the present cycle of generation, the age of man again stood still, and a change opposite to the previous one was the result. The small creatures which had almost disappeared grew in and stature, and the newly born children of the earth became gray and died and sank into the earth again. All things changed, imitating and following the condition of the universe, and of necessity agreeing with that in their mode of conception and generation and nurture; for no animal; was any longer allowed to come into being in the earth through the agency of other creative beings, but as the world was ordained to be the lord of his own progress, in like manner the parts were ordained to grow and generate and give nourishment, as far as they could, of themselves, impelled by a similar movement. And so we have arrived at the real end of this discourse; for although there might be much to tell of the lower animals, and of the condition out of which they changed and of the causes of the change, about men there is not much, and that little is more to the purpose. Deprived of the care of God, who had possessed and tended them, they were left helpless and defenseless, and were torn to pieces by the beasts, who were naturally fierce and had now grown wild. And in the first ages they were still without skill or resource; the food which once grew spontaneously had failed, and as yet they knew not how to procure it, because they had never felt the pressure of necessity. For all these reasons they were in a great strait; consequently also the gifts spoken of in the old tradition were imparted to man by the gods, together with so much teaching and education as was indispensable; fire was given to them by Prometheus, the arts by Hephaestus and his fellow worker, Athene, seeds and plants by others. From these is derived all that has helped to frame human life; since the care of the Gods, as I was saying, had now failed men, and they had to order their course of life for themselves, and were their own masters, just like the universal creature whom they imitate and follow, ever changing, as he changes, and ever living and growing, at one time in one manner, and at another time in another.

On Atlantis

Critias, by Plato. Updated and edited version from the translation by Benjamin Jowett

Timaeus: How thankful I am, Socrates, that I have arrived at last, and, like a weary traveler after a long journey, may be at rest! And I pray the being who always was of old, and has now been by me revealed, to grant that my words may endure in so far as they have been spoken truly and acceptably to him; but if unintentionally I have said anything wrong, I pray that he will impose upon me a just retribution, and the just retribution of him who errs is that he should be set right. Wishing, then, to speak truly in the future concerning the generation of the gods, I pray him to give me knowledge, which of all medicines is the most perfect and best. And now having offered my prayer I deliver up the argument to Critias, who is to speak next according to our agreement.

Critias: And I, Timaeus, accept the trust, and as you at first said that you were going to speak of high matters, and begged that some forbearance might be shown to you, I too ask the same or greater forbearance for what I am about to say. And although I very well know that my request may appear to be somewhat discourteous, I must make it nevertheless. For will any man of sense deny that you have spoken well? I can only attempt to show that I ought to have more indulgence than you, because my theme is more difficult; and I shall argue that to seem to speak well of the gods to men is far easier than to speak well of men to men: for the inexperience and utter ignorance of his hearers about any subject is a great assistance to him who has to speak of it, and we know how ignorant we are concerning the gods. But I should like to make my meaning clearer, if Timaeus, you will follow me. All that is said by any of us can only be imitation and representation. For if we consider the likenesses which painters make of bodies divine and heavenly, and the different degrees of gratification with which the eye of the spectator receives them, we shall see that we are satisfied with the artist who is able in any degree to imitate the earth and its mountains, and the rivers, and the woods, and the universe, and the things that are and move therein, and further, that knowing nothing precise about such matters, we do not examine or analyze the painting; all that is required is a sort of indistinct and deceptive mode of shadowing them forth. But when a person endeavors to paint the human form we are quick at finding out defects, and our familiar knowledge makes us severe judges of anyone who does not render every point of similarity. And we may observe the same thing to happen in discourse; we are satisfied with a picture of divine and heavenly things which has very little likeness to them; but we are more precise in our criticism of mortal and human things. Consequently if at the moment of speaking I cannot suitably express my meaning, you must excuse me, considering that to form approved likenesses of human things is the reverse of easy. This is what I want to suggest to you, and at the same time to beg, Socrates, that I may have not less, but more indulgence conceded to me in what I am about to say. Which favor, if I am right in asking, I hope that you will be ready to grant.

Socrates. Certainly, Critias, we will grant your request, and we will grant the same by anticipation to Hermocrates, as well as to you and Timaeus; for I have no doubt that when his turn comes a little while hence, he will make the same request which you have made. In order, then, that he may provide himself with a fresh beginning, and not be compelled to say the same things over again, let him understand that the indulgence is already extended by anticipation to him. And now, friend Critias, I will announce to you the judgment of the theater They are of the opinion that the last performer was wonderfully successful, and that you will need a great deal of indulgence before you will be able to take his place.

Hermocrates: The warning, Socrates, which you have addressed to him, I must also take to myself. But remember, Critias, that faint heart never yet raised a trophy; and therefore you must go and attack the argument like a man. First invoke Apollo and the Muses, and then let us hear you sound the praises and show forth the virtues of your ancient citizens.

Critias: Friend Hermocrates, you, who are stationed last and have another in front of you, have not lost heart as of yet; the gravity of the situation will soon be revealed to you; meanwhile I accept your exhortations and encouragements. But besides the gods and goddesses whom you have mentioned, I would specially invoke Mnemosyne; for all the important part of my discourse is dependent on her favor, and if I can recollect and recite enough of what was said by the priests and brought here by Solon, I doubt not that I shall satisfy the requirements of this theater And now, making no more excuses, I will proceed.

Let me begin by observing first of all, that nine thousand was the sum of years which had elapsed since the war which was said to have taken place between those who dwelt outside the Pillars of Heracles and all who dwelt within them; this war I am going to describe. Of the combatants on the one side, the city of Athens was reported to have been the leader and to have fought out the war; the combatants on the other side were commanded by the kings of Atlantis, which, as has been said, was an island greater in extent than Libya and Asia, and when afterwards sunk by an earthquake, became an impassable barrier of mud to voyagers sailing from here to any part of the ocean. The progress of the history will unfold the various nations of barbarians and families of Hellenes which then existed, as they successively appear on the scene; but I must describe first of all Athenians of that day, and their enemies who fought with them, and then the respective powers and governments of the two kingdoms. Let us give the precedence to Athens.

In the days of old the gods had the whole earth distributed among them by allotment. There was no quarreling; for you cannot rightly suppose that the gods did not know what was proper for each of them to have, or knowing this, that they would seek to procure for themselves by contention that which more properly belonged to others. They—all of them by just apportionment obtained what they wanted, and peopled their own districts; and when they had peopled them they tended us, their nurslings and possessions, as shepherds tend their flocks, excepting only that they did not use blows or bodily force, as shepherds do, but governed us like pilots from the stern of the vessel, which is an easy way of guiding animals, holding our souls by the rudder of persuasion according to their own pleasure—thus did they guide all mortal creatures. Now different gods had their allotments in different places which they set in order. Hephaestus and Athene, who were brother and sister, and sprang from the same father, having a common nature, and being united also in the love of philosophy and are, both obtained as their common portion this land, which was naturally adapted for wisdom and virtue; and there they implanted brave children of the soil, and put into their minds the order of government; their names are preserved, but their actions have disappeared by reason of the destruction of those who received the tradition, and the lapse of ages. For when there were any survivors, as I have already said, they were men who dwelt in the mountains; and they were ignorant of the art of writing, and had heard only the names of the chiefs of the land, but very little about their actions. The names they were willing enough to give to their children; but the virtues and the laws of their predecessors, they knew only by obscure traditions; and as they themselves and their children lacked for many generations the necessities of life, they directed their attention to the supply of their wants, and of them they conversed, to the neglect of events that had happened in times long past; for mythology and the inquiry into antiquity are first introduced into cities when they begin to have leisure, and when they see that the necessaries of life have already been provided, but not before. And this is the reason why the names of the ancients have been preserved to us and not their actions. This I infer because Solon said that the priests in their narrative of that war mentioned most of the names which are recorded prior to the time of Theseus, such as Cecrops, and Erechtheus, and Erichthonius, and Erysichthon, and the names of the women in like manner. Moreover, since military pursuits were then common to men and women, the men of those days in accordance with the custom of the time set up a figure and image of the goddess in full armor, to be a testimony that all animals which associate together, male as well as female, may, if they please, practice in common the virtue which belongs to them without distinction of sex.

Now the country was inhabited in those days by various classes of citizens—there were artisans, and there were husbandmen, and there was also a warrior class originally set apart by divine men. The latter dwelt by themselves, and had all things suitable for nurture and education; neither had any of them anything of their own, but they regarded all that they had as common property; nor did they claim to receive of the other citizens anything more than their necessary food. And they practiced all the pursuits which we yesterday described as those of our imaginary guardians. Concerning the country the Egyptian priests said what is not only probable but manifestly true, that the boundaries were in those days fixed by the Isthmus, and that in the direction of the continent they extended as far as the heights of Cithaeron and Parnes; the boundary line came down in the direction of the sea, having the district of Oropus on the right, and with the river Asopus as the limit on the left. The land was the best in the world, and was therefore able in those days to support a vast army, raised from the surrounding people. Even the remnant of Attica which now exists may compare with any region in the world for the variety and excellence of its fruits and the suitableness of its pastures to every sort of animal, which proves what I am saying; but in those days the country was fair as now and yielded far more abundant produce. How shall I establish my words? And what part of it can be truly called a remnant of the land that then was? The whole country is only a long peninsula extending far into the sea away from the rest of the continent, while the surrounding basin of the sea is everywhere deep in the neighborhood of the shore. Many great deluges have taken place during the nine thousand years, for that is the number of years which have elapsed since the time of which I am speaking; and during all this time and through so many changes, there has never been any considerable accumulation of the soil coming down from the mountains, as in other places, but the earth has fallen away all around and sunk out of sight. The consequence is, that in comparison of what then was, there are remaining only the bones of the wasted body, as they may be called, as in the case of small islands, all the richer and softer parts of the soil having fallen away, and the mere skeleton of the land being left. But in the primitive state of the country, its mountains were high hills covered with soil, and the plains, as they are termed by us, of Phelleus were full of rich earth, and there was an abundance of wood in the mountains. Of this last the traces still remain, for although some of the mountains now only afford sustenance to bees, not so very long ago there were still to be seen roofs of timber cut from trees growing there, which were of a size sufficient to cover the largest houses; and there were many other high trees, cultivated by man and bearing an abundance of food for cattle. Moreover, the land reaped the benefit of the annual rainfall, not as now losing the water which flows off the bare earth into the sea, but, having an abundant supply in all places, and receiving it into herself and treasuring it up in the close clay soil, it let off into the hollows the streams which it absorbed from the heights, providing everywhere abundant fountains and rivers, of which there may still be observed sacred memorials in places where fountains once existed; and this proves the truth of what I am saying.

Such was the natural state of the country, which was cultivated, as we may well believe, by true husbandmen, who made husbandry their business, and were lovers of honor, and of a noble nature, and had a soil the best in the world, and an abundance of water, and in the heaven above an excellently temperate climate. Now the city in those days was arranged like this. In the first place the Acropolis was not as now. For the fact is that a single night of excessive rain washed away the earth and laid bare the rock; at the same time there were earthquakes, and then occurred the extraordinary inundation, which was the third before the great destruction of Deucalion. But in primitive times the hill of the Acropolis extended to the Eridanus and Ilissus, and included the Pnyx on one side, and the Lycabettus as a boundary on the opposite side to the Pnyx, and was all well covered with soil, and level at the top, except in one or two places. Outside the Acropolis and under the sides of the hill there dwelt artisans, and such of the husbandmen as were tilling the ground near; the warrior class dwelt by themselves around the temples of Athene and Hephaestus at the summit, which moreover they had enclosed with a single fence like the garden of a single house. On the north side they had dwellings in common and had erected halls for dining in winter, and had all the buildings which they needed for their common life, besides temples, but there was no adorning of them with gold and silver, for they made no use of these for any purpose; they took a middle course between meanness and ostentation, and built modest houses in which they and their children's children grew old, and they handed them down to others who were like themselves, always the same. But in summertime they left their gardens and gymnasia and dining halls, and then the southern side of the hill was made use of by them for the same purpose. Where the Acropolis now is there was a fountain, which was choked by the earthquake, and has left only the few small streams which still exist in the vicinity, but in those days the fountain gave an abundant supply of water for all and of suitable temperature in summer and in winter. This is how they dwelt, being the guardians of their own citizens and the leaders of the Hellenes, who were their willing followers. And they took care to preserve the same number of men and women through all time, being so many as were required for warlike purposes, then as now—that is to say, about twenty thousand. Such were the ancient Athenians, and after this manner they righteously administered their own land and the rest of Hellas; they were renowned all over Europe and Asia for the beauty of their persons and for the many virtues of their souls, and of all men who lived in those days they were the most illustrious. And next, if I have not forgotten what I heard when I was a child, I will impart to you the character and origin of their adversaries. For friends should not keep their stories to themselves, but have them in common.

Yet, before proceeding further in the narrative, I ought to warn you, that you must not be surprised if you should perhaps hear Hellenic names given to foreigners. I will tell you the reason of this: Solon, who was intending to use the tale for his poem, inquired into the meaning of the names, and found that the early Egyptians in writing them down had translated them into their own language, and he recovered the meaning of the several names and when copying them out again translated them into our language. My great-grandfather, Dropides, had the original writing, which is still in my possession, and was carefully studied by me when I was a child. Therefore if you hear names such as are used in this country, you must not be surprised, for I have told how they came to be introduced. The tale, which was of great length, began as follows:

I have before remarked in speaking of the allotments of the gods, that they distributed the whole earth into portions differing in extent, and made for themselves temples and instituted sacrifices. And Poseidon, receiving for his lot the island of Atlantis, fathered children by a mortal woman, and settled them in a part of the island, which I will describe. Looking towards the sea, but in the center of the whole island, there was a plain which is said to have been the fairest of all plains and very fertile. Near the plain again, and also in the center of the island at a distance of about fifty stadia, there was a mountain not very high on any side.

In this mountain there dwelt one of the earth born primeval men of that country, whose name was Evenor, and he had a wife named Leucippe, and they had an only daughter who was called Cleito. The maiden had already reached womanhood, when her father and mother died; Poseidon fell in love with her and had intercourse with her, and breaking the ground, enclosed the hill in which she dwelt all around, making alternate zones of sea and land larger and smaller, encircling one another; there were two of land and three of water, which he turned as with a lathe, each having its circumference equidistant every way from the center, so that no man could get to the island, for ships and voyages were not as yet. He himself, being a god, found no difficulty in making special arrangements for the center island, bringing up two springs of water from beneath the earth, one of warm water and the other of cold, and making every variety of food to spring up abundantly from the soil. He also fathered and brought up five pairs of twin male children; and dividing the island of Atlantis into ten portions, he gave to the first-born of the eldest pair his mother's dwelling and the surrounding allotment, which was the largest and best, and made him king over the rest; the others he made princes, and gave them rule over many men, and a large territory. And he named them all; the eldest, who was the first king, he named Atlas, and after him the whole island and the ocean were called Atlantic. To his twin brother, who was born after him, and obtained as his lot the extremity of the island towards the Pillars of Heracles, facing the country which is now called the region of Gades in that part of the world, he gave the name which in the Hellenic language is Eumelus, in the language of the country which is named after him, Gadeirus. Of the second pair of twins he called one Ampheres, and the other Evaemon. To the elder of the third pair of twins he gave the name Mneseus, and Autochthon to the one who followed him. Of the fourth pair of twins he called the elder Elasippus, and the younger Mestor. And of the fifth pair he gave to the elder the name of Azaes, and to the younger that of Diaprepes. All these and their descendants for many generations were the inhabitants and rulers of diverse islands in the open sea; and also, as has been already said, they held sway in our direction over the country within the Pillars as far as Egypt and Tyrrhenia.

Now Atlas had a numerous and honorable family, and they retained the kingdom, the eldest son handing it on to his eldest for many generations; and they had such an amount of wealth as was never before possessed by kings and potentates, and is not likely ever to be again, and they were furnished with everything which they needed, both in the city and country. For because of the greatness of their empire many things were brought to them from foreign countries, and the island itself provided most of what was required by them for the uses of life. In the first place, they dug out of the earth whatever was to be found there, solid as well as fusile, and that which is now only a name and was then something more than a name, orichalcum, was dug out of the earth in many parts of the island, being more precious in those days than anything except gold. There was an abundance of wood for carpenter's work, and sufficient maintenance for tame and wild animals. Moreover, there were a great number of elephants in the island; for as there was provision for all other sorts of animals, both for those which live in lakes and marshes and rivers, and also for those which live in mountains and on plains, so there was for the animal which is the largest and most voracious of all. Also whatever fragrant things there now are in the earth, whether roots, or herbage, or woods, or essences which distill from fruit and flower, grew and thrived in that land; also the fruit which admits of cultivation, both the dry sort, which is given us for nourishment and any other which we use for food—we call them all by the common name pulse, and the fruits having a hard rind, affording drinks and meats and ointments, and good store of chestnuts and the like, which furnish pleasure and amusement, and art fruits which spoil with keeping, and the pleasant kinds of dessert, with which we console ourselves after dinner, when we are tired of eating—all these that sacred island which then beheld the light of the sun, brought forth fair and wondrous and in infinite abundance. With such blessings the earth freely furnished them; meanwhile they went on constructing their temples and palaces and harbors and docks. And they arranged the whole country in the following manner:

First of all they bridged over the zones of sea which surrounded the ancient metropolis, making a road to and from the royal palace. And at the very beginning they built the palace in the habitation of the god and of their ancestors, which they continued to ornament in successive generations, every king surpassing the one who went before him to the utmost of his power, until they made the building a marvel to behold for size and for beauty. And beginning from the sea they dug a canal of three hundred feet in width and one hundred feet in depth and fifty stadia in length, which they carried through to the outermost zone, making a passage from the sea up to this, which became a harbor, and leaving an opening sufficient to enable the largest vessels to find ingress. Moreover, they divided at the bridges the zones of land which parted the zones of sea, leaving room for a single trireme to pass out of one zone into another, and they covered over the channels so as to leave a way underneath for the ships; for the banks were raised considerably above the water. Now the largest of the zones into which a passage was cut from the sea was three stadia in breadth, and the zone of land which came next of equal breadth; but the next two zones, the one of water, the other of land, were two stadia, and the one which surrounded the central island was a stadium only in width. The island in which the palace was situated had a diameter of five stadia. All this including the zones and the bridge, which was the sixth part of a stadium in width, they surrounded by a stone wall on every side, placing towers and gates on the bridges where the sea passed in. The stone which was used in the work they quarried from underneath the center island, and from underneath the zones, on the outer as well as the inner side. One kind was white, another black, and a third red, and as they quarried, they at the same time hollowed out double docks, having roofs formed out of the native rock. Some of their buildings were simple, but in others they put together different stones, varying the color to please the eye, and to be a natural source of delight. The entire circuit of the wall, which went round the outermost zone, they covered with a coating of brass, and the circuit of the next wall they coated with tin, and the third, which encompassed the citadel, flashed with the red light of orichalcum.

The palaces in the interior of the citadel were constructed like this: in the center was a holy temple dedicated to Cleito and Poseidon, which remained inaccessible, and was surrounded by an enclosure of gold; this was the spot where the family of the ten princes first saw the light, and there the people annually brought the fruits of the earth in their season from all the ten portions, to be an offering to each of the ten. Here was Poseidon's own temple which was a stadium in length, and half a stadium in width, and of a proportionate height, having a strange barbaric appearance. All the outside of the temple, with the exception of the pinnacles, they covered with silver, and the pinnacles with gold. In the interior of the temple the roof was of ivory, curiously wrought everywhere with gold and silver and orichalcum; and all the other parts, the walls and pillars and floor, they coated with orichalcum. In the temple they placed statues of gold: there was the god himself standing in a chariot—the charioteer of six winged horses—and of such a size that he touched the roof of the building with his head; around him there were a hundred Nereids riding on dolphins, for such was thought to be the number of them by the men of those days. There were also in the interior of the temple other images which had been dedicated by private persons. And around the temple on the outside were placed statues of gold of all the descendants of the ten kings and of their wives, and there were many other great offerings of kings and of private persons, coming both from the city itself and from the foreign cities over which they held sway. There was an altar too, which in size and workmanship corresponded to this magnificence, and the palaces, in like manner, answered to the greatness of the kingdom and the glory of the temple.

In the next place, they had fountains, one of cold and another of hot water, in gracious plenty flowing; and they were wonderfully adapted for use by reason of the pleasantness and excellence of their waters. They constructed buildings about them and planted suitable trees, also they made cisterns, some open to the heavens, others roofed over, to be used in winter as warm baths; there were the kings' baths, and the baths of private persons, which were kept apart; and there were separate baths for women, and for horses and cattle, and to each of them they gave as much adornment as was suitable. Of the water which ran off they carried some to the grove of Poseidon, where were growing all manner of trees of wonderful height

and beauty, owing to the excellence of the soil, while the remainder was conveyed by aqueducts along the bridges to the outer circles; and there were many temples built and dedicated to many gods; also gardens and places of exercise, some for men, and others for horses in both of the two islands formed by the zones; and in the center of the larger of the two there was set apart a race-course of a stadium in width, and in length allowed to extend all around the island, for horses to race in. Also there were guardhouses at intervals for the guards, the more trusted of whom were appointed to keep watch in the lesser zone, which was nearer the Acropolis while the most trusted of all had houses given them within the citadel, near the persons of the kings. The docks were full of triremes and naval stores, and all things were quite ready for use. Enough of the plan of the royal palace.

Leaving the palace and passing out across the three you came to a wall which began at the sea and went all around: this was everywhere distant fifty stadia from the largest zone or harbor, and enclosed the whole, the ends meeting at the mouth of the channel which led to the sea. The entire area was densely crowded with habitations; and the canal and the largest of the harbors were full of vessels and merchants coming from all parts, who, from their numbers, kept up a multitudinous sound of human voices, and din and clatter of all sorts night and day.

I have described the city and the environments of the ancient palace nearly in the words of Solon, and now I must endeavor to represent the nature and arrangement of the rest of the land. The whole country was said by him to be very lofty and precipitous on the side of the sea, but the country immediately about and surrounding the city was a level plain, itself surrounded by mountains which descended towards the sea; it was smooth and even, and of an oblong shape, extending in one direction three thousand stadia, but across the center inland it was two thousand stadia. This part of the island looked towards the south, and was sheltered from the north. The surrounding mountains were celebrated for their number and size and beauty, far beyond any which still exist, having in them also many wealthy villages of country folk, and rivers, and lakes, and meadows supplying food enough for every animal, wild or tame, and much wood of various sorts, abundant for each and every kind of work.

I will now describe the plain, as it was fashioned by nature and by the labors of many generations of kings through long ages. It was for the most part rectangular and oblong, and where falling out of the straight line followed the circular ditch. The depth, and width, and length of this ditch were incredible, and gave the impression that a work of such extent, in addition to so many others, could never have been artificial. Nevertheless I must say what I was told. It was excavated to the depth of a hundred, feet, and its breadth was a stadium everywhere; it was carried round the whole of the plain, and was ten thousand stadia in length. It received the streams which came down from the mountains, and winding round the plain and meeting at the city, was there let off into the sea. Further inland, likewise, straight canals of a hundred feet in width were cut from it through the plain, and again let off into the ditch leading to the sea: these canals were at intervals of a hundred stadia, and by them they brought down the wood from the mountains to the city, and conveyed the fruits of the earth in ships, cutting transverse passages from one canal into another, and to the city. Twice in the year they gathered the fruits of the earth—in winter having the benefit of the rains of heaven, and in summer the water which the land supplied by introducing streams from the canals.

As to the population, each of the lots in the plain had to find a leader for the men who were fit for military service, and the size of a lot was a square of ten stadia each way, and the total number of all the lots was sixty thousand. And of the inhabitants of the mountains and of the rest of the country there was also a vast multitude, which was distributed among the lots and had leaders assigned to them according to their districts and villages. The leader was required to furnish for the war the sixth portion of a war-chariot, so as to make up a total of ten thousand chariots; also two horses and riders for them, and a pair of chariot-horses without a seat, accompanied by a horseman who could fight on foot carrying a small shield, and having a charioteer who stood behind the man-at-arms to guide the two horses; also, he was bound to furnish two heavy armed soldiers, two slingers, three stone-shooters and three javelin-men, who were light-armed, and four sailors to make up the complement of twelve hundred ships. Such was the military order of the royal city—the order of the other nine governments varied, and it would be wearisome to recount their several differences.

As to offices and honors, the following was the arrangement from the first. Each of the ten kings in his own division and in his own city had the absolute control of the citizens, and, in most cases, of the laws, punishing and slaying whomsoever he would. Now the order of precedence among them and their mutual relations were regulated by the commands of Poseidon which the law had handed down. These were inscribed by the first kings on a pillar of orichalcum, which was situated in the middle of the island, at the temple of Poseidon, where the kings were gathered together every fifth and every sixth year alternately, thus giving equal honor to the odd and to the even number. And when they were gathered together they consulted about their common interests, and inquired if anyone had transgressed in anything and passed judgment and before they passed judgment they gave their pledges to one another in this way: There were bulls who had the range of the temple of Poseidon; and the ten kings, being left alone in the temple, after they had offered prayers to the god that they might capture the victim which was acceptable to him, hunted the bulls, without weapons but with staffs and nooses; and the bull which they caught they led up to the pillar and cut its throat over the top of it so that the blood fell upon the sacred inscription. Now on the pillar, besides the laws, there was inscribed an oath invoking mighty curses on the disobedient. When therefore, after slaying the bull in the accustomed manner, they had burnt its limbs, they filled a bowl of wine and cast in a clot of blood for each of them; the rest of the victim they put in the fire, after having purified the column all around. Then they drew from the bowl in golden cups and pouring a libation on the fire, they swore that they would judge according to the laws on the pillar, and would punish him who in any point had already transgressed them, and that for the future they would not, if they could help, offend against the writing on the pillar, and would neither command others, nor obey any ruler who commanded them, to act otherwise than according to the laws of their father Poseidon. This was the prayer which each of them offered up for himself and for his descendants, at the same time drinking and dedicating the cup out of which he drank in the temple of the god; and after they had supped and satisfied their needs, when darkness came on, and the fire about the sacrifice was cool, all of them put on most beautiful azure robes, and, sitting on the ground, at night, over the embers of the sacrifices by which they had sworn, and extinguishing all the fire about the temple, they received and gave judgment, if any of them had an accusation to bring against any other; and when they had given judgment, at daybreak they wrote down their sentences on a golden tablet, and dedicated it together with their robes to be a memorial.

There were many special laws affecting the several kings inscribed about the temples, but the most important was the following: They were not to take up arms against one another, and they were all to come to the rescue if anyone in any of their cities attempted to overthrow the royal house; like their ancestors, they were to deliberate in common about war and other matters, giving the supremacy to the descendants of Atlas. And the king was not to have the power of life and death over any of his kinsmen unless he had the assent of the majority of the ten.

Such was the vast power which the god settled in the lost island of Atlantis; and this he afterwards directed against our land for the following reasons, as tradition tells: For many generations, as long as the divine nature lasted in them, they were obedient to the laws, and well-affectioned towards the god, whose seed they were; for they possessed true and in every way great spirits, uniting gentleness with wisdom in the various chances of life, and in their intercourse with one another. They despised everything but virtue, caring little for their present state of life, and thinking lightly of the possession of gold and other property, which seemed only a burden to them; neither were they intoxicated by luxury; nor did wealth deprive them of their self-control; but they were sober, and saw clearly that all these goods are increased by virtue and friendship with one another, whereas by too great regard and respect for them, they are lost—and friendship with them. By such reflections and by the continuance in them of a divine nature, the qualities which we have described grew and increased among them; but when the divine portion began to fade away, and became diluted too often and too much with the mortal admixture, and the human nature got the upper hand, they then, being unable to bear their fortune, behaved unseemly, and to him who had an eye to see grew visibly debased, for they were losing the fairest of their precious gifts; but to those who had no eye to see the true happiness, they appeared glorious and blessed at the very time when they were full of avarice and unrighteous power. Zeus, the god of gods, who rules according to law, and is able to see into such things, perceiving that an honorable race was in a woeful plight, and wanting to inflict punishment on them, that they might be chastened and improve, collected all the gods into their most holy habitation, which, being placed in the center of the world, beholds all created things. And when he had called them together, he spoke as follows:

[The rest of the Dialogue of Critias has been lost.]

Soul and World

Excerpt. Timaeus Locrius, The Teacher of Plato, On The Soul And The World. Updated and edited version from the Complete Pythagoras, Translated by Kenneth Sylvan Guthrie and edited by Patrick Rousel

Form and Matter

Timaeus the Locrian asserted this: that of all the things in the Universe, there are, two causes, (one) Mind, (the cause) of things existing according to reason; (the other) Necessity, (the cause) of things (existing) by (some) force, according to the power of the bodies; and that the former of these is the nature of the good and is called God, and the principle of things that are best; but what accessory causes follow, are referred to Necessity. As regards the things in the Universe, there are Form, Matter, and the perceptible; which is, as it were, a resistance of the two others; and that Form is unproduced, and unmoved, and stationary and of the nature of the same, and perceptible by the mind, and a pattern of such things produced, as exist by a state of change; for that some such thing as this is Form, spoken of and conceived to be.

Matter, however, is a mold, and a mother and a nurse, and pro-creative of the third kind of being; for receiving upon itself the resemblances, and as it were remolding them, it perfects these productions. He asserted moreover that Matter, though eternal is not unmoved; and though of itself it is formless and shapeless, yet it receives every kind of form; and that what is around bodies, is divisible, and partakes of the nature of the different; and that Matter is called by the twin names of Plane and Space. These two principles, then, are opposite to each, other; of which Form relates to a male power, and a father; while matter relates to a female, and a mother. Being three, they are recognizable by three marks: Form, by mind, according to knowledge; Matter by a spurious kind of reasoning, because of its not being mentally perceived directly, but by analogy and their productions by sensation and opinion.

Creation Of The World

Before the heavens, then, there existed through reason, Form and Matter, and the God who develops the best. But since the older surpasses the younger and the ordered surpasses the orderless, the deity being good, on seeing that Matter receives Form, and is altered in every way, but without order, the necessity of organizing it, altering the undefined to the defined, so that the differences between bodies might be similarly related, not receiving various turns at haphazard. He therefore made this world out of the whole of Matter, laying it down as a limit to the nature of being, through its containing in itself all the rest of things, being one, only-begotten, perfect, endued with soul and reason, for these qualities are superior to the soulless and the irrational, and of a sphere like body; for this is more perfect than the rest of forms.

Desirous then of making a very good production, he made it a deity, created and never to be destroyed by any cause other than the God, who had put it in order, if indeed he should ever wish to dissolve it. But on the part of the good there is no rushing forward to the destruction of a very beautiful production. Such therefore being the world, it continues without corruption and destruction, being blessed. It is the best of things ordered; since it has been produced by the best cause, that looks not to patterns made by hand, but to Form in the abstract, and to Existence, perceived by the mind to which the created thing, having been carefully adjusted, has become the most beautiful, and to be not wrongly undertaken. It is ever perfect according to the things perceived by sense because the pattern perceived by mind contains in itself all the living things perceived by mind; he left out of itself nothing, as being the limit of the things perceived by mind, as this world is of those perceived by sense.

As being solid, and perceptible by touch and sight, it has a share of earth and fire, and of the things between them, air and water; and it is composed of bodies all perfect, which are in it as wholes so that no part might ever be left out of it, in order that the body of the Universe might be altogether self-sufficient, uninjured by corruption without or within; for apart from these there is nothing else, for the things combined according the best proportions and with equal powers, neither rule over, nor are ruled by each other in turn, so that some receive an increase, others a decrease, remaining indissolubly united according to the very best proportions.

Proportions

For whenever there are any three terms, with mutually equal intervals, that are proportionate, we then perceive that, after the manner of an extended string, the middle is to the first, as is the third to it; and this holds true inversely and alternately, interchanging places and order; so that it is impossible to arrange them numerically without producing an equivalence of results. Likewise the world's shape and movement are well arranged; the shape is a sphere self similar on all sides, able to contain all shapes that are similar; the movement endlessly exhibits the change dependent on a circle.

Now as the sphere is on every side equidistant from the center, it is able to retain its poise whether in movement or at rest; neither leaving its poise, nor assuming another. Its external appearance being exactly smooth, it needs no mortal organs such as are fitted to, and present in all other living beings, because of their wants.

The world-soul's element of divinity radiates out from the center, entirely penetrating the whole world, forming a single mixture of divided substance with undivided form; and this mixture of two forces, the same and the different, became the origin of motion; which indeed was not accomplished in the easiest way, being extremely difficult.

Now all these proportions are combined harmonically according to numbers; which proportions were scientifically divided according to scale which reveals the elements and the means of the soul's combination.

Now seeing that the earlier is more powerful in power and time than the later, the deity did not rank the soul after the substance of the body, but made it older, by taking the first of unities, 384 (12 x [2?]).

Knowing this first, we can easily reckon the double and the triple and all the terms together, with the complements and eighths, must amount to 14,69 and likewise the divisions (sum of the tone sequences of tones, amounting to 384 x 27, the perfect cube).

Revolutions and Time

God the eternal, the chief ruler and creator of the Universe is beheld alone by the mind; but we may behold by sight all that is produced: this world and its parts, how many they [...] in heaven; which as being ethereal, must be divided into kinds, some relating to sameness, others to difference. Sameness draws inward all that is without, along the general eastward movement from the West. Difference draws from within all self-moved portions from West to East, fortuitously rolling around and along by the superior power of sameness.

The different's movement being divided in harmonic proportion, assumes the order of seven circles nearest to the earth. The Moon revolves in a month; while beyond her the Sun completes his revolution in a year. Two planets run a co-equal with that of the Sun: Mercury, and Juno, also called Venus and Lucifer, because shepherds and people generally are not skillful in sacred astronomy, confusing the western and eastern rise. The same star may shine in the West when following the Sun at a distance great enough to be visible in spite of solar splendor; and at another time in the East, when, as herald of the day it rises before the Sun leading it. Because of its running together with the sun, Venus is Lucifer frequently but not always; for there are planets and stars of any magnitude seen above the horizon before sunrise, herald the day.

But the three other planets, Mars,

Jupiter and Saturn have their peculiar velocities and different years, completing their course while making their periods of effulgence, of visibility, of obscuration and eclipse, causing accurate rising and settings. Moreover they complete their appearances conspicuously in the East or West according to their position relative to the Sun, who during the day speeds westward, which during the night it reverses, under the influence of sameness; while its annual revolution is due to its inherent motion. Resulting from these two kinds of motion it rolls out a spiral, creeping according to one portion, in the time of a day, but, whirled around under the sphere of the fixed stars, according to each revolution of darkness and day.

Now these revolutions are by men called portions of time, which the deity arranged together with the world. For before the world the stars did not exist; and hence there was neither year, nor periods of seasons, by which this generated time is measured, and which is the representation of the un-generated time called eternity.

For as this heaven has been produced according to an eternal pattern, so according to the pattern of eternity was our world-time created simultaneously with the world.

Creation By Geometric Figures

The Earth, fixed at the center, becomes the hearth of the gods, and the boundary of darkness and day, producing both settings and risings, according to the occultations produced by the things that form the boundary, just as we improve our sight by making a tube with our closed hand, to exclude refraction. The Earth is the oldest body in the heavens. Water was not produced without Earth, nor air without moisture; nor could fire continue without moisture and the materials that are inflammable; so that the Earth is fixed upon its balance as the root and base of all other substances. Of produced things, the substratum is Matter, while the reason of each shape is abstract Form; of these two the result is Earth, and Water, Air and Fire.

This is how they were created. Each body is composed of surfaces, whose elements are triangles; of which one is right-angled, and the other has all unequal sides, with the greater angle thrice the size of the lesser; while its least angle is the third of a right angle, and the middle one is double of the least; for it is two parts out of three; while the greatest is a right angle, being one and a half greater than the middle one, and the triple of the least. Now this unequal sided triangle is the half of a equilateral triangle, out into two equal parts by a line let down from apex to that base. Now in each of these triangles there is a right angle; but in the one, the two sides about the right angle are equal, and in the other, all the sides are unequal. Now let this be called a scalene triangle; while the other, the half of the square, is the principle of the constitution the Earth. For the square produced from this scalene triangle is composed of four half squares and from such a square is produced the cube, a body the most stationary and steady in every way; having six sides and eight angles, and on this account the Earth is a body the heaviest and most difficult to be moved and its substance is inconvertible because it has no affinity with a triangle of any kind. Only the Earth has as peculiar an element as the square and this is the element of the three other substances, Fire, Air and Water. For when the half triangle is put together six times, it produces a solid equilateral triangle; the exemplar of the pyramid, which has four faces with equal angles, which is the form of Fire, as the easiest to be moved and composed of the finest particles. After this ranks the octahedron, with eight faces and six angles, the element of Air, and the third is the icosahedron, with twenty faces and twelve angles, the element of Water, composed of the most numerous and heaviest particles.

These then, as being composed of the same element, are transmuted. But the deity has made the dodecahedron, as being the nearest to the sphere, the image of the Universe. Fire then, by the fineness of its particles, passes through all things; and Air through the rest of things, with the exception of Fire; and Water through the Earth. All things are therefore full, and have no vacuum. They co-here by the revolving movement of the Universe, and are pressed against, and rubbed by, each other in turn, and produce the never-failing change from production to destruction.

Concretion Of Elements

By making use of these the deity put together this world, sensible to touch through the particles of Earth, and to sight through those of Fire; which two are the extremes. Through the particles of Air and Water he has conjoined the world by the strongest chain, namely, proportion; which restrains not only itself but all its subjects. Now if the conjoined object is a plane surface, one middle term is sufficient; but if a solid, there will be need of two. With two middle terms, therefore, he combined two extremes; so that as Fire is to Air, Air might be to Water, and Water to Earth; and by alternation, as Fire is to Water, Air might be to Earth; and by inversion as Earth is to Water, Water might be to Air, and Air to Fire; and by alternation, as Earth is to Air, so Water might be to Fire. Now since all are equal in power, their ratios are in a state of equality. This world is then one, through the bond of the deity, made according to proportion.

How each of these substances possesses many forms; Fire, those of Flame, and Burning and Luminousness, through the inequality of the triangles in each of them. In the same manner, Air is partly clear and

Mysteries of Reason

dry, and partly turbid and foggy; and Water partly flowing and partly congealed, according as it is Snow, Hoarfrost, Hail or Ice; and that which is Moist, is in one respect flowing as honey and oil; but in another is compact, as pitch and wax; and of compact forms there are some fusible, as gold, silver, copper, tin, lead and steel; and some friable, as sulphur, pitch, nitre, salt, alum, and similar metals.

Composition Of Soul

After putting together the world, the deity planned the creation of living beings, subject to death, so that, himself being perfect, he might perfectly work it out according to his image.

Therefore he mixed up the soul of man out of the same proportions and powers, and after taking the particles and distributing them, he delivered them over to Nature, whose office is to effect change. She then took up the task of working out mortal and ephemeral living beings, whose souls were drawn in from different sources, some from the Moon, others from the Sun, and others from various planets, that cycle within the Difference—with the exception of one single power which was derived from Sameness, which she mixed up in the rational portion of the soul, as the image of wisdom in those of a happy fate.

Now of the soul of man one portion is rational and intellectual; and another irrational and unintellectual.

Of the logical part, the best portion is derived from Sameness, while the worse comes from Difference; and each is situated around the head, so that the other portions of the soul and body may minister to it, as the uppermost of the whole tabernacle.

Of the irrational portion, that which represents passion hangs around the heart, while desire inhabits the liver. The principle of the body, and root of the marrow is the brain, wherein exists leadership; and from this, like an effusion, through the backbone flows what remains, from which are separated the particles for seed and reason; while the marrow's surrounding defenses are the bones, of which the flesh is the covering and concealment. To the nerves he united joints by ligatures, suitable for their movement. Of the internal organs, some exist for the sake of nourishment, and others for safety; of communications, some convey outside movements to the interior intelligent places of perception, while others, not falling under the power of apprehension, are unperceived, either because the affected bodies are too earth-like, or because the movements are too feeble; the painful movements tend to arouse Nature, while the pleasurable lull Nature into remaining within itself.

The Universe

Excerpt. Updated and edited version from the Complete Pythagoras, Trans-

lated by Kenneth Sylvan Guthrie and edited by Patrick Rousel

Ocellus Lucanus has written what follows concerning the nature of the universe; having learned some things through clear arguments from nature herself, but others from opinion, in conjunction with reason, it being his intention to derive what is probable from intellectual perception. Therefore it appears to me, that the universe is indestructible and unbegotten, since it always was, and always will be; for if it had a temporal beginning, it would not always have existed: therefore, the universe is unbegotten and indestructible; for if someone should opine that it was once generated, he would not be able to find anything into which it can be corrupted or dissolved, since that from which it was generated would be the first part of the universe; and again, that into which it would be dissolved would be the last part of it.

But if the universe was generated, it was generated together with all things; and if it should be corrupted, it would be corrupted together with all things. This however is impossible. This universe is therefore without a beginning, and without an end: nor is it possible that it can have any other mode of subsistence.

To which may be added, that everything which, has received a beginning of generation, and which ought also to participate of dissolution, receives two mutations; one of which, indeed proceeds from the less to the greater, and from the worse to the better; and that from which it begins change is denominated "generation", but that at which its length arrives at is called climax. The other mutation, however, proceeds from the greater to the less, and from the better to the worse; but the end of this mutation is called corruption and dissolution.

If therefore the whole and the universe were generated, and are corruptible they must, when generated have been changed from the less to the greater, and from the worse to the better; but when corrupted, they must be changed from the greater to the less, and from the better to the worse. Hence, if the world was generated, it would receive increase and would arrive at its consummation; and again, it would afterwards decrease and end. For every thing which has a progression possesses three boundaries, and two intervals; the three boundaries are generation, consummation and end; and the intervals are, progression from generation to consummation, and from consolation to end.

The whole, however, and the universe, affords as from itself, no indication of anything of this kind; for neither do we perceive it rising into existence, or becoming to be, nor changing to the better and the greater, nor changing to worse or less; but it always continues to subsist in identical manner, and perpetually remains self-identical.

Clear signs and indications of this

are the orders of things, their symmetry, figurations, positions, intervals, powers, swiftness and slowness in respect to each other; and, besides these, their numbers and temporal periods, are clear signs and indications. For all such things as these change and diminish, conforming to the course of generation; for things that are greater and better tend towards consummation through power, but those that are less and worse decay through the inherent weakness of nature.

The whole world is what I call the whole universe; for this word "cosmos" was given it as a result of its being adorned with all things. From itself it is a consummate and perfect system of all things, for there is nothing external to the universe, since whatever exists is contained in the universe, and the universe subsists together with this, comprehending in itself all things, both parts and superfluous.

The things contained in the world are naturally congruous with it; but the world harmonizes with nothing else, harmonizing with itself. Other things do not possess self-subsistence, but require adjustment with the environment. Thus animals require conjunction with air for the purpose of respiration; and with light, in order to see; and similarly the other senses with other environment, to function satisfactorily. A conjunction with earth is necessary for the germination of plants. The sun, moon, planets and fixed stars likewise integrate with the world, as parts of its general arrangement. The world, however, has no conjunction with anything outside of itself. The above is supported by the following. Fire which imparts heat to others, is self-hot; honey which is sweet to the taste, is self-sweet. The principles of demonstrations, which conclude to things unapparent, are self-evident. Therefore the cause of the perfection of other things is itself perfect. That which preserves and renders permanent other things must itself be preserved and permanent. What harmonizes must itself be self-harmonic. Now as the world is the cause of the existence, preservation and perfection of other things, must itself be perpetual and perfect; and because its duration is everlasting, it becomes the cause of the permanence of all other things. In short, if the universe should be dissolved, it would be dissolved either into the existent, or nonexistent. As it could not be dissolved into existence, for in this case the dissolution would not be a corruption; as being is either the universe, or some part of it. Nor can it be dissolved into nonentity, since being cannot possibly arise from non-being; or be dissolved into nonentity. Therefore the universe is incorruptible, and never can be destroyed. If, however, somebody should think that it can be corrupted, it must be corrupted either from something external to, or contained in the universe, but it cannot be corrupted by anything external to it, for nothing such exists, since all other things are comprehended in the universe, and the world is the whole and the all. Nor can it be corrupted by the things it contains, which would imply their greater power. This however is impossible; for all things are led and governed by the universe, and thereby are preserved and adjusted, possessing life and soul. But if the universe can neither be corrupted by anything external to it, nor by anything contained within it, the world must therefore be incorruptible and indestructible; for we consider the world identical with the universe.

Further, the whole of nature surveyed through its own totality, will be found to derive continuity from the first and most honorable bodies, proportionally attenuating this continuity, introducing it to everything mortal, and receiving the progression of its peculiar subsistence; for the first (and most honorable) bodies in the universe revolve according to the same and similarly. The progression of the whole of nature, however, is not successive and continuous, nor yet local, but is subject to mutation. When condensed, fire generates air; air water, and water earth. A return circuit of transformation extends backward from earth to fire, from which it originated. However fruits, and most rooted plants, originate from seeds. When however they fruit and mature, that are again resolved into seed, nature producing a complete circular progression.

In a subordinate manner, men and other animals change the universal boundary of nature; for in these there is no periodical return to the first age; nor is there a transfusion, such as between fire and air, and water and earth; but the mutations of their ages being accomplished in a four-cycled circle, they are dissolved, and reformed.

These therefore are the signs and indications that the universe which comprehends all things, will always endure and be preserved, but that its parts and its nonessential additions are corrupted and dissolved.

Further, it is credible that the universe, without a beginning, and without end, from its figure, motion, time and essence; it may be concluded that the world is begotten and incorruptible; for its figure is circular; and as a circular figure is similar and equal on all sides, it is therefore without a beginning or an end. Circular is also the motion of the universe, but this motion is stable and without transition.

Time, likewise, in which motion exists, infinite; for neither did it have a beginning, nor will it have an end of its revolution. The universe's essence also does not waste elsewhere, and is immutable, because it is not naturally adapted to charge, either from worse to better, or from better to worse. From all these arguments, therefore, it is obviously credible, that the world is unbegotten and incorruptible. So much about the world and the universe.

Creation

Since, however, in the universe there is a difference between generation and the generated, and since generation occurs where there is a mutation and egress from things which rank as subjects, then must the cause of generation subsist as long as the generated matter. The cause of generation must be both efficient and motive, while the recipient must be passive, and moved. The Fates themselves, distinguish and separate the impassive part of the world from that which is perpetually in motion. For the course of the moon is the meeting line of generation and immortality. The region above the moon, as well as the lunar domain, is the residence of the divinities; while sub-lunar regions are the abode of strife and nature; here exists change of the generated things, and regeneration of those that have perished.

So that part of the world, however, in which nature and generation predominate, it is necessary that the three following things be present. In the first place, the body which yields to the touch, and which is the subject of all generated natures. But this will be a universal recipient, a characteristic of generation itself, having the same relation to the things that are generated from it, as water to taste, silence to sound, darkness to light, and the matter of artificial forms to the forms themselves. For water is tasteless and devoid of quality, yet is capable of receiving the sweet and the bitter, the tart and the salt. Air also, which is formless as regards sound, is the recipient of words and melody. Darkness, which is without color, and without form, becomes the recipient of splendor, and of the yellow color, and the white; but white pertains to the statuary's art, and the wax sculptor's art. Matter's relation, however, is different from the sculptor's art, for in matter, prior to generation, all things are in capacity, but they exist in perfection when they are generated, and receive their proper nature. Hence matter (or a universal recipient) is necessary to the existence of generation.

The second necessity is the existence of contrarieties, in order to effect mutations and changes in quality, matter, for this purpose, receiving passive qualities, and an aptitude to the participations of forms. Contrariety is also necessary in order that powers which are naturally mutually repugnant may not finally conquer, or vanquish each other. These powers are hot and cold, dryness and moistness.

In the third place rank essences: and those and fire and water, air and earth, of which heat and cold, dryness and moistness, are powers. But essences differ from powers, essences being locally corrupted or generated, as their reasons or forms are incorporeal.

Of those four powers, however, heat and cold subsist as causes and things of an effective nature; but the dry and the moist rank as matter and things that are passive, though matter is the first recipient of things, for it is that which is spread under all things in common. Hence the body, whose capacity is the object of sense, and ranks as a principle, is the first thing; while contraries, such as heat and cold, moistness and dryness, rank as primary differences; but heaviness and lightness, density and rarity, are related as things produced from primary differences. These amount to sixteen: heat and cold, moistness and dryness, heaviness and lightness, rarity and density, smoothness and roughness, hardness and softness, thinness and thickness, acuteness and obtuseness. Knowledge of all of these is had by touch, which forms a judgment; hence also any body whatsoever which contains capacity for these can be apprehended by touch.

Heat and dryness, rarity and sharpness are the powers of fire; coldness and moistness, density and obtuseness are those of water; those of air are softness, smoothness, light, and the quality of being attenuated; while those of earth are hardness and roughness, heaviness and thickness.

Of these four bodies, however, fire and earth are the intensities of contraries. Fire is the intensity of heat, as ice is of cold; and if ice is a concretion of moisture and frigidity, fire will be the fervor of dryness and heat. That is why neither fire nor ice generate anything. Fire and earth, therefore, are the extremities of the elements, while water and air are the media, for they have a mixed corporeal nature. Nor is it possible that there could be only one of the extremes, a contrary thereto being necessary. Nor could there be two only, for it is necessary to have a medium, as media oppose extremes.

Fire therefore is hot and dry, but air is hot and moist; water is moist and cold, and earth cold and dry. Hence heat is common to air and fire; cold is common to water and earth; dryness to earth and fire, and moisture to water and air. But with respect to the peculiarities of each, heat is the peculiarity of fire, dryness of earth, moisture of air, and frigidity of water. These essences remain permanent, through the possession of common properties; but they change through such as are peculiar, when one contrary overcomes another.

Hence, when the moisture in air overcomes the dryness in fire, or when water's frigidity overcomes air's heat, and earth's dryness, water's moistness, and vice versa, then are effected the mutual mutations and generations of the elements.

The body, however, which is the subject and recipient of mutations, is a universal receptacle, and is in capacity the first tangible substance. But the mutations of the elements are effected either from a change of earth into fire, or from fire into air, or from air into water, or from water into earth. Mutations is also effected, in the third place, when each element's contrariness is corrupted, simultaneously with the preservation of everything kindred and coeval. Generation therefore is effected when one contrary quality is corrupted. For fire, indeed, is hot and dry, but air is hot and moist, and heat is common to both; but the peculiarity of fire is dryness, and of air, moisture. Hence when the moisture in air overcomes the dryness in fire, then fire is changed into air.

Again, since water is moist and cold, but air is moist and hot, moisture is common to both. Water's peculiarity is coldness, and of air, heat. When, therefore, the coldness in water overcomes the heat in air, air is altered into water.

Further, earth is cold and dry, and water cold and moist; coldness being common to both. But earth's peculiarity is dryness, and water's, moisture. When, therefore, earth's dryness overcomes water's moisture, water is altered into earth.

Earth's mutation in the ascending alteration occurs in a contrary way. One alternate mutation is effected when one whole vanquishes another; and two contrary powers are corrupted, nothing being common to them, at the same time. For since fire is hot and dry, while water is cold and moist, when the moisture in water overcomes the dryness in fire, and water's coldness, fire's heat; then fire is altered into water.

Again, earth is cold and dry, while air is hot and moist. When, therefore, earth's coldness overcomes air's heat, and earth's dryness air's moisture, then air is altered into earth.

When air's moisture corrupts fire's heat, then from both of them will be generated fire; for air's heat, and fire's dryness will remain, fire being hot and dry.

When earth's coldness is corrupted, and also water's moisture, then from both of them will be generated earth. For earth's dryness and water's coldness will be left, as earth is cold and dry.

But when air's heat and fire's heat are corrupted, no element will be generated; for in both of these will remain contraries, air's moisture and fire's dryness. Moisture is however contrary to dryness. Again, when earth's coldness, and that of water are corrupted, neither thus will any generation occur; for earth's dryness, and water's moisture will remain. But dryness is contrary to moisture.

Thus we have briefly discussed the generation of the first bodies, and how and from what subjects it is effected.

Since, however, the world is indestructible and unbegotten, and neither had a beginning or generation, nor an end, it is necessary that the nature which produces generation in another thing, and also that which generates in itself, should be simultaneously present. That which produces generation in another thing, is the whole superlunary region; though the more proximate cause is the sun, who by its comings and goings continually changes the air; from cold to heat, which again changes the earth, which alters all its contents.

The obliquity of the zodiac, also,

is well placed in respect to the sun's motion, for it likewise is the cause of generation. This is universally accomplished by the universe's proper order; wherein some things are active, and others passive. Different therefore is the generator, which is superlunary, while that which generated is sublunary; and that which consists of both of these, namely, an over-running body, and an ever-mutable generated nature, is the world itself.

Perpetual World

Man's generation did not originate from the earth, other animals, or plants; but the world's proper order being perpetual, its contained, aptly arranged natures should share with it never-failing subsistence. As primarily the world existed always, its parts must coexist with it; and by these I mean the heavens, the earth, and what is contained between them; which is on high, and is called aerial; for the world does not exist without, but with and from these.

As the world's parts are continually subsistent, their comprehended natures must coexist with them; with the heavens, indeed, the sun, moon, fixed stars and planets; with the earth, animals and plants, gold and silver; with the aerial region, spiritual substances and wind, heating and cooling; for it is the property of the heavens to subsist in conjunction with the natures which it comprehends, and of the earth to support its native plants and animals; of the aerial regions, to be continually subsistent with the natures it has generated. Therefore, in each division of the world there is arranged a certain genus of animals which surpasses its fellows, the heavens are the habitat of the gods, on the earth men, and in the space between, the geniuses. Therefore the race of men must be perpetual, since reason convinces us that not only are the world's parts continually subsistent with it, but also their comprehended natures.

Sudden destructions, and mutations however take place in the parts of the earth; the sea overflows on to the land, or the earth shakes and spits, through the unobserved entrance of wind or water. But an entire destruction of the earth's whole arrangement never took place, nor ever will. Hence the story that Grecian history began with the Argive Inachus is false, if understood to be a first principle, but true, as some mutations of Greek politics; for Greece has frequently been, and will again be barbarous, not only from the introduction of foreigners, but from Nature herself, which, although she does not become greater or less; yet is always younger, and has a beginning in reference to us.

So much about the whole, and the universe; the generation and corruption of natures generated in it; how they subsist, and forever; one part of the universe consisting of a nature which is perpetually moved, and another passive one; the former governing, the latter ever governed.

Chapter 6

Sacred Lotus

Vedic Origins

Hymns 129, 130, and 190 from the Rig Veda. Updated and edited version from the translation by Ralph T.H. Griffith.

From Nothing

Hymn 129. 1 Then was not non-existent nor existent: there was no realm of air, no sky beyond it. What covered in, and where? And what gave shelter? Was water there, unfathomed depth of water? 2 Death was not then, nor was there anything immortal: no sign was there, the day's and night's divider. That One Thing, breathless, breathed by its own nature: apart from it was nothing whatsoever. 3 Darkness there was: at first concealed in darkness, this All was undiscriminated chaos. All that existed then was void and formless: by the great power of Warmth was born that Unit. 4 Thereafter rose Desire in the beginning, Desire, the primal seed and germ of Spirit. Sages who searched with their heart's thought discovered the existent's kinship in the non-existent. 5 Transversely was their severing line extended: what was above it then, and what below it? There were creators, there were mighty forces, free action here and energy up there 6 Who truly knows and who can here declare it, from where it was born and from where comes this creation? The Gods are later than this world's production. Who knows, then, how it first came into being? 7 He, the first origin of this creation, whether he formed it all or did not form it, Whose eye controls this world in highest heaven, he truly knows it, or perhaps he knows not.

The Vault of Heaven

Hymn 130. 1 The sacrifice drawn out with threads on every side, stretched by a hundred sacred ministers and one—This do these Fathers weave, who here have come: they sit beside the warp and cry, weave forth, weave back. 2 The Man extends it and the Man unbinds it: even to this vault of heaven has he weaved it. These pegs are fastened to the seat of worship: they made the Sama-hymns their weaving shuttles. 3 What were the rule, the order and the model? What were the wooden fender and the butter? What were the hymn, the chant, the recitation, when to the God all Deities paid worship? 4 Closely was Gayatri conjoined with Agni, and closely Savitar combined with Usnih. Brilliant with Ukthas, Soma joined Anustup: Brhaspati's voice by Brhati was aided. 5 Viraj adhered to Varuna and Mitra: here Tristup day by day was Indra's portion. Jagati entered all the Gods together: so by this knowledge men were raised to Rishis. 6 So by this knowledge men were raised to Rishis, when ancient sacrifice sprang up, our Fathers. With the mind's eye I think that I behold them who first performed this sacrificial worship. 7 They who were versed in ritual and meter, in hymns and rules, were the Seven Godlike Rishis. Viewing the path of those of old, the sages have taken up the reins like chariot-drivers.

Order Established

Hymn 190. 1 From Fervor kindled to its height, Eternal Law and Truth were born: From this was the Night produced, and from this the billowy flood of sea arose. 2 From that same billowy flood of sea the Year was afterwards produced, Ordainer of the days nights, Lord over all who close the eye. 3 Dhatar, the great Creator, then formed in due order Sun and Moon. He formed in order Heaven and Earth, the regions of the air, and light.

The Origin of All

Excerpt. The Bhagavad Gita, Verses 10:1-42 Updated and edited version from the translation by Swami Swarupananda.

The Blessed Lord said:

1 Again, Oh mighty-armed, do you listen to my supreme word, which I, wishing your welfare, will tell you who are delighted to hear me.

2 Neither the hosts of Devas, nor the great Rishis, know my origin, for in every way I am the source of all the Devas and the great Rishis.

3 He who knows me, birthless and beginningless, the great Lord of worlds—he, among mortals, is undeluded, he is freed from all sins.

4-5 Intellect, knowledge, non-delusion, forbearance, truth, restraint of the external senses, calmness of heart, happiness, misery, birth, death, fear, as well as fearlessness, non-injury, evenness, contentment, austerity, benevolence, good name, and ill-fame—these different kinds of qualities of beings arise from me alone.

6 The seven great Rishis as well as the four ancient Manus, possessed of powers like me due to their thoughts being fixed on me, were born of my

mind; from them are these creatures in the world.

7 He who in reality knows these manifold manifestations of my being and this Yoga power of Mine, becomes established in the unshakable Yoga; there is no doubt about it.

8 I am the origin of all, from me everything evolves—thus thinking the wise worship me with loving consciousness.

9 With their minds wholly in me, with their senses absorbed in me, enlightening one another, and always speaking of me, they are satisfied and delighted.

10 To them, ever steadfast and serving me with affection, I give that Buddhi Yoga by which they come to me.

11 Out of mere compassion for them, I, abiding in their hearts, destroy the darkness (in them) born of ignorance, by the luminous lamp of knowledge.

Arjuna said:

12-13 The Supreme Brahman, the Supreme Abode, the Supreme Purifier, you are. All the Rishis, the Deva-Rishi Nârada as well as Asita, Devala and Vyâsa have declared you as the Eternal, the Self-luminous Purusha, the first Deva, birthless and all-pervading. So also, you yourself say to me.

14 I regard all this that you say to me as true, Oh Keshava. Truly, Oh Bhagavân, neither the Devas nor the Dânavas know your manifestation.

15 Truly, you yourself know yourself by yourself, Oh Purusha Supreme, Oh Source of beings, Oh Lord of beings, Oh Deva of Devas, Oh Ruler of the world.

16 You should indeed speak, without reserve, of your divine attributes by which, filling all these worlds, you exist.

17 How shall I, Oh Yogin, meditate ever to know you? In what things, Bhagavân, are you to be thought of by me?

18 Speak to me again in detail, Jnanârdana, of your Yoga-powers and attributes; for I am never satiated in hearing the ambrosia of your speech.

The Blessed Lord said:

19 I shall speak to you now, Oh best of the Kurus, of my divine attributes, according to their prominence; there is no end to the particulars of my manifestation.

20 I am the Self, Oh Gudâkesha, existent in the heart of all beings; I am the beginning, the middle, and also the end of all beings.

21 Of the Adityas, I am Vishnu; of luminaries, the radiant Sun; of the winds, I am Marichi; of the asterisms, the Moon.

22 I am the Sâma-Veda of the Vedas, and Indra of the gods; of the senses I am Manas, and intelligence in living beings am I.

23 And of the Rudras I am Sankara, of the Yakshas and Râkshasas the Lord of wealth (Kuvera), of the Vasus I am Pâvaka, and of mountains, Meru am I.

24 And of priests, Oh son of Prithâ, know me the chief, Brihaspati; of gen-

erals, I am Skanda; of bodies of water, I am the ocean.

25 Of the great Rishis I am Bhrigu; of words I am the one syllable "Om"; of Yajnas I am the Yajna of Japa (silent repetition); of immovable things the Himâlaya.

26 Of all trees I am the Ashvattha, and Nârada of Deva-Rishis; Chitraratha of Gandharvas am I, and the Muni Kapila of the perfected ones.

27 Know me among horses as Uchchaisshravas, Amrita-born; of lordly elephants Airâvata, and of men the king.

28 Of weapons I am the thunderbolt, of cows I am Kâmadhuk; I am the Kandarpa, the cause of offspring; of serpents I am Vâsuki.

29 And Ananta of snakes I am, I am Varuna of water-beings; and Aryaman of Pitris I am, I am Yama of controllers.

30 And Prahlâda am I of Diti's progeny, of measurers I am Time; and of beasts I am the lord of beasts, and Garuda of birds.

31 Of purifiers I am the wind, Râma of warriors am I; of fishes I am the shark, of streams I am Jâhnavi (the Ganges).

32 Of manifestations I, am the beginning, the middle and also the end; of all knowledges I am the knowledge of the Self, and Vâda of disputants.

33 Of letters the letter A am I, and Dvandva of all compounds; I alone am the inexhaustible Time, I am the Sustainer, the All-formed.

34 And I am the all-seizing Death, and the prosperity of those who are to be prosperous; of the feminine qualities I am Fame, Beauty, Inspiration, Memory, Intelligence, Constancy and Forbearance.

35 Of Sâmas also I am the Brihat-Sâma, of metres Gâyatri am I; of months I am Mârgashirsha, of seasons the flowery season.

36 I am the gambling of the fraudulent, I am the power of the powerful; I am victory, I am effort, I am Sattva of the Sâttvika.

37 Of the Vrishnis I am Vâsudeva; of the Pândavas, Dhananjaya; and also of the Munis I am Vyâsa; of the sages, Ushanas the sage.

38 Of punishers I am the scepter; of those who seek to conquer, I am statesmanship; and also of things secret I am silence, and the knowledge of knowers am I.

39 And whatsoever is the seed of all beings, that also am I, Oh Arjuna. There is no being, whether moving or unmoving, that can exist without me.

40 There is no end of my divine attributes, Oh scorcher of foes; but this is a brief statement by me of the particulars of my divine attributes.

41 Whatever being there is great, prosperous or powerful, that know you to be a product of a part of my splendor

42 Or what avails you to know all this diversity, Oh Arjuna? Know this: that I exist, supporting this whole world by a small part of myself.

The First Cause

Excerpt. From the Svetashvatara Upanishad. The Upanishads. Updated and edited version from the translation by Max Müller.

1 The Brahma-students say: Is Brahman the cause? From where are we born? Whereby do we live, and to where do we go? Oh you who know Brahman, tell us at whose command we abide, whether in pain or in pleasure?

2 Should time, or nature, or necessity, or chance, or the elements be considered as the cause, or he who is called the person (purusha)? It cannot be their union either, because that is not self-dependent, and the self also is powerless, because there is, independent of him, a cause of good and evil.

3 The sages, devoted to meditation and concentration, have seen the power belonging to God himself, hidden in its own qualities (gunas). He, being one, superintends all those causes, time, self, and the rest.

This is That

Excerpt. From the Katha Upanishad versus 2:4:5-9. The Upanishads. Updated and edited version from the translation by Max Müller.

5 He who knows this living soul which eats honey perceives objects as being the Self, always near, the Lord of the past and the future, henceforward fears no more. This is that.

6 He who knows him who was born first from the brooding heat, who, entering into the heart, abides therein, and was perceived from the elements. This is that.

7 He who knows Aditi also, who is one with all deities, who arises with Prâna (breath), who, entering into the heart, abides therein, and was born from the elements. This is that.

8 There is Agni (fire), the all-seeing, hidden in the two fire-sticks, well-guarded like a child by the mother, day after day to be adored by men when they awake and bring oblations. This is that.

9 And that from which the sun rises, and to where it goes to set, there all the Devas are contained, and no one goes beyond. This is that.

Creator of Beings

From Satapatha Brahmana Part 1, Fifth Adhyâya, First Brâhmana, The Kâturmâsyâni, The Vaisvadeva. Updated and edited version from the translation by Julius Eggeling.

In the beginning, Pragâpati alone existed here. He thought within himself, "How can I be propagated?" He toiled and practiced austerities. He created living beings. The living beings created by him passed away: they are those birds. Now man is the nearest to Pragâpati; and man is two-footed: hence birds are two-footed. Pragâpati thought within himself, "Even as formerly I was alone, so also am I now alone." He created a second race of beings; they also passed away: they are those small crawling reptiles other than snakes. He created a third race, they say; they also passed away: they are those snakes. Yâgñavalkya, on his part, declared them to be of two kinds only; but of three kinds they are according to the Rik. While praising and practicing austerities, Pragâpati thought within himself, "How comes it that the living beings created by me pass away?" He then became aware that his creatures passed away from want of food. He made the breasts in the front of their body teem with milk. He then created living beings; and by resorting to the breasts, the beings created by him from then on continued to exist: they are these which have not passed away.

Hence it has been said by the Rishi, "Three generations have passed beyond,"—this is said regarding those that passed away—"Others settled down around the light"—the light doubtless is the fire: those creatures which did not pass away, settled down around the fire; it is with regard to them that this is said. "The great one remained within the worlds"—it is with regard to Pragâpati that this is said, "The blower (or, purifier) entered the regions"—the regions doubtless are the quarters, and these were indeed entered by that blowing wind: it is with regard to them that this verse was uttered. And in like manner as Pragâpati created these living beings, so they are propagated: for whenever the breasts of woman and the udder of cattle swell, then whatever is born is born; and by resorting to the breasts these beings continue to exist. Now that milk is indeed food; for in the beginning Pragâpati produced it for food. But that food also means living beings, since it is by food that they exist: by resorting to the breasts of those who have milk, they continue to exist. And those who have no milk are nursed by the former as soon as they are born; and thus they exist by means of food, and hence food means progeny He who is desirous of offspring, sacrifices with that oblation, and thereby makes himself the sacrifice, which is Pragâpati.

In the first place there is a cake for Agni on eight potsherds. Agni indeed is the root, the progenitor of the deities; he is Pragâpati ("lord of creatures"): hence there is a cake for Agni. Then follows a potful of boiled rice for Soma. Soma doubtless is seed, and that in Agni, the progenitor; he casts the seed Soma: thus there is at the outset a productive union. Then follows a cake on twelve or eight potsherds for Savitri. Savitri indeed is the impeller of the gods; he is Pragâpati, the intermediate progenitor: hence the cake to Savitri. Then follows a potful of boiled rice for Sarasvatî; and another for Pûshan. Sarasvatî doubtless is a woman, and Pûshan is a man: thus there is again a productive union. Through that twofold productive union Pragâpati created the living beings— through the one he created the upright, and through the other those looking to the ground. This is why there are these five oblations.

After that, as a foundation for the curds, a cake on seven potsherds for the Maruts. The Maruts indeed are the people of the gods. They roamed about here entirely unimpeded. Having approached Pragâpati, when he was sacrificing, they said, "We shall destroy those creatures of thine which you are about to create by means of this offering."

Pragâpati reflected, "My former creatures have passed away; and if those Maruts destroy these creatures, then nothing will be left." He accordingly set aside for them that share, the Maruts, cake on seven potsherds; and that is this same cake on seven potsherds for the Maruts. The reason why it is one of seven potsherds, is that the host of the Maruts is of seven each. This is why there is a cake on seven potsherds for the Maruts.

Let him offer it to the "self-strong" Maruts; since they gained that share for themselves. If, however, the priests do not find an invitation and an offering prayer addressed to the "self-strong" Maruts, let it be offered simply to the Maruts. It is offered for the safety of creatures: hence it is offered to the Maruts.

Immediately after follows the oblation of curds. Now it is on milk that the creatures subsist, it was by means of milk that they were preserved: hence he now offers to them that by which they were preserved, and whereon they subsist; and the beings whom he creates by means of the foregoing offerings, subsist on that milk, on that oblation of curds. Therein a union takes place: the curdled milk is female, and the whey is seed. From that union the infinite All was gradually generated; and since the infinite All was gradually generated from that union, it belongs to the All-gods. Then follows a cake on one potsherd for Heaven and Earth. Now when Pragâpati had created the living beings by those offerings, he enclosed them within heaven and earth; and so they are now enclosed within heaven and earth. And in like manner he, who by means of those oblations creates living beings, encloses them within heaven and earth: this is why there is a cake on one potsherd for Heaven and Earth.

Now as to the course of proceeding. They do not raise an uttara-vedi in order that the sacred work may be unobstructed, that it may be entire, that it may be worthy of the All-gods. The barhis is tied up in three bunches, and then again in one; for such is the characteristic form of generation, since father and mother are a productive pair, and what is born forms a third element: hence that which is threefold is again made one. To this flowering shoots are tied: these he uses for the prastara; for this is a productive union, and productive indeed are flowering shoots: this is why he takes flowering shoots for the prastara. On putting the sacrificial dishes in their place, they churn the fire. For it was after Agni was born that Pragâpati's offspring was born; and so for this sacrificer also offspring is born after Agni (fire) has been produced: this is why they churn the fire, after they have deposited the sacrificial dishes in their place.

At the Vaisvadeva offering there are nine fore-offerings and nine after-offerings. Now the virâg meter consists of ten syllables: hence, he obtains both times an inferior virâg for the sake of production, because it was from that lower source of production that Pragâpati twice produced creatures—both the upright and those looking to the ground. This is why the Vaisvadeva has nine fore-offerings and nine after-offerings.

There are three Samishtayagus; for this offering is decidedly greater than an ordinary havir-yagña, since it has nine fore-offerings and nine after-offerings. However, there may also be only a single Samishtayagus, since this is a havir-yagña. The priest's fee for it is the firstborn calf.

And what race, what prosperity accrued to Pragâpati from his offering this sacrifice, that same race he produces, that same prosperity attains the one who, knowing this, offers this sacrifice: let him therefore perform this sacrifice.

Out of the Fire

From Satapatha Brahmana Part 1, Fifth Adhyâya, Third Brâhmana. Updated and edited version from the translation by Julius Eggeling.

Now when Pragâpati, in creating living beings, created Agni, the latter, as soon as born, sought to burn everything here: and so everybody tried to get out of his way. The creatures then existing sought to crush him. Being unable to endure this, he went to man.

He said, "I cannot endure this: come, let me enter into you! Having reproduced me, maintain me; and as you will reproduce and maintain me in this world, even so will I reproduce and maintain you in the other world!" Man replied, "So be it." And having reproduced him, he maintained him.

Now when he establishes the two fires, he reproduces Agni; and having reproduced him, he maintains him; and as he reproduces and maintains him in this world, even so does Agni reproduce and maintain man in the other world. One must not, therefore, remove it prematurely, for too soon it languishes for him; and as it languishes for him too soon in this world, even so does it languish for him too soon in the other world: one must not, therefore, remove it prematurely. And when he dies, and they place him on the fire, then he is reproduced from out of the fire; and Agni who before now was his son, now becomes his father.

Hence it has been said by the Rishis, "A hundred autumns before us, Oh gods, during which you complete the lifetime of our bodies, during which sons become fathers! Do not cut us off midway from reaching the full term of life!" For he who is the son, now in his turn becomes the father: this, then, is why one must establish the fires.

Now the burning sun doubtless is no other than Death; and because he is Death, the creatures that are on this side of him die. But those that are on the other side of him are the gods, and they are therefore immortal. It is by the rays of that sun that all these creatures are attached to the vital airs, and so the rays extend down to the vital airs.

And the breath of whomever the sun wishes, he takes and rises, then that one dies. And whoever goes to the other world not having escaped that Death—him he causes to die repeatedly in the other world, even as in this world, one regards not him that is fettered, but puts him to death whenever one wishes.

Now when, in the evening after sunset, he offers two libations, then he firmly plants himself on that Death with those fore-feet of his; and when, in the morning before sunrise, he offers two libations, then he plants himself on that Death with those hind-feet of his. And when the sun rises, then, in rising, he takes him up and thus the sacrificer escapes that Death. This, then, is the release from death in the Agnihotra: and, truly, he who knows that release from death in the Agnihotra, is freed from death repeatedly.

What the arrowhead is to the arrow, that the Agnihotra is to sacrifices. For to where the head of the arrow flies, there the whole arrow flies: and so are all his works of sacrifice freed by this Agnihotra from that Death.

Now day and night, revolving, destroy man's righteousness in the other world. But day and night are on this side of the sun from him; and so day and night do not destroy his righteousness.

And as, while standing inside a chariot, one would look down from above on the revolving chariot-wheels, even so does he look down from on high upon day and night: and, truly, day and night destroy not the reward of him who thus knows that release from day and night.

The sacrificer having gone round the Âhavanîya, after entering from the east, passes between it and the Gârhapatya. For the gods do not know this man; but when he now passes by them between the fires, they know him, and think, "This is he that now offers to us." Moreover, Agni is the repeller of evil; and these two, the Âhavanîya and Gârhapatya, repel the evil from him who passes between them; and the evil being repelled from him, he becomes very light in splendor and glory.

On the north side is the door of the Agnihotra: thus he approaches it as he would enter a house by a door. If, on the other hand, he were to sit down after approaching from the south, it would be as if he walked outside. The Agnihotra, truly, is the ship that sails heavenwards. The Âhavanîya and Gârhapatya are the two sides of that same heavenward-bound ship; and that milk-offerer is its steersman.

Now when he walks up towards the east, then he steers that ship eastwards towards the heavenly world, and he gains the heavenly world by it. When ascended from the north it makes him reach the heavenly world; but if one were to sit down in it after entering from the south, it would be as if he tried to enter it after it has put off and he were left behind and remained outside.

And again, the stick which he puts on the fire is as a brick, and the formula by with he offers is the Yagus-text, by which he puts on that brick; and when the brick is put on, then a libation is made: hence those same libations of the Agnihotra are offered on his pile of bricks.

The fire, assuredly, is Pragâpati, and Pragâpati is the year. Year after year, therefore, is his Agnihotra consummated with the piled up fire altar; and year after year does he obtain the piled up fire altar—he who, knowing this, offers the Agnihotra.

Seven hundred and twenty eighties of Rik verses he should recite at the Agnihotra in the course of a year. When he offers the Agnihotra in the morning and evening, then there are two libations: hence those libations of his, in the course of a year, amount to seven hundred and twenty. Thus, indeed, his Agnihotra is accomplished, year after year, with the great chant; and year after year does he obtain the great chant, he who, knowing this, offers the Agnihotra.

Gods on Earth

Excerpt. From Satapatha Brahmana Part 2, Fourth Brâhmana. Updated and edited version from the translation by Julius Eggeling.

Now Soma was in the sky, and the gods were here on earth. The gods desired, "Would that Soma came to us: we might sacrifice with him, when come." They created those two illusions, Suparnî and Kadrû. In the chapter on the hearths it is set forth how that affair of Suparnî and Kadrû came to pass.

Gâyatrî flew up to Soma for them. While she was carrying him off, the Gandharva Visvâvasu stole him from her. The gods were aware of this, "Soma has indeed been removed from the sky, but he comes not to us, for the Gandharvas have stolen him."

They said, "The Gandharvas are fond of women: let us send Vâk (speech) to them, and she will return to us together with Soma." They sent Vâk to them, and she returned to them together with Soma.

The Gandharvas came after her and said, "Soma will be yours, and Vâk ours!"

"So be it!" said the gods; "but if she would rather come here, do not carry her off by force: let us woo her!" They accordingly wooed her.

The Gandharvas recited the Vedas to her, saying, "See how we know it, see how we know it!"

The gods then created the lute and sat playing and singing, saying, "Thus we will sing to you, thus we will amuse you!" She turned to the gods; but, in truth, she turned to them vainly, since she turned away from those, engaged in praising and praying, to dance and song. For this reason, even to this day women are given to vain things: for it was because of this that Vâk turned thereto, and other women do as she did. And hence it is to him who dances and sings that they most readily take a fancy. Both Soma and Vâk were thus with the gods.

Supreme Being

Excerpt. From the Mahabharata. Updated and edited version from the translation by Kisari Mohan Ganguli.

Duryodhana said, "In all the worlds Vasudeva is spoken of as the Supreme Being. I desire, oh Grandfather, to know his origin and glory."

Bhishma said, "Vasudeva is the Supreme Being. He is the God of all Gods. None superior to him of eyes like lotus petals is to be seen, oh bull of Bharata's race. Markandeya speaks of Govinda as the Most Wonderful and the Most high, as the All-being, as the All-soul, as the Highest soul, and as the Supreme male Being. Water, Air, and Fire—these three were created by Him. That Divine Master and Lord of all the worlds created this Earth. That Supreme Being of illustrious soul laid himself down on the waters. And that Divine Being made up of all kinds of energy slept thereon in Yoga. From his mouth He created Fire, and from his breath, the Wind. Of unfading glory, He created from his mouth Speech and the Vedas. It was thus that he created first the Worlds and also the gods along with the diverse classes of Rishis. And he created decay and death also of all creatures, as well as birth and growth. He is Righteousness and of righteous soul. He is the giver of boons and the giver of all wishes. He is the Actor and Action, and He is himself the Divine Master. He first made the Past, the Present, and the Future; He is the Creator of the Universe. He is of illustrious soul; He is the Master possessed of unfading glory. He created Sankarshana, the firstborn of all creatures. He created the divine Sesha who is known as Ananta and who upholds all creatures and the Earth with her mountains. Of Supreme Energy, He it is whom the regenerate ones know by Yoga meditation. Sprung from the secretions of his ear, the great Asura known by the name of Madhu, fierce and of fierce deeds and entertaining a fierce intent and about to destroy Brahman, was slain by that Supreme Being. And, oh sire, in consequence of Madhu's slaughter, the gods, the Danavas, and human beings, and Rishis, call Janardana the slayer of Madhu. He is the great Boar. He is the great Lion, and He is the three-stepped Lord. He is the Mother and the Father of all living creatures. There never was, nor will be, any superior to Him of eyes like lotus petals. From His mouth He created the Brahmanas: and from His two arms the Kshatriyas, and from His thighs, oh king, He created the Vaisyas, and from His feet He created the Sudras. One waiting dutifully on Him, observant of vows with ascetic austerities on days of the full moon and the new moon, is sure to obtain the Divine Kesava, that refuge of all embodied creatures, that essence of Brahma and of Yoga. Kesava is the higher Energy, the Grandfather of all the worlds. Him, oh king, the sages call Hrishikesa, the lord of the senses. Him also should all know as the Preceptor, the Father, and the Master. Inexhaustible regions are won by him with whom Krishna is gratified. He also who, in a place of fear, seeks the protection of Kesava, and he who frequently reads this description, becomes happy and endued with every prosperity. Those men who attain to Krishna are never beguiled, Janardana always saves those that are sunk in great terrors. Knowing this truly, oh Bharata, Yudhishthira, with his whole soul, oh king, has sought the shelter of the highly blessed Kesava, the Lord of Yoga, and the Lord of the Earth."

Narayana

Excerpt. From the Mahabharata. Updated and edited version from the translation by Kisari Mohan Ganguli.

The Deity then said, "Oh Brahmana, the gods even do not know me truly! As however, I have been gratified with you, I will tell you how I created the universe! Oh regenerate Rishi, you are devoted to your ancestors and have also sought my protection! You have also beheld me with your eyes, and your ascetic merit also is great! In ancient times I called the waters by the name of Nara; and because the waters have ever been my ayana or home, therefore have I been called Narayana (the waterhomed). Oh best of regenerate ones, I am Narayana, the Source of all things, the Eternal, the Unchangeable. I am the Creator of all things, and the Destroyer also of all. I am Vishnu, I am Brahma and I am Sakra, the chief of the gods. I am king Vaisravana, and I am Yama, the lord of the deceased spirits. I am Siva, I am Soma, and I am Kasyapa, the lord of the created things. And, oh best of regenerate ones, I am he called Dhatri, and he also that is called Vidhatri, and I am Sacrifice embodied. Fire is my mouth, the earth my feet, and the Sun and the Moon are my eyes; the Heaven is the crown of my head, the firmament and the cardinal points are my ears; the waters are born of my sweat. Space with the cardinal points are my body, and the Air is my mind. I have performed many hundreds of sacrifices with gifts in profusion. I am always present in the sacrifices of the gods; and they that are cognizant of the Vedas and officiate therein, make their offerings to me. On earth the Kshatriya chiefs that rule over men, in performing their sacrifices from desire of obtaining heaven, and the Vaisyas also in performing theirs from desire of winning those happy regions, all worship me at such times and by those ceremonials. It is I who, assuming the form of Sesha, support this earth bounded by the four seas and decked by Meru and Mandara. And, oh regenerate one, it is I who, assuming the form of a boar, had raised in days of old this earth sunk in water. And, oh best of Brahmanas, it is I who, becoming the fire that issues out of the Equine mouth, drink up the waters and create them again. In consequence of my energy from my mouth, my arms, my thighs, and my feet gradually sprang Brahmanas and Kshatriyas and Vaisyas and Sudras. It is from me that the Rik, the Sama, the Yajus, and the Atharvan Vedas spring, and it is in me that they all enter when the time comes. Brahmanas devoted to asceticism, they that value Peace as the highest attribute, they that have their souls under complete control, they that are desirous of knowledge, they that are freed from lust and wrath and envy, they that are unwedded to things of the earth, they that have their sins completely washed away, they that are possessed of gentleness and virtue, and are divested of pride, they that have a full knowledge of the Soul, all worship me with profound meditation. I am the flame known as Samvartaka, I am the Wind called by that name, I am the Sun wearing that appellation, and I am the fire that has that designation. And, O best of Brahmanas, those things that are seen in the firmament as stars, know them to be the pores of my skin. The ocean—those mines of gems and the four cardinal points, know, oh Brahmana, are my robes, my bed, and my home. By me have they been distributed for serving the purposes of the gods. And, oh best of men, know also that lust, wrath, joy, fear, and the overclouding of the intellect, are all different forms of myself. And, oh Brahmana, whatever is obtained by men by the practice of truth, charity, ascetic austerities, and peace and harmlessness towards all creatures, and such other handsome deeds, is obtained because of my arrangements. Governed by my ordinance, men wander within my body, their senses overwhelmed by me. They move not according to their will but as they are moved by me. Regenerate Brahmanas that have thoroughly studied the Vedas, that have tranquility in their souls, they that have subdued their wrath, obtain a high reward by means of their numerous sacrifices. That reward, however, is unattainable by men that are wicked in their deeds, overwhelmed by covetousness, mean and disreputable with souls unblessed and impure. Therefore, must you know, oh Brahmana that this reward which is obtained by persons having their souls under control and which is unobtainable by the ignorant and the foolish—this which is attainable by asceticism alone—is productive of high merit. And, oh best of men, at those times when virtue and morality decrease and sin and immorality increase, I create myself in new forms. And, oh Muni, when fierce and malicious Daityas and Rakshasas that are incapable of being slain by even the foremost of the gods, are born on earth, I then take my birth in the families of virtuous men, and assuming human body restore tranquility by exterminating all evils. Moved by my own maya, I create gods and men, and Gandharvas and Rakshasas, and all immobile things and then destroy them all myself. For the preservation of rectitude and morality I assume a human form, and when the season for action comes, I again assume forms that are inconceivable. In the Krita age I become white, in the Treta age I become yellow, in the Dwapara I have become red and in the Kali age I become dark in hue, I the Kali age, the proportion of immorality becomes three-fourths. And when the end of the Yuga comes, assuming the fierce form of Death, alone I destroy all the three worlds with their mobile and immobile existences. With three steps, I cover the whole Universe; I am the Soul of the universe; I am the source of all happiness; I am the humbler of all pride; I am omnipresent; I am infinite; I am the Lord of the senses; and my prowess is great. Oh Brahmana, alone do I set moving the wheel of Time; I am formless; I am the Destroyer of all creatures; and I am the cause of all efforts of all my creatures. Oh best of Munis, my soul completely pervades all my creatures, but, oh foremost of all regenerate ones, no one knows me. It is me that the pious and the devoted worship in all the worlds. Oh regenerate one, whatever of pain you have felt within my stomach, know, oh sinless one, that all that is for your happiness and good fortune. And whatever of mobile and immobile objects you have seen in the world, everything has been ordained by my Soul which is the Spring of all existence. The grandfather of all creatures is half my body; I am called Narayana, and I am bearer of the conch shell, the discus and the mace. Oh regenerate Rishi, for a period measured by a thousand times the length of the Yugas, I who am the Universal Soul sleep overwhelming all creatures in insensibility. And, oh best of regenerate Rishis, I stay here thus for all time, in the form of a boy though I am old, until Brahma wakes up. Oh foremost of Brahmanas, gratified with you, I who am Brahma have repeatedly granted you boons, oh you who are worshiped by regenerate Rishis! Beholding one vast expanse of water and seeing that all mobile and immobile creatures have been destroyed, you were afflicted with melancholy. I know this, and it is for this that I showed you the universe. And while you were within my body, beholding the entire universe, you were filled with wonder and deprived of your senses. Oh regenerate Rishi, it is for this that you were speedily brought out by me through my mouth. I have now told you of that Soul which is incapable of being comprehended by the gods and the Asuras. And as long as that great ascetic, the holy Brahma, does not awake, you, oh regenerate Rishi, can happily and trustfully dwell here. And when that Grandfather of all creatures wakes up, I will then, oh best of Brahmanas, alone create all creatures endued with bodies, the firmament, the earth, light, the atmosphere, water, and indeed all else of mobile and immobile creatures on the earth!"

[...] Having said so to me that wonderful Deity vanished, oh son, from my sight! I then beheld this varied and wondrous creation start into life. Oh king, oh you foremost of the Bharata race, I witnessed all this, so wonderful, oh you foremost of all virtuous men, at the end of the Yuga! And the Deity, of eyes large as lotus leaves, seen by me, in days of old is this tiger among men, this Janardana who has become your relative! It is in consequence of the boon granted to me by this one that memory does not fail me, that the period of my life, oh son of Kunti, is so long and death itself is under my control. This is that ancient and supreme Lord Hari of inconceivable soul who has taken his birth as Krishna of the Vrishni race, and who endued with mighty arms, seems to sport in this world! This one is Dhatri and Vidhatri, the Destroyer of all the Eternal, the bearer of the Sreevatsa mark on his breast, the Lord of the lord of all creatures, the highest of the high, called also Govinda! Beholding this foremost of all gods, this ever-victorious Being, attired in yellow robes, this chief of the Vrishni race, my recollection comes back to me! This Madhava is the father and mother of all creatures! You bulls of the Kuru race, seek you the refuge of this Protector!

Vishnu

Excerpt. From Book 1 of the Vishnu Purána. Updated and edited version from the translation by Horace Hayman Wilson.

OM! GLORY TO VÁSUDEVA— Victory be to you, Pundaríkáksha; adoration be to you, Víswabhávana; glory be to you, Hrishikeśa, Mahápurusha, and Púrvaja.

May that Vishnu, who is the existent, imperishable, Brahma, who is Íswara, who is spirit; who with the three qualities is the cause of creation, preservation, and destruction; who is the parent of nature, intellect, and the other ingredients of the universe; be to us the bestower of understanding, wealth, and final emancipation. Having adored Vishnu, the lord of all, and paid reverence to Brahmá and the rest;

having also saluted the spiritual preceptor; I will narrate a Purána equal in sanctity to the Vedas. Maitreya, having saluted him reverentially, thus addressed Paráśara, the excellent sage, the grandson of Vaśishtha, who was versed in traditional history, and the Puránas; who was acquainted with the Vedas, and the branches of science dependent upon them; and skilled in law and philosophy; and who had performed the morning rites of devotion.

Maitreya said, Master! I have been instructed by you in the whole of the Vedas, and in the institutes of law and of sacred science: through your favor, other men, even though they be my foes, cannot accuse me of having been remiss in the acquirement of knowledge. I am now desirous, oh you who are profound in piety—to hear from you, how this world was, and how in future it will be? What is its substance, oh Brahman, and from what proceeded animate and inanimate things? Into what has it been resolved, and into what will its dissolution again occur? How were the elements manifested? From what proceeded the gods and other beings? What are the situation and extent of the oceans and the mountains, the earth, the sun, and the planets? What are the families of the gods and others, the Menus, the periods called Manwantaras, those termed Kalpas, and their subdivisions, and the four ages: the events that happen at the close of a Kalpa, and the terminations of the several ages: the histories, oh great Muni, of the gods, the sages, and kings; and how the Vedas were divided into branches, after they had been arranged by Vyása: the duties of the Brahmans, and the other tribes, as well as of those who pass through the different orders of life? All these things I wish to hear from you, grandson of Vaśishtha. Incline your thoughts benevolently towards me, that I may, through your favor, be informed of all I desire to know.

PARÁŚARA said, Glory to the unchangeable, holy, eternal, supreme Vishnu, of one universal nature, the mighty over all: to him who is Hiranygarbha, Hari, and Śankara, the creator, the preserver, and destroyer of the world: to Vásudeva, the liberator of his worshipers: to him, whose essence is both single and manifold; who is both subtle and corporeal, indiscreet and discrete: to Vishnu, the cause of final emancipation, Glory to the supreme Vishnu, the cause of the creation, existence, and end of this world; who is the root of the world, and who consists of the world.

Having glorified him who is the support of all things; who is the smallest of the small; who is in all created things; the unchanged, imperishable Purushottama; who is one with true wisdom, as truly known; eternal and incorruptible; and who is known through false appearances by the nature of visible objects: having bowed to Vishnu, the destroyer, and lord of creation and preservation; the ruler of the world; unborn, imperishable, undecaying: I will relate to you that which was originally imparted by the great father of all, Brahmá, in answer to the questions of Daksha and other venerable sages, and repeated by them to Purukutsa, a king who reigned on the banks of the Narmadá. It was next related by him to Sáraswata, and by Sáraswata to me.

Who can describe him who is not to be apprehended by the senses: who is the best of all things; the supreme soul, self-existent: who is devoid of all the distinguishing characteristics of complexion, caste, or the like; and is exempt from birth, transformation, death, or decay: who is always, and alone: who exists everywhere, and in whom all things here exist; and who is therefore named Vásudeva? He is Brahma, supreme, lord, eternal, unborn, imperishable, undecaying; of one essence; ever pure as free from defects. He, that Brahma, was all things; comprehending in his own nature the indiscreet and discrete. He then existed in the forms of Purusha and of Kála. Purusha (spirit) is the first form, of the supreme; next proceeded two other forms, the discrete and indiscreet; and Kála (time) was the last. These four—Pradhána (matter), Purusha (spirit), Vyakta (visible substance), and Kála (time)—the wise consider to be the pure and supreme condition of Vishnu. These four forms, in their due proportions, are the causes of the production of the phenomena of creation, preservation, and destruction. Vishnu being thus discrete and indiscreet substance, spirit, and time, sports like a playful boy, as you shall learn by listening to his frolics.

That chief principle, which is the indiscreet cause, is called by the sages also Prakriti (nature): it is subtle, uniform, and comprehends what is and what is not; is durable, self-sustained, without limit, undecaying, and stable; devoid of sound or touch, and possessing neither color nor form; endowed with the three qualities; the mother of the world; without beginning; and that into which all that is produced is resolved. By that principle all things were invested in the period subsequent to the last dissolution of the universe, and prior to creation.

For Brahmans learned in the Vedas, and teaching truly their doctrines, explain such passages as the following as intending the production of the chief principle. "There was neither day nor night, nor sky nor earth, nor darkness nor light, nor any other thing, save only One, unapprehensible by intellect, or that which is Brahma and Pumán (spirit) and Pradhána (matter)." The two forms which are other than the essence of unmodified Vishnu, are Pradhána (matter) and Purusha (spirit); and his other form, by which those two are connected or separated, is called Kála (time). When discrete substance is aggregated in crude nature, as in a foregone dissolution, that dissolution is termed elemental. The deity as Time is without beginning, and his end is not known; and from him the revolutions of creation, continuance, and dissolution continuously succeed: for when, in the latter season, the equilibrium of the qualities exists, and spirit is detached from matter, then the form of Vishnu which is Time abides. Then the supreme Brahma, the supreme soul, the substance of the world, the lord of all creatures, the universal soul, the supreme ruler, Hari, of his own will having entered into matter and spirit, agitated the mutable and immutable principles, the season of creation being arrived, in the same manner as fragrance affects the mind from its proximity merely, and not from any immediate operation upon mind itself: so the Supreme influenced the elements of creation. Purushottama is both the agitator and the thing to be agitated; being present in the essence of matter, both when it is contracted and expanded. Vishnu, supreme over the supreme, is of the nature of discrete forms in the atomic productions, Brahmá and the rest.

Then from that equilibrium of the qualities, presided over by soul, proceeds the unequal development of those qualities at the time of creation. The Chief principle then invests that Great principle, Intellect, and it becomes threefold, as affected by the quality of goodness, foulness, or darkness, and invested by the Chief principle as seed is by its skin. From the Great principle (Mahat) Intellect, threefold Egotism, (Ahankára), denominated Vaikaríka, "pure;" Taijasa, "passionate;" and Bhútádi, "rudimental," is produced; the origin of the elements, and of the organs of sense; invested, in consequence of its three qualities, by Intellect, as Intellect is by the Chief principle. Elementary Egotism then becoming productive, as the rudiment of sound, produced from it Ether, of which sound is the characteristic, investing it with its rudiment of sound. Ether becoming productive, engendered the rudiment of touch; from where originated strong wind, the property of which is touch; and Ether, with the rudiment of sound, enveloped the rudiment of touch. Then wind becoming productive, produced the rudiment of form; from where light proceeded, of which, form is the attribute; and the rudiment of touch enveloped the wind with the rudiment of color Light becoming productive, produced the rudiment of taste; from where proceed all juices in which flavor resides; and the rudiment of color invested the juices with the rudiment of taste. The waters becoming productive, engendered the rudiment of smell; from where an aggregate originates, of which smell is the property. In each element resides its peculiar rudiment; therefore the property of tanmátratá, is ascribed to these elements. Rudimentary elements are not endowed with qualities, and therefore they are neither soothing, nor terrific, nor stupefying. This is the elemental creation, proceeding from the principle of egotism affected by the property of darkness. The organs of sense are said to be the passionate products of the same principle, affected by foulness;

and the ten divinities proceed from egotism affected by the principle of goodness; as does Mind, which is the eleventh. The organs of sense are ten: of the ten, five are the skin, eye, nose, tongue, and ear; the object of which, combined with Intellect, is the apprehension of sound and the rest: the organs of excretion and procreation, the hands, the feet, and the voice, form the other five; of which excretion, generation, manipulation, motion, and speaking, are the several acts.

Then, ether, air, light, water, and earth, each united with the properties of sound and the rest, existed as distinguishable according to their qualities, as soothing, terrific, or stupefying; but possessing various energies, and being unconnected, they could not, without combination, create living beings, not having blended with each other. Having combined, therefore, with one another, they assumed, through their mutual association, the character of one mass of entire unity; and from the direction of spirit, with the acquiescence of the indiscreet Principle, Intellect and the rest, to the gross elements inclusive, formed an egg, which gradually expanded like a bubble of water. This vast egg, O sage, compounded of the elements, and resting on the waters, was the excellent natural abode of Vishnu in the form of Brahmá; and there Vishnu, the lord of the universe, whose essence is inscrutable, assumed a perceptible form, and even he himself abided in it in the character of Brahmá. Its womb, vast as the mountain Meru, was composed of the mountains; and the mighty oceans were the waters that filled its cavity. In that egg, O Brahman, were the continents and seas and mountains, the planets and divisions of the universe, the gods, the demons, and mankind. And this egg was externally invested by seven natural envelopes, or by water, air, fire, ether, and Ahankára the origin of the elements, each tenfold the extent of that which it invested; next came the principle of Intelligence; and, finally, the whole was surrounded by the indiscreet Principle: resembling thus the coconut, filled interiorly with pulp, and exteriorly covered by husk and rind.

Affecting then the quality of activity, Hari, the lord of all, himself becoming Brahmá, engaged in the creation of the universe. Vishnu with the quality of goodness, and of immeasurable power, preserves created things through successive ages, until the close of the period termed a Kalpa; when the same mighty deity, Janárddana, invested with the quality of darkness, assumes the awful form of Rudra, and swallows up the universe. Having thus devoured all things, and converted the world into one vast ocean, the Supreme reposes upon his mighty serpent couch amidst the deep: he awakes after a season, and again, as Brahmá, becomes the author of creation.

Thus the one only god, Janárddana, takes the designation of Brahmá, Vishnu, and Śiva, accordingly as he creates, preserves, or destroys. Vishnu as creator, creates himself; as preserver, preserves himself; as destroyer, destroys himself at the end of all things. This world of earth, air, fire, water, ether, the senses, and the mind; all that is termed spirit, that also is the lord of all elements, the universal form, and imperishable: hence he is the cause of creation, preservation, and destruction; and the subject of the transformations inherent in elementary nature. He is the object and author of creation: he preserves, destroys, and is preserved. He, Vishnu, as Brahmá, and as all other beings, is infinite form: he is the supreme, the giver of all good, the fountain of all happiness.

The Four Energies

Excerpt from Book 1 of the Vishnu Puránna. Updated, edited, and revised. From the translation by Horace Hayman Wilson

Brahmá, Daksha, time, and all creatures are the four energies of Hari, which are the causes of creation. Vishnu, Manu and the rest, time, and all creatures are the four energies of Vishnu, which are the causes of duration. Rudra, the destroying fire, time, and all creatures are the four energies of Janárddana that are exerted for universal dissolution. In the beginning and the duration of the world, until the period of its end, creation is the work of Brahmá, the patriarchs, and living animals. Brahmá creates in the beginning; then the patriarchs beget progeny; and then animals incessantly multiply their kinds: but Brahmá is not the active agent in creation, independent of time; neither are the patriarchs, nor living animals. So, in the periods of creation and of dissolution, the four portions of the god of gods are equally essential. Whatever, oh Brahman, is engendered by any living being, the body of Hari is cooperative in the birth of that being; so whatever destroys any existing thing, movable or stationary, at any time, is the destroying form of Janárddana as Rudra. Thus Janárddana is the creator, the preserver, and the destroyer of the whole world—being threefold—in the several seasons of creation, preservation, and destruction, according to his assumption of the three qualities: but his highest glory is detached from all qualities; for the fourfold essence of the supreme spirit is composed of true wisdom, pervades all things, is only to be appreciated by itself, and admits of no similitude.

Tripartite

Excerpt. From the Chandogya Upanishad. Updated and edited version from the translation by Max Müller.

Second Khanda

1. "In the beginning," my dear, "there was that only which is, one only, without a second. Others say, in the beginning there was that only which is

not, one only, without a second; and from that which is not, that which is was born.

2. "But how could it be this way, my dear?" the father continued. "How could that which is, be born of that which is not? No, my dear, only that which is, was in the beginning, one only, without a second.

3. "It thought, may I be many, may I grow forth. It sent forth fire.

"That fire thought, may I be many, may I grow forth. It sent forth water.

"And therefore whenever anybody anywhere is hot and perspires, water is produced on him from fire alone.

4. "Water thought, may I be many, may I grow forth. It sent forth food.

"Therefore whenever it rains anywhere, most food is then produced. From water alone is edible food produced.

Third Khanda

1. "Of all living things there are indeed three origins only, that which springs from an egg, that which springs from a living being, and that which springs from a germ.

2. "That Being thought, let me now enter those three beings (fire, water, earth) with this living Self, and let me then reveal names and forms.

3. "Then that Being having said, Let me make each of these three tripartite entered into those three beings with this living Self only, and revealed names and forms.

4. "He made each of these tripartite; and how these three beings become each of them tripartite, that learn from me now, my friend!

Self Alone

Excerpt. From the Brihadaranyaka Upanishad (Fourth Brahmana). Updated and edited version from the translation by Max Müller.

1. In the beginning this was Self alone, in the shape of a person (purusha). He looking round saw nothing but his Self. He first said, "This is I;" therefore he became I by name. Therefore even now, if a man is asked, he first says, "This is I," and then pronounces the other name which he may have. And because before all this, he (the Self) burnt down all evils, therefore he was a person. Truly he who knows this, burns down every one who tries to be before him.

2. He feared, and therefore any one who is lonely fears. He thought, "As there is nothing but myself, why should I fear?" After this his fear passed away. For what should he have feared? Truly fear arises from a second only.

3. But he felt no delight. Therefore a man who is lonely feels no delight. He wished for a second. He was so large as man and wife together. He then made his Self to fall in two, and after that arose husband and wife. Therefore Yâgñavalkya said: "We two are, each of us, like half a shell."

Therefore the void which was there, is filled by the wife. He embraced her, and men were born.

4. She thought, "How can he embrace me, after having produced me from himself? I shall hide myself."

She then became a cow, the other became a bull and embraced her, and hence cows were born. The one became a mare, the other a stallion; the one a male donkey, the other a female donkey. He embraced her, and hence one-hoofed animals were born. The one became a she-goat, the other a he-goat; the one became a ewe, the other a ram. He embraced her, and hence goats and sheep were born. And thus he created everything that exists in pairs, down to the ants.

5. He knew, "I indeed am this creation, for I created all this." Hence he became the creation, and he who knows this lives in this, his creation.

6. Next he produced fire by rubbing. From the mouth, as from the fire-hole, and from the hands he created fire. Therefore both the mouth and the hands are inside without hair, for the fire-hole is inside without hair.

And when they say, "Sacrifice to this or sacrifice to that god," each god is but his manifestation, for he is all gods.

Now, whatever there is moist, that he created from seed; this is Soma. So far truly is this universe either food or eater. Soma indeed is food, Agni eater. This is the highest creation of Brahman, when he created the gods from his better part, and when he, who was then mortal, created the immortals. Therefore it was the highest creation. And he who knows this, lives in this his highest creation.

7. Now all this was then undeveloped. It became developed by form and name, so that one could say, "He, called so and so, is such a one." Therefore at present also all this is developed by name and form, so that one can say, "He, called so and so, is such a one."

He entered there, to the very tips of the finger-nails, as a razor might be fitted in a case, or as fire in a fireplace.

He cannot be seen, for, in part only, when breathing, he is breath by name; when speaking, speech by name; when seeing, eye by name; when hearing, ear by name; when thinking, mind by name. All these are but the names of his acts. And he who regards him as the one or the other, does not know him, for he is apart from this when qualified by the one or the other. Let men worship him as Self, for in the Self all these are one. This Self is the footstep of everything, for through it one knows everything. And as one can find again by footsteps what was lost, he who knows this finds glory and praise.

8. This, which is nearer to us than anything, this Self, is dearer than a son, dearer than wealth, dearer than all else.

And if one were to say to one who declares another than the Self dear, that he will lose what is dear to him, very likely it would be so. Let him worship the Self alone as dear. He who worships the Self alone as dear, the object of his love will never perish.

9. Here they say: "If men think that by knowledge of Brahman they will become everything, what then did that Brahman know, from which all this sprang?"

10. Truly in the beginning this was Brahman, that Brahman knew Self only, saying, "I am Brahman." From it all this sprang. Thus, whatever Deva was awakened, he indeed became that Brahman; and the same with Rishis and men. The Rishi Vâmadeva saw and understood it, singing, "I was Manu (moon), I was the sun." Therefore now also he who thus knows that he is Brahman, becomes all this, and even the Devas cannot prevent it, for he himself is their Self.

Now if a man worships another deity, thinking the deity is one and he another, he does not know. He is like a beast for the Devas. For truly, as many beasts nourish a man, thus does every man nourish the Devas. If only one beast is taken away, it is not pleasant; how much more when many are taken! Therefore it is not pleasant to the Devas that men should know this.

11. Truly in the beginning this was Brahman, one only. That being one, was not strong enough. It created still further the most excellent Kshatra (power), namely those Kshatras among the Devas—Indra, Varuna, Soma, Rudra, Parganya, Yama, Mrityu, Îsâna. Therefore there is nothing beyond the Kshatra, and therefore at the Râgasûya sacrifice the Brâhmana sits down below the Kshatriya. He confers that glory on the Kshatra alone. But Brahman is nevertheless the birthplace of the Kshatra. Therefore though a king is exalted, he sits down at the end of the sacrifice below the Brahman, as his birth-place. He who injures him, injures his own birth-place. He becomes worse, because he has injured one better than himself.

12. He was not strong enough. He created the people, the classes of Devas which in their different orders are called Vasus, Rudras, Âdityas, Visve Devas, Maruts.

13. He was not strong enough. He created the Sûdra color, as Pûshan (nourisher). This earth truly is Pûshan; for the earth nourishes all this whatsoever.

14. He was not strong enough. He created still further the most excellent Law. Law is the power of the Kshatra, therefore there is nothing higher than the Law. From that point forward, even a weak man rules a stronger with the help of the Law, as with the help of a king. Thus the Law is what is called the true. And if a man declares what is true, they say he declares the Law; and if he declares the Law, they say he declares what is true. Both are the same.

15. There are then this Brahman, Kshatra, Vis, and Sûdra. Among the Devas that Brahman existed as Agni only, among men as Brâhmana, as Kshatriya through the divine Kshatriya, as Vaisya through the divine

Vaisya, as Sûdra through the divine Sûdra. Therefore people wish for their future state among the Devas through Agni only; and among men through the Brâhmana, for in these two forms did Brahman exist.

Now if a man departs this life without having seen his true future life in the Self, then that Self, not being known, does not receive and bless him, as if the Veda had not been read, or as if a good work had not been done. No, even if one who does not know that Self, should perform here on earth some great holy work, it will Perish for him in the end. Let a man worship the Self only as his true state. If a man worships the Self only as his true state, his work does not Perish, for whatever he desires, that he gets from that Self.

16. Now truly this Self is the world of all creatures. In so far as man sacrifices and pours out libations, he is the world of the Devas; in so far as he repeats the hymns, he is the world of the Rishis; in so far as he offers cakes to the Fathers and tries to obtain offspring, he is the world of the Fathers; in so far as he gives shelter and food to men, he is the world of men; in so far as he finds fodder and water for the animals, he is the world of the animals; in so far as quadrupeds, birds, and even ants live in his houses, he is their world. And as every one wishes his own world not to be injured, thus all beings wish that he who knows this should not be injured. Truly this is known and has been well reasoned.

17. In the beginning this was Self alone, one only. He desired, "Let there be a wife for me that I may have offspring, and let there be wealth for me that I may offer sacrifices." Truly this is the whole desire, and, even if wishing for more, he would not find it. Therefore now also a lonely person desires, "Let there be a wife for me that I may have offspring, and let there be wealth for me that I may offer sacrifices." And so long as he does not obtain either of these things, he thinks he is incomplete. Now his completeness is as follows: mind is his self; speech the wife; breath the child; the eye all worldly wealth, for he finds it with the eye; the ear his divine wealth, for he hears it with the ear. The body is his work, for with the body he works. This is the fivefold sacrifice, for fivefold is the animal, fivefold man, fivefold all this whatsoever. He who knows this, obtains all this.

Chapter 7

Eastern Star

Of Luminous Space

Excerpt. Fargard 2, Yima. From the Zend Avesta. Bundahis. Updated and edited version from the translation by James Darmesteter.

1 Zarathustra asked Ahura Mazda: "Oh Ahura Mazda, most beneficent Spirit, Maker of the material world, you Holy One! Who was the first mortal, before myself, Zarathustra, with whom you, Ahura Mazda, did converse, whom you did teach the law of Ahura, the law of Zarathustra?"

2 Ahura Mazda answered: "The fair Yima, the great shepherd, Oh holy Zarathustra! He was the first mortal, before you, Zarathustra, with whom I, Ahura Mazda, did converse, whom I taught the law of Ahura, the law of Zarathustra."

3 "To him, Oh Zarathustra, I, Ahura Mazda, spoke, saying: 'Well, fair Yima, son of Vîvanghat, be you the preacher and the bearer of my law!'

And the fair Yima, Oh Zarathustra, replied to me, saying: 'I was not born, I was not taught to be the preacher and the bearer of your law.'

4 "Then I, Ahura Mazda, said this to him, Oh Zarathustra: 'Since you wantest not to be the preacher and the bearer of my law, then make my worlds thrive, make my worlds increase: undertake to nourish, to rule, and to watch over my world.'

5 "And the fair Yima replied to me, Oh Zarathustra, saying: 'Yes! I will make your worlds thrive, I will make your worlds increase. Yes! I will nourish, and rule, and watch over your world. There shall be, while I am king, neither cold wind nor hot wind, neither disease nor death.'

7 "Then I, Ahura Mazda, brought two implements to him: a golden ring and a dagger inlaid with gold. Behold, here Yima bears the royal sway!

8 "Thus, under the sway of Yima, three hundred winters passed away,

and the earth was replenished with flocks and herds, with men and dogs and birds and with red blazing fires, and there was no more room for flocks, herds, and men.

9 "Then I warned the fair Yima, saying: 'Oh fair Yima, son of Vîvanghat, the earth has become full of flocks and herds, of men and dogs and birds and of red blazing fires, and there is no more room for flocks, herds, and men.'

10 Then Yima stepped forward, towards the luminous space, southwards, to meet the sun, and afterwards he pressed the earth with the golden ring, and bored it with the dagger, saying: 'Oh Spenta Ârmaiti, kindly open up and stretch yourself afar, to bear flocks and herds and men.'

11 And Yima made the earth grow larger by one-third than it was before, and there came flocks and herds and men, at his will and wish, as many as he wished.

12 Thus, under the sway of Yima, six hundred winters passed away, and the earth was replenished with flocks and herds, with men and dogs and birds and with red blazing fires, and there was no more room for flocks, herds, and men.

13 And I warned the fair Yima, saying: 'Oh fair Yima, son of Vîvanghat, the earth has become full of flocks and herds, of men and dogs and birds and of red blazing fires, and there is no more room for flocks, herds, and men.'

14 Then Yima stepped forward, towards the luminous space, southwards, to meet the sun, and afterwards he pressed the earth with the golden ring, and bored it with the dagger, saying: 'Oh Spenta Ârmaiti, kindly open up and stretch yourself afar, to bear flocks and herds and men.'

15 And Yima made the earth grow larger by two-thirds than it was before, and there came flocks and herds and men, at his will and wish, as many as he wished.

16 Thus, under the sway of Yima, nine hundred winters passed away, and the earth was replenished with flocks and herds, with men and dogs and birds and with red blazing fires, and there was no more room for flocks, herds, and men.

17 And I warned the fair Yima, saying: 'Oh fair Yima, son of Vîvanghat, the earth has become full of flocks and, herds, of men and dogs and birds and of red blazing fires, and there is no more room for flocks, herds, and men.'

18 Then Yima stepped forward, towards the luminous space, southwards, to meet the sun, and afterwards he pressed the earth with the golden ring, and bored it with the dagger, saying: 'Oh Spenta Ârmaiti, kindly open up and stretch yourself afar, to bear flocks and herds and men.'

19 And Yima made the earth grow larger by three-thirds than it was before, and there came flocks and herds and men, at his will and wish, as many as he wished.

21 The Maker, Ahura Mazda, of high renown in the Airyana Vaêgô, by the good river Dâitya, called together

a meeting of the celestial gods. The fair Yima, the good shepherd, of high renown in the Airyana Vaêgô, by the good river Dâitya, called together a meeting of the excellent mortals. To that meeting came Ahura Mazda, of high renown in the Airyana Vaêgô, by the good river Dâitya; he came together with the celestial gods. To that meeting came, the fair Yima, the good shepherd, of high renown in the Airyana Vaêgô, by the good river Dâitya; he came together with the excellent mortals.

22 And Ahura Mazda spoke to Yima, saying: 'Oh fair Yima, son of Vîvanghat! Upon the material world the fatal winters are going to fall, that shall bring the fierce, foul frost; upon the material world the fatal winters are going to fall, that shall make snow-flakes fall thick, even an aredvî deep on the highest tops of mountains.

23 And all the three sorts of beasts shall perish, those that live in the wilderness, and those that live on the tops of the mountains, and those that live in the bosom of the dale, under the shelter of stables.

24 Before that winter, those fields would bear plenty of grass for cattle: now with floods that stream, with snows that melt, it will seem a happy land in the world, the land wherein footprints even of sheep may still be seen.

25 Therefore, make a Vara, long as a riding-ground on every side of the square, and there bring the seeds of sheep and oxen, of men, of dogs, of birds, and of red blazing fires. Therefore make a Vara, long as a riding-ground on every side of the square, to be an abode for men; a Vara, long as a riding-ground on every side of the square, to be a fold for flocks.

26 There you will make waters flow in a bed a hâthra long; there you will settle birds, by the ever-green banks that bear never-failing food. There you will establish dwelling places, consisting of a house with a balcony, a courtyard, and a gallery.

27 There you will bring the seeds of men and women, of the greatest, best, and finest kinds on this earth; there you will bring the seeds of every kind of cattle, of the greatest, best, and finest kinds on this earth.

28 There you will bring the seeds of every kind of tree, of the greatest, best, and finest kinds on this earth; there you will bring the seeds of every kind of fruit, the fullest of food and sweetest of smell. All those seeds will you bring, two of every kind, to be kept inexhaustible there, so long as those men shall stay in the Vara.

29 There shall be no humpbacked, none bulged forward there; no impotent, no lunatic; no poverty, no lying; no meanness, no jealousy; no decayed tooth, no leprous to be confined, nor any of the brands with which Angra Mainyu stamps the bodies of mortals.

30 In the largest part of the place you will make nine streets, six in the middle part, three in the smallest. To the streets of the largest part you will bring a thousand seeds of men and

women; to the streets of the middle part, six hundred; to the streets of the smallest part, three hundred. That Vara you will seal up with the golden ring, and you will make a door, and a window, self-shining within.'

31 Then Yima said within himself: 'How shall I manage to make that Vara which Ahura Mazda has commanded me to make?' And Ahura Mazda said to Yima: 'Oh fair Yima, son of Vîvanghat! Crush the earth with a stamp of your heel, and then knead it with your hands, as the potter does when kneading the potter's clay.'

32 And Yima did as Ahura Mazda wished; he crushed the earth with a stamp of his heel, he kneaded it with his hands, as the potter does when kneading the potter's clay.

33 And Yima made a Vara, long as a riding-ground on every side of the square. There he brought the seeds of sheep and oxen, of men, of dogs, of birds, and of red blazing fires. He made Vara, long as a riding-ground on every side of the square, to be an abode for men; a Vara, long as a riding-ground on every side of the square, to be a fold for flocks.

34 There he made waters flow in a bed a hâthra long; there he settled birds, by the evergreen banks that bear never-failing food. There he established dwelling places, consisting of a house with a balcony, a courtyard, and a gallery.

35 There he brought the seeds of men and women, of the greatest, best, and finest kinds on this earth; there he brought the seeds of every kind of cattle, of the greatest, best, and finest kinds on this earth.

36 There he brought the seeds of every kind of tree, of the greatest, best, and finest kinds on this earth; there he brought the seeds of every kind of fruit, the fullest of food and sweetest of smell. All those seeds he brought, two of every kind, to be kept inexhaustible there, so long as those men shall stay in the Vara.

37 And there were no humpbacked, none bulged forward there; no impotent, no lunatic; no poverty, no lying; no meanness, no jealousy; no decayed tooth, no leprous to be confined, nor any of the brands with which Angra Mainyu stamps the bodies of mortals.

38 In the largest part of the place he made nine streets, six in the middle part, three in the smallest. To the streets of the largest part he brought a thousand seeds of men and women; to the streets of the middle part, six hundred; to the streets of the smallest part, three hundred. That Vara he sealed up with the golden ring, and he made a door, and a window self-shining within.

39 Oh Maker of the material world, you Holy One! What lights are there to give light in the Vara which Yima made?

40 Ahura Mazda answered: 'There are uncreated lights and created lights. There the stars, the moon, and the sun are only once seen to rise and set, and a year seems only as a day.

41 'Every fortieth year, to every

couple two are born, a male and a female. And thus it is for every sort of cattle. And the men in the Vara which Yima made live the happiest life.'

42 Oh Maker of the material world, you Holy One! Who is he who brought the law of Mazda into the Vara which Yima made? Ahura Mazda answered: 'It was the bird Karshipta, Oh holy Zarathustra!'

43 Oh Maker of the material world, you Holy One! Who is the lord and ruler there? Ahura Mazda answered: 'Urvatad-nara, Oh Zarathustra! and yourself, Zarathustra.'

Original Creation and Antagonism

Bundahis 1-7, 25, 27 Pahlavi Texts. Updated and edited version from the translation by E.W. West.

In the Name of the Creator

The Zand-âkâs (Zand-knowing or tradition-informed), which is first about Ahura Mazda's original creation and the antagonism of the evil spirit and afterwards about the nature of the creatures from the original creation till the end, which is the future existence. As revealed by the religion of the Mazdayasnians, so it is declared that Ahura Mazda is supreme in omniscience and goodness, and unrivaled in splendor; the region of light is the place of Ahura Mazda, which they call "endless light," and the omniscience and goodness of the unrivaled Ahura Mazda is what they call "revelation."

Revelation is the explanation of both spirits together; one is he who is independent of unlimited time, because Ahura Mazda and the region, religion, and time of Ahura Mazda were and are and ever will be; while Aharman in darkness, with backward understanding and desire for destruction, was in the abyss, and it is he who will not be; and the place of that destruction, and also of that darkness, is what they call the "endlessly dark." And between them was empty space, that is, what they call "air," in which is now their meeting.

Both are limited and unlimited spirits, for the supreme is that which they call endless light, and the abyss that which is endlessly dark, so that between them is a void, and one is not connected with the other; and, again, both spirits are limited as to their own selves. And, secondly, on account of the omniscience of Ahura Mazda, both things are in the creation of Ahura Mazda, the finite and the infinite; for this they know is that which is in the covenant of both spirits. And, again, the complete sovereignty of the creatures of Ahura Mazda is in the future existence, and that also is unlimited forever and everlasting; and the creatures of Aharman will perish at the time when the future existence occurs, and that also is eternity.

Ahura Mazda, through omniscience, knew that Aharman exists, and whatever he schemes he infuses with malice and greediness till the end; and because he accomplishes the end by many means, he also produced spiritually the creatures which were necessary for those means, and they remained three thousand years in a spiritual state, so that they were unthinking and unmoving, with intangible bodies.

The evil spirit, on account of backward knowledge, was not aware of the existence of Ahura Mazda; and, afterwards, he arose from the abyss, and came in to the light which he saw. Desirous of destroying, and because of his malicious nature, he rushed in to destroy that light of Ahura Mazda unassailed by fiends, and he saw its bravery and glory were greater than his own; so he fled back to the gloomy darkness, and formed many demons and fiends; and the creatures of the destroyer arose for violence.

Ahura Mazda, by whom the creatures of the evil spirit were seen, creatures terrible, corrupt, and bad, also considered them not commendable. Afterwards, the evil spirit saw the creatures of Ahura Mazda; they appeared many creatures of delight, inquiring creatures, and they seemed to him commendable, and he commended the creatures and creation of Ahura Mazda.

Then Ahura Mazda, with a knowledge of which way the end of the matter would be, went to meet the evil spirit, and proposed peace to him, and said: "Evil spirit! bring assistance to my creatures, and offer praise! so that, in reward for it, you and your creatures may become immortal and undecaying, without hunger and without thirst."

And the evil spirit shouted: "I will not depart, I will not provide assistance for your creatures, I will not offer praise among your creatures, and I am not of the same opinion with you as to good things. I will destroy your creatures forever and everlasting; moreover, I will force all your creatures into disaffection to you and affection for myself." And the explanation thereof is this, that the evil spirit reflected in this manner, that Ahura Mazda was helpless regarding him, therefore He prefers peace; and he did not agree, but bore on even into conflict with Him.

And Ahura Mazda said: "You are not omniscient and almighty, Oh evil spirit! So it is not possible for you to destroy me, and it is not possible for you to force my creatures to not return to my possession."

Then Ahura Mazda, through omniscience, knew that: If I do not grant a period of contest, then it will be possible for him to act so that he may be able to cause the seduction of my creatures to himself. As even now there are many of the intermingling of mankind who practice wrong more than right. And Ahura Mazda spoke to the evil spirit saying: "Appoint a period! so that the intermingling of the conflict may be for nine thousand years." For he knew that by, appointing this period the evil spirit would be undone.

Then the evil spirit, unobservant and through ignorance, was content with that agreement; just like two men quarreling together, who propose a time: Let us appoint such-and-such a day for a fight.

Ahura Mazda also knew this, through omniscience, that within these nine thousand years, for three thousand years everything proceeds by the will of Ahura Mazda, three thousand years there is an intermingling of the wills of Ahura Mazda and Aharman, and the last three thousand years the evil spirit is disabled, and they keep the adversary away from the creatures.

Afterwards, Ahura Mazda recited the Ahunavar, saying: "As a heavenly lord is to be chosen," and others once, and uttered the twenty-one words. He also exhibited to the evil spirit his own triumph in the end, and the impotence of the evil spirit, the annihilation of the demons, and the resurrection and undisturbed future existence of the creatures forever and everlasting. And the evil spirit, who perceived his own impotence and the annihilation of the demons, became confounded, and fell back to the gloomy darkness; even so as is declared in revelation, that, when one of the Ahunavar's three parts was uttered, the evil spirit contracted his body through fear, and when two parts of it were uttered he fell upon his knees, and when all of it was uttered he became confounded and impotent as to the harm he caused the creatures of Ahura Mazda, and he remained three thousand years in confusion.

Ahura Mazda created his creatures in the confusion of Aharman; first he produced Vohûman (good thought), by whom the progress of the creatures of Ahura Mazda was advanced.

The evil spirit first created Mîtôkht (falsehood), and then Akôman (evil thought).

The first of Ahura Mazda's creatures of the world was the sky, and his good thought, by good procedure, produced the light of the world, along with which was the good religion of the Mazdayasnians; this was because the renovation, which happens to the creatures was known to him. Afterwards arose Ardavahist, and then Shatvaîrô, and then Spendarmad, and then Horvadad, and then Amerôdad.

From the dark world of Aharman were Akôman and Andar, and then Sôvar, and then Nâkahêd, and then Tâîrêv and Zâîrîk.

Of Ahura Mazda's creatures of the world, the first was the sky; the second, water; the third, earth; the fourth, plants; the fifth, animals; the sixth, mankind.

Formation of Luminaries

Ahura Mazda produced illumination between the sky and the earth, the constellation stars and those also not of the constellations, then the moon, and afterwards the sun, as I shall relate.

First he produced, the celestial sphere, and the constellation stars are assigned to it by him; especially these twelve whose names are Varak (the Lamb), Tôrâ (the Bull), Dô-patkar (the Two-figures or Gemini), Kalakang (the Crab), Sêr (the Lion), Khûsak (Virgo), Tarâzûk (the Balance), Gazdûm (the Scorpion), Nîmâsp (the Centaur or Sagittarius), Vahîk (Capricornus), Dûl (the Waterpot), and Mâhîk (the Fish); which, from their original creation, were divided into the twenty-eight subdivisions of the astronomers, of which the names are Padêvar, Pêsh-Parvîz, Parviz, Paha, Avêsar, Besn, Rakhvad, Taraha, Avra, Nahn, Miyân, Avdem, Mâshâha, Spûr, Husru, Srob, Nur, Gêl, Garafsa, Varant, Gau, Goî, Muru, Bunda, Kahtsar, Vaht, Miyân, Kaht. And all his original creations, residing in the world, are committed to them; so that when the destroyer arrives they overcome the adversary and their own persecution, and the creatures are saved from those adversities.

As a specimen of a warlike army, which is destined for battle, they have ordained every single constellation of those 6,480,000 small stars as assistance; and among those constellations four chieftains, appointed on the four sides, are leaders. On the recommendation of those chieftains the many unnumbered stars are specially assigned to the various quarters and various places, as the united strength and appointed power of those constellations. As it is said that Tîstar is the chieftain of the east, Satavês the chieftain of the west, Vanand the chieftain of the south, and Haptôk-rîng the chieftain of the north. The great one which they call a Gâh (period of the day), which they say is the great one of the middle of the sky, till just before the destroyer came was the midday (or south) one of the five, that is, the Rapîtvîn.

Ahura Mazda performed the spiritual Yazisn ceremony with the archangels in the Rapîtvîn Gâh, and in the Yazisn he supplied every means necessary for overcoming the adversary. He deliberated with the consciousness and guardian spirits of men, and the omniscient wisdom, brought forward among men, said: "Which seems to you the more advantageous, when I shall present you to the world? That you shall contend in a bodily form with the fiend, and the fiend shall perish, and in the end I shall have you prepared again perfect and immortal, and in the end give you back to the world, and you will be wholly immortal, undecaying, and undisturbed; or that it be always necessary to provide you protection from the destroyer?"

Thereupon, the guardian spirits of men became of the same opinion with the omniscient wisdom about going to the world, on account of the evil that comes upon them, in the world, from the fiend Aharman, and their becoming, at last, again unpersecuted by the adversary, perfect, and immortal, in the future existence, forever and everlasting.

On the rush of the destroyer at the creatures it is said, in revelation, that the evil spirit, when he saw the impotence of himself and the confederate demons, owing to the righteous man, became confounded, and seemed in confusion three thousand years. During that confusion the archfiends of the demons severally shouted, saying: "Rise up, you father of us! for we will cause a conflict in the world, the distress and injury from which will become those of Ahura Mazda and the archangels."

Severally they twice recounted their own evil deeds, and it pleased him not; and that wicked evil spirit, through fear of the righteous man, was not able to lift up his head until the wicked Gêh came, at the completion of the three thousand years. And she shouted to the evil spirit saying: "Rise up, you father of us! For I will cause that conflict in the world for which the distress and injury of Ahura Mazda and the archangels will arise." And she twice recounted her own evil deeds, and it pleased him not; and that wicked evil spirit rose not from that confusion, through fear of the righteous man.

And again, the wicked Gêh shouted: "Rise up, you father of us! for in that conflict I will shed much vexation on the righteous man and the laboring ox that, through my deeds, life will not be wanted, and I will destroy their living souls; I will vex the water, I will vex the plants, I will vex the fire of Ahura Mazda, I will make the whole creation of Ahura Mazda vexed." And she so recounted those evil deeds a second time, that the evil spirit was delighted and started up from that confusion; and he kissed Gêh upon the head, and the pollution which they call menstruation became apparent in Gêh.

He shouted to Gêh saying: "What is your wish? so that I may give it you." And Gêh shouted to the evil spirit, saying: "A man is the wish, so give it to me."

The form of the evil spirit was a log-like lizard's body, and he appeared a young man of fifteen years to Gêh, and that brought the thoughts of Gêh to him.

Afterwards, the evil spirit, with the confederate demons, went towards the luminaries, and he saw the sky; and he led them up, fraught with malicious intentions. He stood upon one third of the inside of the sky, and he sprang, like a snake, out of the sky down to the earth.

In the month Fravardîn and the day Ahura Mazda he rushed in at noon, and thereby the sky was as shattered and frightened by him, as a sheep by a wolf. He came on to the water which was arranged below the earth, and then the middle of this earth was pierced and entered by him. Afterwards, he came to the vegetation, then to the ox, then to Gâyômard, and then he came to fire; so, just like a fly, he rushed out upon the whole creation; and he made the world as injured and dark at midday as though it were in dark night. And noxious creatures. were diffused by him over the earth, biting and venomous, such as the snake, scorpion, frog, and lizard—so that not so much as the point of a needle remained free from noxious creatures. And blight was diffused by him over the vegetation, and it withered away immediately. And avarice, want, pain, hunger, disease, lust, and lethargy were diffused by him abroad upon the ox and Gâyômard.

Before his coming to the ox, Ahura Mazda ground up the healing fruit, which some call "bînâk," small in water openly before its eyes, so that its damage and discomfort from the calamity might be less; and when it became at the same time lean and ill, as its breath went forth and it passed away, the ox also said: "The cattle are to be created, and their work, labor, and care are to be appointed."

And before his coming to Gâyômard, Ahura Mazda brought forth a sweat upon Gâyômard, so long as he might recite a prayer of one stanza; moreover, Ahura Mazda formed that sweat into the youthful body of a man of fifteen years, radiant and tall. When Gâyômard issued from the sweat he saw the world dark as night, and the earth as though not a needle's point remained free from noxious creatures; the celestial sphere was in revolution, and the sun and moon remained in motion: and the world's struggle, owing to the clamor of the Mâzînâkân demons, was with the constellations.

And the evil spirit thought that the creatures of Ahura Mazda were all rendered useless except Gâyômard; and Astô-vîdâd with a thousand demons, causers of death, were let forth by him on Gâyômard, but his appointed time had not come, and he (Astô-vîdâd) obtained no means of noosing him; as it is said that, when the opposition of the evil spirit came, the period of the life and rule of Gâyômard was appointed for thirty years. After the coming of the adversary he lived thirty years, and Gâyômard said: "Although the destroyer has come, mankind will be all of my race; and this one thing is good, when they perform duty and good works."

And, afterwards, the evil spirit came to fire, and he mingled smoke and darkness with it. The planets, with many demons, dashed against the celestial sphere, and they mixed the constellations; and the whole creation was as disfigured as though fire disfigured every place and smoke arose over it. And ninety days and nights the heavenly angels were contending in the world with the confederate demons of the evil spirit, and hurled them confounded to hell; and the rampart of the sky was formed so that the adversary should not be able to mingle with it.

Hell is in the middle of the earth; there where the evil spirit pierced the earth and rushed in upon it, as all the possessions of the world were changing into duality, and persecution, contention, and mingling of high and low became manifest.

This also is said, that when the primeval ox passed away it fell to the right hand, and Gâyômard afterwards, when he passed away, to the left hand. Gôsûrvan, as the soul of the primeval ox came out from the body of the ox, stood up before the ox and cried to Ahura Mazda, as much as a thousand men when they sustain a cry at one time, saying: "With whom is the guardianship of the creatures left by you, when ruin has broken into the earth, and vegetation is withered, and water is troubled? Where is the man of whom it was said by you: I will produce him, so that he may preach carefulness?"

And Ahura Mazda said: "You are made ill, Oh Gôsûrvan! You have the illness which the evil spirit brought on—if it were proper to produce that man in this earth at this time, the evil spirit would not have been oppressive in it."

Gôsûrvan walked to the star station and cried in the same manner, and to the moon station and cried in the same manner, and to the sun station, and then the guardian spirit of Zaratûst was exhibited to her, and Ahura Mazda said: "I will produce for the world him who will preach carefulness." Contented became the spirit Gôsûrvan, and assented: "I will nourish the creatures;" that is, she became again consenting to a worldly creation in the world.

Seven chieftains of the planets have come to the seven chieftains of the constellations, as the planet Mercury (Tîr) to Tîstar, the planet Mars (Vâhrâm) to Haptôk-rîng, the planet Jupiter (Ahura Mazda) to Vanand, the planet Venus (Anâhîd) to Satavês, the planet Saturn (Kêvân) to the great one of the middle of the sky, Gôkîhar and the thievish Mûspar, provided with tails, to the sun and moon and stars. The sun has attached Mûspar to its own radiance by mutual agreement, so that he may be less able to do harm.

Of Mount Albûrz it is declared, that around the world and Mount Têrak, which is the middle of the world, the revolution of the sun is like a moat around the world; it turns back in a circuit owing to the enclosure of Mount Albûrz around Têrak. As it is said that it is the Têrak of Albûrz from behind which my sun and moon and stars return again. For there are a hundred and eighty apertures in the east, and a hundred and eighty in the west, through Albûrz; and the sun, each day, comes in through an aperture, and goes out through an aperture; and the whole connection and motion of the moon and constellations and planets is with it: every day it always lights three regions and a half, as is evident to the eyesight. And twice in every year the day and night are equal, for on the original attack, when it went forth from its first degree, the day and night were equal, it was the season of spring; when it arrives at the first degree of Kalakang (Cancer) the time of day is greatest, it is the beginning of summer; when it arrives at the sign Tarâgûk (Libra) the day and night are equal, it is the beginning of autumn; when it arrives at the sign Vahîk (Capricorn) the night is a maximum, it is the beginning of winter; and when it arrives at Varak (Aries) the night and day have again become equal, as when it went forth from Varak. So that when it comes back to Varak, in three hundred and sixty days and the five Gâtha days, it goes in and comes out through one and the same aperture; the aperture is not mentioned, for if it had been mentioned the demons would have known the secret, and been able to introduce disaster.

From there where the sun comes on the longest day to where it comes on the shortest day is the east region Savah; from there where it comes on the shortest day to where it goes off on the shortest day is the direction of the south regions Fradadafsh and Vîdadafsh; from there where it goes in on the shortest day to where it goes in on the longest day is the west region Arzah; from there where it comes in on the longest day to there where it goes in on the longest day are the north regions Vôrûbarst and Vôrûgarst. When the sun comes on, it lights the regions of Savah, Fradadafsh, Vîdadafsh, and half of Khvanîras; when it goes in on the dark side, it lights the regions of Arzah, Vôrûbarst, Vôrûgarst, and one half of Khvanîras; when it is day here it is night there.

On the conflict of the creations of the world with the antagonism of the evil spirit it is said in revelation, that the evil spirit, even as he rushed in and looked upon the pure bravery of the angels and his own violence, wished to rush back. The spirit of the sky is himself like one of the warriors who has put on Armour; he arrayed the sky against the evil spirit, and led on in the contest, until Ahura Mazda had completed a rampart around, stronger than the sky and in front of the sky. And his guardian spirits of warriors and the righteous, on war horses and spear in hand, were around the sky; such as the hair on the head is the similitude of those who hold the watch of the rampart. And no passage was found by the evil spirit, who rushed back; and he beheld the annihilation of the demons and his own impotence, as Ahura Mazda, did his own final triumph, producing the renovation of the universe forever and everlasting.

The second conflict was waged with the water, because, as the star Tîstar was in Cancer, the water which is in the subdivision they call Avrak was pouring, on the same day when the destroyer rushed in, and came again into notice for mischief in the direction of the west. For every single month is the owner of one constellation; the month Tîr is the fourth month of the year, and Cancer the fourth constellation from Aries, so it is the owner of Cancer, into which Tîstar sprang, and displayed the characteristics of a producer of rain; and he brought on the water aloft by the strength of the wind. Co-operators with Tîstar were Vohûman and the angel Hôm, with the assistance of the angel Bûrg and the righteous guardian spirits in orderly arrangement.

Tîstar was converted into three

forms, the form of a man and the form of a horse and the form of a bull; thirty days and nights he was distinguished in brilliance, and in each form he produced rain ten days and nights; as the astrologers say that every constellation has three forms. Every single drop of that rain became as big as a bowl, and the water stood the height of a man over the whole of this earth; and the noxious creatures on the earth being all killed by the rain, went into the holes of the earth.

And, afterwards, the wind spirit, so that it may not be contaminated, stirs up the wind and atmosphere as the life stirs in the body; and the water was all swept away by it, and was brought out to the borders of the earth, and the wide-formed ocean arose therefrom. The noxious creatures remained dead within the earth, and their venom and stench were mingled with the earth, and in order to carry that poison away from the earth Tîstar went down into the ocean in the form of a white horse with long hoofs.

And Apâôsh, the demon, came meeting him in the likeness of a black horse with clumsy hoofs; a mile away from him fled Tîstar, through the fright which drove him away. And Tîstar begged for success from Ahura Mazda, and Ahura Mazda gave him strength and power, as it is said, that to Tîstar was brought at once the strength of ten vigorous horses, ten vigorous camels, ten vigorous bulls, ten mountains, and ten rivers. A mile away from him fled Apâôsh, the demon, through fright at his strength; on account of this they speak of an arrow-shot with Tîstar's strength in the sense of a mile.

Afterwards, with a cloud for a jar—thus they call the measure which was a means of the work—he seized upon the water and made it rain most prodigiously, in drops like bull's heads and men's heads, pouring in handfuls and pouring in armfuls, both great and small. On the production of that rain the demons Aspengargâk and Apâôsh contended with it, and the fire Vâzist turned its club over; and owing to the blow of the club Aspengargâk made a very grievous noise, as even now, in a conflict with the producer of rain, a groaning and raging are manifest. And ten nights and days rain was produced by him in that manner, and the poison and venom of the noxious creatures which were in the earth were all mixed up in the water, and the water became salty, because there remained in the earth some of those germs which noxious creatures ever collect.

Afterwards, the wind, in the same manner as before, restrained the water, at the end of three days, on various sides of the earth; and the three great seas and twenty-three small seas arose therefrom, and two fountains of the sea thereby became manifest, one the Kêkast lake, and one the Sôvbar, whose sources are connected with the fountain of the sea. And at its north side two rivers flowed out, and went one to the east and one to the west; they are the Arag river and the Vêh river; as it is said: "Through those finger-breadth tricklings do you pour and draw forth two such waters, Oh Ahura Mazda!" Both those rivers wind about through all the extremities of the earth, and intermingle again with the water of the wide-formed ocean. As those two rivers flowed out, and from the same place of origin as theirs, eighteen navigable rivers flowed out, and after the other waters have flowed out from those navigable streams they all flow back to the Arag river and Vêh river, whose fertilization of the world arises therefrom.

Formation of Mountains

As the evil spirit rushed in, the earth shook, and the substance of mountains was created in the earth. First, Mount Albûrz arose; afterwards, the other ranges of mountains of the middle of the earth; for as Albûrz grew forth all the mountains remained in motion, for they have all grown forth from the root of Albûrz. At that time they came up from the earth, like a tree which has grown up to the clouds and its root to the bottom; and their root passed on that way from one to the other, and they are arranged in mutual connection. Afterwards, about that wonderful shaking out from the earth, they say that a great mountain is the knot of lands; and the passage for the waters within the mountains is the root which is below the mountains; they forsake the upper parts so that they may flow into it, just as the roots of trees pass into the earth; a counterpart of the blood in the arteries of men, which gives strength to the whole body. In numbers, apart from Albûrz, all the mountains grew up out of the earth in eighteen years, from which arises the perfection of men's advantage.

Light and Darkness

Excerpt. From Zad-Sparam. Pahlavi Texts. Updated and edited version from the translation by E.W. West.

Chapter 1

In propitiation of the creator Ahura Mazda and all the angels—who are the whole of the heavenly and earthly sacred beings—are the sayings of Herbad Zâd-sparam, son of Yûdân-Yim, who is of the south, about the meeting of the beneficent spirit and the evil spirit.

It is in scripture declared, that light was above and darkness below, and between those two was open space. Ahura Mazda was in the light, and Aharman in the darkness; Ahura Mazda was aware of the existence of Aharman and of his coming for strife; Aharman was not aware of the existence of light and of Ahura Mazda. It happened to Aharman, in the gloom and darkness, that he was walking humbly on the borders, and meditating on other things he came up to the top, and a ray of light was seen by him; and because of its antagonistic nature to him he strove that he might reach it, so that it might also be within his absolute power. And as he came forth to the boundary, accompanied by certain others, Ahura Mazda came forth to the struggle for keeping Aharman away from His territory; and He did it through pure words, confounding witchcraft, and cast him back to the gloom.

For protection from the fiend, the spirits rushed in, the spirits of the sky, water, earth, plants, animals, mankind, and fire He had appointed, and they maintained the protection three thousand years. Aharman, also, ever collected means in the gloom; and at the end of the three thousand years he, came back to the boundary, blustered, and exclaimed: "I will smite you, I will smite the creatures which you think have produced fame for you—you who are the beneficent spirit—I will destroy everything about them."

Ahura Mazda answered, saying: "you are not a doer of everything, Oh fiend!"

And, again, Aharman retorted: "I will seduce all material life into disaffection to you and affection to myself."

Ahura Mazda perceived, through the spirit of wisdom: "Even the blustering of Aharman is capable of performance, if I do not allow disunion during a period of struggle." And he demanded of him a period for friendship, for it was seen by him that Aharman does not rely upon the intervention of any vigorous ones, and the existence of a period is obtaining the benefit of the mutual friendship and just arrangement of both; and he formed it into three periods, each period being three millenniums. Aharman relied upon it, and Ahura Mazda perceived that, though it is not possible to have Aharman sent down, whenever he wants he goes back to his own requisite, which is darkness; and from the poison which is much diffused endless strife arises.

And after the period was appointed by him, he brought forward the Ahûnavar formula; and in his Ahûnavar these kinds of benefit were shown: The first is that, of all things, that is proper which is something declared as the will of Ahura Mazda; so that, since that is proper which is declared the will of Ahura Mazda, where anything exists which is not within the will of Ahura Mazda, it is created injurious from the beginning, a sin of a distinct nature. The second is this, that whoever shall do that which is the will of Ahura Mazda, his reward and recompense are his own; and of him who shall not do that which is the will of Ahura Mazda, the punishment at the bridge, owing thereto, is his own; which is shown from this formula; and the reward of doers of good works, the punishment of sinners, and the tales of heaven and hell are from it. Thirdly, it is shown that the sovereignty of Ahura Mazda increases that which is for the poor, and adversity is removed; by which it is shown that there are treasures for the needy one, and treasures are to be his friends; as the intelligent creations are to the unintelligent, so also are the treasures of a wealthy person to a needy one, treasures liberally given which are his own. And the creatures of the trained hand of Ahura Mazda are contending and angry, one with the other, as the renovation of the universe must occur through these three things. That is, first, true religiousness in one self, and reliance upon a man's original hold on the truly glad tidings, that Ahura Mazda is all goodness without vileness, and his will is a will altogether excellent; and Aharman is all vileness without goodness. Secondly, hope of the reward and recompense of good works, serious fear of the bridge and the punishment of crime, strenuous perseverance in good works, and abstaining from sin. Thirdly, the existence of the mutual assistance of the creatures, or along with and owing to mutual assistance, their collective warfare; it is the triumph of warfare over the enemy which is one's own renovation.

By this formula Aharman was confounded, and he fell back to the gloom; and Ahura Mazda produced the creatures bodily for the world; first, the sky; the second, water; the third, earth; the fourth, plants; the fifth, animals; the sixth, mankind. Fire was in all, diffused originally through the six substances, of which it was as much the confiner of each single substance in which it was established, it is said, as an eyelid when they lay one down upon the other.

Three thousand years the creatures were possessed of bodies and not walking on their navels; and the sun, moon, and stars stood still. In the mischievous incursion, at the end of the period, Ahura Mazda observed: "What advantage is there from the creation of a creature, although without thirst, which is unmoving or mischievous?" And in aid of the celestial sphere he produced the creature Time; and Time is unrestricted, so that he made the creatures of Ahura Mazda moving, distinct from the motion of Aharman's creatures, for the shedders of perfume were standing one opposite to the other while emitting it. And, observantly of the end, he brought forward to Aharman a means out of himself, the property of darkness, with which the extreme limits of Time were connected by him, an envelope of the black-pated and ash-colored kind. And in bringing it forward he spoke: "Through their weapons the co-operation of the serpent dies away, and this which is yours, indeed your own daughter, dies through religion; and if at the end of nine thousand years, as it is said and written, is a time of upheaval, she is upheaved, not ended."

At the same time Aharman came from accompanying Time out to the front, out to the star station; the connection of the sky with the star station was open, which showed, since it hung down into empty space, the strong communication of the lights and glooms, the place of strife in which is the pursuit of both. And having darkness with himself he brought it into the sky, and left the sky so to gloom that the internal deficiency in the sky extends as much as one third over the star station.

Chapter 2

On the coming in of Aharman to the creatures it is declared in revelation, that in the month Fravardîn and the day Ahura Mazda, at noon, he came forth to the frontier of the sky. The sky sees him and, on account of his nature, fears as much as a sheep trembles at a wolf; and Aharman came on, scorching and burning into it. Then he came to the water which was arranged below the earth, and darkness without an eyelid was brought on by him; and he came on, through the middle of the earth, as a snake comes leaping out of a hole; and he stayed within the whole earth. The passage where he came on is his own is the way to hell, through which the demons make the wicked run.

Afterwards, he came to a tree, such as was of a single root, the height of which was several feet, and it was without branches and without bark, juicy and sweet; and to keep the strength of all kinds of trees in its race, it was in the vicinity of the middle of the earth; and at the same time it became quite withered.

Afterwards, he came to the ox, the sole-created, as it stood as high as Gâyômard on the bank of the water of Dâîtih in the middle of the earth; and its distance from Gâyômard being as much as its own height, it was also distant from the bank of the water of Dâîtih by the same measure; and it was a female, white and brilliant as the moon. As the adversary came upon it Ahura Mazda gave it a narcotic, which is also called "bang," to eat, and to rub the "bang" before the eye, so that the annoyance from the assault of crimes may be less; it became lean and ill, and fell upon its right breast trembling.

Before the advance to Gâyômard, who was then about one third the height of Zaratûst, and was brilliant as the sun; Ahura Mazda forms, from the sweat on the man, a figure of fifteen years, radiant and tall, and sends it on to Gâyômard; and, he also brings his sweat on to him as long as one Yathâ-ahû-vairyô is being recited. When he issued from the sweat, and raised his eyes, he saw the world when it was dark as night; on the whole earth were the snake, the scorpion, the lizard, and noxious creatures of many kinds; and so the other kinds of quadrupeds stood among the reptiles; every approach of the whole earth was as though not as much as a needle's point remained, in which there was no rush of noxious creatures. There were the coming of a planetary star into planetary conjunction, and the moon and planets at sixes and sevens; many dark forms with the face and curls of Az-i Dahâk suffered punishment in company with certain non-Iranians; and he was amazed at calling the wicked out from the righteous.

Lastly, Aharman came up to the

fire, and mingled darkness and smoke with it.

Chapter 3

And Gôsûrvan, as she was herself the soul of the primeval ox, when the ox passed away, came out from the ox, even as the soul from the body of the dead, and kept up the clamor of a cry to Ahura Mazda in such fashion as that of an army, a thousand strong, when they cry out together. And Ahura Mazda, in order to be much more able to keep watch over the mingled creatures than in front of Gâyômard, went from the earth up to the sky. And Gôsûrvan continually went after him crying, and she kept up the cry saying: "With whom may the guardianship over the creatures be left by you?"

Chapter 4

This was the highest predominance of Aharman, for he came on, with all the strength which he had, for the disfigurement of the creatures; and he took as much as one third of the base of the sky, in a downward direction, into a confined and captive state, so that it was all dark and apart from the light, for it was itself, at the coming of the adversary, his enemy among the struggles for creation. And this is opposing the renovation of the universe, for the greatest of all the other means of the fiend, when he has come in, are of like origin and strength this day, in the sleep of the renovation, as on that when the enemy, who is fettered on coming in, is kept back.

Amidst all this struggling were mingled the instigations of Aharman, crying: "My victory has come completely, for the sky is split and disfigured by me with gloom and darkness, and taken by me as a stronghold; water is disfigured by me, and the earth, injured by darkness, is pierced by me; vegetation is withered by me, the ox is put to death by me, Gâyômard is made ill by me, and opposed to those revolving are the glooms and planets arranged by me; no one has remained for me to take and pervert in combat except Ahura Mazda, and of the earth there is only one man, who is alone, what is he able to do?"

And he sends Astô-vîdâd upon him with the thousand decrepitudes and diseases which are his own, sicknesses of various kinds, so that they may make him ill and cause death. Gâyômard was not secured by them, and the reason was because it was a decree of appointing Time in the beginning of the coming in of Aharman, that: "Up to thirty winters I appoint Gâyômard to brilliance and preservation of life." And his manifestation in the celestial sphere was through the forgiveness of criminals and instigators of confusion by his good works, and for that reason no opportunity was obtained by them during the extent of thirty years.

For in the beginning it was so appointed that the star Jupiter (Ahura Mazda) was life towards the creatures, not through its own nature, but on account of its being within the band of the luminaries; and Saturn was death towards the creatures. Both were in their supremacy at the beginning of the creatures, as Jupiter was in Cancer on rising, that which is also called Gîvân (living), for it is the place in which life is bestowed upon it; and Saturn was in Libra, in the great subterranean, so that its own venom and deadliness became more evident and more dominant thereby. And it was when both shall not be supreme that Gâyômard was to complete his own life, which is the thirty years Saturn came not again to supremacy, that is, to Libra. And at the time when Saturn came into Libra, Jupiter was in Capricornus, on account of whose own lowness, and the victory of Saturn over Jupiter, Gâyômard suffered through those very defects which came and are to continue advancing, the continuance of that disfigurement which Aharman can bring upon the creatures of Ahura Mazda.

Chapter 5

When in like manner, and equally oppressively, as Ahura Mazda's creatures were disfigured, then through that same deterioration his own great glory was exhibited; for as he came within the sky he maintains the spirit of the sky, like an intrepid warrior who has put on metal armor; and the sky in its fortress spoke these deceitful words to Aharman, saying: "Now when you will have come in I will not let you back;" and it obstructed him until Ahura Mazda prepared another rampart, that is stronger, around the sky, which is called "righteous understanding". And he arranged the guardian spirits of the righteous who are warriors around that rampart, mounted on horses and spear in hand, in such manner as the hair on the head; and they acquired the appearance of prison guards who watch a prison from outside, and would not surrender the outer boundaries to an enemy descended from the inside.

Immediately, Aharman endeavors that he may go back to his own complete darkness, but he found no passage; and he recapitulated, with seeming misgiving, his fears of the worthiness which is to arise at the appearance of the renovation of the universe at the end of the nine thousand years.

As it is said in the Gâthas: "So also both those spirits have approached together to that which was the first creation—that is, both spirits have come to the body of Gâyômard. Whatever is in life is so through this purpose of Ahura Mazda, that is: So that I may keep it alive; whatever is in lifelessness is so through this purpose of the evil spirit, that is: So that I may utterly destroy it; and whatever is thus, is so until the last in the world, so that both spirits come also on to the rest of mankind. And on account of the utter depravity of the wicked their destruction is fully seen, and so is the perfect meditation of him who is righteous, the hope of the eternity of Ahura Mazda." And this was the first contest, that of the sky with Aharman.

Chapter 6

And as Aharman came secondly to the water, together with him rushed in, on the horse Cancer, he who is the most watery Tîstar; the equally watery one, that is called Avrak, gave forth a cloud and went down in the day; that is declared as the movement of the first-comers of the creatures. Cancer became a zodiacal constellation; it is the fourth constellation of the zodiac for this reason, because the month Tîr is the fourth month of the year.

And as Tîstar begged for assistance, Vohûman and Hôm are therefore co-operating with him in command, Bûrg of the waters and the water in mutual aid, and the righteous guardian spirits in keeping the peace. He was converted into three forms, which are the form of a man, the form of a bull, and the form of a horse; and each form was distinguished in brilliance for ten nights, and let its rain fall on the night for the destruction of noxious creatures. The drops became each separately like a great bowl in which water is drawn; and as to that on which they are driven, they kill all the noxious creatures except the reptiles, who entered into the muddiness of the earth.

Afterwards, the wind spirit, in the form of a man, became manifest on the earth; radiant and tall he had a kind of wooden boot on his feet; and as when the life shall stir the body, the body is advancing with like vigor, so that spirit of the wind stirs forth the inner nature of the atmospheric wind, the wind pertaining to the whole earth is forth, and the water in its grasp is flung out from it to the sides of the earth, and from this the wide-formed ocean arose.

The ocean keeps one third of this earth, and among its contents are a thousand sources and fountains, such as are called lakes; a thousand water fountains, whose water is from the ocean, come up from the lakes and are poured forth into it. And the size of all the lakes and all the fountains of water is as much as a fast rider on an Arab horse, who continually compasses and canters around them, will attain in forty days, which is, long leagues, each league being at least, 1000 feet.

And after the noxious creatures died, and the poison was mixed up in the earth, in order to utterly destroy that poison Tîstar went down into the ocean; and Apâôsh, the demon, hastened to meet him, and at the alarm of the first contest Tîstar was in terror. And he applied to Ahura Mazda, who brought such power to Tîstar as arises through propitiation and praise and invoking by name, and they call forth such power to Tîstar as that of ten vigorous horses, ten vigorous camels, ten vigorous bulls, ten mountains when hurled, and ten single-stream rivers when together. And without alarm he drove out Apâôsh, the demon, and kept him away from the sources of the ocean.

And with a cup and measuring bowl, which possessed the diligence even of a guardian spirit, he seized many more handfuls of water, and made it rain down much more prodigiously, for destruction, drops as large as men's heads and bulls' heads, great and small. And in that cloud and rain were the chastisement and beating which Tîstar and the fire Vâzist inflicted on the opposition of Apâôsh; the all-deciding fire Vâzist struck down with a club of fire, all-deciding among the malevolent.

Ten days and nights there was rain, and its darting was the shooting of the noxious creatures; afterwards, the wind drove it to the shore of the wide-formed ocean, and it is portioned out into three, and three seas arose from it; they are called the Pûîtîk, the Kamîrîd, and the Gehân-bûn. Of these the Pûîtîk itself is salt water, in which is a flow and ebb; and the control of its flow and ebb is connected with the moon, and by its continual rotation, in coming up and going down, that of the moon is manifested. The wide-formed ocean stands forth on the south side as to Albûrz, and the Pûîtîk stands contiguous to it, and amidst it is the gulf of Satavês, whose connection is with Satavês, which is the southern quarter. In the activity of the sea, and in the increase and decrease of the moon, whose circuit is the whole of Iran, are the flow and ebb; of the curving tails in front of the moon two issue forth, and have an abode in Satavês; one is the up-drag and one the down-drag; through the up-drag occurs the flood, and through the down-drag occurs the ebb. And Satavês itself is a gulf and side arm of the wide-formed ocean, for it drives back the impurity and turbidity which come from the salt sea, when they are continually going into the wide-formed ocean, with a mighty high wind, while that which is clear through purity goes into the Arêdvîvsûr sources of the wide-formed ocean. Besides these four there are the small seas. And, afterwards, there were made to flow from Albûrz, out of its northern border, two rivers, which were the Arvand—that is, the Diglît, and the flow of that river was to those of the setting sun —and the Vêh was the river of the first-comers to the sun; formed as two horns they went on to the ocean. After them eighteen great rivers came out from the same Albûrz; and these twenty rivers, whose source is in Albûrz, go down into the earth, and arrive in Khvanîras.

Afterwards, two fountains of the sea are opened out for the earth, which are called the Kêkast—a lake which has no cold wind, and on whose shore rests the triumphant fire Gûsnasp and, secondly, the Sôvar which casts on its shores all turbidity, and keeps its own salt lake clear and pure, for it is like the semblance of an eye which casts out to its edges every ache and every impurity; and on account of its depth it is not reached to the bottom, for it goes into the ocean; and in its vicinity rests the beneficial fire Bûrzîn-Mitrô. And this was the second contest, which was with the water.

Chapter 7

And as Aharman came thirdly to the earth, which arrayed the whole earth against him—since there was an animation of the earth through the shattering—Albûrz grew up, which is the boundary of the earth, and the other mountains, which are amidst the circuit of the earth, came up in number. And by them the earth was bound together and arranged, and on them was the sprouting and growth of plants, from which came the nourishment of cattle, and from which came the great advantage of assistance to men.

Even so it is declared that before the coming of the destroyer to the creatures, for a thousand years the substance of mountains was created in the earth—especially as antagonism came on the earth, and settled on it with injury—and it came up over the earth just like a tree whose branch has grown at the top, and its root at the bottom. The root of the mountains is passed on from one to the other, and is arranged in connection with them, and through it is produced the path and passage of water from below to above, so that the water may flow in it in such a manner as blood in the veins, from all parts of the body to the heart, the latent vigor which they possess. And, moreover, in six hundred years, at first, all the mountains apart from Albûrz were completed. Albûrz was growing during eight hundred years; in two hundred years it grew up to the star station, in two hundred years up to the moon station, two hundred years up to the sun station, and two hundred years up to the sky. After Albûrz the Aparsên mountain is the greatest, as it is also called the Avarrôyisn (up-growth) mountain, whose beginning is in Sagastân and its end to Pârs and to Kînîstân.

This, too, is declared, that after the great rain in the beginning of creation, and the wind's sweeping away the water to the ocean, the earth is in seven portions, a little above it, as the compact earth, after the rain, is torn up by the noise and wind in various places. One portion, moreover, as much as one-half the whole earth, is in the middle, and in each of the six portions around is as much as Sagastân; moreover, as much as Sagastân is the measure of what is called a keshvar (region) for the reason that one was defined from the other by a kêsh (furrow). The middle one is Khvanîras, of which Pârs is the center, and those six regions are like a coronet around it. One part of the wide-formed ocean wound around it, among those six regions; the sea and forest seized upon the south side, and a lofty mountain grew up on the north, so that they might become separate, one from the other, and imperceptible. This is the third contest, about the earth.

Chapter 8

As Aharman came fourthly to the plants—which have struggled against him with the whole vegetation—because the vegetation was quite dry, Amerôdad, by whom the essence of the world's vegetation was seized upon, pounded it up small, and mixed it up with the rain water of Tîstar. After the rain the whole earth is discerned sprouting, and ten thousand special species and a hundred thousand additional species so grew as if there were a species of every kind; and those ten thousand species are provided for keeping away the ten thousand diseases.

Afterwards, the seed was taken up from those hundred thousand species of plants, and from the collection of seed the tree of all germs, amid the wide-formed ocean, was produced, from which all species of plants continually grow. And the griffin bird has his resting place upon it; when he wanders forth from within it, he scatters the dry seed into the water, and it is rained back to the earth with the rain.

And in its vicinity the tree was produced which is the white Hôm, the counteractor of decrepitude, the reviver of the dead, and the immortalizer of the living. This was the fourth contest, about the plants.

Chapter 9

As Aharman came fifthly to cattle—which struggled against him with all the animals—and likewise as the primeval ox passed away, from, the nature of the vegetable principle it possessed, fifty-five species of grain and twelve species of medicinal plants grew from its various members; and since they should see from which member each one proceeds, it is declared in the Dâmdâd Nask. And every plant grown from a member promotes that member, as it is said that there where the ox scattered its marrow on to the earth, grain afterwards grew up, corn and sesame, vetches and peas; so sesame, on account of its marrow quality, is itself a great thing for developing marrow. And it is also said that from the blood is the vine, a great vegetable thing—as wine itself is blood—for more befriending the sound quality of the blood. And it is said that from the nose is the pulse which is called dônak, and was a variety of sesame, and it is for other noses.

And it is also said that from the lungs are the rue-like herbs which heal, and are for the lung disease of cattle. This, rooted in the heart, is thyme, from which is Vohûman's thorough withstanding of the stench of Akôman, and it is for that which proceeds from the sick and yawners.

Afterwards, the brilliance of the seed, seized upon, by strength, from the seed which was the ox's, they would carry off from it, and the brilliance was entrusted to the angel of the moon; in a place therein that seed was thoroughly purified by the light of the moon, and was restored in its many qualities, and made fully infused with life. Forth from there it produced for Aîrân-vêg, first two oxen, a pair, male and female, and afterwards, other species, until the completion of the species; and they were discernible as far as two long leagues on the earth. Quadrupeds walked forth on the land, fish swam in the water, and birds flew in the atmosphere; in every two, at the time good eating is enjoyed, a longing arose therefrom, and pregnancy and birth.

Secondly, their subdivision is as follows: First, they are divided into three, that is, quadrupeds walking on the earth, fish swimming in the water, and birds flying in the atmosphere. Then, into five classes, that is, the quadruped which is round-hoofed, the double-hoofed, the five-clawed, the bird, and the fish, whose dwellings are in five places, and which are called aquatic, burrowing, oviparous, wide-traveling, and suitable for grazing. The aquatic are fish and every beast of burden, cattle, wild beast, dog, and bird which enters the water; the burrowing are the marten and musk animals, and all other dwellers and movers in holes; the oviparous are birds of every kind; the wide-traveling sprang away for help, and are also those of a like kind; those suitable for grazing are whatever are kept grazing in a flock.

And afterwards, they were divided into genera, as the round-hoofed are one, which is all called "horse;" the double-hoofed are many, as the camel and ox, the sheep and goat, and others double-hoofed; the five-clawed are the dog, hare, musk animals, marten, and others; then are the birds, and then the fish. And then they were divided into species, as eight species of horse, two species of camel, ten species of ox, five species of sheep, five species of goat, ten of the dog, five of the hare, eight of the marten, eight of the musk animals, one hundred and ten of the birds, and ten of the fish; some are counted for the pigs, and with all those declared and all those undeclared there were, at first, species; and with the species within species there were a thousand varieties.

The birds are distributed into eight groups, and from that which is largest to that which is smallest they are so spread about as when a man, who is sowing grain, first scatters abroad that of heavy weight, then that which is middling, and afterwards that which is small.

And of the whole of the species, as enumerated a second time in the Dâmdâd Nask, and written by me in the manuscript of "the summary enumeration of races"—this is a lordly summary—the matter which is shown is, about the species of horses, that the first is the Arab, and the chief of them is white and yellow-eared, and secondly the Persian, the mule, the ass, the wild ass, the water-horse, and others.

Of the camel there are specially two, that for the plain, and the mountain one which is double-humped.

Among the species of ox are the white, mud-colored, red, yellow, black, and dappled, the elk, the buffalo, the camel-leopard, the ox-fish, and others.

Among sheep are those having tails and those which are tailless, also the ram and the Kûrisk which, because of its trampling the hills, its great horn, and also being suitable for ambling, became the steed of Mânûskîhar.

Among goats are the ass-goat, the Arab, the fawn, the roe, and the mountain goat.

Among martens are the white ermine, the black marten, the squirrel, the beaver, and others.

Of musk animals with a bag, one is the Bîsh-musk—which eats the Bîsh poison and does not die from it—and it is created for the great advantage that it should eat the Bîsh, and less of it should succeed in poisoning the creatures—and one is a musk animal of a black color which they desired who were bitten by the fanged serpent—as the serpent of the mountain watercourses is called—which is numerous on the riverbanks; one throws the same to it for food, which it eats, and then the serpent enters its body, when his serpent, at the time this happens, feeds upon the same belly in which the serpent is, and he will become clear from that malady.

Among birds two were produced of a different character from the rest, and those are the griffin bird and the bat, which have teeth in the mouth, and suckle their young with animal milk from the teat.

This is the fifth contest, as to animals.

Chapter 10

As Aharman came sixthly to Gâyômard there was arrayed against him, with Gâyômard, the pure propitious liturgy, as heard from Gâyômard; and Ahura Mazda, in pure meditation, considered that which is good and righteousness as destruction of the fiend. And when Gâyômard passed away eight kinds of mineral of a metallic character arose from his various members; they are gold, silver, iron, brass, tin, lead, quicksilver, and adamant; and on account of the perfection of gold it is produced from the life and seed. Spendarmad received the gold of the dead Gâyômard, and it was forty years in the earth. At the end of the forty years, in the manner of a Rîvâs-plant, Mashya and Mashyôî came up, and, one joined to the other, were of like stature and mutually adapted; and its middle, on which a glory came, through their like stature, was such that it was not clear which is the male and which the female, and which is the one with the glory which Ahura Mazda created. This is that glory for which man is, indeed, created, as it is said in revelation: "Which existed before, the glory or the body?" And Ahura Mazda spoke: "The glory was created by me before; afterwards, for him who is created, the glory is given a body so that it may produce activity, and its body is created only for activity." And, afterwards, they changed from the shape of a plant into the shape of man, and the glory went spiritually into them.

Chapter 11

As Aharman came seventhly to fire, which was all together against him, the fire separated into five kinds, which are called the Propitious, the Good diffuser, the Aûrvâzîst, the Vâzîst, and the Supremely-benefiting. And it produced the Propitious fire itself in heaven; its manifestation is in the fire which is burning on the earth, and its propitiousness is this, that all the kinds are of its nature. The Good diffuser is that which is in men and animals, and its business consists in the digestion of the food, the sleeping of the body, and the brightening of the eyes. The Aûrvâzîst is that which is in plants, in whose seed it is formed, and its business consists in piercing the earth, warming the chilled water and producing the qualities and fragrance of plants and blossoms therefrom, and elaborating the ripened produce into many fruits. And the Vâzîst is that which has its motion in a cloud, and its business consists in destroying the atmospheric gloom and darkness, and making the thickness of the atmosphere fine and propitious in quality, sifting the hail, moderately warming the water which the cloud holds, and making sultry weather showery. The Supremely-benefiting, like the sky, is that glory whose location is in the Behrâm fire, as the master of the house is over the house, and whose propitious power arises from the growing brightness of the fire, the blazing forth in the purity of the place, the praise of God, and the practice of good works. And its business is that it struggles with the spiritual fiend, it watches the forms of the witches—who walk up from the river, wear woven clothing, disturb the luminaries by the concealment of stench, and by witchcraft injure the creatures—and the occurrences of destruction, burning, and celebration of witchcraft, especially at night; being an assistant of Srôsh the righteous.

And in the beginning of the creation the whole earth was delivered over into the guardianship of the sublime Frôbak fire, the mighty Gûsnasp fire, and the beneficial Bûrzîn-Mitrô fire, which are like priest, warrior, and husbandman. The place of the fire Frôbak was formed on the Gadman-hômand (glorious) mountain in Khvârizem, the fire Gûsnasp was on the Asnavand mountain in Âtarô-pâtakân, and the fire Bûrzîn-Mitrô on the Rêvand mountain which is in the Ridge of Vistâsp, and its material manifestation in the world was the most complete.

In the reign of Hôshâng, when men were continually going forth to the other regions on the ox Srûvô, one night, while admiring the fires, the fire-stands which were prepared in three places on the back of the ox, and in which the fire was, fell into the sea, and the substance of that one great fire which was manifest is divided into three, and they established it on the three fire stands, and it became itself three glories whose locations are in the Frôbak fire, the Gûsnasp fire, and the Bûrzîn-Mitrô.

Light and Darkness

Excerpt. From The Holy Qur'an. Sūra XV. Al-Hijr, or The Rocky Tract. Updated and edited version from the translation by Yusuf Ali.

16. It is We who have set out the Zodiacal Signs in the heavens, and made them fair-seeming to all beholders;

17. And We have guarded them from every evil spirit accursed:

18. But any that gains a hearing by stealth, is pursued by a flaming fire, bright (to see).

19. And the earth We have spread out; set thereon mountains firm and immovable; and produced therein all kinds of things in due balance.

20. And We have provided therein means of subsistence—for you and for those for whose sustenance you are not responsible.

21. And there is not a thing but its treasures (Inexhaustible) are with Us; But We only send down thereof in due and ascertainable measures.

22. And We send the fertilizing winds, then cause the rain to descend from the sky, therewith providing you with water in abundance, though you are not the guardians of its stores.

23. And truly, it is We who give life, and who give death: it is We who remain Inheritors after all else passes away.

24. To Us are known those of you who hasten forward, and those who lag behind.

25. Assuredly it is your Lord who will gather them together: for He is perfect in Wisdom and Knowledge.

26. We created man from sounding clay, from mud molded into shape;

27. And the Jinn race, we had created before, from the fire of a scorching wind.

28. Behold! Your Lord said to the angels: "I am about to create man, from sounding clay from mud molded into shape;"

29. "When I have fashioned him (in due proportion) and breathed into him of My spirit, fall down in obeisance to him."

30. So the angels prostrated themselves, all of them together:

31. Not so Iblīs: he refused to be among those who prostrated themselves.

32. God said: "O Iblīs! What is your reason for not being among those who prostrated themselves?"

33. Iblīs said: "I am not one to prostrate myself to man, whom You did create from sounding clay, from mud molded into shape."

34. God said: "Then leave from here; for you are rejected, accursed."

35. "And the curse shall be on you till the Day of Judgment."

36. Iblīs said: "O my Lord! Give me then respite till the day the dead are raised."

37. God said: "Respite is granted you."

39. Iblīs said: "O my Lord! Because You have put me in the wrong, I will make (wrong) fair-seeming to

them on the earth, and I will put them all in the wrong,"

40. "Except Your servants among them, sincere and purified (by Your grace)."

41. God said: "This (way of my sincere servants) is indeed a way that leads straight to Me."

42. "For over My servants no authority will you have, except such as put themselves in the wrong and follow you."

Chapter 8

Northern Heroes

Beginning of Things

Excerpt. Story of Creation. Updated and edited version of the text from Teutonic Myth and Legend, by Donald A. Mackenzie

In the Ages, when nothing else was, there stretched in space a vast and empty gulf called Ginnunga-gap. Length it had, and breadth immeasurable, and there was depth beyond comprehension. No shore was there, nor cooling wave; for there was yet no sea, and the earth was not made nor the heavens above.

There in the gulf was the beginning of things. There time first dawned. And in the perpetual twilight was All-father, who governs every realm and sways all things both great and small.

First of all there was formed, northward of the gulf, Nifel-heim, the immense home of misty darkness and freezing cold, and to the south, Muspel-heim, the luminous home of warmth and of light.

In the midst of Nifel-heim burst forth the great fountain from where all waters flow, and to which all waters return. It is named Hvergelmer, "the roaring cauldron", and from it surged, at the beginning, twelve tremendous rivers called Elivagar, that washed southward towards the gulf. A vast distance they traversed from their source, and then the venom that was swept with them began to harden, as does waste pouring from a surface, until they congealed and became ice. Whereupon the rivers grew silent and ceased to move, and gigantic blocks of ice stood still. Vapor arose from the ice-venom and was frozen to rime; layer upon layer heaped up in fantastic forms one above another.

That part of the gulf which lay northward was a region of horror and of strife. Heavy masses of black vapor enveloped the ice, and within were screaming whirlwinds that never ceased, and dismal banks of fleeting mist. But southward, Muspelheim glowed with intense radiance, and sprayed forth beautiful flakes and sparks of shining fire. The intervening space between the region of tempest and gloom and the region of warmth and light was a peaceful twilight, serene and still as is windless air.

Now when the sparks from Muspelheim fell through the frozen vapor, and the heat was sent there by the might of the All-father, drops of moisture began to fall from the ice. It was then and there that life began to be. The drops were quickened and a formless mass took human shape. Thus came into being the great lumbering clay-giant who was named Ymer.

Rough and ungainly was Ymer, and as he stretched himself and began to move about he was tortured by the pangs of immense hunger. So he went forth ravenously to search for food; but there was yet no substance of which he could partake. The whirlwinds went past him and over, and the dark mists enveloped him like a shroud.

More drops fell through the gloomy vapors, and next there was formed a gigantic cow, which was named Audhumla, "void darkness". Ymer beheld it standing in the gloom beside blocks of ice, and groped weakly towards it. Wondering, he found that milk ran from its teats in four white streams, and greedily he drank and drank until he was filled with the seeds of life and was satisfied.

Then a great heaviness came over Ymer, and he lay down and fell into deep and dreamless slumber. Warmth and strength possessed him, and sweat gathered in the pit of his left arm, from which, by the might of All-father, were formed a son named Mimer and a daughter named Bestla. From Mimer were descended the Vana-gods. Under the feet of Ymer arose a monstrous six-headed son, who was the ancestor of the evil frost giants, the dreaded Hrimthursar. Then Ymer awoke.

For Audhumla, the great cow, there was no vegetation upon which to feed. She stood on the verge of gloom, and found sustenance by licking constantly the huge boulders that were encrusted by salt and rime. For the space of a day she fed in this manner, until the hair of a great head appeared. On the second day the cow returned to the boulder, and when she had ceased to lick, a head of human semblance was laid bare. On the third day a noble form leapt forth. He was endowed with great beauty, and was nimble and powerful. The name he received was Bure, and he was the first of the Asa-gods.

There followed in time more beings—noble giants and wicked giants, and gods. Mimer, who is Mind and Memory, had daughters, the chief of whom was Urd, Goddess of Fate and Queen of Life and Death. Bure had a son named Bor, who took for his wife Bestla, the sister of wise Mimer. Three sons were born to them, and the first was called Odin (spirit), the second Ve whose other name is Honer, and the third Vile, whose other names are Lodur and Loke. Odin became the chief ruler of the Asa-gods, and Honer was chief of the Vans until Loke, the usurper, became their ruler.

Now Ymer and his evil sons were moved with wrath and enmity against the family of gods, and soon warfare broke out between them. To neither side was there early victory, and the fierce conflicts were waged through the long ages before the earth was formed. But, at length, the sons of Bor prevailed over their enemies and drove them back. In time there followed a great slaughter, which diminished the army of evil giants until one alone remained.

It was thus that the gods achieved their triumph. Ymer was stricken down, and the victors leapt upon him and then slit open the bulging veins of his neck. A great deluge of blood gushed forth, and the whole race of giants was drowned save Bergelmer, "The Mountain-old", who with his wife took refuge on the timbers of the great World-mill, and remained there. From these are descended the Jotuns, who forever harbored enmity against the gods.

The great World-mill of the gods was under care of Mundilfore (Lodur-Loke). Nine giant maids turned it with much violence, and the grinding of the stones made such fearsome clamor that the loudest tempests could not be heard. The great mill is larger than is the whole world, for out of it the mold of earth was ground.

When Ymer was dead, the gods took counsel among themselves, and set forth to frame the world. They laid the body of the clay-giant on the mill, and the maids ground it. The stones were smeared with blood, and the dark flesh came out as mold. Thus was earth produced, and the gods shaped it to their desire. From Ymer's bones were made the rocks and the mountains; his teeth and jaws were broken asunder, and as they went round at their labor the giant maids flung the fragments here and there, and these are the pebbles and boulders. The ice-cold blood of the giant became the waters of the vast engulfing sea.

Nor did the giant maids cease their labors when the body of Ymer was completely ground, and the earth was framed and set in order by the gods. The body of giant after giant was laid upon the mill, which stands beneath the floor of Ocean, and the flesh-grist is the sand which is ever washed up round the shores of the world. Where the waters are sucked through the whirling eye of the millstone is a fearsome maelstrom, and the sea ebbs and flows as it is drawn down to Hvergelmer, "the roaring cauldron", in Nifel-heim and thrown forth again. The very heavens are made to swing by the great World-mill, round Veraldar Nagli, "the world spike", which is the Polar Star.

Now when the gods had shaped the earth they set Ymer's skull over it to be the heavens. At each of the four corners they put as sentinels the strong dwarfs East and West and North and South. The skull of Ymer rests upon their broad shoulders.

As yet the sun knew not her home, nor the moon her power, and the stars had no fixed dwelling place.

Now the stars are bright fire-sparks sprayed from Muspel-heim over the great gulf, and these the gods fixed in the heavens to give light to the world and to shine over the sea. To these and to every wandering fire-flake they assigned due order and motion, so that each has its set place and time and season.

The sun and the moon were also regulated in their courses, for these are the greater fire-disks that were sprayed from Muspel-heim, and to bear them over the paths of the heavens the gods caused the elf-smiths, the sons of Ivalde and the kinsmen of Sindre, to fashion chariots of fine gold.

Mundilfore, who has care of the World-mill, aspired to rival Odin. He had two beautiful children, and one he called Mani (moon), and the other Sol (sun). The gods were filled with anger because of Mundilfore's presumption, and to punish him they took from him his two children, of whom he was exceedingly boastful, to drive the heavenly chariots and count the years for men. Fair Sol they set to drive the sun-chariot. Her steeds are Arvak, which is "Early Dawn", and Alsvid, which signifies "scorching heat". Under their withers were placed skins of ice-chilled air for coolness and refreshment. They enter the eastern heaven at Hela-gate, through which the souls of dead men pass to the world beneath.

Then the gods set Mani, the handsome youth, to drive the chariot of the moon. With him are two fair children whom he carried away from earth—a boy who was called Hyuki, and a girl whose name is Bil. They had been sent out in the darkness of night by Vidfinner, their father, to draw song-mead from the mountain spring Byrger, "the hidden", which broke forth from the source of Mimer's fount; and they filled their pail Saegr to the brink, so that the precious mead spilled over as they raised it on the pole Simul. When they began to descend the mountain, Mani seized them and took them away. The spots that are ever seen by night on the fair-faced moon are Hyuki and Bil, and beautiful Bil do poets invoke, so that hearing them she may sprinkle from the moon the magic song-mead upon their lips.

In Mani's keeping is a bundle of thorns from which evildoers among men must suffer the punishment of piercing pains.

The sun is ever in flight, and so also is the moon. They are pursued by bloodthirsty enemies, who seek to compass their destruction when they reach the sheltering forest of the Varns, behind the western horizon. These are two fierce and gigantic wolves. The one whose name is Skoll, "the adherer", chases the sun, whom one day it will devour; the other is Hati, "the hater", who races in front of "the bright maiden of heaven", in ceaseless pursuit of the moon.

Skoll and Hati are giants in wolf-guise. They were sent forth by the Mother of Evil, the dark and fearsome Hag, Gulveig-Hoder, whose children they are. She dwells in the Iarnvid, the black forest of iron trees, on the world's edge, which is the habitation of a witch family dreaded both by gods and by men. Of the Hag's wolf-sons the most terrible is Hati, who is also called Managarm, "the moon devourer". He feeds on the blood of dying men. The seers have foretold that when he comes to swallow the moon, the heavens and the earth shall turn red with blood. Then too, must the seats of the mighty gods be reddened with gore, and the sunshine of summer be made dim, while great storms burst in fury to rage across the world.

Again and again, at the dreaded eclipse, would these giant wolves have swallowed now the sun and now the moon, had not their evil designs been thwarted by spells which were wrought against them, and the clamor of frightened men.

Now Nat, which is Night, is the dark-skinned daughter of the Vana-giant Narve, "the Binder", whose other name is Mimer. Dark is her hair like all her race, and her eyes are soft and benevolent. She brings rest to the toiler, and refreshment to the weary, and sleep and dreams to all. To the warrior she gives strength so that he may win victory, and care and sorrow she loves to take away. Nat is the beneficent mother of gods. Three times was she wed. Her first husband was Nagelfare of the stars, and their son was Aud of bountiful riches. Her second husband was Annar, "Water", and their daughter, Jörd, the earth-goddess, was Odin's wife and the mother of Thor. Her third husband was Delling, the red elf of dawn, and their son was Dagr, which is Day.

To mother Nat and her son Dagr were given jewelled chariots to drive across the world, one after the other, in the space of twelve hours. Nat is first to set forth. Her steed is called Hrim Faxi, "frosted mane". Swiftly it gallops over the heavens, and every morn the sweet foam from its bit falls as dewdrops upon the earth beneath. Dagr's fair steed is called Skin Faxi, "shining mane". From its golden neck is shed radiance and beauty upon the heavens and over all the world. Of all coursers that are, he is praised most by faring men.

There are two seasons, and these are Winter and Summer. Vindsval, son of gloomy Vasud, "the ice wind", was father of grim Winter, and the mild and beneficent Svasud was the sire of fair Summer, beloved by all.

It is the wonder of men, from where comes the wind that shakes the ocean with fear, that fans the low spark into bright flame, and that no eye can behold. At the northern summit of heaven there sits in eagle-guise a great giant called Hraesvelgur, "the swallower of dead men's flesh". When his wide pinions are spread for flight the winds are stirred beneath them and rush down upon the earth. When coming or going, or travelling here and there across the heavens, the winds are driven from his wings.

As yet there were no men who had their dwelling upon the earth, although the sun and moon were set in their courses, and the days and seasons were marked out in due order. There came a time, however, when the sons of Bor were walking on the world's shores, and they beheld two logs of wood. They were grown from Ymer's hair, which sprang up as thick forests and verdure abundant from the mold of his body, which is the earth. One log was of an ash tree, and from it the gods shaped a man; and the other, which was an alder tree, they made into a fair woman. They had but life like a tree which grows until the gods gave them mind and will and desire. Then was the man named Ask and the woman Embla, and from them are descended the entire human race, whose habitation is called Midgard, "middle ward", and Mana-heim, "home of men".

Round Midgard is the embracing sea, and beyond, on the outward shores, is Jotun-heim, the home of giants. Against these the gods raised an ice bulwark shaped from the eyebrows of turbulent Ymer, whose brains they cast high in heaven, where they became heavy masses of scattered cloud, tossing here and there.

The Nine Worlds

Excerpt. The Nine Worlds. Updated and edited version of the text from Teutonic Myth and Legend, by Donald A. Mackenzie

The Asa-gods built for themselves Asgard, the celestial city, which is set high above the heavens. It stands there in beauty and in glory upon a holy island in the midst of a dark broad river flowing from the thunder-vapors that rise through the great World-tree from Hvergelmer, "the roaring cauldron", the mother of waters. The river is ever troubled with eddies and fierce currents, and above it hover dark, thick banks of kindling mist called "Black Terror Gleam", from which leap everlastingly tongues of vapor-flame (lightning), filling the air and darting like white froth from whirling billows.

Around Asgard is a dark and lofty wall, and the great boiling river breaks angrily at its base. There is no entry-way except by Odin's mighty gate. And if anyone who is unworthy, be he god or giant or mortal, should cross the river unscathed by the vapor-flames, and seek to open the gate of Asgard, he would be caught suddenly by a chain which springs from the lock of strange mechanism, and crushed and utterly destroyed.

In the middle of Asgard was built stately Idavoll, the Court of Judgment, the High Forum of the Gods, in which their own divine affairs are discussed and arranged. The beauty of the great hall is unequaled in the nine worlds, for its roof is of shining silver and it is resplendent without and within with polished and graven gold. Therein was set the great golden throne of Odin, the chief ruler of Asgard, and around it were placed twelve golden seats for the gods who sit with him in judgment, and to whom the All-father gave power to rule and to issue decrees.

When Odin sits on his high golden throne he looks over the homes of giants and elves and mortals and sees all things. He is silent and he listens.

Another fair and stately structure did the gods cause to be made as a sanctuary for the goddesses, and by singers of songs who echo its praises it is called Vingolf, "the abode of friends".

In Asgard was shaped a smithy which was furnished with anvils and hammers and tongs. With these the gods had made for them, by the cunning elf-smiths, Ivalde's sons and Sindre's kinsmen, every instrument they had need of. They worked in fine metals, and so great was the treasure of gold that all movables were made of it.

On a green place in the celestial city were found the golden tablets with which was played the Game of the Gods. This was in the Golden Age, which lasted until there came from Jotun-heim three giant maids, who brought corruption.

To the gods in ages past it became known that there dwelt in Midgard a race of dwarfs. In the deep, dark mold of Ymer's body they swarmed as do maggots in rotted flesh, and they went here and there with no purpose or knowledge. All the gods assembled in their high Forum, with Odin seated on his golden throne, and there took counsel one with another. To the dwarfs they gave human shape, but their hue was the blackness of earth in which they had being. Over them the gods set Modsognir, who is Mimer, to be king. In the mounds of the earth dwell one tribe of these dark elves, within rocks another, and a third have their habitation inside high and precipitous mountains. Besides these are the Trolls, who fly here and there carrying bundles of sticks, and have power to change their shape. Now the wonder of the Universe, which was set in order by the will of All-father, is the great ash tree, Ygdrasil, the Tree of Existence, which nourishes and sustains all spiritual and physical life. Its roots are spread through the divisions of the worlds that fill the yawning gulf, and its boughs are above the high celestial city of the gods. It grows out of the past, it lives in the present, and it reaches towards the future.

The World-ash has three great roots. In the realms below Midgard is one root, which receives warmth and life in Hela's glittering plains from the deep fountain of Urd, the goddess of fate and of death; another root reaches the egg-white well of Mimer, who is Wisdom and Memory; and the last root is in gloomy Nifel-heim, where it finds hardening sustenance in

Hvergelmer, "the roaring cauldron", the fountain of primeval waters, ice-cold and everlasting, which springs up on Hvergelmer mountain.

In the realm of Urd, which is Hela, the souls of good men dwell. Near it, in the underworld, is Mimer's well in Mimer's grove, where dwells the race which will regenerate the world of men. Below cold and dark Nifel-heim are the nine divisions of torture in which the souls of the wicked are punished. At Hvergelmer the watchman of the root of Ygdrasil is Ivalde, who, with his sons, contends against the storm-giants who threaten Hela.

The roots of the great World-tree suck up the waters of the three eternal fountains, and these mixed together give imperishable life. In the well of wise Mimer the fibers are made white with the holy mead which gives wisdom to men, and poetry also, and is the very elixir of life eternal.

On the high branches of Ygdrasil, which overshadow Asgard, sits a wise eagle, and between its eyes is perched a hawk named Vedfolner. On the topmost bough is Goldcomb, the "cock of the north", which awakens the gods from sleep and puts the demons to flight. From Hela answers the red cock, whose fire purifies what is good and destroys what is evil.

But the great World-tree bears a more painful burden than mortals can conceive. In the well of Hvergelmer, in the black realm of Nifel-heim, is the corpse-eating dragon Nidhog, "the lower one", which chews constantly at the root; above, four giant deer are ever biting its buds and its leaves; on its side, age rots it; and many serpents gnaw its tender fibers in the dark underworld. For there never was good to which evil came not, nor growth which has known not decay and the wasting of time.

The Norns of Hela sprinkle the great ash-tree each morning with precious mead from Urd's fountain of life so that its leaves may ever be green. From there comes the honey-dew, which drips upon the world and is stored by the bees. And in Urd's fountain are the two mystic swans which are the ancestors of the swan race in Midgard.

Up and down the World-tree runs constantly the squirrel Ratatosk, which bears gossip between the eagle on the highest branches and the dragon Nidhog at the root, and is thus ever the cause of strife. Greatly dreaded is Nidhog, who flies to the rocks and cliffs of the lower world with the bodies of dead men beneath its wings.

The three Fates, who are called Norns, are Urd and her two sisters–Urd, "present"; Verdande, "past"; and Skuld, "future". By them are spun at will the fates of men and women. There are also Dises, who are maids of Urd, to whom various duties are assigned. The Hamingjes are those Dises who are guardians of men through their lives, and appear to them in dreams to give warnings and noble counsel, and he whom the holy elf deserts for wrongdoing is indeed lost. The decrees of Urd are executed by the Giptes, and men who are favored are suddenly awarded good fortune and treasure; other Dises attend upon families and even upon tribes. There are also the sweet elf-maids who have care of babes unborn in the fair realms of Urd, and find them kind mothers in the world of men; and there are maids who conduct the souls of the dead to Hela's glittering plain.

Now in Hela is the lower-world Forum of the gods, where the souls of the dead are judged, and rewards and punishments are meted out by Odin. There is but one road there from Asgard for all the gods save Thor, and that is over the curved bridge Bif-rost, "the rainbow", which has its foundation beyond the edge of the world of men. The southern span reaches to the fountain of Urd in the realms of green vegetation that never know decay.

Bif-rost is built of air and water, and is protected by red fire flaming on its edge. Frost giants and mountain giants ever seek to capture the bridge, so that they may ascend to Asgard and overcome the gods; but its sentinel, Heimdal, is constantly on guard against them.

The gods set Heimdal, son of the waves, to protect the bridge forever against the enemy. He is clad in silver armor, and on his head is a polished helmet with ram's horns. Horsed on his swift steed, Gull-top, he now watches at the highest point of Bif-rost from his fortified citadel, Himinbjorg, "the ward of heaven", where his hall is supplied with precious mead. Shortly he crosses over from side to side of the bridge. His sight is so keen that he can see by night as well as by day the length of a hundred leagues, and he listens so keenly that he can hear the grass growing. He sleeps as little and as lightly as a bird. When the giants and monsters come to assail the gods at Ragnarok, Heimdal shall blow a thunder-blast on Gjallar-horn which is hidden in the deepest shade of the World-tree. With his great sword he shall combat with the Evil One in the Last Battle.

Heimdal is loved both by gods and by men, and he is also called Gullintani because his teeth are of gold. There was a time when he went to Midgard as a child; he grew up to be a teacher among men, and was named Scef.

Every day the horses of the gods thunder over Bif-rost as they descend to and return from the lower-world Forum. Thor, the thunder god, cannot travel this way because the fire of his thunder chariot might set the bridge aflame and destroy it. He must wade across the four great girdling rivers in the underworld to reach Hela's glittering plains.

When the gods come to Hela they leap from their horses and take their seats in the Forum. The dead are then brought before them.

A weary and long way these dead men and women have traveled Down the valley of thorns they came, and those who were given hel-shoes in their graves, because they had shown mercy to others while they lived, suffered indeed little; but the feet of the wicked were torn and bleeding. Then they crossed a river full of weapons. The just walked over on boards, but the unjust waded, and were sorely wounded and covered with scars, so that their bodies dripped blood.

To the Forum come men and women in full attire, with the jewels and ornaments which those who loved them placed on their bodies when they were laid in grave chambers. Warriors carry their weapons, and all are clad so that they may be recommended to the gods as the well-beloved among men. But silent are the dead, save the happy ones under whose tongues were placed, before they were laid in their graves, magic runes, so that they might make answer when accused, and give reasons to justify their deeds. But the Hamingjes can also speak for the dead, and those who have not Hamingjes to speak for them are known to have done evil and to be deserted by their Dises in sorrow and wrath. Those who are justified pass to the eternal realms of Hela, where joy prevails, because they have lived upright lives, and have been honorable and full of pity and have helped others; because they were brave and feared not to die; and also because they worshiped the gods and gave offerings in the temples.

But those who are condemned are sent to Nifel-hel, the region of torture.

They are judged to be unworthy if they injured others by falsehoods or wicked deeds, if they were adulterers, or murderers, or despoilers of graves, or cowards, or were traitors, and profaners of the temples.

Those who are to share eternal joy are given to drink from the horn of Urd, which imparts to them enduring strength. In it are mixed the three meads from the wells which sustain Ygdrasil, the World-ash. But the doomed are given a draft of burning venom which changes them to monsters. Their tongues are then for ever bereft of speech and they can only moan.

The happy dead disport themselves on the green plains of Hela, where they meet lost friends and ancestors from the earliest years of the world. And many beautiful ways they travel, and wonderful tales they hear. The children are cared for in the realm of Mimer, "memory", where joy is theirs forever and their food is honeydew.

The doomed are fettered and are driven towards Nifel-hel by black elves, who carry thorny rods with which they lash those who falter or seek to turn back. Their first punishment is received when they must pass through the regions of eternal bliss, and behold with grief unutterable the joy of the blessed. Then they cross the rivers which girdle Hela, and climb towards the dark mountains of Nifel-hel. The wolf dog barks at them in the shadowy valley where it guards the borders of

Hela, and there is blood on its breast. And as they climb tortuous paths and tread the narrow path on the edge of dizzy precipices they hear the barking of the terrible watchdogs at Nifel-hel's gates. The dreaded dragon, Nidhog, hovers near them, and ferocious birds of prey sit on the rocks.

Then they enter the Na-gates and die the second death. Punishment is given in the nine realms of torture according to the sins that were committed. Some are seized by the dragon and some by the birds of prey, according to their deserts. Others are tempted forever by illusions of sinful things they sought in life, and there are those who are torn to pieces by the great wolf.

In the Venom-dale is a river called Slid, and it is full of daggers and sharp spears. Through it must wade the perjurers and murderers and adulterers, who are continually suffering new and fierce wounds. Others sit together on benches of iron, while venom drips on them, within a hall which is full of stench unbearable. Traitors are hung on trees, and cowards are drowned in pools of foulness. Eternal night broods over all.

Naglefar, the "ship of death", lies in the Gulf of Black Grief, in the outer regions of Nifel-hel, made fast to a dark island with chains that shall not sever until Ragnarok, "the dusk of the gods". It is constructed of the parings of dead men's nails–the wicked men, hated by their kind because of their evil deeds, whose bodies were cleansed not at life's end, and whose nails were not pared when they were laid in grave-chambers. When Naglefar breaks loose the avenging hosts shall sail in it to battle against the gods.

The warriors who are slain in battle, or drowned at sea, are borne to Valhal in Asgard by the maids of Urd, who are called Valkyries. They are horsed on swift steeds, and first they pass to Hela, where the gods give judgment and reject the unworthy. Then they are carried by the Valkyries over Bif-rost, and the hoofs of their steeds resound in Asgard. In great Valhal the heroes feast with Odin in eternal triumph and happiness.

Now these are the divisions of the Universe. In the midst is the earth, Midgard, which is encircled by the ocean. On high, and above all else, is Asgard, and below it is the realm of white elves, who flit between the branches of the great World-tree. Then Vana-heim, the home of the Vana-gods, is in the air and in the sea; and in the depths of the western sea is the hall of Aeger, god of Ocean. Alf-heim, the home of elves, is to the east. In the lower world, below Nifelheim, are the Nifel-hel regions of torture, and under Midgard are the Hela realms of Mimer and of Urd. Far below the path of the gods towards Hela's fields of bliss are Surtur's deep dales on the borders of Muspel-heim, where the great giant Surtur, the swarthy sentinel, keeps watch with his flaming sword. Jotun-heim is to the north and the east, beyond the world's edge.

Billing is the elf-guardian of the western heaven, and when the cars of Day and of Night and of the Sun and of the Moon enter the forest of the Varns, "the protectors", they pass through the lower-world realms of Mimer and of Urd towards the gates of Delling, the elf of dawn, in the east. When Nat reaches Hela, where she must rest, darkness falls around her, and the blessed are given sleep, and light comes again with Dagr, as Nat covers the earth above with shadow and deep slumber.

From Holy Races

Excerpt. Voluspo. Updated and edited version from The Poetic Edda, Volume I, by Henry Adams Bellows.

1 Hearing I ask from the holy races, From Heimdall's sons, both high and low; You will, Valfather, that well I relate, Old tales I remember of men long ago.

2 I remember yet the giants of old, Who gave me bread in the days gone by; Nine worlds I knew, the nine in the tree, With mighty roots beneath the mold.

3 Of old was the age when Ymir lived; Sea nor cool waves nor sand there were; Earth had not been, nor heaven above, But a yawning gap, and grass nowhere.

4 Then Bur's sons lifted the level land, Mithgarth the mighty there they made; The sun from the south warmed the stones of earth, And green was the ground with growing leeks.

5 The sun, the sister of the moon, from the south, Her right hand cast over heaven's rim; No knowledge she had where her home should be, The moon knew not what might was his, The stars knew not where their stations were.

6 Then sought the gods their assembly-seats, The holy ones, and council held; Names then gave they to noon and twilight, Morning they named, and the waning moon, Night and evening, the years to number.

7 At Ithavoll met the mighty gods, Shrines and temples they timbered high; Forges they set, and they smithed ore, Tongs they wrought, and tools they fashioned.

8 In their dwellings at peace they played at tables, Of gold no lack did the gods then know, Till there came up giant-maids three, Huge of might, out of Jotunheim.

9 Then sought the gods their assembly-seats, The holy ones, and council held, To find who should raise the race of dwarfs, Out of Brimir's blood and the legs of Blain.

10 There was Motsognir the mightiest made, Of all the dwarfs, and Durin next; Many a likeness of men they made, The dwarfs in the earth, as Durin said.

11 Nyi and Nithi, Northri and Suthri, Austri and Vestri, Althjof, Dvalin, Nar and Nain, Niping, Dain, Bifur, Bofur, Bombur, Nori, An and Onar, Ai, Mjothvitnir.

12 Vigg and Gandalf, Vindalf, Thrain, Thekk and Thorin, Thror, Vit and Lit, Nyr and Nyrath, now have I told– Regin and Rathsvith– the list aright.

13 Fili, Kili, Fundin, Nali, Heptifili, Hannar, Sviur, Frar, Hornbori, Fraeg and Loni, Aurvang, Jari, Eikinskjaldi.

14 The race of the dwarfs in Dvalin's throng, Down to Lofar the list must I tell; The rocks they left, and through wet lands, They sought a home in the fields of sand.

15 There were Draupnir and Dolgthrasir, Hor, Haugspori, Hlevang, Gloin, Dori, Ori, Duf, Andvari, Skirfir, Virfir, Skafith, Ai.

16 Alf and Yngvi, Eikinskjaldi, Fjalar and Frosti, Fith and Ginnar; So for all time shall the tale be known, The list of all the forbears of Lofar.

17 Then from the throng did three come forth, From the home of the gods, the mighty and gracious; Two without fate on the land they found, Ask and Embla, empty of might.

18 Soul they had not, sense they had not, Heat nor motion, nor good hue; Soul gave Othin, sense gave Hönir, Heat gave Lothur and good hue.

19 An ash I know, Yggdrasil its name, With water white is the great tree wet; From there come the dews that fall in the dales, Green by Urth's well does it ever grow.

20 From there come the maidens mighty in wisdom, Three from the dwelling down beneath the tree; Urth is one named, Verthandi the next, On the wood they scored, and Skuld the third. Laws they made there, and life allotted, To the sons of men, and set their fates.

21 The war I remember, the first in the world, When the gods with spears had smitten Gollveig, And in the hall of Hor had burned her, Three times burned, and three times born, Oft and again, yet ever she lives.

22 Heith they named her who sought their home, The wide-seeing witch, in magic wise; Minds she bewitched that were moved by her magic, To evil women a joy she was.

23 On the host his spear did Othin hurl, Then in the world did war first come; The wall that girdled the gods was broken, And the field by the warlike Wanes was trodden.

24 Then sought the gods their assembly-seats, The holy ones, and council held, Whether the gods should tribute give, Or to all alike should worship belong.

25 Then sought the gods their assembly-seats, The holy ones, and council held, To find who with venom the air had filled, Or had given Oth's bride to the giants' brood.

26 In swelling rage then rose up Thor, Seldom he sits when he such things hears, And the oaths were broken, the words and bonds, The mighty pledges between them made.

27 I know of the horn of Heimdall, hidden, Under the high-reaching holy tree; On it there pours from Valfather's pledge, A mighty stream: would you know yet more?

28 Alone I sat when the Old One

sought me, The terror of gods, and gazed in mine eyes: "What have you to ask? Why do you come here? Othin, I know where your eye is hidden."

29 I know where Othin's eye is hidden, Deep in the wide-famed well of Mimir; Mead from the pledge of Othin each morn, Does Mimir drink: would you know yet more?

30 Necklaces had I and rings from Heerfather, Wise was my speech and my magic wisdom; [...] Widely I saw over all the worlds.

31 On all sides saw I Valkyries assemble, Ready to ride to the ranks of the gods; Skuld bore the shield, and Skogul rode next, Guth, Hild, Gondul, and Geirskogul. Of Herjan's maidens the list have ye heard, Valkyries ready to ride over the earth.

32 I saw for Baldr, the bleeding god, The son of Othin, his destiny set: Famous and fair in the lofty fields, Full grown in strength the mistletoe stood.

33 From the branch which seemed so slender and fair, Came a harmful shaft that Hoth should hurl; But the brother of Baldr was born before long, And one night old fought Othin's son.

34 His hands he washed not, his hair he combed not, Till he bore to the bale-blaze Baldr's foe. But in Fensalir did Frigg weep sore, For Valhall's need: would you know yet more?

35 One did I see in the wet woods bound, A lover of ill, and to Loki like; By his side does Sigyn sit, nor is glad, To see her mate: would you know yet more?

36 From the east there pours through poisoned vales, With swords and daggers the river Slith. [...] [...]

37 Northward a hall in Nithavellir, Of gold there rose for Sindri's race; And in Okolnir another stood, Where the giant Brimir his beer-hall had.

38 A hall I saw, far from the sun, On Nastrond it stands, and the doors face north, Venom drops through the smoke-vent down, For around the walls do serpents wind.

39 I saw there wading through rivers wild, Treacherous men and murderers too, And workers of ill with the wives of men; There Nithhogg sucked the blood of the slain, And the wolf tore men; would you know yet more?

40 The giantess old in Ironwood sat, In the east, and bore the brood of Fenrir; Among these, one in monster's guise, Was soon to steal the sun from the sky.

41 There feeds he, full on the flesh of the dead, And the home of the gods he reddens with gore; Dark grows the sun, and in summer soon, Come mighty storms: would you know yet more?

42 On a hill there sat, and smote on his harp, Eggther the joyous, the giants' warder; Above him the cock in the bird-wood crowed, Fair and red did Fjalar stand.

43 Then to the gods crowed Gollinkambi, He wakes the heroes in Othin's hall; And beneath the earth does another crow, The rust-red bird at the bars of Hel.

44 Now Garm howls loud before Gnipahellir, The fetters will burst, and

the wolf run free; Much do I know, and more can see, Of the fate of the gods, the mighty in fight.

45 Brothers shall fight and fell each other, And sisters' sons shall kinship stain; Hard is it on earth, with mighty whoredom; Axe-time, sword-time, shields are sundered, Wind-time, wolf-time, when the world falls; Never shall men each other spare.

46 Fast move the sons of Mim, and fate, Is heard in the note of the Gjallarhorn; Loud blows Heimdall, the horn is aloft, In fear quake all who on Hel-roads are.

47 Yggdrasil shakes, and shiver on high, The ancient limbs, and the giant is loose; To the head of Mim does Othin give heed, But the kinsman of Surt shall slay him soon.

48 How fare the gods? how fare the elves? All Jotunheim groans, the gods are at council; Loud roar the dwarfs by the doors of stone, The masters of the rocks: would you know yet more?

49 Now Garm howls loud before Gnipahellir, The fetters will burst, and the wolf run free, Much do I know, and more can see, Of the fate of the gods, the mighty in fight.

50 From the east comes Hrym with shield held high; In giant-wrath does the serpent writhe; Over the waves he twists, and the tawny eagle, Gnaws corpses screaming; Naglfar is loose.

51 Over the sea from the north there sails a ship, With the people of Hel, at the helm stands Loki; After the wolf do wild men follow, And with them the brother of Byleist goes.

52 Surt fares from the south with the scourge of branches, The sun of the battle-gods shone from his sword; The crags are sundered, the giant-women sink, The dead throng Hel-way, and heaven is cloven.

53 Now comes to Hlin yet another hurt, When Othin fares to fight with the wolf, And Beli's fair slayer seeks out Surt, For there must fall the joy of Frigg.

54 Then comes Sigfather's mighty son, Vithar, to fight with the foaming wolf; In the giant's son does he thrust his sword, Full to the heart: his father is avenged.

55 Here there comes the son of Hlothyn, The bright snake gapes to heaven above; [...] Against the serpent goes Othin's son.

56 In anger smites the warder of earth, Forth from their homes must all men flee;- Nine paces fares the son of Fjorgyn, And, slain by the serpent, fearless he sinks.

57 The sun turns black, earth sinks in the sea, The hot stars down from heaven are whirled; Fierce grows the steam and the life-feeding flame, Till fire leaps high about heaven itself.

58 Now Garm howls loud before Gnipahellir, The fetters will burst, and the wolf run free; Much do I know, and more can see, Of the fate of the gods, the mighty in fight.

59 Now do I see the earth anew, Rise all green from the waves again; The cataracts fall, and the eagle flies, And fish he catches beneath the cliffs.

60 The gods in Ithavoll meet to-

gether, Of the terrible girdler of earth they talk, And the mighty past they call to mind, And the ancient runes of the Ruler of Gods.

61 In wondrous beauty once again, Shall the golden tables stand mid the grass, Which the gods had owned in the days of old [...]

62 Then fields unsowed bear ripened fruit, All ills grow better, and Baldr comes back; Baldr and Hoth dwell in Hropt's battle-hall, And the mighty gods: would you know yet more?

63 Then Hönir wins the prophetic wand, [...] And the sons of the brothers of Tveggi abide, In Vindheim now: would you know yet more?

64 More fair than the sun, a hall I see, Roofed with gold, on Gimle it stands; There shall the righteous rulers dwell, And happiness ever there shall they have.

65 There comes on high, all power to hold, A mighty lord, all lands he rules. Rule he orders, and rights he fixes, Laws he ordains that ever shall live.

66 From below the dragon dark comes forth, Nithhogg flying from Nithafjoll; The bodies of men on his wings he bears, The serpent bright: but now must I sink.

Baldr's Dreams

Excerpt. Baldrs Draumar. Updated and edited version from The Poetic Edda, Volume I, by Henry Adams Bellows.

1 Once were the gods together met, And the goddesses came and council held, And the far-famed ones the truth would find, Why baleful dreams to Baldr had come.

2 Then Othin rose, the enchanter old, And the saddle he laid on Sleipnir's back; From there rode he down to Niflhel deep, And the hound he met that came from hell.

3 Bloody he was on his breast before, At the father of magic he howled from afar; Forward rode Othin, the earth resounded, Till the house so high of Hel he reached.

4 Then Othin rode to the eastern door, There, he knew well, was the wise-woman's grave; Magic he spoke and mighty charms, Till spell-bound she rose, and in death she spoke:

5 "What is the man, to me unknown, That has made me travel the troublesome road? I was snowed on with snow, and smitten with rain, And drenched with dew; long was I dead."

Othin spoke:

6 "Vegtam my name, I am Valtam's son; Speak you of hell, for of heaven I know: For whom are the benches bright with rings, And the platforms happily bedecked with gold?"

The Wise-Woman spoke:

7 "Here for Baldr the mead is brewed, The shining drink, and a shield lies over it; But their hope is gone from the mighty gods. Unwilling I spoke, and now would be still."

Othin spoke:

8 "Wise-woman, cease not! I seek from you, All to know that I fain would

ask: Who shall the bane of Baldr become, And steal the life from Othin's son?"

The Wise-Woman spoke:

9 "Hoth there bears the far-famed branch, He shall the bane of Baldr become, And steal the life from Othin's son. Unwilling I spoke, and now would be still."

Othin spoke:

10 "Wise-woman, cease not! I seek from you, All to know that I fain would ask: Who shall vengeance win for the evil work, Or bring to the flames the slayer of Baldr?"

The Wise-Woman spoke:

11 "Rind bears Vali in Vestrsalir, And one night old fights Othin's son; His hands he shall wash not, his hair he shall comb not, Till the slayer of Baldr he brings to the flames. Unwilling I spoke, and now would be still."

Othin spoke:

12 "Wise-woman, cease not! I seek from you, All to know that I fain would ask: What maidens are they who then shall weep, And toss to the sky the yards of the sails?"

The Wise-Woman spoke:

13 "Vegtam you are not, as formerly I thought; Othin you are, the enchanter old."

Othin spoke:

"No wise-woman are you, nor wisdom have; Of giants three the mother are you."

The Wise-Woman spoke:

14 "Home ride, Othin, be ever proud; For no one of men shall seek me more, Till Loki wanders loose from his bonds, And to the last strife the destroyers come."

Chapter 9

Glimmering Waters

Of Heaven and Earth

Koh Nga Tama A Rangi. Updated and edited version of the text from Polynesian Mythology and Ancient Traditional History Of The New Zealanders as Furnished by Their Priests And Chiefs, by Sir George Grey

Men had but one pair of primitive ancestors; they sprang from the vast heaven that exists above us, and from the earth which lies beneath us. According to the traditions of our race, Rangi and Papa, or Heaven and Earth, were the source from which, in the beginning, all things originated. Darkness then rested upon the heaven and upon the earth, and they still both clung together, for they had not yet been torn apart; and the children they had begotten were ever thinking amongst themselves what might be the difference between darkness and light; they knew that beings had multiplied and increased, and yet light had never broken upon them, but it ever continued dark. Hence these sayings are found in our ancient religious services: "There was darkness from the first division of time, to the tenth, to the hundredth, to the thousandth", that is, for a vast space of time; and these divisions of times were considered as beings, and were each termed "a Po"; and on their account there was as yet no world with its bright light, but darkness only for the beings which existed.

At last the beings who had been begotten by Heaven and Earth, worn out by the continued darkness, consulted amongst themselves, saying: "Let us now determine what we should do with Rangi and Papa, whether it would be better to slay them or to tear them apart." Then spoke Tu-matauenga, the fiercest of the children of Heaven and Earth: "It is well, let us slay them."

Then spoke Tane-mahuta, the father of forests and of all things that inhabit them, or that are constructed from trees: "No, not so. It is better to tear them apart, and to let the heaven stand far above us, and the earth lie under our feet. Let the sky become as a stranger to us, but the earth remains close to us as our nursing mother."

The brothers all consented to this proposal, with the exception of Tawhiri-ma-tea, the father of winds and storms, and he, fearing that his kingdom was about to be overthrown, grieved greatly at the thought of his parents being torn apart. Five of the brothers willingly consented to the separation of their parents, but one of them would not agree to it.

Hence, also, these sayings of old are found in our prayers: "Darkness, darkness, light, light, the seeking, the searching, in chaos, in chaos"; these signified the way in which the offspring of heaven and earth sought for some mode of dealing with their parents, so that human beings might increase and live.

So, also, these sayings of old time. "The multitude, the length," signified the multitude of the thoughts of the children of Heaven and Earth, and the length of time they considered whether they should slay their parents, that human beings might be called into existence; for it was in this manner that they talked and consulted amongst themselves.

But at length their plans having been agreed on, Rongo-ma-tane, the god and father of the cultivated food of man, rises up, that he may tear apart the heavens and the earth; he struggles, but he tears them not apart. Next, Tangaroa, the god and father of fish and reptiles, rises up, that he may tear apart the heavens and the earth; he also struggles, but he tears them not apart. Next, Haumia-tikitiki, the god and father of the food of man which springs without cultivation, rises up and struggles, but ineffectually. Then, Tu-matauenga, the god and father of fierce human beings, rises up and struggles, but he, too, fails in his efforts. Then, at last, slowly uprises Tane-mahuta, the god and father of forests, of birds, and of insects, and he struggles with his parents; in vain he strives to tear them apart with his hands and arms. Then he pauses; his head is now firmly planted on his mother the earth, his feet he raises up and rests against his father the skies, he strains his back and limbs with mighty effort. Now are torn apart Rangi and Papa, and with cries and groans of woe they shriek aloud: "Why do you slay your parents? Why do you commit so dreadful a crime as to slay us, as to tear your parents apart?" But Tane-mahuta pauses not, he regards not their shrieks and cries; far beneath him he presses down the earth; far, far above him he thrusts up the sky.

Hence these sayings of olden time: "It was the fierce thrusting of Tane which tore the heaven from the earth, so that they were torn apart, and darkness was made manifest, and so was the light."

No sooner was heaven torn from earth than the multitude of human beings were discovered whom they had begotten, and who had previously lain concealed between the bodies of Rangi and Papa.

Then, also, there arose in the breast of Tawhiri-ma-tea, the god and father of winds and storms, a fierce desire to wage war with his brothers, because they had torn apart their common parents. He, from the first, had refused to consent to his mother being torn from her lord and children; it was his brothers alone that wished for this separation, and desired that Papa-tu-a-nuku, or the Earth alone, should be left as a parent for them.

The god of hurricanes and storms dreads also that the world should become too fair and beautiful, so he rises, follows his father to the realm above, and hurries to the sheltered hollows in the boundless skies; there he hides and clings, and nestling in this place of rest he consults long with his parent, and as the vast Heaven listens to the suggestions of Tawhiri-ma-tea, thoughts and plans are formed in his breast, and Tawhiri-ma-tea also understands what he should do. Then, by himself and the vast Heaven, were begotten his numerous brood, and they rapidly increased and grew. Tawhiri-ma-tea dispatches one of them to the west, and one to the south, and one to the east, and one to the north; and he gives corresponding names to himself and to his progeny, the mighty winds.

He next sends forth fierce squalls, whirlwinds, dense clouds, bulky clouds, dark clouds, gloomy thick clouds, fiery clouds, clouds which precede hurricanes, clouds of fiery black, clouds reflecting glowing red light, clouds wildly drifting from all quarters and wildly bursting, clouds of thunderstorms, and clouds hurriedly flying. in the midst of these Tawhiri-ma-tea himself sweeps wildly on. Alas! alas! then rages the fierce hurricane; and while Tane-mahuta and his gigantic forests still stand, unconscious and unsuspecting, the blast of the breath of the mouth of Tawhiri-ma-tea smites them, the gigantic trees are snapped off right in the middle. Alas! Alas! They are torn to atoms, dashed to the earth, with boughs and branches torn and scattered, and lying on the earth, trees and branches all alike left for the insect, for the grub, and for loathsome rottenness.

From the forests and their inhabitants Tawhiri-ma-tea next swoops down upon the seas, and lashes in his wrath the ocean. Ah! Ah! Waves steep as cliffs arise, whose summits are so lofty that to look from them would make the beholder giddy; these soon eddy in whirlpools, and Tangaroa, the god of ocean, and father of all that dwell therein, flies frightened through his seas; but before he fled, his children consulted together how they might secure their safety, for Tangaroa had begotten Punga, and he had begotten two children, Ika-tere, the father of fish, and Tu-te-wehiwehi, or Tu-te-wanawana, the father of reptiles.

When Tangaroa fled for safety to the ocean, then Tu-te-wehiwehi and Ika-tere, and their children, disputed together as to what they should do to escape from the storms, and Tu-te-wehiwehi and his party cried aloud: "Let us fly inland"; but Ika-tere and his party cried aloud: "Let us fly to the sea." Some would not obey one order, some would not obey the other, and they escaped in two parties: the party of Tu-te-wehiwehi, or the reptiles, hid themselves ashore; the party of Punga rushed to the sea. This is what, in our ancient religious services, is called the separation of Tawhiri-ma-tea.

Hence these traditions have been handed down: Ika-tere, the father of things which inhabit water, cried aloud to Tu-te-wehiwehi: "Ho, ho, let us all escape to the sea."

But Tu-te-wehiwehi shouted in answer: "No, nay, let us rather fly inland."

Then Ika-tere warned him, saying: "Fly inland, then; and the fate of you and your race will be, that when they catch you, before you are cooked, they will singe off your scales over a lighted wisp of dry fern."

But Tu-te-wehiwehi answered him, saying: "Seek safety, then, in the sea; and the future fate of your race will be, that when they serve out little baskets of cooked vegetable food to each person, you will be laid upon the top of the food to give a relish to it."

Then without delay these two races of beings separated. The fish fled in confusion to the sea, the reptiles sought safety in the forests and scrubs.

Tangaroa, enraged at some of his children deserting him, and, being sheltered by the god of the forests on dry land, has ever since waged war on his brother Tane, who, in return, has waged war against him.

Hence Tane supplies the offspring of his brother Tu-matauenga with canoes, with spears and with fish-hooks made from his trees, and with nets woven from his fibrous plants, that they may destroy the offspring of Tangaroa; while Tangaroa, in return, swallows up the offspring of Tane, overwhelming canoes with the surges of his sea, swallowing up the lands, trees, and houses that are swept off by floods, and ever wastes away, with his lapping waves, the shores that confine him, that the giants of the forests may be washed down and swept out into his boundless ocean, that he may then swallow up the insects, the young birds, and the various animals which inhabit them— all which things are recorded in the prayers which were offered to these gods.

Tawhiri-ma-tea next rushed on to attack his brothers Rongo-ma-tane and Haumia-tikitiki, the gods and progenitors of cultivated and uncultivated food; but Papa, to save these for her other children, caught them up, and hid them in a place of safety; and so well were these children of hers concealed by their mother Earth, that Tawhiri-ma-tea sought for them in vain.

Tawhiri-ma-tea having thus vanquished all his other brothers, next rushed against Tu-matauenga, to try his strength against his; he exerted all his force against him, but he could neither shake him nor prevail against him. What did Tu-matauenga care for his brother's wrath? He was the only one of the whole party of brothers who had planned the destruction of their parents, and had shown himself brave and fierce in war; his brothers had yielded at once before the tremendous assaults of Tawhiri-ma-tea and his progeny—Tane-mahuta and his offspring had been broken and torn in pieces—Tangaroa and his children had fled to the depths of the ocean or the recesses of the shore—Rongo-ma-tane and Haumia-tikitiki had been hidden from him in the earth—but Tu-matauenga, or man, still stood erect and unshaken upon the breast of his mother Earth; and now at length the hearts of Heaven and of the god of storms became tranquil, and their passions were assuaged.

Tu-matauenga, or fierce man, having thus successfully resisted his brother, the god of hurricanes and storms, next took thought how he could turn upon his brothers and slay them, because they had not assisted him or fought bravely when Tawhiri-ma-tea had attacked them to avenge the separation of their parents, and because they had left him alone to show his prowess in the fight. As yet death had no power over man. It was not until the birth of the children of Taranga and of Makea-tu-tara, of Maui-taha, of Maui-roto, of Maui-pae, of Maui-waho, and of Maui-tikitiki-o-Taranga, the demi-god who tried to beguile Hine-nui-te-po, that death had power over men. If that goddess had not been deceived by Maui-tikitiki, men would not have died, but would in that case have lived forever; it was from his deceiving Hine-nui-te-po that death obtained power over mankind, and penetrated to every part of the earth.

Tu-matauenga continued to reflect upon the cowardly manner in which his brothers had acted, in leaving him to show his courage alone, and he first sought some means of injuring Tane-mahuta, because he had not come to aid him in his combat with Tawhiri-ma-tea, and partly because he was aware that Tane had numerous progeny, who were rapidly increasing, and might at last prove hostile to him, and injure him, so he began to collect leaves of the whanake tree, and twisted them into nooses, and when his work was ended, he went to the forest to put up his snares, and hung them up. Ha! Ha! The children of Tane fell before him, none of them could any longer fly or move in safety.

Then he next determined to take revenge on his brother Tangaroa, who had also deserted him in the combat; so he sought for his offspring, and found them leaping or swimming in the water; then he cut many leaves from the flax-plant, and netted nets with the flax, and dragged these, and hauled the children of Tangaroa ashore.

After that, he determined also to get revenge upon his brothers Rongo-ma-tane and Haumia-tikitiki; he soon found them by their peculiar leaves, and he scraped into shape a wooden hoe, and plaited a basket, and dug in the earth and pulled up all kinds of plants with edible roots, and the plants which had been dug up withered in the sun.

Thus Tu-matauenga devoured all his brothers, and consumed the whole of them, in revenge for their having deserted him and left him to fight alone against Tawhiri-ma-tea and Rangi.

When his brothers had all thus been overcome by Tu, he assumed several names, namely, Tu-ka-riri, Tu-ka-nguha, Tu-ka-taua, Tu-whaka-heke-tan-gata, Tu-mata-wha-iti, and Tu-matauenga; he assumed one name for each of his attributes displayed in the victories over his brothers. Four of his brothers were entirely deposed by him, and became his food; but one of them, Tawhiri-ma-tea, he could not vanquish or make common, by eating him for food, so he, the last born child of Heaven and Earth, was left as an enemy for man, and still, with a rage equal to that of man, this elder brother ever attacks him in storms and hurricanes, endeavoring to destroy him alike by sea and land.

Now, the meanings of these names of the children of the Heaven and Earth are as follows:

Tangaroa signifies fish of every kind; Rongo-ma-tane signifies the sweet potato, and all vegetables cultivated as food; Haumia-tikitiki signifies fern root, and all kinds of food which grow wild; Tane-mahuta signifies forests, the birds and insects which inhabit them, and all things fashioned from wood; Tawhiri-ma-tea signifies winds and storms; and Tu-matauenga signifies man.

Four of his brothers having, as before stated, been made common, or articles of food, by Tu-matauenga, he assigned for each of them fitting incantations, that they might be abundant, and that he might easily obtain them.

Some incantations were proper to Tane-mahuta, they were called Tane.

Some incantations were for Tangaroa, they were called Tangaroa.

Some were for Rongo-ma-tane, they were called Rongo-ma-tane.

Some were for Haumia-tikitiki, they were called Haumia.

The reason that he sought out these incantations was so that his brothers might be made common by him, and serve for his food. There were also incantations for Tawhiri-ma-tea to cause favorable winds, and prayers to the vast Heaven for fair weather, as also for mother Earth that she might produce all things abundantly. But it was the great God that taught these prayers to man.

There were also many prayers and incantations composed for man, suited to the different times and circumstances of his life—prayers at the baptism of an infant; prayers for abundance of food, for wealth; prayers in illness; prayers to spirits, and for many other things. The bursting forth of the wrathful fury of Tawhiri-ma-tea against his brothers, was the cause of the disappearance of a great part of the dry land; during that contest a great part of mother Earth was submerged. The names of those beings of ancient days who submerged so large a portion of the earth were—Terrible-rain, Long-continued rain, Fierce-hailstorms; and their progeny were, Mist, Heavy-dew, and Light-dew, and these together submerged the greater part of the earth, so that only a small portion of dry land projected above the sea.

From that time clear light increased upon the earth, and all the beings which were hidden between Rangi and Papa before they were separated, now multiplied upon the earth. The first beings begotten by Rangi and Papa were not like human beings; but Tu-matauenga bore the likeness of a man, as did all his brothers, as also did a Po, a Ao, a Kore, te Kimihanga and Runuku, and thus it continued until the times of Ngainui and his generation, and of Whiro-te-tupua and his generation, and of Tiki-tawhito-ariki and his generation, and it has so continued to this day.

The children of Tu-matauenga were begotten on this earth, and they increased and continued to multiply, until we reach at last the generation of Maui-taha, and of his brothers Maui-roto, Maui-waho, Maui-pae, and Maui-tikitiki-o-Taranga.

Up to this time the vast Heaven has still ever remained separated from his spouse the Earth. Yet their mutual love still continues—the soft warm sighs of her loving bosom still ever rise up to him, ascending from the woody mountains and valleys... and men can see these mists; and the vast Heaven, as he mourns through the long nights his separation from his beloved, drops frequent tears upon her bosom, and men seeing these, call them dewdrops.

Oceanic Origin

Excerpt. Various Fragments. Updated and edited version of text from Oceanic Mythology by Roland B. Dixon.

Prefiguration

Unsteadily, as in dim moon-shimmer,
From out Makalii's night-dark veil of cloud Thrills, shadow-like, the prefiguration of the world to be.

Conception

From the conception the increase;
From the increase the swelling;
From the swelling the thought;
From the thought the remembrance;
From the remembrance the consciousness, the desire.
The word became fruitful: It dwelt with the feeble glimmering;
It brought forth night; The great night, the long night,

The lowest night, the loftiest night,
The thick night, the night to be felt,
The night touched, the night unseen.
 The night following on, The night ending in death.
 From the nothing, the begetting, From the nothing the increase;
 From the nothing the abundance, The power of increasing, the living breath;
 It dwelt with the empty space, It produced the atmosphere which is above us.
 The atmosphere which floats above the earth, The great firmament above us, The spread out space dwelt with the early dawn, Then the moon sprang forth;
 The atmosphere above dwelt with the glowing sky, Without delay, was produced the sun,
 They were thrown up above as the chief eyes of Heaven: Then the Heavens became light, the early dawn, the early day, The midday.
 The blaze of day from the sky. The sky which floats above the earth dwelt with Hawaiki.

Existing Alone

He existed. Taaroa was his name. In the immensity there was no earth, there was no sky, There was no sea, there was no man. Taaroa calls, but nothing answers. Existing alone, he became the universe.
 Taaroa is the root, the rocks (foundation). Taaroa is the sands. It is thus that he is named. Taaroa is the light. Taaroa is within. Taaroa is the germ. Taaroa is the support. Taaroa is enduring. Taaroa is wise. He erected the land of Hawaii, Hawaii, the great and sacred, As a body or shell for Taaroa.
 The earth is moving. Oh Foundations, oh Rocks, oh Sands, here, here, brought here, pressed together the earth. Press, press again. They do not unite. Stretch out the seven heavens, let ignorance cease. Create the heavens, let darkness cease. Let immobility cease. Let the period of messengers cease. It is the time of the speaker.
 Completed the foundations, completed the rocks, completed the sands, the heavens are enclosing, the heavens are raised. In the depths is finished the land of Hawaii.

The Chorus of Life

(New Zealand) Seeking, earnestly seeking in the gloom. Searching—yes, on the coastline—on the bounds of light of day. Looking into night, night had conceived, the seed of night. The heart, the foundation of night, had stood forth self-existing even in the gloom. It grows in gloom—the sap and succulent parts, the life pulsating, and the cup of life. The shadows screen the faintest gleam of light. The procreating power, the ecstasy of life first known, and joy of issuing forth, from silence into sound. Thus the progeny of the Great Extending filled the heaven's expanse. The chorus of

life rose and swelled into ecstasy, then rested in bliss of calm and quiet.

Lift the Universe

(Chasam Islands) Oh Son! Oh Son! Raise my son! Raise my son! Lift the Universe! Lift the Heavens! The Heavens are lifted! It is moving! It moves! It moves!

Work Complete

Come, Oh Ru-taki-nuhu, who has propped up the Heavens. The Heavens were fast, but are lifted. The Heavens were fast, but are lifted. Our work is completed.

The Creation

Excerpt. From the Kumulipo. Updated and edited version of the translation by Queen Liliuokalani.

The First Era

First Verse. At the time that turned the heat of the earth, At the time when the heavens turned and changed, At the time when the light of the sun was subdued To cause light to break forth, At the time of the night of Makalii (winter) Then began the slime which established the earth, The source of deepest darkness. Of the depth of darkness, of the depth of darkness, Of the darkness of the sun, in the depth of night, It is night, So was night born.

Second Verse. Kumulipo was born in the night, a male. Poele was born in the night, a female. A coral insect was born, from which was born perforated coral. The earth worm was born, which gathered earth into mounds, From it were born worms full of holes. The starfish was born, whose children were born starry. The phosphorous was born, whose children were born phosphorescent. The Ina was born Ina (sea egg). The Halula was born Halula (sea urchin). Shellfish. The Hawae was born, the Wana-ku was its offspring. The Haukeuke was born, the Uhalula was its offspring. The Pioe was born, the Pipi was its offspring (clam oyster). The Papaua was born, the Olepe was its offspring (pearl and oyster). The Nahawele was born, the Unauna was its offspring (muscle and crab in a shell). The Makaiaulu was born, the Opihi was its offspring. The Leho was born, the Puleholeho was its offspring (cowry). The Naka was born, its offspring was Kupekala (rock oysters). The Makaloa was born, the Pupuawa was its offspring. The Ole was born, the Oleole was its offspring (conch). The Pipipi was born, the Kupee was its offspring (limpets).

Kane was born to Waiololi, a female to Waiolola. The Wi was born, the Kiki was its offspring. The Akaha's home was the sea; Guarded by the Ekahakaha that grew in the forest. A night of flight by noises Through a channel; water is life to trees; So the gods may enter, but not man.

Third Verse. Seaweed and grasses

Man by Waiololi, woman by Waiolola, The Akiaki was born and lived in the sea; Guarded by the Manienie Akiaki that grew in the forest. A night of flight by noises Through a channel; water is life to trees; So the gods may enter, but not man.

Fourth Verse. Man by Waiololi, woman by Waiolola, The Aalaula was born and lived in the sea; Guarded by the Alaalawainui that grew in the forest. A night of flight by noises Through a channel; water is life to trees; So the gods may enter, but not man.

Fifth Verse. Man by Waiololi, woman by Waiolola, The Manauea was born and lived in the sea; Guarded by the Kalo Manauea that grew in the forest. A night of flight by noises Through a channel; water is life to trees; So the gods may enter, but not man.

Sixth Verse. Seaweed and grasses Man by Waiololi, woman by Waiolola, The Koeleele was born and lived in the sea; Guarded by the Ko punapuna Koeleele that grew in the forest. A night of flight by noises Through a channel; water is life to trees; So the gods may enter, but not man.

Seventh Verse. Man by Waiololi, woman by Waiolola, The Puaiki was born and lived in the sea; Guarded by the Lauaki that grew in the forest. A night of flight by noises Through a channel; water is life to trees; So the gods may enter, but not man.

Eighth Verse. Man by Waiololi, woman by Waiolola, The Kikalamoa was born and lived in the sea; Guarded by the Moamoa that grew in the forest. A night of flight by noises Through a channel; water is life to trees; So the gods may enter, but not man.

Ninth Verse. Man by Waiololi, woman by Waiolola, The Limukele was born and lived in the sea; Guarded by the Ekele that grew in the forest. A night of flight by noises Through a channel; water is life to trees; So the gods may enter, but not man.

Tenth Verse. Man by Waiololi, woman by Waiolola, The Limukala was born and lived in the sea; Guarded by the Akala that grew in the forest. A night of flight by noises Through a channel; water is life to trees; So the gods may enter, but not man.

Eleventh Verse. Man by Waiololi, woman by Waiolola, The Lipuupuu was born and lived in the sea; Guarded by the Lipuu that grew in the forest. A night of flight by noises Through a channel; water is life to trees; So the gods may enter but not man.

Twelfth Verse. Seaweed and grasses Man by Waiololi, woman by Waiolola, The Loloa was born and lived in the sea; Guarded by the Kalamaloloa that grew in the forest. A night of flight by noises Through a channel; water is life to trees; So the gods may enter, but not man.

Thirteenth Verse. Seaweed and grasses Man by Waiololi, woman by Waiolola, The Ne was born and lived in the sea; Guarded by the Neneleau that grew in the forest. A night of flight by noises Through a channel;

Glimmering Waters

water is life to trees; So the gods may enter, but not man.

Fourteenth Verse. Man by Waiololi, woman by Waiolola, The Hulu-waena was born and lived in the sea; Guarded by the Huluhulu Ieie that grew in the forest. A night of flight by noises Through a channel; water is life to trees; So the gods may enter, but not man.

Fifteenth Verse. A husband of gourd, and yet a god, A tendril strengthened by water and grew A being, produced by earth and spread, Made deafening by the swiftness of Time Of the Hee that lengthened through the night, That filled and kept on filling Of filling, until, filled To filling, it is full, And supported the earth, which held the heaven On the wing of Time, the night is for Kumulipo (creation), It is night.

The Second Era

First Verse. The First child born of Powehiwehi (dusky night) Tossed up land for Pouliuli (darkest night), For Mahiuma or Maapuia, And lived in the land of Pohomiluamea (sloughy hill of Mea); Suppressed the noise of the growth of unripe fruit, For fear Uliuli would cause it to burst, and the stench To disagree and turn sour, For pits of darkness and pits of night. Then the seven waters became calm. Then was born a child (kama), 'twas a Hilu and swam. The Hilu is a fish with standing fins, On which Pouliuli sat. So undecided seemed Powehiwehi, For Pouliuli was husband And Powehiwehi his wife. Fish. And fish was born, the Naia (porpoise) was born in the sea and swam. The Mano (shark) was born, the Moana was born in the sea and swam. The Mau was born, the Maumau was born in the sea and swam. The Nana was born, the Mana was born in the sea and swam. The Nake was born, the Make was born in the sea and swam. The Napa was born, the Nala was born in the sea and swam. The Pala was born, the Kala was born in the sea and swam. The Paka (an eel) was born, the Papa (crab) was born in the sea and swam. The Kalakala was born, the Huluhulu was born in the sea and swam. The Halahala was born, the Palapala was born in the sea and swam. The Pea (starfish) was born, the Lupe was born in the sea and swam. The Ao was born, the Awa was born in the sea and swam. The Aku (bonito) was born, the Ahi (same kind) was born in the sea and swam. The Opelu (same as above) was born, the Akule was born in the sea and swam. The Amaama (mullet) was born, the Anae (large kind) was born in the sea and swam. The Ehu was born, the Nehu was born in the sea and swam. The Iao (used for bait) was born, the Aoao was born in the sea and swam. The Ono (large fish) was born, the Omo was born in the sea and swam. The Pahau (striped flatfish) was born, the Lauhau was born in the sea and swam. The Moi was born, the Loiloi was born in the sea and swam. The Mao was born, the Maomao was born in the sea and swam. The Kaku was born, the A'ua'u was born in the sea and swam. The Kupou was born, the Kupoupou was born in the sea and swam. The Weke was born, the Lele was born in the sea and swam. The Palani was born, the Nuku Moni was born in the sea and swam. The Ulua was born, the Hahalua was born in the sea and swam. The Aoaonui was born, the Pakukui was born in the sea and swam. The Maiii was born, the Alaihi was born in the sea and swam. The Oo was born, the Akilolo was born in the sea and swam.

Second Verse. Fish and vine. The Nenue was born and lived in the sea; Guarded by the Lauhue that grew in the forest. A night of flight by noises Through a channel; salt water is life to fish; So the gods may enter, but not man.

Third Verse. Fish and vine. Man by Waiololi, woman by Waiolola, The Haha was born and lived in the sea; Guarded by the Puhala that grew in the forest. A night of flight by noises Through a channel; salt water is life to fish; So the gods may enter, but not man.

Fourth Verse. Fish and shrub. Man by Waiololi, woman by Waiolola, The Pahau was born in the sea; Guarded by the Lauhau that grew in the forest. A night of flight by noises Through a channel; salt water is life to fish; So the gods may enter, but not man.

Fifth Verse. Fish and shrub. Man by Waiololi, woman by Waiolola, The Hee was born and lived in the sea; Guarded by the Walahee that grew in the forest. A night of flight by noises Through a channel; salt water is life to fish; So the gods may enter, but not man.

Sixth Verse. Sea and water fish. Man by Waiololi, woman by Waiolola, The Oopukai was born and lived in the sea; Guarded by the Oopuwai that lived in the forest. A night of flight by noises Through a channel; salt water is life to fish; So the gods may enter, but not man.

Seventh Verse. Eel and tree. Man by Waiololi, woman by Waiolola, The Puhi kauwila was born and lived in the sea; Guarded by the Uwila that lived in the forest. A night of flight by noises Through a channel; salt water is life to fish; So the gods may enter, but not man.

Eighth Verse. Fish and bread-fruit. Man by Waiololi, woman by Waiolola, The Umaumalei was born and lived in the sea; Guarded by the Ulei that grew in the forest. A night of flight by noises Through a channel; salt water is life to fish; So the gods may enter, but not man.

Ninth Verse. Eel and tree. Man by Waiololi, woman by Waiolola, The Pakukui was born and lived in the sea; Guarded by Laukukui that grew in the forest. A night of flight by noises Through a channel; salt water is life to fish; So the gods may enter, but not man.

Tenth Verse. Eel and tree. Man by Waiololi, woman by Waiolola, The

Laumilo was born and lived in the sea; Guarded by the Milo that grew in the forest. A night of flight by noises Through a channel; salt water is life to fish; So the gods may enter, but not man.

Eleventh Verse. Fish and large tree. Man by Waiololi, woman by Waiolola, The Kapoou was born and lived in the sea; Guarded by Kou that grew in the forest. A night of flight by noises Through a channel; salt water is life to fish; So the gods may enter, but not man.

Twelfth Verse. Fish and yam or Uhi (Impomea batatas). Man by Waiololi, woman by Waiolola, The Hauliuli was born and lived in the sea; Guarded by the Uhi that grew in the forest. A night of flight by noises Through a channel; water is life to fish; So the gods may enter, but not man.

Thirteenth Verse. Man by Waiololi, woman by Waiolola, The Weke was born and lived in the sea; Guarded by the Wauke that grew in the forest. A night of flight by noises Through a channel; water is life to fish; So the gods may enter, but not man.

Fourteenth Verse. Fish and Awa (Kawa). Man by Waiololi, woman by Waiolola, The Aawa was born and lived in the sea; Guarded by the Awa that grew in the forest. A night of flight by noises Through a channel; water is life to fish; So the gods may enter, but not man.

Fifteenth Verse. Fish and grass. Man by Waiololi, woman by Waiolola, The Ulae was born and lived in the sea; Guarded by the Mokae that grew in the forest. A night of flight by noises Through a channel; salt water is life to fish; So the gods may enter, but not man.

Sixteenth Verse. Man by Waiololi, woman by Waiolola, The Palaoa (sea-elephant) was born and lived in the sea; Guarded by the Aoa that grew in the forest. A night of flight by noises Through a channel; salt water is life to fish; So the gods may enter, but not man.

Seventeenth Verse. The train of Palaoa (walrus) that swim by Embracing only the deep blue waters, Also the Opule that move in schools, The deep is as nothing to them. And the Kumimi (a crab) and Lohelohe (a locust) cling together To the rolling motion of their cradle On their path so narrow, so slim, to move, Till Pimoe (a mermaid) is found in the depth of her cave, With Hikawainui, and Hikawaina Amongst piles of heated coral That were thrown in piles unevenly, So thin and scraggy in the blue tide. Surely it must be dismal, that unknown deep; It is a sea of coral from the depth of Paliuli, And when the land recedes from them The east is still in darkness of night, It is night.

The Third Era

First Verse. He was the man and she the woman; The man that was born in the dark age, And the woman was born in the age of bubbles. The sea spread, the land spread, The waters spread, the mountains spread, The Poniu grew tall with advancing time, The Haha grew and had nine leaves, And the Palai (fern) sprout that shot forth leaves of high chiefs Brought forth Poeleele, a man (darkness), Who lived with Pohaha, a woman (bubbles), And brought forth generations of Haha (kalo tops). The Haha was born.

Second Verse. Insects. The Haha was born and became parent; His offspring, a Hahalelelele, was born. The Peelua (caterpillar) was born and became parent; Its offspring was a flying Pulelehua (butterfly). The Naonao (an ant) was born and became parent; Its offspring was a Pinao (dragonfly). The Unia was born and became parent; Its offspring was an Uhini, and flew (grasshopper). The Naio was born and became parent (waterworms); Its offspring was a Nalo, and flew (flies). Birds. The Hualua was born and became parent; Its offspring was a bird, and flew. The Ulili was born and became parent (snipe); Its offspring was a Kolea, and flew (plover). The A-o was born and became parent; Its offspring was an Au, and flew (a species of plover). The Akekeke was born and became parent (sea-bird); Its offspring was Elepaio, and flew (woodpecker). The Alae was born and became parent (mud hen); Its offspring was an Apapane, and flew (red woodpecker). The Alala was born and became parent (crow); Its offspring was an Alawi, and flew. The Eea was born and became parent; Its offspring was a Alaiaha, and flew. The Mamo was born and became parent (the royal bird); Its offspring was the Oo, and flew (black woodpecker). The Moha was born and became parent (wingless bird); Its offspring was a Moli, and flew. Sea-birds. The Kiki was born and became parent; Its offspring was the Ukihi, and flew. The Kioea was born and became parent (stork); Its offspring was a Kukuluaeo, and flew (crane). The Ka Iwa was born and became parent (sea-bird); Its offspring was a Koae, and flew (man-of-war hawk). The Kala was born and became parent (sea-bird); Its offspring was a Kaula, and flew (sea-bird). Then was born the Unauna (shell-fish, part crab); Its offspring was an Aukuu, and flew. These birds fly together in flocks And usually light on the sea beach And array themselves in line.

Third Verse. They covered the land of Kanehunamoku. These were born birds of the land And birds of the sea. Man was born of Waiololi, woman Waiolola, The Lupe was born and lived in the sea; Guarded by the Lupe that grew in the forest. A night of flight by noises Through a channel; the Io is life to birds; So the gods may enter, but not man. Fourth Verse. Man by Waiololi, woman by Waiolola, The Noio lived on the sea, Guarded by the Io that lived in the forest. A night of flight by noises. Eggs and the Io are life to birds, So the gods may enter, but not man.

Fifth Verse. Man by Waiololi, woman by Waiolola, The Kolea of the island lived on the sea, Guarded by the Kolea that flew on land. A night of flight by noises. Eggs and Io are life to birds, So the gods may enter, but not man.

Sixth Verse. Man by Waiololi, woman by Waiolola, The Hehe was born and lived on the sea, Guarded by the Nene that lived in the forest. A night of flight by noises. Eggs and Io are life to birds, So the gods may enter, but not man.

Seventh Verse. Man by Waiololi, woman by Waiolola, The Aukuu was born and lived on the sea (Pewit), Guarded by the Ekupuu that grew on land. A night of flight by noises. Eggs and Io are life to birds, So the gods may enter, but not man.

Eighth Verse. Man by Waiololi, woman by Waiolola, The Noeo was born and lived on the sea, Guarded by the Pueo that lived in the forest. A night of flight by noises. Eggs and Io are food for birds, So the gods may enter, but not man.

Ninth Verse. This is the leaping point of the bird Halulu Of Kiwaa, the bird of many notes, And of those birds that fly closely together as to shade the sun, They cover the land with their young to the rock's edge, Their gall burst easily with a smack As the Ape sprout whose delicate shoots Shoot forth their young sprouts and spread And bring forth in their birth many branches. It was so on that night, It was so this night, It was dark at the time with Poeleele, And darkest age— of bubbly night. It is night.

The Fourth Era

First Verse. Established in the dawn of Laa's light The Ape aumoa with faintest strife Envied the sea that washed the land, As it crept up and yet crept down And brought forth creeping families That crept on their backs and crept on their front, With pulses that beat in front and rounding backs, With faces in front and claws to feel Of darkness, of darkness, For Kaneaka Papanopano is born (dawn). So Popanopano the man And Polalowehi his wife, Man was born to increase— To increase in the night by the thousands. At this age there is a lull— At this age take your children to the beach. Children play at heaping sands. They are the children born of night. Night was born.

Second Verse. Night was born of great delight, Night was rolled for the pleasure of gods, Night gave birth to the split-back turtle. Watch in the night for the land turtle. Night gave birth to the brown lobster, The night of commotion for the Alii (?) lobster, The birth night of the lazy monster Was a wet night for the rolling monster. Night gave birth to clinging beings, And Night loudly called for roughness. Night gave birth to wailing A night of drawback to oblivion, Night gave birth to high noses, Night dug deep for jelly fish, Night gave birth to slush, So the night must wait for motion.

Third Verse. Man by Waiololi, woman by Waiolola, The earth was born and lived by the sea; Guarded by the Kuhonua that grew in land (a shrub). A night of flight by noises Through a channel; the la-i is food, and creeps.

Fourth Verse. Man by Waiololi, woman by Waiolola, The Wili was born and lived in the sea; Guarded by the Wiliwili that grew on land (tiger's claws tree). A night of flight by noises Through a channel; la-i is food, and creeps; So the gods may enter, but not man.

Fifth Verse. Man by Waiololi, woman by Waiolola, The Aio was born and lived in the sea; Guarded by the Naio that grew in the forest (mock sandalwood). A night of flight by noises Through a channel; la-i is food, and creeps; So the gods may enter, but not man.

Sixth Verse. Man was created by Waiololi, woman by Waiolola, The Okea was born and lived in the sea; Guarded by the Ahakea that grew in the forest. A night of flight by noises Through a channel; the la-i is food, and creeps; So the gods may enter, but not man.

Seventh Verse. Man by Waiololi, woman by Waiolola, The Wawa was born and lived in the sea; Guarded by the Wanawana that lived in the forest. A night of flight by noises Through a channel, la-i is food, and creeps; So the gods may enter, but not man.

Eighth Verse. Man by Waiololi, woman by Waiolola, The Nene was born and lived in the sea (geese); Guarded by the Manene that lived in the forest (weed). A night of flight by noises Through a channel; la-i is food, and creeps; So the gods may enter, but not man.

Ninth Verse. Man by Waiololi, woman by Waiolola, The Liko was born and lived in the sea; Guarded by the Piko that grew in the forest. A night of flight by noises Through a channel; the la-i is food, and creeps; So the gods may enter, but not man.

Tenth Verse. Man by Waiololi, woman by Waiolola, The Okeope was born and lived in the sea; Guarded by the Oheohe that grew in the forest (bamboo). A night of flight by noises Through a channel; la-i is food and creeps; So the gods may enter, but not man.

Eleventh Verse. Man by Waiololi, woman by Waiolola, The Nananana was born and lived in the sea (spider); Guarded by the Nonanona that lived in the forest (ants). A night of flight by noises Through a channel; la-i is food, and creeps; So the gods may enter, but not man.

Twelfth Verse. The dancing motion till creeping crept With long and waving lengyour tail, And with humpy lumpy lashes sweeps And trails along in filyour places. These live on dirt and mire; Eat and rest, eat and throw up; They exist on filth, are low-born beings, Till to earth they become a burden Of mud that's made, Made unsafe, until one reels And is unsteady., Go you to the land of creepers, Where families of creepers were born in one night. It is night.

The Fifth Era

First Verse. The advance of age when Kapokanokano (night of strength) Established heaps in the Polalouli (depth of night), And the dark fresh color of the earth thrown up Was the darkness of the famous Polalouli (night in the deep), Who married for wife Kapokanokano. His snout was of great size and with it dug the earth; He dug until he raised a great mound, He raised a hill for his gods, A hill, a precipice in front, For the offspring of a pig which was born; Built a house and paid the forest And rested by the patches of Loiloa, For Umi who is to possess the land, For Umi who is to reign soon; The land where Kapokanokano dwelt, To which place laid a path of frailest trail, A trail as fine as the choicest hair of this pig, A being was born half pig, half god, At the time of life of Kapokanokano, Who became the wife of Polalouli. Night was born.

Second Verse. The Poowaawaa was born, his head was uneven. The Poopahapaha was born, his head was flat and spread. The Poohiwahiwa was born, he appeared noble. The Poohaole was born, he became a haole (foreigner). The Poomahakea was born, his skin was fair. The Pooapahu was born, was a hairy man. The Poomeumeu was born, is a short man. The Pooauli was born, is dark complexioned. The Hewahewa was born, and he remained so (light-headed). The Lawalawa was born, becomes a lawalawa. The Hooipo was born, and became hooipoipo (loving). The Hulu was born, and became a-aia (demented). The Hulupii was born, and became piipii (curly-headed). The Meleuli was born, and became melemele (yellow-haired). The Haupo was born, and became hauponuinui (noble-chested). The Hilahila was born, and became hilahila (very bashful). The Kenakena was born, and became kenakena (bitter). The Luheluhe was born, and became luheluhe (limber). The Awaawa was born, and became awaawa (sour disposed). The Aliilii was born, and became liilii (puny). The Makuakua was born, and became kuakua (great). The Halahala was born, decorated with lei Hala. The Eweewe was born, who was proud of his pedigree. The Huelo Maewa was born, with very long tail. The Hulu liha was born, and became lihelihe (hairy eggs). The Pukaua was born, and became a warrior. The Meheula was born, and became red. The Puuwelu was born, and became weluwelu (ragged). That is his, this is in shreds. Then came the children of Loiloa, And the land grew and spread, And the goblet of wish was lowered Of affections for the tribe of relations, Of songs that grasp of Oma's friends Till relations are enrolled from Kapokanokano At yester eve. It is night.

The Sixth Era

A sacred emblem is the kahili of Kuakamano That sends out its stiff branches as a sacred frill, Which fills the fainthearted with awe, But brings such ones to claim friendship. Those are beings who eat by gushing waters, Who eat also by the dashing sea, They live in nests inside ditches, There in hollow places the parent rats dwell, There huddle together the little mice. It is they who keep the changes of the month.

The mites of the land, The mites of the water, It is Mehe the reddish seaweed Whose lashes stand, That hides and peeps. There are rats inland, there are rats at sea. There are also rabbits That were born in the night of the crash– They were born in the night that moved away. The tiniest mice move by crawling; The tiny mice spring as they move. They run over the pebbles, The propagating pebbles where no inland ohia bear. A puny child born in the night of the crash. They gave birth to beings that leaped in the night, that moved away The child of Uli-a-kama last night. It is night.

The Seventh Era

Over the mountains silence reigns– The silence of night that has moved away, And the silence of night that comes, The silence of night filled with people, And the silence of night of dispersing. It is fearful the steps and narrow trails– It is fearful the amount eaten and left– It is fearful the night past and gone, The awful stillness of the night that came– The night that went by and brought forth an offspring, That offspring a dog, A yellow dog, a tiny dog, A dog without hair, sent by the gods, A dog sent for sacrifice. A speckled bird was First sacrificed, Else he'd repent for having no hair, Else he'd repent for having no covering, And go naked on the road to Malama, The easiest path for children, From great to small, From tall to short, He is equal to the blowing breeze, The younger brother of the god From which sprang the gods of the bats– The hairy bats. Sprang the bat with many claws– Sprang the bat and moved away, That the rising surf might give it birth. It is night.

The Eighth Era

The child of Uli, of Uli of Ke, The child in the time of numerous night, The child in the time of riding distant surf in the night. Beings were born to increase. Male was born of Waiololi, Female was born of Waiolola, Then was born the night of gods, Men that stood, Of men lying down, They slept long sleep in the distant time, And went staggering when they walked. The forehead of the gods is red. That of man is dark. Their chins are light. Then calmness spread in the time of Kapokinikini– Calm in the time of Kapoheenalu mamao, And it was called there Lailai. Lailai was born a woman, Kii was born a man. Kane a god was born. Kanaloa was born a god, the great Kaheehaunawela (Octopus). It is day.

Glimmering Waters

The drums were born, Called Moanaliha. Kawaomaaukele came next. The last was Kupololiiliali-imuaoloipo, A man of long life and very high rank. Oh night! Oh God of Night! Oh kupa, Kupakupa kupa, the settler! Then Kupakupa the settler, the woman who sat sideway, That woman was Lailai of the distant night, Lailai, the woman. Kapokinikini Dwelt with people of Kapokinikini. Hahapoele was born a woman, Hapopo was born a woman. Maila was born and called Lopalapala (ingenious), Her other name was void or nakedness, And lived in the land of Lua (deep hole). So the place was called Olohelohe lua. Then Olohelohe was born in the day a man, And Olohelohe was born at the time, a woman, And lived with Kane. Laiolo was born by Kane. Kapopo was born a woman, Poelei and Poelea were born twins. After them was born Wehiloa. From them these were born, The little beings who were cross-eyed, That stood in numbers and moved in myriads. These men that flew naked were the men of the day. It is day

The Ninth Era

Lailai, of the quaking earth, Of great heat and noise, and opening heavens, This woman ascending to heaven, Climbed to heaven by the forest. Onehenehe flew where the earth rose. Children of Kii that were born from the brain, Were born and flew, both flew to heaven. Then the signs appeared and cast their shadow On their forehead, a bread fruit was impressed, On their chins shot roots of fire. This woman was from a race of delusions (myth), A woman with dark skin, from the land of Iipakalani, Where numbers of men lived in the heat. This woman lived in Nuumealani, Land where the Aoa thrived, Who stripped with great ease the leaves of the Koa; A woman whose person was never seen, From her to Kii, from him to Kane, From her to Kane of Kapokinikini. The times of those people came to naught. A tribe, a generation of great strength, She alone flew to her abode, And on the boughs of the Aoa tree, in Nuumealani stayed, Became pregnant, and the earth was born. Haha Poele was born a woman, Hapopo was born, Lohelohe was born last of all. These were the children of this woman. It is day.

The Tenth Era

Maila, with Lailai for protection, And Kane of Kapokinikini was support, Kii was helpless. Laioloolo was born and lived at Kapapa. Kamahaina was born a man, Kamamale was born a man, Kamakalua a woman, Poeleieholo a child, Poeleaaholo a child, Then Wehiwelawehi loa. Lailai went back to Kane, Hai was born a woman, Halia was born a woman, Hakea was born a man, The Muki, Muka, and Mukekeke were born (kisses, smacks, chirruping), Smacks, boils, and other weaknesses, Moku, Monu, mumuleana (strife, broils, and huffiness), The men became speechless from sulkiness, Became cross from envy of ours, Of the woman who is brave and fearless, Then hid and dared not claim kin, To claim kin with her child. The heavens deny the right of kin (being of younger branch), Yield the sacred right to Kii; For to be with Kii, it is his to claim. Kane then taunts her eldest for this, Kii retaliates through Lailai for his being the younger branch; He flings a stone and hits Kane; Then is heard the sound of the drum, The sign of life for the younger. Kane, furious with jealous anger, struck her for faithlessness For the younger child of the younger branch. That is why First-born are always hakus (superiors, lords), First through Lailai, next by Kii, Their First-born with sacred birthright Is born.

The Eleventh Era

She that lived in the heavens and Piolani (married her brother), She that was full of enjoyments and lived in the heavens, Lived up there with Kii and became his wife, Brought increase to the world. Kamahaina was born a man, Kamamule his brother; Kamainau was born next, Kamakulua was born, the youngest a woman; Kamahaina lived with Hali. Loaa was born a man, Loaa was the husband, Nakelea the wife; Le was the husband, Kanu the wife; Kalawe was the husband, Kamau the wife; Kulou was the husband, Halau the wife. [...]

Haumea Discovered

Haumea of mythical form, Haumea with eight different forms, Haumea of several forms, Haumea in form of a shark. Whose many forms took different shapes, And at the birth of Hikapuanaiea her breasts were caught by the heavens. This woman of Nuumea was discovered by a dog. Nuumea was the land, Nuupapakini the earth, Where Haumea's grandchildren increased. In Kio sickness ended, the brains began to roll. This woman that gave birth from her head, Children were born from her brains. This woman of the darkest night, of Nuumea, And lived at Mulinaha, Gave birth to Laumiha through the brain; Gave birth to Kahaula, a woman, through the brain; Gave birth to Kahakauakoko through the brain. Haumea was the same woman Who lived with Kanaloaakua. Kauakahiakua was born from the brains; Her children were mostly born from the brains; With great slime was the birth from the brain By "Papa who sought the earth" (people), By "Papa who sought the heavens" (chief), By Papa the great producer of lands, By Papa who lived with Wakea. Haalolo was born a woman. Accompanying its birth were anger and jealousy. Wakea became false to Papa. Changed the days and months, Ordered the nights of Kane towards the last of the month And the nights of Hilo to be First; And established sacred tabus across his threshold. Such was the house that Wakea lived in. The food of the parent chief became sacred; The Ape, so bitter, became sacred; The Akia (sour) became sacred; The Auhuhu (pungent and bitter) became sacred; The Uhaloa for its life-giving properties became sacred; The Laalo, so acid, became sacred; The Haloa that grow by the edge of the patch became sacred. Plant the Haloa, the leaves will grow tall; So grew the sprout of Haloa in the day and Thrived.

Chapter 10

Nature's Spirit

Olelbis

Olelbis. Native American origin. Updated and edited version of the text by Jeremiah Curtin.

The first that we know of Olelbis is that he was in Olelpanti. Whether he lived in another place is not known, but in the beginning he was in Olelpanti (on the upper side), the highest place. He was in Olelpanti before there was anything down here on the earth, and two old women were with him always. These old women he called grandmother, and each of them we call Pakchuso Pokaila.

There was a world before this one in which we are now. That world lasted a long, long time, and there were many people living in it before the present world and we, the present people, came.

One time, the people of that first world who were living then in the country around here were talking of those who lived in one place and another. Down in the southwest was a person whose name was Katkatchila. He could kill game wonderfully, but nobody knew how he did it, nor could anyone find out. He did not kill as others did; he had something that he aimed and threw; he would point a hollow stick which he had, and something would go out of it and kill the game. In that time a great many people lived about this place where we are now, and their chief was Torihas Kiemila; these people came together and talked about Katkatchila.

Someone said: "I wonder if he would come up here if we sent for him."

"Let us send for him," said Torihas; "let us ask him to come; tell him that we are going to have a great dance. Tomorrow we will send some one down to invite him."

The next morning Torihas sent a messenger to invite Katkatchila; he sent Tsaroki Sakahl, a very quick traveller. Though it was far, Tsaroki went there in one day, gave the invitation, and told about Torihas and his people.

"I agree," said Katkatchila. "I will go in the morning."

Tsaroki went home in the night, and told the people that Katkatchila would come on the following day.

"What shall we do?" they asked.

"First, we will dance one night," said the chief; "then we will take him out to hunt and see how he kills things."

Katkatchila had a sister; she had a husband and one child. She never went outdoors herself. She was always in the house. Nobody ever saw the woman or her child.

When Katkatchila was ready to start he told his sister that he was going, and said to his brother-in-law: "I am going. You must stay at home while am gone."

The sister was Yonot. Her husband was Tilikus.

Katkatchila came to a hill up here, went to the top of it, and sat down. From the hill he could see the camp of the people who had invited him. He stayed there awhile and saw many persons dancing. It was in summer and about the middle of the afternoon. At last Katkatchila went down to where they were dancing, and stopped a little way off. Torihas, who was watching, saw him and said,

"Come right over here, Katkatchila, and sit by me."

Olelbis was looking down from Olelpanti at this moment, and said to the old women, "My grandmothers, I see many people collected on earth; they are going to do something."

Katkatchila sat down and looked on. Soon all the people stopped dancing and went to their houses. Torihas had food brought to Katkatchila after his journey. While he was eating, Torihas said to him,

"My grandson, I and all my people have lived here very long. My people want to dance and hunt. I sent one of them to ask you to come up here. They will dance tonight and go hunting tomorrow."

Tori has stood up then and said,

"You my people, we will all dance tonight and tomorrow morning we will go to hunt. Do not leave home, any of you. Let all stay. We will have a great hunt. Katkatchila, will you stay with us?" he asked. "I shall be glad if you go and hunt with us."

"I will go with you," said Katkatchila. "I am glad to go."

They danced all night. The next morning, after they had eaten, and just as they were starting off to hunt, the chief said to his people,

"I will send my grandson with Katkatchila, and some of you, my sons, stay near him."

Some said to others: "When Katkatchila shoots a deer, let us run right up and take out of the deer the thing with which he killed it, and then we won't give it back to him."

"You stay with him, too," said Torihas to Kaisus, who was a swift runner. The whole party, a great many people, went to Hau Buli to hunt. When they got onto the mountain they saw ten deer. Katkatchila shot without delay; as soon as he shot a deer fell, and Kaisus, who was ready, made a rush and ran up to the deer, but Katkatchila was there before him and had taken out the weapon.

He killed all ten of the deer one after another, and Kaisus ran each time to be first at the fallen body, but Katkatchila was always ahead of him. When they went home Kaisus carried one deer, and told of all they had done, saying,

"Now you people, go and bring in the other deer. I don't believe any man among us can run as fast as Katkatchila; he is a wonderful runner. I don't know what he uses to kill game, and I don't think we can get it away from him."

That night Hau spoke up among his friends and said, "I will go with Katkatchila tomorrow and see what I can do."

A great many of the people talked about Katkatchila that night, saying,

"We do not think that he will ever come to us again, so we must all do our best to get his weapon while he is here."

Katkatchila was ready to go home after the hunt, but Torihas persuaded him, saying: "Stay one day more. Hunt with us tomorrow."

Katkatchila agreed to stay. The next morning they went to hunt. Hau went among others, and stayed near Katkatchila all the time.

On the mountain they saw ten deer again. Katkatchila stood back to shoot. Hau was ready to spring forward to get the weapon. The moment the weapon was shot, Hau ran with all his strength, reached the deer first, took out the weapon and hid it in his ear.

That moment Katkatchila was there. "You have taken my flint!" he cried. "Give it back!"

"I have not taken it," said Hau. "I have nothing of yours. I have just come."

"You have it. I saw you take it," said Katkatchila.

"I took nothing. I only put my hand on the deer's head."

"I saw you take it."

"No, you did not. I haven't it."

Katkatchila kept asking all day for his flint, but Hau would neither give it back nor own that he had it. At last, when the sun was almost down. Katkatchila turned to Hau and said,

"I saw you take my flint. It would be better for you to give it back to me, better for you and very much better for your people. You want to keep the flint; well, keep it. You will see something in pay for this, something that will not make you glad."

He left the hunt and went away in great anger, travelled all night and was at home next morning.

Torihas's people went back from the hunt, and Hau with the others. He went into the sweat house, took the flint out of his ear and held it on his palm. Everyone came and looked at it. It was just a small bit of a thing. "When I took this," said Hau, "Katkatchila got very angry; he left us on the mountain and went home."

All the people stood around looking at the flint in Hau's hand.

"You have done wrong, you people," said Patsotchet. "Katkatchila is very strong and quick; you will see what he will do. He has great power, more power than you think, and he will have vengeance. He will make us suffer terribly. He is stronger than we are. He can do anything. You will see something dreadful before long."

"Now, my people," said Torihas, "come into the sweat house and we will see what we can do with that flint."

All went in. Hau went last, for he had the flint. He held it out, showed it again, and said, "I took this because you people wanted it."

They passed the flint from one to another; all looked at it, all examined it. One old man said: "Give it to me here, let me see it." He got it in his hand, and said: "Now all go outside of the sweat house."

This was Hilit Kiemila. They went out, leaving him alone. Patsotchet kept on repeating, "Katkatchila is angry, he is malicious; before long we shall see what will happen."

As soon as Hilit was alone in the sweat house, he began to rub the flint with his hands and roll it with his legs (Hilit was turned afterward into a house-fly, and that is why house-flies keep rubbing their legs against each other to this day). He wanted to make the flint large. After he had rolled and rubbed the flint all night, it was four or five feet long, and as thick and wide. He let the block fall to the ground and it made a great noise, a very loud noise; people heard it for a long distance. Hilit went out then and said,

"Go in, all you people, and look at that good flint."

They went and looked. It was almost daylight at the time, and each one said,

"Well. I don't know what is best to do; perhaps it would be best to send this off. It may be bad for us to keep it here; bad for us to have it in the sweat house or the village."

They did not know who could carry the great block. It was so heavy. "Perhaps Patsotchet can carry it," they said.

Torihas went outside and called Patsotchet, saying: "Come into the sweat house a little while. You come seldom; but come now."

Patsotchet left his house, which was near by, and went into the sweat house.

"What are you going to do?" he asked. "It is too late to do anything now. I have known a long time about Katkatchila. He is very strong. He will do something terrible as soon as daylight comes."

"Patsotchet," said Torihas, "you are a good man. I wish you would take this big flint and carry it far away off north."

Nature's Spirit

"I don't want to take it," said Patsotchet. "It is too heavy." Torihas went to Karili, who lived a little way off, and said: "Come into the sweat house. I wish to talk with you."

Karili went in. "Take this block," said Torihas. "No one is willing to carry it away, but you are strong. Carry it north for me."

Karili took up the flint, but when he had it outside the house he said: "I cannot carry this. It is too heavy. I am not able to carry it."

Torihas called in Tichelis, and said: "My uncle, will you take this north for me?"

"Why will not others take it? Why are they unwilling to carry it?" asked Tichelis. "Well, I will take it he said, after thinking a little; and he made ready."

"Take it and start right away," said Torihas.

"Daylight is coming. Go straight. I will go, too, and when I am on the top of Toriham Pui Toror I will shout, and show you where to put the block."

Tichelis put the flint on his back and hurried away with it.

When Katkatchila reached home he told his brother-in-law, Tilikus, and his brother-in-law's brother, Poharamas, and Yonot, his sister, how his flint had been stolen.

It was just before sunrise. Tilikus and Poharamas went out in front of the house and swept a space clean and smooth; then they ran off to the east and got pine as full of pitch as they could find it. They brought a great deal of this, split some very fine, and made a large pile there on the smooth place. Just at this time Torihas's people were in his sweat house talking about the theft. "Nothing will happen," said most of them; "old Patsotchet is always talking in that way, foretelling trouble. We will dance today. Tichelis has carried that thing far away; all will be well now."

Yonot, Katkatchila's sister, had one child, a little baby which she called Pohila (fire child). The woman never left the house herself, and never let anyone carry the child out.

"Now, my sister," said Katkatchila, "bring your child here; bring my nephew out, and put him on that nice, smooth place which we have swept clean; it will be pleasant there for him."

She brought the boy out, put him on the smooth place. Poharamas was on the southeast side all ready, and Tilikus on the southwest side. As soon as Yonot put down the baby, they pushed pitch-pine sticks toward it. That instant fire blazed up. When the fire had caught well Poharamas took a large burning brand of pitch-pine and rushed off to the southeast; Tilikus took another and ran to the southwest. Poharamas, when he reached the southeast where the sky comes to the earth, ran around northward close to the sky; he held the point of his burning brand on the ground, and set fire to everything as he ran. When Tilikus reached the southwest, at the place where the sky touches the earth, he ran northward near the sky. The two brothers went swiftly, leaving a line of flame behind them, and smoke rose in a cloud with the fire.

After the two had started Yonot snatched up Pohila, and as she raised the boy a great flame flashed up from the spot. She ran into the house with her son, and put him into the basket where she had kept him till that morning.

Torihas's people had begun to dance. Some time after sunrise they saw a great fire far away on the east and on the west as well.

"Oh, look at the fire on both sides!" said one.

"It is far off and won't come here," said another.

"I feel the heat already!" cried a third.

Soon all saw that the fire was coming toward them from the east and the west like waves of high water, and the line of it was going northward quickly. The fire made a terrible roar as it burned; soon everything was seething. Everywhere people were trying to escape, all were rushing toward the north. By the middle of the morning the heat and burning were so great that people began to fall down, crying out,

"Oh, I'm hot! Ah. I'm hot!"

Torihas made a rush toward the north, and reached the top of Toriham Pui Toror. When he saw the fire coming very near he called out to Tichelis, who was struggling along with the great block of flint on his back,

"Go ahead with the flint! Go on, go on, the fire is far from here, far behind us!"

Tichelis heard the shouting, but said nothing and kept going northward steadily. When he was northeast of Bohem Puyuk, he saw the fire coming very fast, a mighty blaze roaring up to the sky. It was coming from the south, east, west. Tichelis could go no farther; there was no place for escape above ground; the fire would soon be where he was. The flint had grown very hot from the burning; he threw it down; it had skinned his back, it was so hot and heavy. He ran under the ground, went as far as he could, and lay there. Presently he heard the fire roaring above him, the ground was burning, he was barely alive; soon all blazed up, earth, rocks, everything.

Tichelis went up in flames and smoke toward the sky.

When the brothers Tilikus and Poharamas had carried the fire around the world and met in the north, just half-way between east and west, they struck their torches together and threw them on the ground. The moment before they joined the burning brands two persons rushed out between them. One was Klabus and the other Tsaroki, who had carried the invitation from Torihas to Katkatchila. They just escaped.

The flint rock that Tichelis dropped lies there yet, just where it fell, and when the Wintu people want black flint they find it in that place.

Nature's Spirit

Poharamas and Tilikus ran home as soon as they struck their torches together.

Katkatchila had a little brother. He put the boy on his back, and went beyond the sky where it touches the earth in the south.

Yonot, the mother of Pohila, took her son and went behind the sky; her husband, Tilikus, went with her. Poharamas went to Olelpanti. He flew up to where Olelbis is. Olelbis looked down into the burning world. He could see nothing but waves of flame; rocks were burning, the ground was burning, everything was burning. Great rolls and piles of smoke were rising; fire flew up toward the sky in flames, in great sparks and brands. Those sparks became kolchituh (sky eyes), and all the stars that we see now in the sky came from that time when the first world was burned. The sparks stuck fast in the sky, and have remained there ever since the time of the wakpohas (world fire). Quartz rocks and fire in the rocks are from that time. There was no fire in the rocks before the wakpohas.

When Klabus escaped he went east outside the sky, went to a place called Pom Wai Hudi Pom. Tsaroki went up on the eastern side of the sky, ran up outside.

Before the fire began Olelbis spoke to the two old women and said: "My grandmothers, go to work for me and make a foundation. I wish to build a sweat house."

They dug out and cleared a place for the sweat house the day before the world-fire began. Olelbis built it in this way: When the two women had dug the foundation, he asked,

"What kind of wood shall I get for the central pillar of the house?"

"Go far down south," said the old grandmothers, "and get a great young white oak, pull it up with the roots, bring it, and plant it in the middle to support the house."

He went, found the tree, and brought it. "Now, my grandmothers, what shall I do next?"

"Go north and bring a black oak with the roots. Go then to the west, put your hand out, and there you will touch an oak different from others."

He went north and west, and brought the two trees.

"Now," said Olelbis, "I want a tree from the east."

"Go straight east to a live-oak place, you can see it from here, get one of those live-oaks." He brought it with the roots and said,

"Now I want two trees more."

"Go to the southeast," they said, "where white oaks grow, and get two of them."

He went and got two great white oak trees, pulled them up with the roots, brought them with all the branches, which were covered with acorns.

Olelbis put the great white oak from the south in the middle as the central pillar; then he put the northern black oak on the north side; he put it sloping, so that its branches were on the south side of the house;

over against this he put a southeastern white oak sloping in like manner, so that its head came out on the north side. The western oak he planted on the west side, sloping so that its branches hung on the east side; then he put up the two white oaks from the southeast on the east side: six trees in all. The top of each tree was outside opposite its roots; acorns from it fell on the opposite side. Olelbis wished to fasten the trees firmly together so they should never loosen. "Stop, grandson," said one of the old women.

"How will you bind the top?"

"I have nothing to bind it with," answered Olelbis.

She put her hand toward the south, and on it came humus koriluli (a plant with beautiful blossoms). She took it with roots, stem, and blossoms and made a long narrow mat, the stem and roots all woven together inside and the blossoms outside. "Here, grandson," said she, "put this around the top of the house and bind the trees with it firmly."

He did this. The binding was beautiful and very fragrant. He wrapped it around the trees where they came together at the top of the house inside.

The two old women made four very large mats now, one for each side of the house. They wove first a mat of yosoŭ (a plant about a foot high, which has no branches and only a cluster of red flowers at the top). When they had finished it they told Olelbis to put it on the north side of the house.

"Now, my grandmothers," said Olelbis, "I want a cover for the east side."

"My grandson," said each, "we are sorry that you are alone, sorry that you have no one to help you in building this house. Now take this mat and put it on the east side."

They gave him a mat made of the same plant that was used for a binding to hold the top of the house.

"I want a cover now for the south side." The old women put their hands to the east, and a plant came to them a foot high with white blossoms, of very sweet odor. A great deal of this plant came, and they made a mat of it. They put all the blossoms outside. The mat covered the south side.

"Now, how shall I cover the west side?"

"We have the covering here already, made of kin-tekchi-luli" (a plant with blue and white blossoms).

They put that mat on the west side, the blossoms turned outward.

The old women gave him all kinds of beautiful plants now, and flowers to form a great bank around the bottom of the sweat house. All kinds of flowers that are in the world now were gathered around the foot of that sweat house, an enormous bank of them; every beautiful color and every sweet odor in the world was there.

When they went into the sweat house, the perfume was delightful. The two old women said then:

"All people to come in the world below will talk of this house, and call it Olelpanti Hlut when they tell about it and praise the house on high."

Olelbis said: "I want to lay something lengthwise on each side of the door. What shall I get?"

The two said: "We will get sau" (acorn bread made in a great round roll like a tree-trunk).

They got sau, and put a roll at each side of the door; these rolls were put there for people to sit on.

Olelbis walked around, looked at everything, and said,

"I want this house to grow, to be wide and high, to be large enough for all who will ever come to it."

Then the house began to extend and grow wider and higher, and it became wonderful in size and in splendor. Just as daylight was coming the house was finished and ready. It stood there in the morning dawn, a mountain of beautiful flowers and oak-tree branches; all the colors of the world were on it, outside and inside. The tree in the middle was far above the top of the house, and filled with acorns; a few of them had fallen on every side.

That sweat house was placed there to last forever, the largest and most beautiful building in the world, above or below. Nothing like it will ever be built again.

"Now, my grandson," said the old women, "the house is built and finished. All the people in the world will like this house. They will talk about it and speak well of it always. This house will last forever, and these flowers will bloom forever; the roots from which they grow can never die."

The world fire began on the morning after the sweat house was finished. During the fire they could see nothing of the world below but flames and smoke. Olelbis did not like this.

"Grandson," said the old women, "we will tell you what to do to put out that terrible wakpohas. There is a very old man, Kahit Kiemila, and he lives far north toward the east, outside the first sky. He stays there in one little place; he is all alone, and always in the same place. Tell him what to do, and he will do it. If you don't like the fire and smoke down below, tell the old man to turn his face toward you, to come this way and to bring with him Mem Loimis. He sits with his head between his hands and his face to the north, and never looks up. The place where he sits is called Waiken Pom Pui Humok Pom."

The first person who came to Olelbis on the day of the fire was Kiriu Herit. He came about daylight.

"You have finished the sweat house, my nephew," he said.

"I have," said Olelbis, "but we are going to have trouble, and will you, my uncle, go up on the west side of the sweat house, look around everywhere, and tell me what you see."

Kiriu went to the top of the house and looked. Soon another man came and said, "My brother, you have finished the sweat house."

"Yes," said Olelbis, "and will you, my brother, go up on the east side of the house, stand there, and call to Kahit."

This was Lutchi Herit. Two more came and saluted Olelbis. "Go into the sweat house," he said. These were the two brothers, Tilichi. A fifth person came, Kuntihle, and then a sixth, Sutunut, a great person. Lutchi kept darting around, looking toward the north and calling: "Kahit cannot take me! Kahit cannot take me!" Kahit was getting angry by this time, and thinking to turn and look at Lutchi, for though far away, he heard the noise of his darting and his calling. "That old Kahit may come out, but he cannot catch me!" called Lutchi, as he darted around, always watching the north.

Now Olelbis called Lutchi and Sutunut, and said: "You, Lutchi, go north, pry up the sky and prop it; here is a sky pole and a sky prop." Turning to Sutunut, he plucked a feather from each of his wings and said: "Go to Kahit in Waiken Pom Pui Humok Pom; tell him to come south with Mem Loimis. She lives not far from him. Her house is in the ground. And tell him to blow his whistle with all his breath. Put these two feathers on his cheeks just in front of his ears."

Lutchi went quickly. No one could travel as fast as he. He reached the sky on the north, raised and propped it. Sutunut gave the message to Kahit, who raised his head from between his hands slowly and turned toward the south. Sutunut put the feathers in his cheeks then, as Olelbis had commanded.

One person, Sotchet, who lived just south of Kahit, spoke up now and said, "Go ahead, Kahit. I am in a hurry to see my father, Olelbis. I will follow you. I am drinking my mother's milk." (He was doing that to bring great water.) His mother was Mem Loimis.

"Come with me, Mem Loimis," said Kahit to Sotchet's mother. "When I start, go ahead a little. I will help you forward."

Olelbis was watching, and thought, "Kahit is ready to start, and Mem Loimis is with him."

Olelbis made then an oak paddle, and hurled it to where Sotchet was. Sotchet caught the paddle, made a tail of it, put it on, and went plashing along through the water. Not far from Kahit lived an old woman, Yoholmit Pokaila. She made a basket of white willow, and finished it just as Mem Loimis was ready to start. In the same place was Sosini Herit, just ready to move. In one hand he held a bow and arrows, with the other he was to swim.

Olelbis saw all this, saw and knew what people were doing or preparing to do. "Grandmothers," he said, "Mem Loimis is ready to move. Kahit is ready. All the people around them will follow."

The great fire was blazing, roaring all over the earth. Burning rocks, earth, trees, people, burning everything.

Mem Loimis started, and with her Kahit. Water rushed in through the open place made by Lutchi when he raised the sky. It rushed in like a crowd of rivers, covered the earth, and put out the fire as it rolled on toward the south. There was so much water outside that could not come through that it rose to the top of the sky and rushed on toward Olelpanti.

Olelbis went to the top of the sweat house and stood looking toward the north. Sula Kiemila and Toko Kiemila had come that morning. "Take your places north of the sweat house," said Olelbis, and they did so. Olelbis saw everything coming toward him in the water from the north, all kinds of people who could swim. They were so many that no one could count them. Before he had built the sweat house, the two grandmothers had said to Olelbis: "Go far south and get pilok, which is a tall plant with a strong fibre, and make a cord." He did so, and twisted a strong cord from pilok. Of this he made a sling. He put his hand to the west, and kilson came on it, a round white stone an inch and a half in diameter. He put the stone in the sling, tied the sling around his head, and kept it there always.

He took this sling in his hand now, and stood watching ready to throw the stone at something that was coming in the water. Olelbis threw with his left hand. He was left-handed, and for this reason was called Nomhlyestawa (throwing west with the left hand).

Mem Loimis went forward, and water rose mountains high. Following closely after Mem Loimis came Kahit. He had a whistle in his mouth; as he moved forward he blew it with all his might, and made a terrible noise. The whistle was his own; he had had it always. He came flying and blowing. He looked like an enormous bat, with wings spread. As he flew south toward the other side of the sky, his two cheek feathers grew straight out, became immensely long, waved up and down, grew till they could touch the sky on both sides.

While Kahit flew on and was blowing his whistle, old Yoholmit lay in her basket; she floated in it high on the great waves, and laughed and shouted, "Ho! Ho!"

"How glad my aunt is to see water; hear how she laughs!" said Olelbis. And he gave her two new names, Surut Womulmit (hair-belt woman) and Mem Hlosmulmit (water-foam woman). "Look at my aunt," said Olelbis again. "She is glad to see water!"

As Yoholmit was laughing and shouting she called out,

"Water, be big! Grow all the time! Be deep so that I can float and float on, float all my life."

Olelbis was watching everything closely. Sosini Herit was coming. He held a bow and arrows in one hand and swam with the other. He was next behind old Yoholmit.

"Look at my brother, Sosini, look at him swimming," said Olelbis. When mountains of water were coming near swiftly, Olelbis said to the two old women, "Go into the sweat house." The two brothers, Kuntihle and Tede Wiu, went in also. Olelbis stood ready to use his sling. When Yoholmit was coming near, he hurled a stone at her. He did not hit her. He did not wish to hit her. He hit the basket and sent her far away east in it until the basket struck the sky.

When the water reached Toko, it divided, went east and west, went no farther south in Olelpanti. At this time Olelbis saw a hollow log coming from the north. On it were sitting a number of Tede Memtulit and Bisus people. Just behind the log came someone with a big willow-tree in his mouth, sometimes swimming east, sometimes swimming west. He slapped the water with his new tail, making a loud noise. This was Sotchet, the son of Mem Loimis. Olelbis struck the log with a stone from his sling, and threw it far away west with all the Memtulits on it except one, which came to the sweat house and said,

"My brother, I should like to stay with you here." This was Tede Memtulit.

"Stay here," said Olelbis.

The next came Wokwuk. He was large and beautiful, and had very red eyes. When Kahit came flying toward the sweat house, and was still north of it, Olelbis cried to him,

"My uncle, we have had wind enough and water enough; can you not stop them?"

Kahit flew off toward the east and sent Mem Loimis back. "Mem Loimis," he said, "you are very large and very strong, but I am stronger. Go back! If not, I will stop you. Go home!"

Mem Loimis went back north, went into the ground where she had lived before. Kahit went east, then turned and went north to where he had been at first, and sat down again in silence with his head between his hands.

When Mem Loimis and Kahit had gone home, all water disappeared; it was calm, dry, and clear again everywhere. Olelbis looked down on the earth, but could see nothing: no mountains, no trees, no ground, nothing but naked rocks washed clean. He stood and looked in every direction, looked east, north, west, south, to see if he could find anything. He found nothing. After a time he saw in the basin of a great rock some water, all that was left. The rock was in Tsarau Heril. "My grandmothers," asked Olelbis, "what shall I do now? Look everywhere, there is nothing in the world below but naked rocks. I don't like it."

"Wait a while, grandson," they said. "We will look and see if we can find something somewhere. Perhaps we can."

On this earth there was no river. No creek, no water in any place but that water at Tsarau Heril. This was the morning after Mem Loimis had gone home.

Now a person came from the east to Olelpanti, Klabus Herit. "My uncle," said Olelbis to Klabus, "I am looking all over the world below, but can see nothing on it. Do you know any place beyond the sky on the north, south, east, or west, where there is earth?"

"I know no place where there is earth," said Klabus.

Soon another person, Yilahl Herit, was seen coming from the west. When he came up, Olelbis asked,

"My uncle, do you know of earth, or trees, or people in any place beyond the sky?"

"I do not," answered Yilahl. "But are you all well here?"

"We are well and unharmed," answered Olelbis.

"How did you come here? Which way did you come? Where did you stay that the world fire did not burn you?" asked Klabus of Yilahl.

"I will tell you," said Yilahl. "When the fire began. I went west, I went under the sky where it touches the lower world. I went out to the other side. The fire did not go there. There is earth now in that place."

"My uncles", said Olelbis, "I want you both to go down, to go west, and get that earth for me."

"I will go," said Klabus; and turning to the two old women he said: "Give me two baskets, very large round baskets."

The old women made two very large baskets. Klabus took these and went west with Yilahl. As soon as they started Olelbis took a great sky net (kolchi koro), and spread it out; it reached to the ends of the sky in every direction; it was full of small, fine holes, like a sieve. He spread it out in Olelpanti; put it under his sweat house. It is above this world still, but we cannot see it.

Klabus and Yilahl went west to where the earth was. Klabus dug it up and filled the baskets quickly; went to the north side of the sweat house and threw the earth into the great net, then hurried back and brought more earth and threw it on the net. It went through the net and fell down here, fell on the rocks in this world like rain.

Klabus hurried back and forth very quickly, carrying one basket on each arm. He was going and coming for five days and five nights; fine earth was falling all this time, till the rocks were covered, and there was plenty of earth everywhere.

Yilahl gave no help. He went down the first time with Klabus, showed him the earth, and stayed there, but he did not help to carry earth or to dig it. When Klabus had covered all the rocks with good earth, Olelbis told him to rest.

"Go west and tell Yilahl to help you," said Olelbis to Klabus the next morning, after he had rested. "Tell him to work with you, fixing the earth which you have thrown down. Go, both of you; make mountains, hills, and level country; arrange everything."

No fire was visible anywhere; every bit had been quenched by the flood which came in after Lutchi propped up the sky. Yilahl came out into this world below from under the edge of the sky in the west, and Klabus came out from under it in the east. Both met and went to work. Yilahl made the small hills and fixed the rolling country.

Klabus raised the great mountains and mountain ranges. There was nothing but earth and rock yet; no people at work only these two, Klabus and Yilahl.

Olelbis stood watching and looking; he looked five days, and found no fire in any place. The next day he saw a little smoke in the southwest coming straight up as if through a small opening. Olelbis had a Winishuyat on his head tied in his hair, and the Winishuyat said to him,

"My brother, look; there is a little fire away down south; a woman there has fire in a small basket."

This woman was Yonot, the mother of Pohila, who had gone back to live in her old house.

"My brother," said Olelbis, turning to Tede Wiu, "do you see that place there? Go and bring fire from it." Tede Wiu went quickly to the place where Olelbis had seen the smoke. He found a house, and looking through a crack he saw the glow of fire, but not the fire itself.

Tede Wiu stayed five days and nights watching. He could not get into the house where the basket was. That house was closed firmly, and had no door. At last he went back to Olelpanti without fire.

"I should like to catch the fish which I see jumping in that southern water," said Kuntihle, "but we could not cook fish if we had it, for we have no fire."

"You would better go yourself and try to get fire," said Olelbis.

Kuntihle went and watched five days. He could not get into the house, and no fire fell out. He went back to Olelpanti.

"We need fire," said Olelbis, "but how are we to get it? Go again and try," he said to Tede Wiu; "watch till fire falls out, or go in and take some."

Klabus and Yilahl were at work still. Tede Wiu went and crept under the house, watched five days and nights, stayed right under the basket in which Pohila was. On the sixth morning, very early, just at daybreak, a spark of fire fell out. Tede Wiu caught the spark, ran off quickly to Olelbis, and gave it to him.

They had fire in Olelpanti now, and were glad. Neither Yonot, the mother, nor Tilikus, the father of Pohila, knew that fire had been carried away to Olelpanti. Klabus and Yilahl were still at work making the mountains and valleys, and had almost finished.

Now that there was fire in Olelpanti, Kuntihle said: "I will go and see that fish. Tilitchi, will you come with me?"

Tilitchi went. Before they started Olelbis gave them a fish net. They caught a fish, and went back, dressed, cooked, and ate it.

"This is a good fish," said Olelbis. "How did it get into that water? That pond in the rock is small and round; there is no water to run into it. Grandmothers, what shall we do with this pond and the fish in it?"

"We will tell you," said the old

women. "Go to the west under the sky, break off a strip of the sky, bring it here, and make a pointed pole of it."

Klabus and Yilahl were just putting the top on Bohem Puyuk; all the other mountains in the world were finished.

Olelbis went west, got the sky pole, and pointed one end of it. He stuck the pole down at the foot of Bohem Puyuk, drew the point of it along southward, making a deep furrow. Then he stuck the pole far north, and made a second furrow to join the eastern end of the first one. There was no water in either furrow yet, and Olelbis said,

"Now, my grandmothers, what shall I do next?"

"Take this grapevine root," they said. "Throw it to the place where you thrust in the pole at the foot of Bohem Puyuk."

He threw the root. One end of it went into the mountain, the other hung out; from this water flowed.

"This will be called Wini Mem," said the grandmothers. "The country around it will be good; many people will go there to live in the future."

The grandmothers gave a second root, a tule root, and Olelbis threw this far up north, where one end stuck in the ground as had the grapevine root, and from the other end flowed Pui Mem—there is much tule at the head of Pui Mem to this day.

Olelbis took his sky pole again and made deep furrows down southward from Bohema Mem, large ones for large rivers and smaller ones for creeks. Water flowed and filled the furrows, flowed southward till it reached the place where Kuntihle found the first fish; and when the large river reached that little pond, fish went out of it into the river, and from the river into all creeks and rivers.

When the rivers were finished, and water was running in them, Olelbis saw an acorn tree in the east, outside the sky. He looked on the north side of the tree and saw someone hammering. He hurled a stone from his sling, struck down the person, and sent Tilitchi to bring him. Tilitchi brought him.

"Of what people is this one?" he asked of the old women.

"He is of a good people," they answered. "Put him on the central pillar of the sweat house; we call him Tsurat." Tsurat was only stunned. When Tsurat was taken to the central pillar, he climbed it, stopping every little while and hammering. The sound which he made, "Ya-tuck! Ya-tuck!" was heard outside the sweat house, a good sound; all liked to hear it.

Olelbis saw on the same tree another of the same family. When he was brought, the old women said, "This is Min Taitai; put him on the ground east of the fire"—the fire was in the middle.

Min Taitai began to talk to himself. They could hear two words, "Wit, wit!" (coming back, coming back).

Olelbis stunned a third person, who was brought by Tilitchi. The old women said, "He, too, is of a good people, he is Hessiha; let him be with Min Taitai, and put a basket of red earth and water near them."

Min Taitai talked on to himself, "Wit, wit!"

"Who is 'Wit, wit?'" asked Hessiha.

"Sas" (the sun), answered Min Taitai, "was going down, and now he is coming back; that is who 'Wit, wit' is."

"Who is coming back?" asked Hessiha.

"Sas is coming back."

"Sas is not coming back, he is going on."

(In winter Sas goes down south, and in summer he comes back north. Min Taitai was saying Sas is coming back, up north. Hessiha thought he was saying Sas has gone down toward the west, and now is coming back east without setting.)

"Wit, wit" (coming back, coming back), said Min Taitai. "Cherep, cherep!" (going on, going on), said Hessiha.

Soon they came to blows, began to fight; when fighting, Hessiha took red mud from the basket and threw it. Min Taitai took mud, too, and threw it at Hessiha. Both were soon covered with mud and water.

Clover, beautiful grasses, and plants of all kinds were growing around the sweat house in Olelpanti. The whole place was a mass of blossoms. "Now, my grandmothers," said Olelbis, "tell me what you think. All that ground below us is bare; there is nothing on it. What can we do for it?"

"My grandson, in a place southeast of this is a house in which people live. The place is called Hlihli Pui Hlutton (acorn eastern sweat house place). An old man lives there. Send Tsurat to bring that old man to us."

"I will," said Olelbis; and he sent Tsurat, who brought Hlihli Kiemila, who had lived all his life in that eastern sweat house. When Olelbis looked at the old man, he said to Tsurat: "Go to the world beneath us with Hlihli. Carry him all over it, north, south, east, and west."

Hlihli was like an old worm-eaten acorn outside; inside he was like meal or snuff, and when he moved this inside sifted out of him. He had a daughter, Hlihli Loimis, and she had many sons.

Tsurat carried Hlihli all over the world, and when he had carried him five days little oak bushes were springing up everywhere from the dust which fell from him. They took seeds of clover growing around the sweat house in Olelpanti and scattered them; clover grew up in every place. Olelbis threw down all kinds of flower seeds from the flowers blossoming in Olelpanti.

A little way east of Olelbis's sweat house lived Sedit. At the time of the fire he ran through under the sky in the south and went up on the sky to Olelpanti. He stayed there with Olelbis until the fire and water stopped. Then he went east a short distance, and made a house for himself During the great water Sedit caught Wokwuk, and afterward built a house near his own for him.

There was a big rock east of Sedit's house. Olelbis saw Chuluhl sitting on this rock, and he said,

"My brother, I have put clover on the earth. I want you to go down there and stay with that clover, stay with it always. The place is a good one for you." This place was Tokuston on Pui Mem. "Take this pontcheuchi (headband made of dew), wear it around your head, wear it always, guard the clover, put your head among its leaves, and keep the grass and clover wet and green all the time. I will take that rock from near Sedit's house, and put it down on the earth for you." (The rock stands now about fifty miles above Paspuisono. It is called Pui Toleson—rock leaning east.)

Wokwuk at the time of the great water lost the middle and longest finger on one hand; it went far north, and after a time became a deer, and from that deer came all the deer in the world after the fire. When Kahit and Mem Loimis went east on the way home, Wokwuk lost a small feather from above one of his eyes. It went west and was turned into the beautiful shells tsanteris. He also lost two neck feathers. They went west and became kalas, and from that came all pearl shells. He lost the tip of his little finger. It went west and became the Wokwuk bird down here. He lost some spittle. It went east on the water and turned to blue beads, such as people wear now around their necks. Wokwuk lost a small bit of his intestines. It went south on the water and became mempak; from that come all mempak (water bone). He lost a piece of his backbone. It went east on the water and became an elk, and from that elk came all elks.

One day Sedit said to Olelbis, when all were telling Olelbis what they were going to do: "Grandson, I am going to take off my skin and let it go to the world below."

"Do so," said Olelbis.

Sedit took off his skin as he would a coat, and threw it down to this world.

"Now there will be Sedits all over down there," he said.

While Olelbis was gathering into Olelpanti all the people from every place outside this sky above us, Min Taitai and Hessiha were disputing and throwing red mud at each other.

Olelbis gathered people from every side till he had gathered them all at his house. They were there in crowds and in thousands, singing and talking inside and outside, everywhere in Olelpanti.

One morning Olelbis said to the old women, "My grandmothers, I cannot tell what to do nor how to get what I want, but far west of here is a ridge that stretches from the south to the north, and on that ridge people of some kind come from the south and hurry north; they do that every day; they go north along that ridge, and I do not know what kind of people they are. When they are on the top of the ridge, they run north very swiftly. As soon as Klabus and Yilahl finished the level ground and the hills and mountains in the world below, these people began to travel along the ridge in this way, and they have been going north ever since."

"You do not know those people," said the old women, "but we know them, the Katkatchila brothers know them; they are Kahsuku, the cloud dogs, the cloud people. If you wish to know more about these cloud people, ask the elder Katkatchila; he knows them; he lives far west at this time; go and ask him, go yourself."

Olelbis set out the next morning early, and just before he reached Katkatchila's house in the west he came upon someone who was stooping and looking toward the south. It was the elder Katkatchila, who was watching the cloud people.

"Stop, my brother," said Katkatchila, "and watch with me."

The two looked along the ridge toward the south—it was before sunrise then—and they saw a person come a little way in sight, then turn and go back. He did not come nearer because he saw Olelbis. The cloud people are very timid; they can see a long distance, and have a very keen scent. When he saw Olelbis, this one ran away home.

"My brother," said Katkatchila to Olelbis, "we have been watching here to drive back these cloud people. We have watched night and day, I and my little brother. My brother is near the eastern slope of this ridge which runs north and south; he stays there and watches."

"What do you mean by cloud people?" asked Olelbis; "what kind of people are they? I have seen only the head and neck of one; what I saw looked well, seemed good. I wish you, my brothers, would catch one of these people, if you can."

"How is it that you do not know these people?" asked Katkatchila. "You ought to know them; you have seen every place, every person, everything; you ought to know these people. I will tell you how they came. My sister and I made the great world fire; we made the wakpohas because Torihas and his people stole my flint. I was angry. I told my sister to put her baby outside the house. We put pitch-pine around it, and fire blazed up from the baby. When the fire was burning all over the earth and there were great flames and smoke, a big water and a strong wind came; the water filled the whole world with steam, and the wind drove the steam and smoke from the great fire, and carried them far off to the south, where they became a people, the cloud people. These people are red or white or black, all of them, and they are going north always. They have good heads and long necks."

"I should like to stand near some of these people and look at them," said Olelbis.

"I do not like to see them go north," said Katkatchila. "My brother and I are here trying to drive them back;

but they go north in spite of us. My brother is on the other slope over there to frighten them back; but they turn to the east a little and go around him."

"Bring your brother here," said Olelbis.

Katkatchila brought his brother, and the two said,

"These cloud people are very wild; we cannot go near them. But we should like to drive them back or catch them."

"Go west. my brothers," said Olelbis. "and get something to stop that gap on the east where the cloud people pass you and go north. Stop that opening on the east, and stop the western slope also, leaving only a narrow place for them to go through. Get yew wood, make a very high fence with it, and stop the eastern slope."

They brought the yew wood and made a very high fence on the eastern slope, and then one on the west, leaving only a narrow gap open.

"Go to the east now," said Olelbis, "get katsau, which is a strong, fibrous plant, and make strings of it. Make a rope of the string and set a snare in the opening of the fence across the western slope to catch those cloud people."

The elder brother was on the ridge near the western slope, and the younger on the ridge near the eastern slope. The brothers made the snare and set it on the western slope. Both watched and waited for the clouds to come.

"Now, my brother," said Olelbis, when he saw this work, "watch these people well, frighten them into the trap, and I will go back to Olelpanti."

The next morning early the two brothers were watching, and very soon they saw a great many cloud people coming. Both brothers were lying flat on the middle of the ridge, so that the clouds could not see them. The clouds watched closely. They came to the place where they had always turned east to go past little Katkatchila; they ran against the fence and could not pass. They turned and went toward the west to pass northward along the central ridge; but when both brothers stood up, the clouds rushed to the western slope and fell into the trap.

Olelbis saw this and said: "Now, my brothers are driving them in. I must go and see!" And he ran off quickly.

"Oh, my brother," said the Katkatchilas when he came, "we have caught one cloud. All the rest went through the fence. They broke it—we caught one; the others burst away."

Olelbis looked at the cloud and said,

"This is a black one! They broke down the fence and ran away! They are a strong people." "Now, my brother," said the elder Katkatchila, "we will skin this cloud, and you may have the skin. We will give it to you."

"I shall be glad to have it," said Olelbis.

They stripped the skin from the cloud, and, when giving it to Olelbis, the elder one said, "You must tan this carefully."

"Make another fence," said Olelbis, "but make it stronger. You will catch more of these people."

"A great many clouds have broken through our fence today and gone north. Others went before we made the fence. We shall see these people by and by," said Katkatchila. (He meant that clouds would stay in the north and become another people; stay there always.)

Olelbis took the skin, turned toward home, and travelled on. He was rubbing it in his hands, tanning it as he went. The brothers put the body in a hole and buried it, not caring for the flesh. They wanted only the skin.

Olelbis went along tanning the skin of the black cloud, and he walked around everywhere as he tanned. He went away west, then north, then south, then east. At last he came home with the skin well tanned. He spread it and stretched it smooth. The two Katkatchila brothers had not been able yet to catch another of the cloud people, but they were working at it all the time. After Olelbis spread the skin on the ground, he took it up and said to one of the old women,

"My grandmother is always cold; let us give her this skin;" and he gave it to her. Each of the two old women said,

"My grandson, we are glad to have this skin. We shall sleep warm now."

"I must go," said Olelbis, "and see my brothers drive in more of the cloud people." And he went.

"We cannot catch these clouds," said the older brother; "they go through our fence, they escape, we cannot catch them; they have gone to the north, they will stay there and become a new people. We have caught only one, a white cloud. Those that have escaped will become a new people; they will be Yola Ka" (snow clouds).

The Katkatchilas stripped the skin from the white cloud and gave it to Olelbis. He went around north, south, east, and west, tanning it in the same way that he had tanned the black skin. After he had tanned it well he spread the skin, stretched it, straightened it; then he gave it to the other grandmother.

Both old women were glad now. Both said: "We shall sleep warm at night now all the time."

The next day the two brothers caught a third cloud, a red one, but they kept that skin for themselves. They did not give it to Olelbis, because he told them to keep it. We see this skin now often enough, for the brothers hang it up when they like in the west and sometimes in the east.

"Now," said the two old women, "we have this white skin and this black one. When we hang the white skin outside this house, white clouds will go from it, will go away down south, where its people began to live, and then they will come from the south and travel north to bring rain. When they come back, we will hang out the black skin, and from it a great many black rain clouds will go out, and from these clouds heavy rain will fall on all the world below."

From that time the old women hang out the two skins, first the white, then the black skin, and when clouds enough have gone from them they take the skins into the sweat house again; and from these two skins comes all the rain to people in this world.

"The cloud people who went north will stay in the northwest," said Olelbis, "and from them will come snow to people hereafter."

All this time the people in Olelpanti were singing and talking. Any one could hear them from a distance. Olelbis had brought in a great many different kinds of people, others had come themselves, and still others were coming. After the tanning of the two cloud skins a man came and took his place above the sweat house door, and sat there with his face to the east. This was Kar Kiemila. Right after him came Tsararok, and took his place at the side of Kar. The next came Kau; then the two brothers Hus came, and Wehl Dilidili. All these people in the sweat house and around it asked one another,

"What shall we do? Where shall we live? We should like to know what Olelbis will do with us."

"You will know very soon where we are going," said Toko and Sula. "Olelbis will put us in our places; he is chief over all."

The next morning Olelbis said: "Now, my grandmothers, what do you think best? What are we to do with the people here? Is it best for them to stay in Olelpanti?"

"Our grandson," answered the old women, "send all that are not needed here to the lower world; turn them into something good for the people who are to come soon, those fit for this place up here. The great people, the best ones, you will keep in Olelpanti, and send down only a little part of each of them to turn into something in the world below and be of use to people there."

Olelbis called all who were in the sweat house to come out, and he began to send them to their places.

To Kar he said: "Go and live on Wini Mem. Be a gray heron there; that is a good country for you." (Before white people came there were many of these birds on that river.)

To Toko he said: "Go to Kawiken on Pui Mem. Be a sunfish and live there always. You, Sula, go to the south of Bohem Puyuk on Wini Mem. Be a trout, and live at Sulanharas."

To Torihas he said: "You will be a blue crane," and to Chalilak: "You will be a goose. You both will have two places to live in, one in the south and the other in the north. You will go north in the spring and live there all summer; you will go south in the fall and live in the south all winter. Do this always; travel that way every year." To Kiriu he said: "Go and live along the water. You will be a loon, and you will go up and down great rivers all your life."

To Katsi he said: "You will be a fish hawk, catch fish and eat them, live along rivers."

Olelbis plucked one small feather from the neck of Moihas. This he threw down and said, "Be an eagle, and live on high mountains." All bald eagles on earth came from that feather, but the great Moihas remained above with Olelbis, where he is now.

From Lutchi Olelbis plucked one feather, threw it down, and said: "You will be a humming-bird. Fly around in spring when the green grass comes and the trees and flowers bloom. You will be on blossoms and dart from one to another everywhere." Lutchi himself stayed in Olelpanti.

Olelbis pulled a feather from Kau, threw it down, and said: "You will fly along rivers, be a white crane, and live near them always." The great Kau stayed in Olelpanti with Olelbis.

From the elder Hus brother Olelbis plucked a feather from the right side, sent the feather down on this earth, and said,

"You will be a buzzard down there, and in spring go up on Wini Mem. and look for dead salmon and other fish along Pui Mem, Bohema Mem, and other rivers, eat dead salmon and other fish. When people kill a snake or something else which they do not like, you will go and eat the snake or other dead thing. The Wintu, the coming people, will feed you always with what is dead."

Tilitchi had been sent for three persons, and now he brought the first.

"Who is this?" asked Olelbis of the old women.

"This is Dokos", they said; "he is bad."

Dokos was placed a little northeast of the sweat house. He sat looking toward the west. Tilichi brought in a second and third person.

"Who are these?" asked Olelbis.

"These are both bad people," said the old women. "These are Wima Loimis and Klak Loimis."

"Put them with Dokos," said Olelbis. After he had called all the people out of the sweat house to send them to their proper places, Olelbis had put something on their teeth to make them harmless.

"Come here, Wima Loimis," said Olelbis. "I have something to put on your teeth so that they may harm no one."

"I want nothing on my teeth," said Wima Loimis. "If something were put on them I could not eat." He asked again, but she shook her head, saying: "I want nothing on my teeth, I could not eat if anything were put on them."

"If she will not come, come you, Klak Loimis." Klak Loimis would not go to him.

"Why not come when I call you?" asked Olelbis.

"My sister Wima will not go. She says that she could not eat if her teeth were touched. I want nothing on my teeth. I am afraid that I could not eat."

"Very well," answered Olelbis, "you, Wima, and you, Klak, want to be different from others. Come, Dokos, I will touch your teeth."

"My sisters, Klak and Wima, want nothing on their teeth. I want nothing on mine. I am angry at my sisters; my heart hates them. I do not wish to be good. I am angry at my sisters. I will be wicked as well as they." Then turning to his sisters he said: "After a while people will employ me against you whenever they are angry at you. Whenever you bite people or hurt them, they will call me to fight against you, and I will go with them. I will go into your bodies and kill you. Then you will be sorry for what you have done today. Olelbis asked you to be good. He wants you to be good, but you are not willing. I will be bad to punish you."

When the two women heard these words they cried, and Wima said, "Well, my brother, we can put something on our teeth yet."

Dokos placed his head between his hands and sat awhile in that posture. Then he straightened himself and said,

"You two have talked enough; you would better stop. You are not like me; I am stronger than both of you, and I shall be so always. You, Wima, and you, Klak, will hate people only, but I shall hate all living things. I shall hate you, hate everyone; kill you, kill everyone. I want nothing of anyone. I want no friend in any place."

"Well," said Olelbis, "you go as you are."

"I will go first," said Dokos. "Go," said Olelbis, "to Koiham Nomdaltopi, be flint there, and spread all around the place. You, Klak Loimis, will go to Klak Kewilton, be a rattlesnake there, increase and spread everywhere. I will send you, Wima, to Wima Wai Tsarauton; you will be a grizzly bear there. After a while a great family will come from you and spread over all the country. You will be bad; and, Klak, you will be bad, but, Dokos, you will be the worst, always ready to hurt and kill; always angry, always hating your sisters and everyone living."

"You, Klak, and you, Wima, when you see people you will bite them, and people will take Dokos to kill you, and Dokos will go into your bodies, and you will die. Wima, you will be sorry that you would not let me change your teeth. You, Klak, will be sorry. You will bite people, and they will kill you because you cannot run away from them. Your dead body will lie on the ground, and buzzards will eat it."

"Dokos, you will go to your place and increase. People will go there and get you to kill your sisters and others for them, and when you have pleased them and killed all the people they wished you to kill, when they want you no longer, they will throw you down on a rock and break you to pieces, then you will be nothing. You will be dead forever. Now go!"

To all those who let their teeth be made innocent, Olelbis said: "You will go to where I send you, one here, another there." And he gave their places to all. To some he said: "After a while the new people will use you for food," and to the others he said: "The new people will use your skins, and you will be of service to them, you will be good for them."

The first person taken up to Olelbis's sweat house was Tsurat; and now Olelbis spoke to Tsurat last of all and said,

"Pluck one feather from your back."

Tsurat plucked it.

Olelbis threw the feather to the earth and said,

"The place where this falls will be called Tsuratton Mem Puisono. This feather will become woodpeckers, and their place will be there. Their red feathers will be beautiful, and everyone will like their red scalps and will use them for headbands. The woodpeckers will be also called Topi chilchihl" (bead birds).

All people that were good on this earth only, of use only here, Olelbis sent down to be beasts, birds, and other creatures. The powerful and great people that were good in Olelpanti and useful there he kept with himself, and sent only a feather or a part of each to become something useful down here. The good people themselves, the great ones, stayed above, where they are with Olelbis now.

Creation of Men

Iroquois story of the Creation of Men. Updated and edited version from Seneca Indian Myths by Jeremiah Curtin, as told by Esq Johnson.

Shagodyoweg is often translated False Face, but the literal meaning is "The Great One Who Protects Them (Mankind)" from sickness and pestilence, and is considered to be of the Wind People. Above, in the center of the Blue, people lived before there was any earth down here. In the middle of the village up there stood a tree covered with white blossoms; when the tree was in bloom, its blossoms gave light to the people and when the blossoms fell, there was darkness.

One time a woman in that village dreamed and in her dream an oñgwe said to her, "That tree with white blossoms on it must be pulled up by the roots."

When the woman told her dream, the people were silent, Some time passed and the woman dreamed again.

The oñgwe in her dream, said, "A circle must be dug, around the tree and the tree pulled up by the roots, then something giving more and better light will come"

The woman told her dream a second time, but still the people took no heed of it. She dreamed a third time and again was told that the tree must be pulled up. Then a man said, "I think we should give heed to this dream; we have better light and the people will have cause to rejoice." His advice was listened to, men cut around the roots of the tree; when the roots were loosened the tree sank down, and disappeared.

The chief of the people said, "I did not heed this dream for I knew something would happen to the people if the tree were pulled up." He was angry and ordered that the woman, who had the dream, should be brought and pushed into the hole left by the tree. Men caught her and threw her into the hole. Now that the tree with white blossoms was gone it was dark all the time.

The woman fell and fell. The hole was deep and long, but at last she came out into bright light, into our sky, and looking down she saw only water.

It is well known that in very ancient days all animals had the gift of speech by which they communicated with one another as freely as human beings do at the present time.

Down under the Blue there was just one enormous body of water on which there were multitudes of various kinds of water fowl and aquatic animals amusing themselves after their own fashion. One of the duck family looked up and saw a dark object coming down from the sky.

The duck cried out to the other birds and animals, "Some strange being is coming down to us."

A council was called at once to decide how they could prepare a resting place for this being, who might not be fitted to live on the water as they did. A duck said, "I'll dive and find if there is any bottom to this water." After a time, the duck came to the surface, shot into the air and fell back, lifeless. Several water birds made the same attempt with a similar result.

All the people that lived in the water were there.

Loon said to fish-hawk, "Go and meet that creature in the air and hold it till we are ready for you to come down."

Fish-hawk went and they saw him meet the woman, for it was a woman.

Turtle said, "I'll take care of her."

Loon said, "You can't, you are too fond of eating."

Horned snake said, "I'll take care of her. She can sit between my horns. I'll carry her wherever I go." Loon said, "You can't care for her. You are poisonous, you would kill her."

Meanwhile one person after another was trying to bring earth from the bottom of the sea. At last Hell-diver brought up a little. Loon was chief and when Hell-diver came up, he sent all that kind of people after more dirt. Loon said, "Put the dirt on Turtle's back." Turtle was willing, and as fast as the divers brought dirt, Beaver with his tail, pounded it down on Turtle's back, to make it solid. When Loon thought there was enough dirt, Fish-hawk came down with the woman.

The beaver and duck people kept at work making the earth larger and larger. As it grew, more Beavers and Ducks were ordered to work. Bushes began to grow, little red bushes, like water reeds.

Soon the woman gave birth to a child, a girl. The child quickly grew to be a young woman and to be very active. She walked here and there and watched the birds and animals and once when she was wandering around she met a nice looking young man. They fell in love with each other and by their union came night and day. At daybreak the young woman went to meet her husband, at twilight she came home and the man went away.

One evening, after they had parted, the young woman turned to look at her husband, and saw a big Turtle walking along where the man had just been. She thought, "A Turtle has deceived me!"

She told her mother about the man, and said "I am going to die, you must put my body in the ground and cover it up well. Two stalks will grow from my breasts and on each stalk an ear will come. When the ears are ripe you must pick them and give one to each of the boys that are born to me."

The younger woman gave birth to twin boys, and died. The mother buried her daughter and soon two stalks came up out of her grave. And this was the origin of corn.

The boys grew quickly; they were strong and healthy, but the younger was an awkward, ugly looking, disagreeable fellow, with a head like a lump of rough flint.

Once when the elder brother was off by himself, he was lonesome and he thought he would try to make something, so he took mud and when he had molded it into the shape he wanted, he put it down, and asked, "Can't you jump?"

It didn't move, then he blew on it till at last it jumped. And he had created the grasshopper. Then he thought he would make something that would fly higher, so of red clay he made the cherry bird. After he had the clay molded, he set it up and told it to fly in the air. The bird flew and lighted on a bough—this was the first bird. One after another he made all of the birds of the air.

Then he thought he would make something that would run on the ground, so he shaped a deer, brought it to life, and said to it, "You must run fast and go everywhere in the world." He blew on it, and pushed it, and it ran off. In the same way he made different kinds of animals. Then he thought, "Maybe I can make something like myself." Out of the mud he made something that looked like himself, but now, in some way, he found that he had a spirit in his body and he wanted the thing he had lying on the ground to have a spirit too. He wanted to give it some of his own but didn't know how. At last he bent down and blew into its mouth. He hadn't blown into the mouth of any other creature he had made. The image began to move; the young man raised it up, made it stand on its feet, and told it to whoop.

The new man whooped; he had a fine voice. Then he walked off a little way and turned and looked at the young man.

The elder brother had a special place to sit when he made all these creatures. About the time he made man, the younger brother found the place and, while watching his brother, he thought, "I will make a man too." He went away alone, made something as nearly like himself as he could and brought it to life. It didn't look like a man. It was a strange creature, and when its maker saw that it wasn't a man, but some ugly, deformed thing, he said to it, "My brother has made a man, he is over there, go and kill him."

The elder brother was watching the younger, for he was afraid he would make some harmful animal. When he heard him tell the creature he had made to go and destroy man, he went back to his own place, caught the cherry bird and pulling out the hind leg of grasshopper, gave it to the bird, and said, "Go and scare my brother." As the bird took up the leg the bird became very large and the leg was like the leg of a man, and it was bloody. The bird flew near, perched on a limb and called out, "Gowa! Gowa!" When the younger brother saw what the bird had in its beak, he left his work, ran home and said to his grandmother, "A bird came and perched just where I was at work. My brother made it frighten me. I was afraid it would pull my leg out, so I ran."

When the elder brother came the grandmother said, "You shouldn't frighten your brother."

The first man made was wandering about alone. The young man saw him once in a while and saw that he was lonesome. Then he said to himself, "I will make something like my grandmother." He made it out of mud, breathed into it and told it to walk; then he found the man, and said, "I give you this one, you must always go together."

When the woman sat down by the man he thought that her arm was in the way and his was also. He said, "We will cut them off." They cut them off and laid them one side. When the elder brother came along and saw what they had done he said to himself, "This won't do. I will give them blood and pain," and from himself he gave them blood and pain, then he put their arms on and healed them (before that they had neither blood nor pain).

To the man and woman, he said, "I have made you, you will have children like yourselves. You must hunt the animals I have made, kill them and eat their flesh; that will be your food. I am going above the Blue. You will not live forever. You will die and your spirit will go above the Blue."

Creation of the World

Updated and edited version from Myths of the Cherokee by James Mooney.

The earth is a great island floating in a sea of water, and suspended at each of the four cardinal points by a cord hanging down from the sky vault, which is of solid rock. When the world grows old and worn out, the people will die and the cords will break and let the earth sink down into the ocean, and all will be water again. The Indians are afraid of this.

When all was water, the animals were above in Gälûñ'lätï, beyond the arch; but it was very much crowded, and they were wanting more room. They wondered what was below the water, and at last Dâyuni'sï, "Beaver's Grandchild," the little Water-beetle, offered to go and see if it could learn. It darted in every direction over the surface of the water, but could find no firm place to rest. Then it dove to the bottom and came up with some soft mud, which began to grow and spread on every side until it became the island which we call the earth. It was afterward fastened to the sky with four cords, but no one remembers who did this.

At first the earth was flat and very soft and wet. The animals were anxious to get down, and sent out different birds to see if it was yet dry, but they found no place to descend and came back again to Gälûñ'lätï. At last it seemed to be time, and they sent out the Buzzard and told him to go and make ready for them. This was the Great Buzzard, the father of all the buzzards we see now. He flew all over the earth, low down near the ground, and it was still soft. When he reached the Cherokee country, he was very tired, and his wings began to flap and strike the ground, and wherever they struck the earth there was a valley, and where they turned up again there was a mountain. When the animals above saw this, they were afraid that the whole world would be mountains, so they called him back, but the Cherokee country remains full of mountains to this day.

When the earth was dry and the animals came down, it was still dark, so they got the sun and set it in a track to go each day across the island from east to west, just overhead. It was too hot this way, and Tsiska'gïlï', the Red Crawfish, had his shell scorched a bright red, so that his meat was spoiled; and the Cherokee do not eat it. The conjurers put the sun another hand-breadth higher in the air, but it was still too hot. They raised it another time, and another, until it was seven handbreadths high and just under the sky arch. Then it was right, and they left it so. This is why the conjurers call the highest place Gûlkwâ'gine Di'gälûñ'lätiyûñ', "the seventh height," because it is seven hand-breadths above the earth. Each day the sun goes along under this arch, and returns at night on the upper side to the starting place.

There is another world under this, and it is like ours in everything—animals, plants, and people—save that the seasons are different. The streams that come down from the mountains are the trails by which we reach this underworld, and the springs at their heads are the doorways by which we enter it, but to do this one must fast and go to water and have one of the underground people for a guide. We know that the seasons in the underworld are different from ours, because the water in the springs is always warmer in winter and cooler in summer than the outer air.

When the animals and plants were first made—we do not know by whom—they were told to watch and keep awake for seven nights, just as young men now fast and keep awake when they pray to their medicine. They tried to do this, and nearly all were awake through the first night, but the next night several dropped off to sleep, and the third night others were asleep, and then others, until, on the seventh night, of all the animals only the owl, the panther, and one or two more were still awake. To these were given the power to see and to go about in the dark, and to make prey of the birds and animals which must sleep at night. Of the trees only the cedar, the pine, the spruce, the holly, and the laurel were awake to the end, and to them it was given to be always green and to be greatest for medicine, but to the others it was said: "Because you have not endured to the end you shall lose your hair every winter."

Men came after the animals and plants. At first there were only a brother and sister until he struck her with a fish and told her to multiply, and so it was. In seven days a child was born to her, and thereafter every seven days another, and they increased very fast until there was danger that the world could not keep them. Then it was made that a woman should have only one child in a year, and it has been so ever since.

The First Fire

Updated and edited version from Myths of the Cherokee by James Mooney.

In the beginning there was no fire, and the world was cold, until the Thunders (Ani'-Hyûñ'tĭkwälâ'skĭ), who lived up in Gälûñ'lätĭ, sent their lightning and put fire into the bottom of a hollow sycamore tree which grew on an island. The animals knew it was there, because they could see the smoke coming out at the top, but they could not get to it on account of the water, so they held a council to decide what to do. This was a long time ago.

Every animal that could fly or swim was anxious to go after the fire. The Raven offered, and because he was so large and strong they thought he could surely do the work, so he was sent first. He flew high and far across the water and alighted on the sycamore tree, but while he was wondering what to do next, the heat had scorched all his feathers black, and he was frightened and came back without the fire. The little Screech-owl (Wa'huhu') volunteered to go, and reached the place safely, but while he was looking down into the hollow tree a blast of hot air came up and nearly burned out his eyes. He managed to fly home as best he could, but it was a long time before he could see well, and his eyes are red to this day. Then the Hooting Owl (U'guku') and the Horned Owl (Tskĭlĭ') went, but by the time they got to the hollow tree the fire was burning so fiercely that the smoke nearly blinded them, and the ashes carried up by the wind made white rings around their eyes. They had to come home again without the fire, but with all their rubbing they were never able to get rid of the white rings.

Now no more of the birds would venture, and so the little Uksu'hï snake, the black racer, said he would go through the water and bring back some fire. He swam across to the island and crawled through the grass to the tree, and went in by a small hole at the bottom. The heat and smoke were too much for him, too, and after dodging about blindly over the hot ashes until he was almost on fire himself he managed by good luck to get out again at the same hole, but his body had been scorched black, and he has ever since had the habit of darting and doubling on his track as if trying to escape from close quarters. He came back, and the great blacksnake, Gûle'gï, "The Climber," offered to go for fire. He swam over to the island and climbed up the tree on the outside, as the blacksnake always does, but when he put his head down into the hole the smoke choked him so that he fell into the burning stump, and before he could climb out again he was as black as the Uksu'hï.

Now they held another council, for still there was no fire, and the world was cold, but birds, snakes, and four-footed animals all had some excuse for not going, because they were all afraid to venture near the burning sycamore, until at last Känäne'skï Amai'yëhï (the Water Spider) said she would go. This is not the water spider that looks like a mosquito, but the other one, with black downy hair and red stripes on her body. She can run on top of the water or dive to the bottom, so there would be no trouble to get over to the island, but the question was, How could she bring back the fire? "I'll manage that," said the Water Spider; so she spun a thread from her body and wove it into a tusti bowl, which she fastened on her back. Then she crossed over to the island and through the grass to where the fire was still burning. She put one little coal of fire into her bowl, and came back with it, and ever since we have had fire, and the Water Spider still keeps her tusti bowl.

The Flood

Updated and edited version from Myths of the Cherokee *by James Mooney.*

A long time ago a man had a dog, which began to go down to the river each day and look at the water and howl. At last the man was angry and scolded the dog, which then spoke to him and said: "Very soon there is going to be a great freshet and the water will come so high that everybody will be drowned; but if you will make a raft to get upon when the rain comes you can be saved, but you must first throw me into the water." The man did not believe it, and the dog said,

"If you want a sign that I speak the truth, look at the back of my neck." He looked and saw that the dog's neck had the skin worn off so that the bones stuck out.

Then he believed the dog, and began to build a raft. Soon the rain came and he took his family, with plenty of provisions and they all got upon it. It rained for a long time, and the water rose until the mountains were covered and all the people in the world were drowned. Then the rain stopped and the waters went down again, until at last it was safe to come off the raft. Now there was no one alive but the man and his family, but one day they heard a sound of dancing and shouting on the other side of the ridge. The man climbed to the top and looked over; everything was still, but all along the valley he saw great piles of bones of the people who had been drowned, and then he knew that the ghosts had been dancing.

Coming of Earth

Excerpt. Updated and edited version from Kato Texts by Pliny Earle Goddard.

Water came they say. The waters completely joined everywhere. There was no land or mountains or rocks, but only water. Trees and grass were not. There were no fish, or land animals, or birds. Human beings and animals alike had been washed away.

The wind did not then blow through the portals of the world, nor was there snow, nor frost, nor rain. It did not thunder nor did it lightening. Since there were no trees to be struck, it did not thunder. There were neither clouds nor fog, nor was there a sun. It was very dark.

Then it was that this earth with its great, long horns got up and walked down this way from the north. As it walked along through the deep places the water rose to its shoulders.

When it came up into shallower places, it looked up. There is a ridge in the north upon which the waves break. When it came to the middle of the world, in the east under the rising of the sun it looked up again.

There where it looked up will be a large land near to the coast. Far away to the south it continued looking up. It walked under the ground.

Having come from the north it traveled far south and lay down. Nagaitcho, standing on earth's head, had been carried to the south. Where earth lay down Nagaitcho placed its head as it should be and spread gray clay between its eyes and on each horn. Upon the clay he placed a layer of reeds and then another layer of clay. In this he placed upright blue grass, brush, and trees. "I have finished," he said. "Let there be mountain peaks here on its head. Let the waves of the sea break against them."

The Sandstone Sky

Excerpt. Updated and edited version from Kato Texts by Pliny Earle Goddard.

The sandstone rock which formed the sky was old they say. It thundered in the east; it thundered in the south; it thundered in the west; it thundered in the north. "The rock is old, we will fix it," he said. There were two, Nagaitcho and Thunder. "We will stretch it above far to the east," one of them said. They stretched it. They walked on the sky.

In the south he stood on the end of a large rock. In the west he stood on the end of a large rock. In the north he stood on the end of a large, tall rock. In the east he stood on the end of a large, tall rock. He made everything properly. He made the roads. He made a road to the north (where the sun travels in summer).

"In the south there will be no trees but only many flowers," he said. "Where will there be a hole through?" he asked. At the north he made a hole through. East he made a large opening for the clouds. West he made an opening for the fog. "To the west the clouds shall go," he said.

He made a knife. He made it for splitting the rocks. He made the knife very strong.

"How will it be?" he considered. "You go north; I will go south," he said. "I have finished already," he said. "Stretch the rock in the north. You untie it in the west, I will untie it in the east."

"What will be clouds?" he asked. "Set fires about here," he told him. On the upland they burned to make clouds. Along the creek bottoms they burned to make mist. "It is good," he said. He made clouds so the heads of coming people would not ache.

There is another world above where Thunder lives. "You will live here near by," he told Nagaitcho.

"Put water on the fire, heat some water," he said. He made a person out of earth. "Well I will talk to him," he said. He made his right leg and his left leg. He made his right arm and his left arm. He pulled off some grass and wadded it up. He put some of it in place for his belly. He hung up some of it for his stomach. When he had slapped some of the grass he put it in for his heart. He used a round piece of clay for his liver. He put in more clay for his kidneys. He cut a piece into parts and put it in for his lungs. He pushed in a reed (for a trachea).

"What sort will blood be?" he enquired. He pounded up ochre. "Get water for the ochre," he said. He laid him down. He sprinkled him with water. He made his mouth, his nose, and two eyes. "How will it be?" he said. "Make him privates," he said. He made them. He took one of the legs, split it, and made woman of it.

Clouds arose in the east. Fog came up in the west. "Well, let it rain, let the wind blow," he said. "Up in the sky there will be none, there will be only gentle winds. Well, let it rain in the fog," he said. It rained. One could not see. It was hot in the sky. The sun came up now. "What will the sun be?" he said. "Make a fire so it will be hot. The moon will travel at night." The moon is cold.

He came down. "Who, I wonder, can kick open a rock?" he said. "Who can split a tree?" "Well, I will try," said Nagaitcho. He couldn't split the tree. "Who, I wonder, is the strongest?" said Thunder. Nagaitcho didn't break the rock. "Well, I will try," said Thunder. Thunder kicked the rock. He kicked it open. It broke to pieces. "Go look at the rock," he said. "He kicked the rock open," one reported. "Well, I will try a tree," he said. He kicked the tree open. The tree split to pieces.

Thunder and Nagaitcho came down. "Who can stand on the water? You step on the water," Thunder told Nagaitcho. "Yes, I will," Nagaitcho said. He stepped on the water and sank into the ocean. "I will try," said Thunder. He stepped on the water. He stood on it with one leg. "I have finished quickly," he said.

It was evening. It rained. It rained. Every day, every night it rained. "What will happen, it rains every day," they said. The fog spread out close to the ground. The clouds were thick. The people then had no fire. The fire became small. All the creeks were full. There was water in the valleys. The water encircled them.

"Well, I have finished," he said.

"Yes," Nagaitcho said. "Come, jump up. You must jump up to another sky," he told him. "I, too, will do that." "At night when every kind of thing is asleep we will do it," he said.

Every day it rained, every night it rained. All the people slept. The sky fell. The land was not. For a very great distance there was no land. The waters of the oceans came together. Animals of all kinds drowned. Where the water went there were no trees. There was no land.

People became. Seal, sea lion, and grizzly built a dance house. They looked for a place in vain. At Usal they built it, for there the ground was good. There are many sea-lions there. Whale became a human woman. That is why women are so fat. There were no grizzlies. There were no fish. Blue lizard was thrown into the water and became sucker. Bull-snake was thrown into the water and became black salmon. Salamander was thrown into the water and became hook-bill salmon. Grasssnake was thrown into the water and became steel-head salmon. Lizard was thrown into the water and became trout.

Trout cried for his net. "ckak'e, ckak'e," (my net, my net) he said. They offered him every kind of thing in vain. It was "my net" he said when he cried. They made a net and put him into it. He stopped crying. They threw the net and trout into the water. He became trout.

"What will grow in the water?" he asked. Seaweeds grew in the water. Abalones and mussels grew in the water. Two kinds of kelp grew in the ocean. Many different kinds grew there.

"What will be salt?" he asked. They tasted many things. The ocean foam became salt. The Indians tried their salt. They will eat their food with it. They will eat clover with it. It was good salt.

"How will the water of this ocean behave? What will be in front of it?" he asked. "The water will rise up in ridges. It will settle back again. There will be sand. On top of the sand it will glisten," he said. "Old kelp will float ashore. Old whales will float ashore."

"People will eat fish, big fish," he said. "Sea lions will come ashore. They will eat them. They will be good. Devil-fish, although they are ugly looking, will be good. The people will eat them. The fish in the ocean will be fat. They will be good."

"There will be many different kinds in the ocean. There will be water-panther. There will be stone-fish. He will catch people. 'Long-tooth-fish,' gesLcun, will kill sea lion. He will feel around in the water."

"Sea lion will have no feet. He will have a tail. His teeth will be large. There will be no trees in the ocean. The water will be powerful in the ocean," he said.

He placed redwoods and firs along the shore. At the tail of the earth, at the north, he made them grow. He placed land in walls along in front of the ocean. From the north he put down rocks here and there. Over there the ocean beats against them. Far to the south he did that. He stood up pines along the way. He placed yellow pines. Far away he placed them. He placed mountains along in front of the water. He did not stop putting them up even way to the south.

Redwoods and various pines were growing. He looked back and saw them growing. The redwoods had become tall. He placed stones along. He made small creeks by dragging along his foot. "Wherever they flow this water will be good." he said. "They will drink this. Only the ocean they will not drink."

He made trees spring up. When he looked behind himself he saw they had grown. When he came near 'water-head-place' (south) he said to himself, "It is good that they are growing up."

He made creeks along. "This water they will drink," he said. That is why all drink, many different kinds of animals. "Because the water is good, because it is not salt deer, elk, panther, and fishers will drink of it," he said. He caused trees to grow up along. When he looked behind himself he saw they had grown up. "Birds will drink, squirrels will drink," he said. "Many different kinds will drink. I am placing good water along the way."

Many redwoods grew up. He placed water along toward the south. He kicked out springs. "There will be springs," he said. "These will belong to the deer," he said of the deer-licks.

He took along a dog. "Drink this water," he told his dog. He, himself, drank of it. "All, many different kinds of animals and birds, will drink of it," he said.

Tanbark oaks he made to spring up along the way. Many kinds, redwoods, firs, and pines he caused to grow. He placed water along. He made creeks with his foot. To make valleys for the streams he placed the land on edge. The mountains were large. They had grown.

"Let acorns grow," he said. He looked back at the ocean, and at the trees and rocks he had placed along. "The water is good, they will drink it," he said. He placed redwoods, firs, and tanbark oaks along the way. He stood up land and made the mountains. "They shall become large," he said of the redwoods.

He went around the earth, dragging his foot to make the streams and placing redwoods, firs, pines, oaks, and chestnut trees. When he looked back he saw the rocks had become large. And the mountains loomed up. He drank of the water and called it good. "I have arranged it that rocks shall be around the water," he said. "Drink," he told his dog. "Many animals will drink this good water." He placed rocks and banks. He put along the way small white stones. He stood up white and black oaks. Sugar-pines and firs he planted one in a place.

"I will try the water," he said. "Drink, my dog." The water was good. He dragged along his foot, making creeks. He placed the rocks along and turned to look at them. "Drink, my dog," he said. "I, too, will drink. Grizzlies, all kinds of animals, and human beings will drink the water which I have placed among the rocks." He stood up the mountains. He placed the trees along, the firs and the oaks. He caused the pines to grow up. He placed the redwoods one in a place.

He threw salamanders and turtles into the creeks. "Eels will live in this stream," he said. "Fish will come into it. Hook-bill and black salmon will run up this creek. Last of all steel-heads will swim in it. Crabs, small eels, and day-eels will come up."

"Grizzlies will live in large numbers on this mountain. On this mountain will be many deer. The people will eat them. Because they have no gall they may be eaten raw. Deer meat will be very sweet. Panthers will be numerous. There will be many jackrabbits on this mountain," he said.

He did not like yellow jackets. He nearly killed them. He made blue-flies and wasps.

His dog walked along with him. "There will be much water in this stream," he said. "This will be a small creek and the fish will run in it. The fish will be good. There will be many suckers and trout in this stream."

"There will be brush on this mountain," he said. He made manzanita and white-thorn grow there. "Here will be a valley. Here will be many deer. There will be many grizzlies at this place. Here a mountain will stand. Many rattlesnakes, bull snakes, and water-snakes will be in this place.

Here will be good land. It shall be a valley."

He placed fir trees, yellow-pines, oaks, and redwoods one at a place along the way. He put down small grizzly bears. "Water will be bad. It will be black here," he said. "There will be many owls here, the barking-owl, the screech-owl, and the little owl. There shall be many blue jays, grouse, and quails. Here on this mountain will be many wood-rats. Here shall be many varied robins. There shall be many woodcocks, yellowhammers, and sapsuckers. Here will be many mocking-birds and meadowlarks. Here will be herons and blackbirds. There will be many turtle-doves and pigeons. The kingfishers will catch fish. There will be many buzzards and ravens. There will be many chicken-hawks. There will be many robins. On this high mountain there will be many deer," he said.

"Let there be a valley here," he said. "There will be fir trees, some small and some large. Let the rain fall. Let it snow. Let there be hail. Let the clouds come. When it rains let the streams increase, let the water be high, let it become muddy. When the rain stops let the water become good again," he said.

He came back. "Walk behind me, my dog," he said. "We will look at what has taken place." Trees had grown. Fish were in the streams. The rocks had become large. It was good.

He traveled fast. "Come, walk fast, my dog," he said. The land had become good. The valleys had become broad. All kinds of trees and plants had sprung up. Springs had become and the water was flowing. "Again I will try the water," he said. "You, too, drink." Brush had sprung up. He traveled fast.

"I have made a good earth, my dog," he said. "Walk fast, my dog." Acorns were on the trees. The chestnuts were ripe. The hazelnuts were ripe. The manzanita berries were getting white. All sorts of food had become good. The buckeyes were good. The pepper nuts were black. The bunch grass was ripe. The grasshoppers were growing. The clover was in bloom. The bear-clover was good. The mountains had grown. The rocks had grown. All kinds that are eaten had become good. "We made it good, my dog," he said. Fish for the people to eat had grown in the streams.

"We have come to tosidun (south) now," he said. All the different kinds were matured. They started back, he and his dog. "We will go back," he said. "The mountains have grown up quickly. The land has become flat. The trout have grown. Good water is flowing. Walk fast. All things have become good. We have made them good, my dog. It is warm. The land is good."

The brush had grown. Various things had sprung up. Grizzlies had increased in numbers. Birds had grown. The water had become good. The grass was grown. Many deer for the people to eat walked about. Many kinds of herbs had grown. Some kinds remained small.

Rattlesnakes had multiplied. Water snakes had become numerous. Turtles had come out of the water and increased in numbers. Various things had grown. The mountains had grown. The valleys had become.

"Come fast. I will drink water. You, too, drink," he told his dog. "Now we are getting back, we are close to home, my dog. Look here, the mountains have grown. The stones have grown. Brush has come up. All kinds of animals are walking about. All kinds of things are grown."

"We are about to arrive. We are close to home, my dog," he said. "I am about to get back north," he said to himself. "I am about to get back north. I am about to get back north. I am about to get back north," he said to himself.

That is all.

Chapter 11

Of Anahuac

From Primeval Waters

Excerpt. Creation Story of the Mixtecs. Updated and edited version from The Myths of Mexico and Peru by Lewis Spence.

When the earth had arisen from the primeval waters, one day the deer-god, who bore the surname Puma-Snake, and the beautiful deer-goddess, or Jaguar-Snake, appeared. They had human form, and with their great knowledge (that is, with their magic) they raised a high cliff over the water, and built on it fine palaces for their dwelling. On the summit of this cliff they laid a copper axe with the edge upward, and on this edge the heavens rested. The palaces stood in Upper Mixteca, close to Apoala, and the cliff was called *Place Where the Heavens Stood*. The gods lived happily together for many centuries, when it chanced that two little boys were born to them, beautiful of form and skilled and experienced in the arts. From the days of their birth they were named Wind of Nine Snakes (Viento de Neuve Culebras) and Wind of Nine Caves (Viento de Neuve Cavernas). Much care was given to their education, and they possessed the knowledge of how to change themselves into an eagle or a snake, to make themselves invisible, and even to pass through solid bodies.

After a time these youthful gods decided to make an offering and a sacrifice to their ancestors. Taking incense vessels made of clay, they filled them with tobacco, to which they set fire, allowing it to smolder. The smoke rose heavenward, and that was the first offering to the gods. Then they made a garden with shrubs and flowers, trees and fruit-bearing plants, and sweet-scented herbs. Adjoining this they made a grass-grown level place, and equipped it with everything necessary for sacrifice. The pious brothers lived contentedly on this piece of ground, tilled it, burned tobacco, and with prayers, vows, and promises they supplicated their ancestors to let the light appear, to let the water collect in certain places and the earth be freed from its covering, for they had no more than that little garden for their subsistence. In order to strengthen their prayer they pierced their ears and their tongues with pointed knives of flint, and sprinkled the blood on the trees and plants with a brush of willow twigs.

The deer-gods had more sons and daughters, but there came a flood in which many of these perished. After the catastrophe was over the god who is called the Creator of All Things formed the heavens and the earth, and restored the human race.

Ixtlilxochitl

Excerpt. Ixtlilxochitl's Legend of the Creation. Updated and edited version from The Myths of Mexico and Peru by Lewis Spence.

Ixtlilxochitl states that the Toltecs credited a certain Tloque Nahuaque (Lord of All Existence) with the creation of the universe, the stars, mountains, and animals. At the same time he made the first man and woman, from whom all the inhabitants of the earth are descended. This "first earth" was destroyed by the "water-sun."

At the commencement of the next epoch the Toltecs appeared, and after many wanderings settled in Huehue Tlapallan (Very Old Tlapallan). Then followed the second catastrophe, that of the "wind-sun."

The remainder of the legend recounts how mighty earthquakes shook the world and destroyed the earth giants.

The Flood

Excerpt. Compilation. Account of Flood. Updated and edited version from texts from The Myths of Mexico and Peru by Lewis Spence and Atlantis, the Antediluvian World by Ignatius Donnelly. From the Codex Chimalpopoca translated by Abbé Brasseur.

This is the sun called Nahuiatl (four water). Now the water was tranquil for forty years, plus twelve, and men lived for the third and fourth times. When the sun Nahuiatl came, there had passed away four hundred years, plus two ages, plus seventy-six years. Then all mankind was lost and drowned—and found themselves changed into fish. The sky came nearer the water. In a single day all was lost, and the day Nahuixochitl (four flower) destroyed all our flesh.

And this year was that of Ce-calli, and on the first day all was lost. The mountain itself was submerged in the water, and the water remained tranquil for fifty-two springs.

Now toward the close of the year Titlacahuan had forewarned the man named Nata and his wife Nena, saying,

"Make no more pulque, but straightway hollow out a large cypress, and enter it when in the month Tozoztli the water shall approach the sky." They entered it, and when Titlacahuan had closed the door he said, "You will eat but a single ear of maize and your wife but one also."

As soon as they had finished eating, they went forth, and the water was tranquil; for the log did not move any more; and opening it they saw many fish.

Then they built a fire, rubbing together pieces of wood, and they roasted fish. The gods Citallinicue and Citallatonac, looking below, exclaimed, "Divine Lord, what is the meaning of that fire below? Why do they thus smoke the heavens?"

Straightway descended Titlacahuan-Tezcatlipoca, and commenced to scold, saying, "What is this fire doing here?" And seizing the fishes he molded their hinder parts and changed their heads, and they were at once transformed into dogs.

Viracocha

Inca Creation Story. Updated and edited version from History of the Incas by Pedro Sarmiento De Gamboa, translated by Clements Markham.

Viracocha and The Coming of The Incas

The natives of this land affirm that in the beginning, and before this world was created, there was a being called Viracocha. He created a dark world without sun, moon or stars. Owing to this creation he was named Viracocha Pachayachachi, which means "Creator of all things." And when he had created the world he formed a race of giants of disproportioned greatness painted and sculptured, to see whether it would be well to make real men of that size. He then created men in his likeness as they are now; and they lived in darkness.

Viracocha ordered these people that they should live without quarreling, and that they should know and serve him. He gave them a certain precept which they were to observe on pain of being confounded if they should break it. They kept this precept for some time, but it is not mentioned what it was. But as there arose among them the vices of pride and covetousness, they transgressed the precept of Viracocha Pachayachachi and falling, through this sin, under his indignation, he confounded and cursed them. Then some were turned into stones, others into other things, some were swallowed up by the earth, others by the sea, and over all there came a general flood which they call uñu pachacuti, which means "water that overturns the land." They say that it rained days and nights, that it drowned all created things, and that there alone remained some vestiges of those who were turned into stones, as a memorial of the event, and as an example to posterity, in the edifices of

Pucara, which are leagues from Cuzco.

They say that in the time of the deluge called uñu pachacuti there was a mountain named Guasano in the province of Quito and near a town called Tumipampa. The natives still point it out. Up this mountain went two of the Cañaris named Ataorupagui and Cusicayo. As the waters increased the mountain kept rising and keeping above them in such a way that it was never covered by the waters of the flood. In this way the two Cañaris escaped. These two, who were brothers, when the waters abated after the flood, began to sow. One day when they had been at work, on returning to their hut, they found in it some small loaves of bread, and a jar of chicha, which is the beverage used in this country in place of wine, made of boiled maize. They did not know who had brought it, but they gave thanks to the Creator, eating and drinking of that provision. Next day the same thing happened. As they marveled at this mystery, they were anxious to find out who brought the meals. So one day they hid themselves, to spy out the bringers of their food. While they were watching they saw two Cañari women preparing the victuals and putting them in the accustomed place. When about to depart the men tried to seize them, but they evaded their would-be captors and escaped. The Cañaris, seeing the mistake they had made in molesting those who had done them so much good, became sad and prayed to Viracocha for pardon for their sins, entreating him to let the women come back and give them the accustomed meals. The Creator granted their petition. The women came back and said to the Cañaris—"The Creator has thought it well that we should return to you, lest you should die of hunger." They brought them food. Then there was friendship between the women and the Cañari brothers, and one of the Cañari brothers had connection with one of the women. Then, as the elder brother was drowned in a lake which was near, the survivor married one of the women, and had the other as a concubine. By them he had ten sons who formed two lineages of five each, and increasing in numbers they called one Hanansaya which is the same as to say the upper party, and the other Hurinsaya, or the lower party. From these all the Cañaris that now exist are descended.

Of The Second Age

It is related that everything was destroyed in the flood called uñu pachacuti. Viracocha Pachayachachi, when he destroyed that land as has been already recounted, preserved three men, one of them named Taguapaca, that they might serve and help him in the creation of new people who had to be made in the second age after the deluge, which was done in this manner.

The flood being passed and the land dry, Viracocha determined to people it a second time, and, to make it more perfect, he decided upon creating luminaries to give it light. With this object he went, with his servants, to a great lake in the Collao, in which there is an island called Titicaca, the meaning being "the rock of lead," of which we shall treat in the first part. Viracocha went to this island, and presently ordered that the sun, moon, and stars should come forth, and be set in the heavens to give light to the world, and it was so. They say that the moon was created brighter than the sun, which made the sun jealous at the time when they rose into the sky. So the sun threw over the moon's face a handful of ashes, which gave it the shaded color it now presents. This frontier lake of Chucuito, in the territory of the Collao, is leagues to the south of Cuzco. Viracocha gave various orders to his servants, but Taguapaca disobeyed the commands of Viracocha. So Viracocha was enraged against Taguapaca, and ordered the other two servants to take him, tie his hands and feet, and launch him in a balsa on the lake. This was done. Taguapaca was blaspheming against Viracocha for the way he was treated, and threatening that he would return and take vengeance, when he was carried by the water down the drain of the same lake, and was not seen again for a long time. This done, Viracocha made a sacred idol in that place, as a place for worship and as a sign of what he had there created.

Leaving the island, he passed by the lake to the main land, taking with him the two servants who survived. He went to a place now called Tiahuanacu in the province of Collasuyu, and in this place he sculptured and designed on a great piece of stone, all the nations that he intended to create. This done, he ordered his two servants to charge their memories with the names of all tribes that he had depicted, and of the valleys and provinces where they were to come forth, which were those of the whole land. He ordered that each one should go by a different road, naming the tribes, and ordering them all to go forth and people the country. His servants, obeying the command of Viracocha, set out on their journey and work. One went by the mountain range or chain which they call the heights over the plains on the South Sea. The other went by the heights which overlook the wonderful mountain ranges which we call the Andes, situated to the east of the South Sea. By these roads they went, saying with a loud voice "Oh you tribes and nations, hear and obey the order of Ticci Viracocha Pachayachachi, which commands you to go forth, and multiply and settle the land." Viracocha himself did the same along the road between those taken by his two servants, naming all the tribes and places by which he passed. At the sound of his voice every place obeyed, and people came forth, some from lakes, others from fountains, valleys, caves, trees, rocks and hills, spreading over the land and multiplying to form the nations.

They say that Viracocha was made

from the Titicaca site where, having originally formed some shapes of large strong men which seemed to him out of proportion, he made them again of his stature which was, as they say, the average height of men, and being made he gave them life. Then they set out to people the land. As they spoke one language previous to starting, they built those edifices, the ruins of which may still be seen, before they set out. This was for the residence of Viracocha, their maker. After departing they varied their languages, noting the cries of wild beasts, insomuch that, coming across each other afterwards, those could not understand who had before been relations and neighbors

After Creation

After Viracocha had created all people, he went on his way and came to a place where many men of his creation had congregated. This place is now called Cacha. When Viracocha arrived there, the inhabitants were estranged owing to his dress and bearing. They murmured at it and proposed to kill him from a hill that was near. They took their weapons there, and gathered together with evil intentions against Viracocha. Viracocha fell on his knees on some plain ground, with his hands clasped. Fire from above came down upon those on the hill, and covered all the place, burning up the earth and stones like straw. Those bad men were terrified at the fearful fire. They came down from the hill, and sought pardon from Viracocha for their sin. Viracocha was moved by compassion. He went to the flames and put them out with his staff. But the hill remained quite parched, the stones being rendered so light by the burning that a very large stone which could not have been carried on a cart, could be raised easily by one man. This may be seen at this day, and it is a wonderful sight to behold this hill, which is a quarter of a league in extent, all burnt up. It is in the Collao.

After this Viracocha continued his journey and arrived at a place called Urcos, leagues to the south of Cuzco. Remaining there some days he was well served by the natives of that area. At the time of his departure, he made them a celebrated huaca or statue, for them to offer gifts to and worship; to which statue the Incas, in later times, offered many rich gifts of gold and other metals, and above all a golden bench.[1]

Viracocha continued his journey, working his miracles and instructing his created beings. In this way he reached the territory on the equinoctial line, where are now Puerto Viejo and Manta. Here he was joined by his servants. Intending to leave the land of Peru, he made a speech to those he had created, apprising them of the things that would happen. He told them that people would come, who

---

[1] When the Spaniards entered Cuzco they found it and took it, according to the author. The Marquis Don Francisco Pizarro took it for himself.

would say that they were Viracocha their creator, and that they were not to believe them; but that in the time to come he would send his messengers who would protect and teach them. Having said this he went to sea with his two servants, and went traveling over the water as if it was land, without sinking. For they appeared like foam over the water, and the people, therefore, gave them the name of Viracocha which is the same as to say the grease or foam of the sea. At the end of some years after Viracocha departed, they say that Taguapaca, whom Viracocha ordered to be thrown into the lake of Titicaca in the Collao, as has already been related, came back and began, with others, to preach that he was Viracocha. Although at first the people were doubtful, they finally saw that it was false, and ridiculed them.

Mayan Dawn

Excerpt. Mayan Creation Story. Updated and edited version from The Myths of Mexico and Peru, by Lewis Spence.

We are told that the god Hurakan, the mighty wind, passed over the universe, still wrapped in gloom. He called out "Earth", and the solid land appeared. Then the chief gods took counsel among themselves as to what should next be made. These were Hurakan, Gucumatz or Quetzalcoatl, and Xpiyacoc and Xmucane, the mother and father gods. They agreed that animals should be created. This was accomplished, and they next turned their attention to the framing of man. They made a number of mannikins carved out of wood. But these were irreverent and angered the gods, who resolved to bring about their downfall. Then Hurakan (The Heart of Heaven) caused the waters to be swollen, and a mighty flood came upon the mannikins. Also a thick resinous rain descended upon them. The bird Xecotcovach tore out their eyes, the bird Camulatz cut off their heads, the bird Cotzbalarn devoured their flesh, the bird Tecumbalam broke their bones and sinews and ground them into powder. Then all sorts of beings, great and small, abused the mannikins. The household utensils and domestic animals jeered at them, and made game of them in their plight. The dogs and hens said: "Very badly have you treated us and you have bitten us. Now we bite you in turn." The millstones said: "Very much were we tormented by you, and daily, daily, night and day, it was squeak, screech, screech, holi, holi, huqi, huqi, for your sake. Now you shall feel our strength, and we shall grind your flesh and make meal of your bodies." And the dogs growled at the unhappy images because they had not been fed, and tore them with their teeth. The cups and platters said: "Pain and misery you gave us, smoking our tops and sides, cooking us over the fire, burning and hurting us as if we had no feeling."

Now it is your turn, and you shall burn." The unfortunate mannikins ran here and there in their despair. They mounted upon the roofs of the houses, but the houses crumbled beneath their feet; they tried to climb to the tops of the trees, but the trees hurled them down; they were even repulsed by the caves, which closed before them. Thus this ill-starred race was finally destroyed and overthrown, and the only vestiges of them which remain are certain of their progeny, the little monkeys which dwell in the woods.

Vukub-Cakix

When the earth had recovered from the wrathful flood which had descended upon it there lived a being haughty and full of pride, called Vukub-Cakix. His teeth were of emerald, and other parts of him shone with the brilliance of gold and silver. In short, it is evident that he was a sun-and-moon god of prehistoric times. He boasted dreadfully, and his conduct so irritated the other gods that they resolved upon his destruction. His two sons, Zipacna and Cabrakan (Cockspur or Earth-heaper, and Earthquake), were earth giants. These also were prideful and arrogant, and to cause their downfall the gods dispatched the heavenly twins Hun-Apu and Xbalanque to earth, with instructions to chastise the trio.

Vukub-Cakix prided himself upon his possession of the wonderful nanze-tree, the tapal, bearing a fruit round, yellow, and aromatic, which he ate every morning. One morning he mounted to its summit, from where he could best see the choicest fruits, when he was surprised and infuriated to observe that two strangers had arrived there before him, and had almost stripped the tree of its produce.

On seeing Vukub, Hun-Apu raised a blow-pipe to his mouth and blew a dart at the giant. It struck him on the mouth, and he fell from the top of the tree to the ground. Hun-Apu leaped down upon Vukub and grappled with him, but the giant in terrible anger seized the god by the arm and wrenched it from the body. He then returned to his house, where he was met by his wife, Chimalmat, who inquired for what reason he roared with pain. In reply he pointed to his mouth, and so full of anger was he against Hun-Apu that he took the arm he had wrenched from him and hung it over a blazing fire. He then threw himself down to bemoan his injuries, consoling himself, however, with the idea that he had avenged himself upon the disturbers of his peace.

While Vukub-Cakix moaned and howled with the dreadful pain which he felt in his jaw and teeth the arm of Hun-Apu hung over the fire, and was turned round and round and basted by Vukub's spouse, Chimalmat. The sun-god rained bitter imprecations upon the interlopers who had penetrated to his paradise and had caused him such woe, and he gave vent to dire threats of what would happen if he succeeded in getting them into his power.

But Hun-Apu and Xbalanque were not minded that Vukub-Cakix should escape so easily, and the recovery of Hun-Apu's arm must be made at all cost. So they went to consult two great and wise magicians, Xpiyacoc and Xmucane, who advised them to proceed with them in disguise to the dwelling of Vukub, if they wished to recover the lost arm. The old magicians resolved to disguise themselves as doctors, and dressed Hun-Apu and Xbalanque in other garments to represent their sons.

Shortly they arrived at the mansion of Vukub, and while still some way off they could hear his groans and cries. Presenting themselves at the door, they accosted him. They told him that they had heard someone crying out in pain, and that as famous doctors they considered it their duty to ask who was suffering.

Vukub appeared quite satisfied, but closely questioned the old wizards concerning the two young men who accompanied them.

"They are our sons," they replied.

"Good," said Vukub. "Do you think you will be able to cure me?"

"We have no doubt whatsoever upon that head," answered Xpiyacoc. "You have sustained very bad injuries to your mouth and eyes."

"The demons who shot me with an arrow from their, blow-pipe are the cause of my sufferings," said Vukub. "If you are able to cure me I shall reward you richly."

"Your Highness has many bad teeth, which must be removed," said the wily old magician. "Also the balls of your eyes appear to me to be diseased."

Vukub appeared highly alarmed, but the magicians speedily reassured him.

"It is necessary," said Xpiyacoc, "that we remove your teeth, but we will take care to replace them with grains of maize, which you will find much more agreeable in every way."

The unsuspicious giant agreed to the operation, and very quickly Xpiyacoc, with the help of Xmucane, removed his teeth of emerald, and replaced them by grains of white maize. A change quickly came over the giant. His brilliancy speedily vanished, and when they removed the balls of his eyes he sank into insensibility and died.

All this time the wife of Vukub was turning Hun-Apu's arm over the fire, but Hun-Apu snatched the limb from above the brazier, and with the help of the magicians replaced it upon his shoulder. The discomfiture of Vukub was then complete. The party left his dwelling feeling that their mission had been accomplished.

The Earth Giants

But in reality it was only partially accomplished, because Vukub's two sons, Zipacna and Cabrakan, still remained to be dealt with. Zipacna was daily employed in heaping up mountains, while Cabrakan, his brother, shook them in earthquake. The vengeance of Hun-Apu and Xbalanque was first directed against Zipacna, and they conspired with a band of young men to bring about his death.

The young men, four hundred in number, pretended to be engaged in building a house. They cut down a large tree, which they made believe was to be the roof-tree of their dwelling, and waited in a part of the forest through which they knew Zipacna must pass. After a while they could hear the giant crashing through the trees. He came into sight, and when he saw them standing round the giant tree-trunk, which they could not lift, he seemed very much amused.

"What have you there, Oh little ones?" he said laughing.

"Only a tree, your Highness, which we have felled for the roof-tree of a new house we are building."

"Cannot you carry it?" asked the giant disdainfully.

"No, your Highness," they made answer; "it is much too heavy to be lifted even by our united efforts."

With a good-natured laugh the giant stooped and lifted the great trunk upon his shoulder. Then, bidding them lead the way, he trudged through the forest, evidently not disconcerted in the least by his great burden. Now the young men, incited by Hun-Apu and Xbalanque, had dug a great ditch, which they pretended was to serve for the foundation of their new house. Into this they requested Zipacna to descend, and, scenting no mischief, the giant readily complied. On his reaching the bottom his treacherous acquaintances cast huge trunks of trees upon him, but on hearing them coming down he quickly took refuge in a small side tunnel which the youths had constructed to serve as a cellar beneath their house.

Imagining the giant to be killed, they began at once to express their delight by singing and dancing, and to lend color to his stratagem Zipacna dispatched several friendly ants to the surface with strands of hair, which the young men concluded had been taken from his dead body. Assured by the seeming proof of his death, the youths proceeded to build their house upon the tree trunks which they imagined covered Zipacna's body, and, producing a quantity of pulque, they began to make merry over the end of their enemy. For some hours their new dwelling rang with revelry.

All this time Zipacna, quietly hidden below, was listening to the hubbub and waiting his chance to revenge himself upon those who had entrapped him.

Suddenly arising in his giant might, he cast the house and all its inmates high in the air. The dwelling was utterly demolished, and the band of youths were hurled with such force into the sky that they remained there, and in the stars we call the Pleiades we can still discern them wearily waiting an opportunity to return to earth.

The Undoing of Zipacna

But Hun-Apu and Xbalanque, grieved that their comrades had so perished, resolved that Zipacna must not be permitted to escape so easily. Zipacna, carrying the mountains by night, sought his food by day on the shore of the river, where he wandered catching fish and crabs. The brothers made a large artificial crab, which they placed in a cavern at the bottom of a ravine. They then cunningly undermined a huge mountain, and awaited events. Very soon they saw Zipacna wandering along the side of the river, and asked him where he was going.

"Oh, I am only seeking my daily food," replied the giant.

"And what may that consist of?" asked the brothers.

"Only of fish and crabs," replied Zipacna.

"Oh, there is a crab down yonder," said the crafty brothers, pointing to the bottom of the ravine. "We spotted it as we came along. Truly, it is a great crab, and will furnish you with a capital breakfast."

"Splendid!" cried Zipacna, with glistening eyes. "I must have it at once," and with one bound he leaped down to where the cunningly contrived crab lay in the cavern.

No sooner had he reached it than Hun-Apu and Xbalanque cast the mountain upon him; but so desperate were his efforts to get free that the brothers feared he might rid himself of the immense weight of earth under which he was buried, and to make sure of his fate they turned him into stone. Thus at the foot of Mount Meahuan, near Vera Paz, perished the proud Mountain-Maker.

The Shame of Cabrakan

Now only the third of this family of boasters remained, and he was the most proud of any.

"I am the Overturner of Mountains!" he said.

But Hun-Apu and Xbalanque had made up their minds that not one of the race of Vukub should be left alive.

At the moment when they were plotting the overthrow of Cabrakan he was occupied in moving mountains. He seized the mountains by their bases and, exerting his mighty strength, cast them into the air; and of the smaller mountains he took no account at all. While he was so employed he met the brothers, who greeted him cordially.

"Good day, Cabrakan," they said. "What may you be doing?"

"Bah! Nothing at all," replied the giant. "Can't you see that I am throwing the mountains about, which is my usual occupation? And who may you be that ask such stupid questions? What are your names?"

"We have no names," they replied. "We are only hunters, and here we have our blow-pipes, with which we shoot the birds that live in these mountains. So you see that we do not require names, as we meet no one."

Cabrakan looked at the brothers disdainfully, and was about to depart when they said to him: "Stay; we should like to behold these mountain-throwing feats of yours."

This aroused the pride of Cabrakan.

"Well, since you wish it," said he, "I will show you how I can move a really great mountain. Now, choose the one you would like to see me destroy, and before you are aware of it I shall have reduced it to dust."

Hun-Apu looked around him, and spotting a great peak pointed toward it. "Do you think you could overthrow that mountain?" he asked.

"Without the least difficulty," replied Cabrakan, with a great laugh. "Let us go toward it."

"But first you must eat," said Hun-Apu. "You have had no food since morning, and so great a feat can hardly be accomplished fasting."

The giant smacked his lips. "You are right" he said, with a hungry look. Cabrakan was one of those people who are always hungry. "But what have you to give me?"

"We have nothing with us," said Hun-Apu.

"Umph!" growled Cabrakan, "you are a pretty fellow. You ask me what I will have to eat, and then tell me you have nothing," and in his anger he seized one of the smaller mountains and threw it into the sea, so that the waves splashed up to the sky.

"Come," said Hun-Apu, "don't get angry. We have our blow-pipes with us, and will shoot a bird for your dinner."

On hearing this Cabrakan grew somewhat quieter. "Why did you not say so at first?" he growled.

"But be quick, because I am hungry."

Just at that moment a large bird passed overhead, and Hun-Apu and Xbalanque raised their blow-pipes to their mouths. The darts sped swiftly upward, and both of them struck the bird, which came tumbling down through the air, falling at the feet of Cabrakan.

"Wonderful, wonderful!" cried the giant. "You are clever fellows indeed!" And, seizing the dead bird, he was going to eat it raw when Hun-Apu stopped him.

Wait a moment, said he. "It will be much nicer when cooked," and, rubbing two sticks together, he ordered Xbalanque to gather some dry wood, so that a fire was soon blazing.

The bird was then suspended over the fire, and in a short time a savory odor mounted to the nostrils of the giant, who stood watching the cooking with hungry eyes and watering lips.

Before placing the bird over the fire to cook, however, Hun-Apu had smeared its feathers with a thick coating of mud. [2] But Hun-Apu had done this with a purpose. The mud that he spread on the feathers was that

---

[2] Original content continues, adding: The Indians in some parts of Central America still do this, so that when the mud dries with the heat of the fire the feathers will come off with it, leaving the flesh of the bird quite ready to eat.

of a poisoned earth, called tizate, the elements of which sank deeply into the flesh of the bird.

When the savory mess was cooked, he handed it to Cabrakan, who speedily devoured it.

"Now" said Hun-Apu, "let us go toward that great mountain and see if you can lift it as you boast."

But already Cabrakan began to feel strange pangs.

"What is this?" said he, passing his hand across his brow. "I do not seem to see the mountain you mean."

"Nonsense," said Hun-Apu. "Yonder it is, see, to the east there."

"My eyes seem dim this morning," replied the giant.

"No, it is not that," said Hun-Apu. "You have boasted that you could lift this mountain, and now you are afraid to try."

"I tell you," said Cabrakan, "that I have difficulty in seeing. Will you lead me to the mountain?"

"Certainly," said Hun-Apu, giving him his hand, and with several strides they were at the foot of the mountain.

"Now," said Hun-Apu, "see what you can do, boaster."

Cabrakan gazed stupidly at the great mass in front of him. His knees shook together so that the sound was like the beating of a war-drum, and the sweat poured from his forehead and ran in a little stream down the side of the mountain.

"Come," cried Hun-Apu derisively, "are you going to lift the mountain or not?"

"He cannot," sneered Xbalanque. "I knew he could not."

Cabrakan shook himself into a final effort to regain his senses, but all to no purpose. The poison rushed through his blood, and with a groan he fell dead before the brothers.

Thus perished the last of the earth giants of Guatemala, whom Hun-Apu and Xbalanque had been sent to destroy.

Perishable Gods

Excerpt. Mayan. Updated and edited version from the Book Of Chilam Balam of Chumayel by Ralph L. Roys.

It is most necessary to believe this. These are the precious stones which our Lord, the Father, has abandoned. This was his first repast, this fermented drink, with which we, the ruling men revere him here. Very rightly they worshiped as true gods these precious stones, when the true God was established, our Lord God, the Lord of heaven and earth, the true God. Nevertheless, the first gods were perishable gods. Their worship came to its inevitable end. They lost their efficacy by the benediction of the Lord of Heaven, after the redemption of the world was accomplished, after the resurrection of the true God, the true Dios, when he blessed heaven and earth. Then was your worship abolished, Maya men. Turn away your hearts from your old religion.

This is the history of the world in those times, because it has been written down, because the time has not yet ended for making these books, these many explanations, so that Maya men may be asked if they know how they were born here in this country, when the land was founded.

It was Katun Ahau when the Ah Mucenca came forth to blindfold the faces of the Oxlahun-ti-ku; but they did not know his name, except for his older sister and his sons. They said his face had not yet been shown to them also. This was after the creation of the world had been completed, but they did not know it was about to occur. Then Oxlahun-ti-ku was seized by Bolon-ti-ku. Then it was that fire descended, then the rope descended, then rocks and trees descended. Then came the beating of things with wood and stone. Then Oxlahun-ti-ku was seized, his head was wounded, his face was buffeted, he was spit upon, and he was thrown on his back as well. After that he was despoiled of his insignia and his smut. Then shoots of the yaxum tree were taken. Also Lima beans were taken with crumbled tubercles, hearts of small squash-seeds, large squash-seeds and beans, all crushed. He wrapped up the seeds composing this first Bolon cacab, and went to the thirteenth heaven. Then a mass of maize-dough with the tips of corn-cobs remained here on earth. Then its heart departed because of Oxlahun-ti-ku, but they did not know the heart of the tubercle was gone.

After that the fatherless ones, the miserable ones, and those without husbands were all pierced through; they were alive though they had no hearts. Then they were buried in the sands, in the sea.

There would be a sudden rush of water when the theft of the insignia of Oxlahun-ti-ku occurred. Then the sky would fall, it would fall down upon the earth, when the four gods, the four Bacabs, were set up, who brought about the destruction of the world. Then, after the destruction of the world was completed, they placed a tree to set up in its order the yellow cock oriole. Then the white tree of abundance was set up. A pillar of the sky was set up, a sign of the destruction of the world; that was the white tree of abundance in the north. Then the black tree of abundance was set up in the west for the black-breasted picoy to sit upon. Then the yellow tree of abundance was set up in the south, as a symbol of the destruction of the world, for the yellow-breasted picoy to sit upon, for the yellow cock oriole to sit upon, the yellow timid mut. Then the green tree of abundance was set up in the center of the world as a record of the destruction of the world.

The plate of another Katun was set up and fixed in its place by the messengers of their lord. The red Piltec was set at the east of the world to conduct people to his lord. The white Piltec was set at the north of the world to conduct people to his lord. Lahun Chaan was set at the west to bring things to his lord. The yellow Piltec was set at the south to bring things to his lord. But it was over the whole world that Ah Uuc Cheknal was set up. He came from the seventh stratum of the earth, when he came to fecundate Itzam-kab-ain, when he came with the vitality of the angle between earth and heaven. They moved among the four lights, among the four layers of the stars. The world was not lighted; there was neither day nor night nor moon. Then they perceived that the world was being created. Then creation dawned upon the world. During the creation thirteen infinite series added to seven was the count of the creation of the world. Then a new world dawned for them.

The two-day throne was declared, the three-day throne. Then began the weeping of Oxlahun-ti-ku. They wept in this reign. The reign became red; the mat became red; the first tree of the world was rooted fast. The entire world was proclaimed by Uuc-yol-zip; but it was not at the time of this reign that Bolon-ti-ku wept. Then came the counting of the mat in its order. Red was the mat on which Bolon-ti-ku sat. His buttock is sharply rounded, as he sits on his mat. Then descended greed from the heart of the sky, greed for power, greed for rule.

Then the red foundation was established; the white foundation of the ruler was established; the black foundation was established; the yellow foundation was established. Then the Red Ruler was set up, he who was raised upon the mat, raised upon the throne. The White Ruler was set up, he who was raised upon the mat, raised upon the throne. The Black Ruler was set up, he who was raised upon the mat, raised upon the throne. The Yellow Ruler was set up, he who was raised upon the mat, raised upon the throne.

As a god, it is said; whether or not gods, their bread is lacking, their water is lacking. There was only a portion of what was needed for them to eat together... but there was nowhere from which the quantity needed for existence could come. Compulsion and force were the tidings, when he was seated in authority; compulsion was the tidings, compulsion by misery; it came during his reign, when he arrived to sit upon the mat... Suddenly on high, fire flamed up. The face of the sun was snatched away, taken from earth. This was his garment in his reign. This was the reason for mourning his power, at that time there was too much vigor. At that time there was the riddle for the rulers. The planted timber was set up. Perishable things are assembled at that time. The timber of the grave-digger is set up at the crossroads, at the four resting places. Sad is the general havoc, at that time the butterflies swarmed. Then there came great misery, when it came about that the sun in Katun Ahau was moved from its place for three months. After three years it will come back into place in Katun Ahau. Then another Katun will put in its place. The ramon fruit is their bread, the ramon fruit is their drink; the jícama cimarrona is their bread, the jícama cimarrona is their drink; what they eat and what they drink. The ix-batun, the chimchim-chay, are what they eat. These things were present here when misery settled, father, in Tun 9. At that time there were the foreigners. The charge of misery was sought for all the years of Katun Ahau.

Then it was that the lord of Katun Ahau spread his feet apart. Then it was that the word of Bolon cacab descended to the tip of his tongue. Then the charge of the Katun was sought; nine was its charge when it descended from heaven. Kan was the day when its burden was bound to it. Then the water descended, it came from the heart of the sky for the baptism of the House of Nine Bushes. With it descended Bolon Mayel; sweet was his mouth and the tip of his tongue. Sweet were his brains. Then descended the four mighty supernatural jars, this was the honey of the flowers. Then there grew up for it the red unfolded calyx, the white unfolded calyx, the black unfolded calyx and the yellow unfolded calyx, those which were half a palm broad and those which were a whole palm in breadth. Then there sprang up the five-leafed flower, the five drooping petals, the cacao with grains like a row of teeth, the ix-chabil-tok, the little flower, Ix Macuil Xuchit, the flower with the brightly colored tip, the laurel flower, and the limping flower. After these flowers sprang up, there were the vendors of fragrant odors, there was the mother of the flowers. Then there sprang up the bouquet of the priest, the bouquet of the ruler, the bouquet of the captain; this was what the flower-king bore when he descended and nothing else, so they say. It was not bread that he bore. Then it was that the flower sprang up, wide open, to introduce the sin of Bolon-ti-ku. After three years was the time when he said he did not come to create Bolon cacab as the god in hell. Then descended Ppizlimtec to take the flower; he took the figure of a humming-bird with green plumage on its breast, when he descended. Then he sucked the honey from the flower with nine petals. Then the five-petaled flower took him for her husband, and shortly after the heart of the flower came forth to set itself in motion. Four-fold was the plate of the flower, and Ah Kin Xocbiltun was set in the center. At this time Oxlahun-ti-ku came forth, but he did not know of the descent of the sin of the mat, when he came into his power. The flower was his mat, the flower was his chair. He sat in envy, he walked in envy. Envy was his plate, envy was his cup. There was envy in his heart, in his understanding, in his thought and in his speech. Ribald and insolent was his speech during his reign. At that time his food cries out, his drink cries out, from the corner of his mouth when he eats, from the back of his claw when he bites his food. He holds in his hand a piece of wood, he holds in his hand a stone. Mighty are his teeth; his face is that of Lahun Chan, as he sits. Sin is in his face, in his speech, in his talk, in his understanding and in his walk. His eyes are blindfolded. He seizes, he demands as his right, the mat on which he sits during his reign. Forgotten is his father, forgotten is his mother, nor does his mother know her offspring. The heart is on fire alone in the fatherless one who despises his father, in the motherless one. He shall walk abroad giving the appearance of one drunk, without understanding, in company with his father, in company with his mother. There is no virtue in him, there is no goodness in his heart, only a little on the tip of his tongue. He does not know in what manner his end is to come; nor does he know what will be the end of his reign, when the period of his power shall terminate.

This is Bolon-ti-ku. Like that of Bolon Chan is the face of the ruler of men, the two day occupant of the mat and throne. He came in Katun Ahau. After that there will be another lord of the land who will establish the law of another Katun, after the law of the lord of Katun Ahau shall have run its course. At that time there shall be few children; then there shall be mourning among the Itza who speak our language brokenly. Industry and vigor finally take the place, in the first tun of the new Katun, of the sin of the Itzá who speak our language brokenly. It is Bolon-ti-ku who shall come to his end with the law of the lord of Katun Ahau. Then the riddle of the rulers of the land shall end the law of the Katun. Then those of the lineage of the noble chiefs shall come into their own, with the other men of discretion and with those of the lineage of the chiefs. Their faces had been trampled on the ground, and they had been overthrown by the unrestrained upstarts of the day and of the Katun, the son of evil and the offspring of the harlot, who were born when their day dawned in Katun Ahau. Thus shall end the power of those who are two-faced toward our Lord God.

But when the law of the Katun shall have run its course, then God will bring about a great deluge again which will be the end of the world. When this is over, then our Lord Jesus Christ shall descend over the valley of Jehoshaphat beside the town of Jerusalem where he redeemed us with his holy blood. He shall descend on a great cloud to bear true testimony that he was once obliged to suffer, stretched out on a cross of wood. Then shall descend in his great power and glory the true God who created heaven and earth and everything on earth. He shall descend to level off the world for the good and the bad, the conquerors and the captives.

The Uinal

Excerpt. Mayan. Updated and edited version from the Book Of Chilam Balam of Chumayel by Ralph L. Roys.

Thus it was recorded by the first sage, Melchise, the first prophet, Napuc Tun, the priest, the first priest. This is a song of how the uinal came to be created before the creation of the world. Then he began to march by his own effort alone. Then said his maternal grandmother, then said his maternal aunt, then said his paternal grandmother, then said his sister-in-law: "What shall we say when we see man on the road?" These were their words as they marched along, when there was no man as yet. Then they arrived there in the east and began to speak. "Who has passed here? Here are footprints. Measure it off with your foot." So spoke the mistress of the world. Then he measured the footstep of our Lord, God the Father. This was the reason it was called counting off the whole earth, lahca (12) Oc. 11 This was the count, after it had been created by the day 13 Oc, after his feet were joined evenly, after they had departed there in the east. Then he spoke its name when the day had no name, after he had marched along with his maternal grandmother, his maternal aunt, his paternal grandmother and his sister-in-law. The uinal was created, the day, as it was called, was created, heaven and earth were created, the stairway of water, the earth, rocks and trees; the things of the sea and the things of the land were created.

On 1 Chuen, he raised himself to his divinity, after he had made heaven and earth.

On 2 Eb, he made the first stairway. It descended from the midst of the heavens, in the midst of the water, when there were neither earth, rocks nor trees.

On 3 Ben, he made all things, as many as there are, the things of the heavens, the things of the sea and the things of the earth.

On 4 Ix, sky and earth were tilted.

On 5 Men, he made everything.

On 6 Cib, the first candle was made; it became light when there was neither sun nor moon.

On 7 Caban, honey was first created, when we had none.

On 8 Ecnab, his hand and foot were firmly set, then he picked up small things on the ground.

On 9 Cauac, hell was first considered.

On 10 Ahau, wicked men went to hell because of God the Father, that they might not be noticed.

On 11 Imix, rocks and trees were formed; this he did within the day.

On 12 Ik, the breath of life was created. The reason it was called Ik was because there was no death in it.

On 13 Akbal, he took water and watered the ground. Then he shaped it and it became man.

On 1 Kan, he first created anger because of the evil he had created.

On 2 Chicchan, occurred the discovery of whatever evil he saw within the town.

On 3 Cimi, he invented death; it happened that our Lord God invented the first death.

On 5 Lamat, he established the seven great waters of the sea.

On 6 Muluc, all valleys were submerged, when the world was not yet created. Then occurred the invention of the word of our Lord God, when there was no word in heaven, when there were neither rocks nor trees.

Then they went to consider what they were, and the voice spoke as follows: "Thirteen entities, seven entities, one." So it spoke when the word came forth, at the time when there was no word. Then the reason was sought by the first ruling day (the first day Ahau) why the meaning of the word to them was not revealed so that they could declare themselves. Then they went to the center of heaven and joined hands. Then the following were set up in the middle of the land: the Burners, four of them:

4 Chicchan, the Burner.
4 Oc, the Burner.
4 Men, the Burner.
4 Ahau, the Burner.
These are the four Rulers.
8 Muluc 5 Cauac
9 Oc 6 Ahau
10 Chuen 7 Imix
11 Eb 8 Ik
12 Ben 9 Akbal
13 Ix 10 Kan
1 Men 11 Chicchen
2 Cib 12 Cimi
3 Caban 13 Manik
4 Ecnab 1 Lamat

The uinal was created, the earth was created; sky, earth, trees and rocks were set in order; all things were created by our Lord God, the Father. Thus he was there in his divinity, in the clouds, alone and by his own effort, when he created the entire world, when he moved in the heavens in his divinity. Thus he ruled in his great power. Every day is set in order according to the count, beginning in the east, as it is arranged.

Chapter 12

Land Without Cold

The Beginning

From the Yoruba people of Nigeria. Excerpt. Updated and edited version from Myths of Ífè by John Wyndham.

The Órní of Ífè speaks: Oíbo, you have asked to hear our lore, The legends of the World's young hours—and where could truth in greater surety have its home than in the precincts of the shrines of those who made the World, and in the mouths of priests to whom their doings have been handed down from sire to son? Arámfè reigns in Heaven; Before this World was made there reigned Arámfè in the realm of Heaven amidst his sons. Old were the hills around him; The Sun had shone upon his vines and cornfields since time past reckoning. Old was Arámfè, The father of the Gods: his youth had been the youth of Heaven.

Once when the King reclined upon the dais, and his sons lay prostrate in veneration at his feet, he spoke tells his sons of the creation of Heaven; Of the great things he purposed: "My sons, you know but fair things which I made for you, before I called your spirits from the dusk: for always your eyes have watched the shadows and the wind on waving corn, and I have given you the dances and the chorus of the night—An age of mirth and sunrise (the wine of Heaven) is your existence. You have not even heard of the gray hour when my young eyes first opened to gaze upon a herbless Mass, unshaped and unadorned. But I knew well the heart of Him-Who-Speaks-Not, the far-felt purpose that gave me birth; I labored and the grim years passed: Streams flowed along their sunny beds; I set The stars above me, and the hills about; I fostered budding trees, and taught the birds their song— the unshapely I had formed to beauty, And as the ages came I loved to make the beautiful more fair... All went not well: A noble animal my mind conceived emerged in loathsome form to prey upon my gentle creatures; a river, born to bask in sunlit channels and mirror the steep hills, Tore down its banks and ravaged field and plain; While cataract and jagged precipice, Now grand with years, remind me of dread days when Heaven tottered, and wide rifts sundered my young Fair hills, and all seemed lost. Yet—I prevailed. Think, now, if the accomplished whole be Heaven, How wonderful the anxious years of slow And hazardous achievement—a destiny for Gods. But yours it has not been to lead Creation by the cliff's edge way from Mass to Paradise." He paused on the remembrance, And great Orísha cried: "Can we do naught? What use in godhead without deeds to do? Where yearns a helpless region for a hand to guide it?" And old Arámfè answered him: sends them to make the World. "My son, your day approaches. Far-off, the haze Rests always on the outer waste which skirts Our realm; beyond, a nerveless Mass lies cold beneath floods which some malign unreason heaves. Odúwa, first-born of my sons, to you I give the five-clawed Bird, the sand of power. Go now, Call a despairing land to smiling life Above the jealous sea, and found sure homesteads for a new race whose destiny is not the eternal life of Gods. You are their judge; Yours is the kingship, and to you all Gods and men are subject. Wisest of my sons, Orísha, yours is the grateful task to loose vague spirits waiting for the Dawn—to make the race that shall be; and to you I give this bag of Wisdom's guarded lore and arts for Man's well-being and advancement. And you, My younger sons, the chorus and the dance, The voice of worship and the crafts are yours to teach—that the new thankful race may know the mirth of Heaven and the joys of labor."

Then Odúwa said: "Happy our life has been, And I would gladly roam these hills forever, Your son and servant. But to your command I yield; and in my kingship pride oversteps Sorrow and heaviness. Yet, Lord Arámfè, I am your first-born: why do you give the arts and wisdom to Orísha? I, The King, will be obeyed; the hearts of men will turn in wonder to the God who spells strange benefits." But Arámfè said "Enough; To each is fitting task is given. Farewell." The Gods leave Heaven. Here the Beginning was: from Arámfè's vales through the desert regions the exiled Gods approached the edge of Heaven, and into blackness plunged—A sunless void over godless water lying—To seize an empire from the Dark, and win amidst ungoverned waves a sovereignty.

Odúwa steals the bag and causes war on Earth. But by the roadside while Orísha slept Odúwa came by stealth and bore away the bag Arámfè gave. Thus was the will of God undone: for thus with the charmed sand Cast wide on the unmastered sea, his sons Called forth a World of envy and of war.

Of Man's Creation, and of the restraint Olókun placed upon the chafing sea, Of the unconscious years which passed in darkness till dazzling sunshine touched the unused eyes of men, of war and magic—my priest shall tell you, And all the Great Ones did before the day they vanished to return to the calm hills life in Ífè is as it was in the time of the Gods of old Arámfè's realm... They went away; But still with us their altars and their priests remain, and from their shrines the hidden Gods Peer forth with joy to watch the dance they taught, And hear each night their chorus with the drum: For changeless here the early World endures In this first stronghold of humanity, And, constant as the buffets of the waves of Queen Olókun on the shore, the song, The dance of those old Gods abide, the mirth, The life... I, too, am born of the Beginning: Odúm'la speaks for the Gods; For, when from the sight of men the Great Gods passed, They left on Earth Órní Odúm'la charged to be a father to a mourning people, To tend the shrines and utter solemn words inspired by those invisible. And when Odúm'la's time had come to yield the crown, To wait upon the River's brink, and cross to old Arámfè—Ífa, in his wisdom, and lives forever in the person of the Órní. Proclaimed that son with whom Odúm'la's soul lives. Thus has it ever been; and now with me that Being is—about, within—And on our sacred days these lips pronounce the words of Odudúwa and Orísha.

The Descent

From the Yoruba people of Nigeria. Excerpt. Updated and edited version from Myths of Ífè By John Wyndham.

Arába speaks: I am the voice of Ífa, messenger of all the Gods: to me the histories are known, and I will tell you of the days of the Descent.

How old Arámfè sent the Gods from Heaven, and Odudúwa stole the bag—my king has told you...

For many days across unwatered plains the Great Ones journeyed, and sandy deserts—for such is the stern bar set by Arámfè—between his smiling vales the Gods arrive at the edge of Heaven. And the stark cliff's edge which his sons approached with trembling, till from the sandy brink they peered down the sheer precipice.

Behind them lay the parched, forbidding leagues; but yet the Sun was there, and breezes soft, and yet the mountains—A faded line beyond the shimmering waste—Called back to mind their ancient home.

Beneath hung chaos—dank blackness and the threatening roar of untamed waters. Then Odudúwa spoke: "Orísha, what did we? And what fault was ours? Outcasts today; tomorrow we must seek our destiny in dungeons, and beneath that yawning blackness we must found a city for unborn men. Better a homeless life in desert places: dare we turn and flee to some lost valley of the hills? Orísha, What do you think?" Then spoke Orísha whom men call The Great: "Is this

Odúwa that I hear—My mother's son who stole Arámfè's gift, and thought to filch away the hearts of men with blessings which were mine to give? For me, the ares I know I long to use, and yearn to see the first of toiling, living men that I shall make. Forbidding is our task, you say—but think, were we return to peace and Heaven's calm, how boundless is the fate you flinch from! Besides, is Godhead blind? You think Arámfè would not know? Has Might no bodes with eyes and ears? Dumb spirits hungering Odúwa sends Ojúmu with the bird, for life await us: let us go." So spoke Orísha; and Odúwa hung a chain over the cliff to the dark water's face, and sent Ojúmu, the wise priest, to pour the magic sand upon the sea and loose the five-clawed bird to scatter far and wide triumphant land.

But, as Earth's ramparts grew, ever in the darkness came the waves and sucked away the crumbling shore, while foot by foot lagoons crept up, and turned to reedy swamps the soil of hope. So Odudúwa called Olókun and Olóssa to the cliff, and thus he spoke: "Beneath, the waters wrestle with the new-rising World, and would destroy our kingdom and undo Arámfè's will. Go to the fields of men to be, the homes that they shall make. Olókun! To the sea! For there your rule and your dominion shall be: To curb the hungry waves upon the coast lands forever. And thus, in our first queen of cities and secret sanctuaries on lonely shores through every eon as the season comes, shall men bring gifts in homage to Olókun. And you, Olóssa, where your ripple laps the fruitful bank, shall see continually the offerings of thankful men."

The months of Heaven passed by, while in the moonless night the Bird makes the Earth, Beneath the Bird toiled on until the bounds, The corners of the World were steadfast. And then Odúwa called Orísha and the Gods to the cliff's edge, and spoke these words of sorrow: "We go to our sad kingdom. Such is the will of old Arámfè: so let it be. But before the hour the wilderness which gapes for us engulf us utterly, before the lingering sight of those loved hills can gladden us no more—May we not dream awhile of smiling days gone by?

Fair was drenched morning in the Sun when dark the hilltops rose over misty hollows; Fair were the leafy trees of night beneath the silvering Moon, and beautiful the wind upon the grasslands. Good-bye, you plains we roamed. The Gods descend. Good-bye to sunlight and the shifting shadows Cast on the crags of Heaven's blue hills. Ah! wine of Heaven, farewell"...

So came the Gods to Ífè. Then of an age of passing months told by wanings of the Moon our lore repeats A sunless World. The dirge of wasting hopes and the lament of a people in a strange World shuddering Beneath the thunder of the unseen waves on crumbling shores around. Always the marsh pressed eagerly on Ífè; but ever the Bird returned with the unconquer-

Land Without Cold

able sand Ojúmu poured from his enchanted shell, And the marsh yielded. Then young Ógun asked the Forest to grow her whispering trees—but she budded the pallid shoots of hopeless night, And all was sorrow round the sodden town where Odudúwa reigned. Yet for live men Orísha creates man. Orísha, the Creator, yearned, and called to him the longing shades from other glooms; He threw their images into the wombs of Night, Olókun and Olóssa, and all the wives of the great Gods bore babes with eyes of those born blind—unknowing of their want—And limbs to feel the heartless wind which blew from outer nowhere to the murk beyond...

But as the unconscious years wore by, Orísha, The Creator, watched the unlit Dawn of Man wistfully—as one who follows the set flight of a lone sea-bird when the sunset fades Beyond a marshy wilderness—and spoke to Odudúwa: "Our day is endless night, and deep, weak woods enclose our weeping children. The Ocean menaces, chill winds moan through our moldering homes. Our guardian Night, who spoke to us with her strange sounds in the still hours of Heaven is here; yet she can but bewail Her restless task. And where is Evening? Oh! Where is Dawn?" He ceased, and Odudúwa sent Ífa, the Messenger, to his old sire to crave the Sun and the warm flame that lit the torch of Heaven's Evening and the dance...

A deep compassion moved thunderous Arámfè, The Father of the Gods, and he sent down the vulture with red fire upon his head For men; and, by the Gods' command, the bird still wears no plumage where those embers burned him—A mark of honor for remembrance. Again the Father spoke the word, and the pale Moon sought out the precincts of calm Night's retreat to share her watch on Darkness; and Day took wings, And flew to the broad spaces of the sky—To roam benignant from the floating mists which cling to hillsides of the Dawn—to Eve who calls the happy toilers home. And all the Age of Mirth was changed: for when the terror of bright Day had lifted from the unused eyes of men, sparks flew from Ládi's anvil, while Ógun taught the use of iron, and wise Obálufon made brazen vessels and showed how wine streams out from the slim palms. And in the night the Gods set torches in their thronging courts to light the dance, and Heaven's music touched the drum once more as in its ancient home. And mirth with Odudúwa reigned.

The Yoruba Kingdom

Excerpt. Updated and edited version from Yoruba Legends by M.I. Ogumefu.

The ancient King Oduduwa had a great many grandchildren, and on his death he divided among them all his possessions. But his youngest grandson, Oranyan, was at that time away hunting, and when he returned home he learned that his brothers and cousins had inherited the old King's money, cattle, beads, native cloths, and crowns, but that to himself nothing was left but twenty-one pieces of iron, a cock, and some soil tied up in a rag.

At that time the whole earth was covered with water, on the surface of which the people lived.

The resourceful Oranyan spread upon the water his pieces of iron, and upon the iron he placed the scrap of cloth, and upon the cloth the soil, and on the soil the cock. The cock scratched with his feet and scattered the soil far and wide, so that the ocean was partly filled up and islands appeared everywhere. The pieces of iron became the mineral wealth hidden under the ground.

Now Oranyan's brothers and cousins all desired to live on the land, and Oranyan allowed them to do so on payment of tribute. He thus became King of all the Yorubas, and was rich and prosperous through his grandfather's inheritance.

Modes of Life

Excerpt. Updated and edited version from South-African Folk-Tales, by James A. Honey.

In the beginning there were two. One was blind, the other was always hunting. This hunter found at last a hole in the earth from which game proceeded and killed the young. The blind man, feeling and smelling them, said, "They are not game, but cattle."

The blind man afterwards recovered his sight, and going with the hunter to this hole, saw that they were cows with their calves. He then quickly built a kraal (fence made of thorns) round them, and anointed himself, just as Hottentots (in their native state) are still accustomed to doing.

When the other, who now with great trouble had to seek his game, came and saw this, he wanted to anoint himself also. "Look here!" said the other, "you must throw the ointment into the fire, and afterwards use it." He followed this advice, and the flames flaring up into his face, burnt him most miserably; so that he was glad to make his escape. The other, however, called to him: "Here, take the kirri (a knobstick), and run to the hills to hunt there for honey." Hence sprung the race of Bushmen.

The Glory of Kings

Excerpt. Updated and edited version from The Kebra Nagast, by E.A. Wallis Budge.

Concerning the Glory of Kings

The interpretation and explanation of the Three Hundred and Eighteen Orthodox Fathers concerning splendor, and greatness, and dignity, and how God gave them to the children of Adam, and especially concerning the greatness and splendor of Zion, the Tabernacle of the Law of God, of which He Himself is the Maker and Fashioner, in the fortress of His holiness before all created things, both angels and men.

For the Father, and the Son, and the Holy Spirit with good fellowship and right good will and cordial agreement together made the Heavenly Zion to be the place of habitation of their Glory. And then the Father, and the Son, and the Holy Spirit said, "Let Us make man in Our similitude and likeness," and with ready agreement and good will They were all of this opinion. And the Son said, "I will put on the body of Adam," and the Holy Spirit said, "I will dwell in the hearts of the Prophets and the Righteous," and this common agreement and covenant was fulfilled in Zion, the City of their Glory. And David said, "Remember Your agreement which You did make of old for salvation, the rod of Your inheritance, in Mount Zion in which You dwell."

And He made Adam in His own image and likeness, so that He might remove SATAN because of his pride, together with his host, and might establish Adam—His own plant—together with the righteous, His children, for His praises. For the plan of God was decided upon and decreed in that He said, "I will become man, and I will be in everything which I have created, I will abide in flesh." And in the days that came after, by His good pleasure there was born in the flesh of the Second Zion the second Adam, Who was our Savior Christ. This is our glory and our faith, our hope and our life, the Second Zion.

Concerning the Kingdom of Adam

And I go up from Adam and I say, God is King in truth, for Him praise is meant, and He appointed under Him Adam to be king over all that He had created. And He drove him out of the Garden, because of his apostasy through the sin of the Serpent and the plotting of the Devil.

And at that sorrowful moment Cain was born, and when Adam saw that the face of Cain was ill-tempered and his appearance evil he was sad.

And then Abel was born, and when Adam saw that his appearance was good and his face good-tempered he said, "This is my son, the heir of my kingdom."

Concerning Noah

Now Noah was a righteous man. He feared God, and kept the righteousness and the Law which his fathers had declared to him—now Noah was the tenth generation from Adam—and he kept in remembrance and did what was good, and he preserved his body from fornication, and he admonished his children, bidding them not to mingle with the children of Cain, the arrogant tyrant, the divider of the kingdom, who walked in the counsel of the Devil, who makes evil to flourish. And he taught them everything that God hated—pride, boastfulness of speech, self-adulation, calumniation, false accusation, and the swearing of false oaths.

And besides these things, in the wickedness of their uncleanness, which was unlawful and against rule, man wrought pollution with man, and woman worked with woman the abominable thing.

Concerning the Flood

And this thing was evil before God, and He destroyed them with the water of the Flood, which was colder than ice. He opened the doors of heaven, and the cataracts of the Flood poured down; and He opened the fountains that were under the earth, and the fountains of the Flood appeared on the earth.

And the sinners were blotted out, for they reaped the fruit of their punishment. And with them perished all beasts and creeping things, for they were all created for the gratification of Adam, and for his glory, some to provide him with food, and some for his pleasure, and some for the names to the glorification of his Creator so that he might know them, even as David said, "And You have set everything under his feet"; for his sake they were created, and for his sake they were destroyed, with the exception of Eight Souls, and seven of every kind of clean beasts and creeping things, and two of every kind of unclean beast and creeping thing.

Concerning the Ark

And as concerning the Ark: God saved Noah in the Ark. And God held conversation with Abraham in the wood of Manbar, that is to say the wood that cannot be destroyed; and He saved Isaac by means of the ram which was caught in the thicket; and He made Jacob rich by means of three rods of woods which he laid in running water; and through the top of his staff Jacob was blessed. And He said to Moses, "Make a tabernacle of wood which cannot be destroyed, in the similitude of Zion, the Tabernacle of the Covenant." And when David took it from the city of Samaria, he placed the Tabernacle of the Law in a new Tabernacle, and rejoiced before it.

For from the beginning God had made the Tabernacle the means of salvation, and very many signs and wonders were performed through it by its form and similitude. Listen you now to me, and I will show you plainly how God had ordained salvation through the wood of His Cross, in the Tabernacle of His Law, from the beginning to the end.

Salvation came to Adam through the wood. For Adam's first transgression came through the wood, and from the beginning God ordained salvation for him through the wood.

For God Himself is the Creator and Giver of life and death, and everything is performed by His Word, and He created everything, and He makes righteous him that serves Him in purity in His pure Tabernacle of the Law. For it is called "mercy-seat", and it is also called "place of refuge", and it is also called "altar", and it is also called "place of forgiveness of sins", and it is called "salvation", and it is called "gate of life", and it is called "glorification", and it is called "city of refuge", and it is called "ship", and it is called "haven of salvation", and it is called "house of prayer", and it is called "place of forgiveness of sins for him that prays in purity in it", so that men may pray therein in purity and not defile their bodies. God loves the pure, for He is the habitation for the pure.

Those who come into His habitation, and are accepted in the holy Tabernacle, and who pray to Him with all their hearts, He will hear and will save in the day of their tribulation, and He will fulfill their desire. For He has made the holy Tabernacle to be a similitude of His throne. But there are some among those whom you have brought to us who are like to us Christians, but who have not abandoned the sin which their father the Devil has made to spring up in them. And he said, "Thus it is right that we should pray in Zion, the Tabernacle of the Law of God; she was at the first and is even now. The similitude thereof and the fruit thereof are the Mother of the Redeemer, Mary; it is right that we should worship her, for in her name is blessed the Tabernacle of the Law of God. And it is right that we should worship Michael and Gabriel." [...]

Concerning Abraham

And Terah begot a son and called him "Abraham". And when Abraham was twelve years old his father Terah sent him to sell idols. And Abraham said, "These are not gods that can make deliverance"; and he took away the idols to sell even as his father had commanded him. And he said to those to whom he would sell them, "Do you wish to buy gods that cannot make deliverance, things made of wood, and stone, and iron, and brass, which the hand of an artificer has made?" And they refused to buy the idols from Abraham because he himself had defamed the images of his father. And as he was returning he stepped aside from the road, and he set the images down, and looked at them, and said to them, "I wonder now if you are able to do what I ask you at this moment, and whether you are able to give me bread to eat or water to drink?" And none of them answered him, for they were pieces of stone and wood; and he abused them and heaped insults upon them, and they spoke never a word. And he buffeted the face of one, and kicked another with his feet, and a third he knocked over and broke to pieces with stones, and he said to them, "If you are unable to deliver yourselves from him that buffets you, and you cannot requite with injury him that injures you, how can you be called 'gods'? Those who worship you do so in vain, and as for myself I utterly despise you, and you shall not be my gods."

Then he turned his face to the East, and he stretched out his hands and said, "Be You my God, Oh Lord, Creator of the heavens and the earth, Creator of the sun and the moon, Creator of the sea and the dry land, Maker of the majesty of the heavens and the earth, and of that which is visible and that which is invisible; Oh Maker of the universe, be You my God. I place my trust in You, and from this day forth I will place my trust in no other except Yourself." And then there appeared to him a chariot of fire which blazed, and Abraham was afraid and fell on his face on the ground; and God said to him, "Fear you not, stand upright." And He removed fear from him.

Concerning the Beginning

As David prophesied by the mouth of the Holy Spirit, saying, "With You was the headship on the day of might." Now what do these words, "day of might" mean? Is it not the day whereon Christ, the Word of the Father, created heaven and earth? For Moses said in the beginning of the Book, "In the beginning God made the heavens and the earth." Understand then "In the beginning" means "in Christ"; the interpretation of "beginning" is Christ. John the Apostle, the son of Zebedee, said concerning Christ, "This is the first Whom we have heard and seen, Whom we have known, and Whom our hands have felt." And we will relate to you how we have a portion with Him, and you who believe our words shall have a portion with us. And Luke the disciple said in the Acts of the Apostles, "In the beginning we make speech concerning everything," and this that he said showed that Christ was the redemption of all, and we believe in Him. And Mark the Evangelist in the beginning of his Book wrote, saying, "The beginning of the Gospel is Jesus Christ, the Son of God"; and these words mean that Christ was the glad tidings for the Prophets and the Apostles, and that we all have participated in His grace. And again John the Evangelist wrote, saying, "In the beginning was the Word, and that Word was with God"; and in another place his word shows this plainly, and he said, "And likewise in the beginning was God the Word." And now observe that that Word of the Father is Christ, whereby He made the heavens and the earth and every created thing. It is He Who created, and without Him nothing that came came into being, nothing whatsoever: "He spoke, and they came into being; He commanded, and they were created." And the third glorious thing, hearken to it: "Through the breath of His mouth He created all their host." This makes manifest the Holy Spirit, Who is clearly referred to. [...]

Origins of Death

Excerpt. Updated and edited version from Specimens of Bushman Folklore, by W.H.I. Bleek and L.C. Lloyd.

The Moon and the Hare 1

We, when the Moon has newly returned alive, when another person has shown us the Moon, we look towards the place at which the other has shown us the Moon, and, when we look there, we perceive the Moon, and when we perceive it, we shut our eyes with our hands, we exclaim: "!kabbi-a yonder! Take my face yonder! You will give me your face yonder! You will take my face yonder! That which does not feel pleasant. You will give me your face—with which you, when you have died, you do again, living return, when we did not perceive you, you dost again lying down come—that I may also resemble you. For, the joy yonder, you do always possess it yonder, that is, that you want again to return alive, when we did not perceive you; while the hare told you about it, that you should do thus. You did formerly say, that we should also again return alive, when we died."

The hare was the one who thus did. He spoke, he said, that he would not be silent, for, his mother would not again living return; for his mother was altogether dead. Therefore, he would cry greatly for his mother.

The Moon replying, said to the hare about it that the hare should leave off crying; for, his mother was not altogether dead. For, his mother meant that she would again living return. The hare replying, said that he was not willing to be silent; for, he knows that his mother would not again return alive. For, she was altogether dead.

And the Moon became angry about it, that the hare spoke thus, while he did not assent to him (the Moon). And he hit with his fist, cleaving the hare's mouth; and while he hit the hare's mouth with his fist, he exclaimed: "This person, his mouth which is here, his mouth shall altogether be like this, even when he is a hare; he shall always bear a scar on his mouth; he shall spring away, he shall do-doubling return. The dogs shall chase him; they shall, when they have caught him, they shall grasping tear him to pieces, he shall altogether die.

"And they who are men, they shall—altogether dying—go away when they die. For, he was not willing to agree with me, when I told him about it, that he should not cry for his mother; for, his mother would again live; he said to me, that, his mother would not again living return. Therefore, he shall altogether become a hare. And the people, they shall altogether die. For, he was the one who said that his mother would not again living return. I said to him about it, that they (the people) should also be like me; that which I do; that I, when I am dead, I again living return. He contradicted me, when I had told him about it."

Therefore, our mothers said to me, that the hare was formerly a man; when he had acted in this manner, then it was that the Moon cursed him, that he should altogether become a hare. Our mothers told me, that, the hare has human flesh at his katten-ttu; therefore, we, when we have killed a hare, when we intend to eat the hare, we take out the "biltong flesh" yonder, which is human flesh, we leave it; while we feel that he who is the hare, his flesh it is not. For, flesh belonging to the time when he formerly was a man, it is.

Therefore, our mothers were not willing for us to eat that small piece of meat; while they felt that it is this piece of meat with which the hare was formerly a man. Our mothers said to us about it, did we not feel that our stomachs were uneasy if we ate that little piece of meat, while we felt that it was human flesh; it is not hare's flesh; for, flesh which is still in the hare it is; while it feels that the hare was formerly a man.

Therefore, it is still in the hare; while the hare's doings are those on account of which the Moon cursed us; that we should altogether die. For, we should, when we died, we should have again living returned; the hare was the one who did not assent to the Moon, when the Moon was willing to talk to him about it; he contradicted the Moon.

Therefore, the Moon spoke, he said: "You who are people, you shall, when you die, altogether dying vanish away. For, I said, that, you should, when you died, you should again arise, you should not altogether die. For, I, when I am dead, I again living return. I had intended, that, you who are men, you should also resemble me and do the things that I do; that I do not altogether dying go away. You, who are men, are those who did this deed; therefore, I had thought that I would give you joy. The hare, when I intended to tell him about it—while I felt that I knew that the hare's mother had not really died, for, she slept— the hare was the one who said to me, that his mother did not sleep; for, his mother had altogether died. These were the things that I became angry about; while I had thought that the hare would say: 'Yes; my mother is asleep.'"

For, on account of these things, he (the Moon) became angry with the hare; that the hare should have spoken in this manner, while the hare did not say: "Yes, my mother lies sleeping; she will presently arise."

If the hare had assented to the Moon, then, we who are people, we should have resembled the Moon; for, the Moon had formerly said, that we should not altogether die. The hare's doings were those on account of which the Moon cursed us, and we die altogether; on account of the story which the hare was the one who told him. That story is the one on account of which we altogether die and go away;

on account of the hare's doings; when he was the one who did not assent to the Moon; when the Moon intended to tell him about it; he contradicted the Moon, when the Moon intended to tell him about it.

The Moon spoke, saying that he (the hare) should lie upon a bare place; vermin should be those who were biting him, at the place where he was lying; he should not inhabit the bushes; for, he should lie upon a bare place; while he did not lie under a tree. He should be lying upon a bare place. Therefore, the hare is used, when he springs up, he goes along shaking his head; while he shakes out, making to fall the vermin from his head, in which the vermin had been hanging; while he feels that the vermin hung abundantly in his head. Therefore, he shakes his head, so that the other vermin may fall out for him.

The Moon, the Insect, and the Hare

Excerpt. From South-African Folk-Tales, by James A. Honey. Updated, edited, and revised.

The Moon, it is said, sent once an Insect to Men, saying, "Go you to Men, and tell them, 'As I die, and dying live, so you shall also die, and dying live.'"

The Insect started with the message, but while on his way was overtaken by the Hare, who asked: "On what errand are you bound?" The Insect answered: "I am sent by the Moon to Men, to tell them that as she dies, and dying lives, they also shall die, and dying live." The Hare said, "As you are an awkward runner, let me go." With these words he ran off, and when he reached Men, he said, "I am sent by the Moon to tell you, 'As I die, and dying perish, in the same manner you shall also die and come wholly to an end.'" Then the Hare returned to the Moon, and told her what he had said to Men. The Moon reproached him angrily, saying, "Dare you tell the people a thing which I have not said?"

With these words she took up a piece of wood, and struck him on the nose. Since that day the Hare's nose is slit.

The Moon and the Hare 2

Excerpt. From South-African Folk-Tales, by James A. Honey. Updated, edited, and revised.

The Moon dies, and rises to life again. The Moon said to the Hare, "Go you to Men, and tell them, 'Like as I die and rise to life again, so you also shall die and rise to life again.'" The Hare went to the Men, and said, "Like as I die and do not rise to life again, so you shall also die, and not rise to life again."

When he returned the Moon asked him, "What have you said?" "I have told them, 'Like as I die and do not rise to life again, so you shall also die and not rise to life again.'" "What," said the Moon, "have you said that" And she took a stick and beat the Hare on his mouth, which was slit by the blow. The Hare fled, and is still fleeing.

The Chameleon and the Salamander

Excerpt. From South-African Folk-Tales, by James A. Honey. Updated, edited, and revised.

God (Unknlunkulu) arose from beneath (the seat of the spiritual world, according to the Zulu tradition), and created in the beginning men, animals, and all things. He then sent for the Chameleon, and said, "Go, Chameleon, and tell Men that they shall not die." The Chameleon went, but it walked slowly, and loitered on the way, eating of a shrub called Bukwebezane.

When it had been away some time, God sent the Salamander after it, ordering him to make haste and tell Men that they should die. The Salamander went on his way with this message, outran the Chameleon, and, arriving first where the Men were, told them that they must die.

Source Text Index

African, 323
African, Ethiopian, Kebra Nagast, 318
African, South-African, 318
African, Yoruba, 313, 315, 317

Babylonian, 25, 30, 32, 57
Babylonian, Enuma Elish, 9

Egyptian, 35–37, 40

Hesiod, Theogony, 84
Hesiod, Works and Days, 78
Hindu, Bhagavad Gita, 164
Hindu, Mahabharata, 173, 174
Hindu, Rig Veda, 163
Hindu, Satapatha Brahmana, 167, 170, 172
Hindu, Upanishads, 167, 182, 183
Hindu, Vishnu Purána, 177, 182

Incan, 295
Islam, Qur'an, 213

Jewish, Genesis, 44, 65

Mayan, 299

Mayan, Chilam Balam of Chumayel, 305, 309
Mexican, 293, 294

Native American, Cherokee, 281, 283, 284
Native American, Iroquois, 278
Native American, Kato, 285, 286
Native American, Olelbis, 255
Norse, Poetic Edda, 226, 230
Norse, Teutonic Myth and Legend, 215, 220

Plato, Critias, 137
Plato, Statesman, 132
Plato, Timaeus, 107
Polyhistor, 32, 33, 43, 57, 59, 61, 63, 65, 73, 77, 104
Polynesian, Fragments, 239
Polynesian, Koh Nga Tama A Rangi, 233
Polynesian, Kumulipo, 241
Pythagoras, 150, 155

Zoroastrian, Bundahis, 191
Zoroastrian, Zad-Sparam, 200
Zoroastrian, Zend Avesta, 187

Index

A
abated, 52, 62, 296
abel, 48, 49, 319
abide, 167, 230, 319
abides, 167, 180
able, 38, 39, 61, 67, 69, 108, 114, 116, 125, 133, 135, 138, 140, 149, 151, 152, 156, 192, 195–198, 204, 259, 274, 284, 301, 321
abode, 30, 81, 159, 181, 189, 190, 207, 221, 251
abraham, 65, 70, 320–322
abram, 56, 65–70
abroad, 36, 55, 56, 83–85, 196, 210, 309
abundance, 17, 23, 57, 84, 135, 141, 144, 213, 238, 240, 306
abundant, 140–142, 147, 220, 238
abyss, 34, 60, 191, 192
acab, 306, 309
accept, 68, 114, 121, 137, 138
accord, 41, 112, 114
account, 43, 44, 60–62, 64, 65, 127, 133, 154, 191, 192, 194, 199, 203, 205, 207, 209, 211, 233, 283, 303, 324, 325
accursed, 37, 213

acorns, 83, 261–263, 289, 290
acropolis, 141, 142, 146
across, 146, 147, 219, 220, 223, 252, 273, 282–284, 298, 305, 315
act, 21, 38, 77, 148, 192
action, 107, 108, 110, 163, 173, 176
actions, 57, 60, 107, 109, 139, 140
acts, 181, 184, 322
adah, 49
adam, 48, 49, 318–320
adapted, 115, 122, 127, 139, 146, 158, 211
added, 60, 62, 74, 156, 307
addressed, 13, 27, 75, 122, 138, 169, 178
admah, 55, 67, 68
admits, 129, 131, 144, 182
advance, 12, 14–16, 29, 203
advanced, 18, 29, 193
advancing, 123, 124, 205, 206, 246
advantage, 79, 112, 200, 202, 208, 211
advice, 13, 75, 278, 318
aeetes, 103, 104
aegis, 85, 98, 102–104
aeon, 73
aerial, 34, 162
affected, 118, 125, 155, 181

affection, 192, 201
affirm, 113, 121, 130, 295
afflicted, 11, 96, 176
afraid, 15, 47, 58, 276, 281, 282, 284, 305, 322
afterward, 55, 258, 271, 282
age, 60, 80, 81, 89, 96, 107, 108, 115, 116, 134–136, 158, 176, 221, 222, 226, 245, 247, 296, 313, 316, 317
aged, 82, 107, 108, 111, 134
ages, 25, 33, 132, 137, 139, 147, 158, 178, 181, 215, 217, 221, 294
agni, 164, 167, 168, 170, 171, 184
agnihotra, 171, 172
ago, 108, 110, 111, 141, 226, 283, 284
agree, 82, 192, 234, 256, 323
agreed, 57, 111, 234, 257, 299, 301
agreement, 127, 137, 193, 197, 319
aharman, 191, 193, 194, 200–206, 208, 209, 211, 212
ahau, 306, 309, 311
ahead, 257, 260, 264
ai, 66, 226, 227
aid, 26, 97, 100, 112, 202, 206, 237
air, 30, 33, 34, 38, 42, 59, 61, 62, 76, 78, 97, 115, 120, 123, 124, 126–128, 130–132, 135, 151, 153–155, 157–161, 164, 173, 175, 181, 182, 191, 216, 218, 220, 223, 226, 227, 279, 280, 282, 283, 302–304
airyana, 189
akôman, 193, 209
akin, 110, 113, 123, 125, 127
albûrz, 197, 200, 207, 208
alike, 78, 91, 97, 227, 235, 238, 285

alive, 38, 51, 56, 205, 260, 285, 303, 306, 323
allies, 29, 75, 77, 100
allotted, 88, 99, 227
allow, 40, 130, 201
allowed, 23, 58, 116, 125, 136, 146, 318
almighty, 84, 94, 192
almost, 111, 136, 257, 258, 268, 284, 300
alone, 46, 59, 111, 119, 129, 133, 148, 152, 164, 166–168, 176, 177, 179, 183, 185, 204, 217, 228, 235, 237, 238, 240, 251, 258, 262, 263, 281, 295, 309, 311
aloud, 29, 58, 100, 234, 236
altar, 53, 62, 66, 84, 146, 172, 321
always, 91, 92, 95, 96, 98, 109, 112, 113, 115, 122, 126, 128–131, 133, 137, 142, 152, 156, 158, 162, 165, 167, 174, 175, 179, 194, 197, 252, 255–257, 259, 263–265, 271–277, 281, 283, 284, 304, 313, 314, 316, 318, 323
ambrosia, 96, 99
amid, 88, 89, 113, 209
amidst, 25, 181, 204, 207, 208, 313, 314
amount, 144, 160, 172, 250
ancestors, 112, 121, 134, 144, 149, 174, 222, 224, 233, 293, 294
ancient, 32, 33, 43, 107–109, 112, 132, 138, 142, 144, 147, 164, 174, 177, 229, 230, 233, 236, 239, 279, 315, 317

angels, 196, 198, 200, 213, 319
anger, 11, 23, 27, 79, 83, 88, 96,
    101, 123, 218, 229, 252,
    257, 300, 304
angle, 153, 307
angles, 154
angrily, 59, 220, 325
angry, 26, 36, 37, 48, 78, 81, 90, 94,
    95, 102, 202, 258, 264,
    272, 277, 279, 284, 304,
    323, 324
animal, 45–47, 51–53, 60, 114–116,
    120, 122, 123, 136, 140,
    144, 147, 211, 281, 283,
    314
annedotus, 63
anshar, 11–13, 22, 25, 27, 28
answer, 26, 27, 38, 57, 129, 135,
    179, 224, 236, 302
answered, 10, 87, 95, 146, 187, 190,
    191, 201, 236, 262, 267,
    269, 270, 275, 276, 301,
    314, 321, 325
antiquity, 108, 140
ants, 184, 248, 302
anu, 12, 13, 15, 17, 18, 20–23, 25,
    27–30, 40, 57–59
anunnaki, 11–13, 15, 16, 21
anvil, 98, 317
anxious, 64, 282, 283, 296, 314
anywhere, 183, 267
apart, 59, 81, 91, 99, 102, 140, 146,
    151, 163, 184, 200, 204,
    208, 233–235, 309
apep, 35–37
aphrodite, 76, 79, 84, 88, 100, 103,
    104
apollo, 76, 84, 86, 91, 102, 138
apparel, 12, 14
appear, 41, 58, 121, 126, 129, 137,
    139, 223, 294, 301
appeared, 33, 36, 60–63, 66, 120,
    149, 192, 195, 216, 249,
    251, 293, 294, 299, 301,
    318, 320, 322
appears, 126, 128, 129, 156
apples, 60, 88, 91
appoint, 15, 90, 99, 192, 193, 204
appointed, 18, 20, 48, 57, 58, 63,
    91, 92, 119, 123, 125, 135,
    146, 194, 196, 201, 204,
    319
apsu, 9–12, 25–27
aquatic, 210, 279
arámfè, 313–317
arch, 282
ares, 81, 102, 316
argument, 128, 129, 137, 138
arise, 84, 99, 118, 126, 157, 164,
    195, 205, 235, 324
arisen, 97, 127, 293
arises, 167, 183, 200, 201, 206, 212
arising, 108, 122, 302
arjuna, 165, 166
ark, 57, 320
arm, 29, 92, 207, 216, 267, 281,
    286, 300, 301
armenia, 57, 62, 63
armor, 81, 88, 140, 205, 223
arms, 37, 80, 81, 87, 93, 94, 97, 98,
    100, 102, 149, 174, 175,
    177, 234, 281
army, 26, 65, 83, 140, 194, 204, 217
arose, 28, 35, 64, 98, 100, 164, 184,
    192, 193, 196, 199, 200,
    206, 207, 210, 211, 215,
    216, 235, 286, 295, 326
arranged, 112, 132, 141, 144, 151,
    153, 162, 178, 195, 200,
    203–205, 208, 221, 289,

311

array, 10, 68, 246
arrive, 156, 207, 291, 315
arrived, 75, 136, 137, 180, 298, 300, 301
arrow, 171, 301
arrows, 84, 102, 264, 265
art, 74, 94, 100, 139, 144, 159
artificer, 113, 121, 122, 321
arts, 60, 74, 94, 95, 137, 293, 314
asa-gods, 216, 217, 220
ascetic, 174, 175, 177
asgard, 220–223, 225
ash, 220, 221
ashore, 236, 238, 288
asia, 91, 110, 139, 142
ask, 113, 137, 220, 227, 228, 231, 255, 256, 272, 301, 303, 304, 321
asked, 62, 108, 111, 113, 256, 258, 259, 261, 266, 267, 269, 270, 272, 275–277, 280, 286–288, 302–304, 306, 313, 317, 325
asking, 113, 138, 257
assembled, 13, 29, 57, 86, 221
assembly, 10, 12, 14, 15, 58, 86, 88, 92
asserted, 43, 108, 150
assigned, 94, 116, 119, 122, 147, 194, 218, 223, 238
assisted, 64, 105, 237
assume, 113, 176
assumed, 61, 128, 181, 238
assuming, 113, 152, 175, 176
assyria, 46
assyrians, 104, 105
astarte, 76
ate, 47, 81, 268, 300, 324
athena, 75, 77, 102

athene, 79, 84, 90, 95, 101, 102, 108, 137, 139, 142
athenians, 107, 108, 112, 139, 142
athens, 109, 112, 139
atlantic, 110, 143
atlantis, 111, 139, 143, 149
atlas, 75, 94, 104, 143, 144, 149
attached, 17, 76, 125, 171, 197
attack, 11, 12, 14–16, 26, 27, 76, 115, 138, 197, 236
attain, 120, 121, 130, 174, 206
attempt, 121, 129, 137, 279
attempted, 75, 105, 149
attend, 78, 108, 223
attribute, 118, 128, 131, 175, 181
aunt, 265
author, 78, 132, 181, 182, 298
authority, 28, 107, 125, 214
avenge, 11, 27, 75, 237
avenged, 42, 49, 229, 300
avenger, 15, 26–28, 30
awake, 77, 126, 167, 177, 283
aware, 168, 172, 192, 200, 237, 304
awful, 88, 90, 91, 98, 99, 102, 181, 250

B

babel, 56, 64
baby, 259, 272
babylon, 21, 60–62, 64, 65
babylonia, 60, 62, 64, 65
backward, 158, 191, 192
backwards, 54, 123
bad, 82–84, 114, 192, 258, 276, 277, 290, 298, 301, 309
bag, 211, 314
balance, 131, 133, 153, 194, 213
baldr, 228, 230, 231
band, 24, 205, 302
bank, 57, 203, 262, 316

banks, 32, 102, 145, 179, 189, 190, 216, 220, 289, 314
bare, 76, 103, 141, 216, 270, 325
base, 64, 153, 204, 220
basket, 238, 260, 264–268, 270
baskets, 236, 267
bat, 211, 250, 265
baths, 146
battle, 10–12, 14–16, 18, 21, 26–29, 68, 75, 78, 81, 92, 97, 98, 194, 223, 225
bear, 47, 61, 67, 82, 83, 85, 93, 101, 149, 188–190, 218, 230, 250, 277, 309, 323
bearer, 176, 177, 187
bearing, 45, 61, 69, 76, 88, 141, 298, 300
bears, 45, 79, 81, 83, 187, 222, 230, 231, 290
beast, 12, 14, 15, 185, 210, 320
beasts, 31, 38, 41, 58, 60, 74, 75, 84, 136, 166, 185, 189, 278, 298, 320
beautiful, 50, 85, 101, 114, 149, 151, 216, 218, 224, 235, 262, 263, 266, 270, 271, 278, 293, 316
beauty, 75, 95, 142, 144, 146, 147, 166, 216, 219–221, 313
beaver, 211, 279
become, 28, 38, 48, 83, 115, 119, 124, 133, 151, 162, 171, 176, 177, 183, 185, 188, 192, 195, 198, 208, 211, 231, 234, 235, 248, 274, 278, 288–291, 319, 323, 324
becomes, 22, 113, 119, 128, 130, 153, 157, 159, 165, 170, 171, 174, 176, 181, 249
becoming, 113, 115, 119, 131, 134, 156, 175, 181, 194
bed, 85, 94, 99, 102, 175, 189, 190
beg, 114, 128, 138
began, 33, 49, 54, 58, 108, 118, 132, 142, 146, 149, 162, 215, 216, 218, 237, 241, 252, 258, 260, 261, 263, 267, 269, 270, 272, 274, 275, 279, 280, 282, 284, 285, 296, 299, 302, 305, 307
begin, 55, 85, 109, 128, 130, 139, 140
begotten, 73–75, 77, 86, 132, 134, 158, 233, 235, 239
beheld, 13, 18, 26, 27, 29, 44, 58, 59, 144, 152, 174, 177, 198, 216, 220
behind, 18, 35, 37, 77, 88, 93, 121, 148, 172, 197, 213, 219, 260, 261, 265, 266, 288, 290, 315
behold, 37–39, 45, 48, 53, 55, 68–70, 78, 86, 121, 127, 144, 152, 164, 187, 213, 220, 225, 298, 304
beholding, 131, 176, 177
beings, 9, 37, 43, 60, 95, 114, 122, 130, 133, 136, 152, 155, 164–170, 174, 178, 181–183, 200, 217, 233–236, 239, 247, 248, 250, 251, 279, 285, 289, 298, 299
bel, 20, 23–25, 57, 59
believe, 121, 141, 257, 284, 299, 302, 305, 322
belly, 9, 17, 47, 93, 101, 102, 211, 286
belong, 131, 134, 227, 288

belongs, 22, 41, 42, 140, 169
beloved, 41, 42, 219, 239
below, 32, 60, 100, 101, 109, 124, 163, 195, 200, 203, 208, 222, 225, 226, 230, 262, 263, 266, 267, 270–272, 275, 282, 295, 302
belus, 61, 76, 104, 105
beneath, 25, 86, 88, 90, 93, 96–98, 100–102, 143, 217–220, 222, 226–229, 233, 234, 270, 300, 302, 314–316, 326
benefit, 21, 126, 141, 147, 201
benefits, 92, 127, 314
berossus, 60
beside, 30, 59, 83, 85, 116, 164, 216, 309
besides, 82, 91, 130, 138, 142, 148, 157, 207, 221, 316, 320
best, 84, 109, 113–115, 118, 123, 126, 128, 132, 137, 140, 141, 143, 150, 151, 155, 174–177, 179, 189, 190, 257, 258, 275, 283, 300
bestow, 15, 42, 116, 118
better, 40, 83, 84, 109, 110, 112, 114, 123, 127, 135, 156–158, 184, 230, 233, 234, 257, 268, 277, 278, 315
between, 47, 54, 59, 60, 64–67, 69, 70, 84, 115, 117, 126, 139, 142, 151, 158, 159, 162, 171, 191, 193, 200, 216, 217, 222, 225, 227, 233, 235, 239, 260, 263, 264, 266, 277, 279, 285, 296, 297, 307, 315
beyond, 59, 80, 84, 87–90, 100, 121, 147, 152, 163, 167, 168, 215, 220, 223, 226, 261, 266, 267, 282, 314, 315, 317
bharata, 174, 177
bidding, 80, 302, 319
bif-rost, 223, 225
big, 199, 258, 265, 266, 271, 272, 280, 288
bil, 218
billowy, 88, 164
bind, 27, 40, 115, 262
binding, 262
bird, 45, 46, 52, 53, 82, 94, 191, 209–211, 223, 228, 246, 247, 250, 271, 280, 281, 299, 304, 305, 314, 316, 317
birth, 33, 36, 37, 39, 48–50, 56, 60, 76, 82, 85, 86, 88, 89, 93, 102, 120, 122, 123, 132, 164, 173, 176, 177, 179, 182, 210, 237, 247, 250, 252, 279, 280, 293, 313
bit, 219, 258, 267, 271
bite, 277, 299
bitten, 39, 211, 299
bitter, 82, 96–98, 159, 249, 253, 300
black, 33, 34, 81, 87, 93, 145, 199, 211, 216, 219, 220, 222, 225, 229, 235, 246, 260, 261, 272–275, 283, 284, 287, 289, 290, 306, 307, 309
blackness, 221, 314, 315
blameless, 89
blast, 90, 98, 235, 283
blasts, 78, 89, 101
blazed, 259, 260, 272, 322

blazing, 40, 90, 100, 101, 188–190, 212, 264, 300, 304
blessed, 33, 34, 45, 46, 49, 54, 66, 68, 80, 81, 85–87, 116, 123, 134, 149, 151, 164, 165, 174, 225, 226, 305, 320, 321
blessings, 134, 144, 316
blew, 265, 280, 300, 317
blind, 93, 316–318
block, 258–260
blood, 12, 14, 15, 17, 20, 21, 26, 28, 30, 34, 48, 53, 61, 74, 76, 148, 200, 208, 209, 217, 219, 224–226, 228, 281, 286, 294, 305, 309
bloody, 88, 230, 281
bloom, 134, 263, 276, 278, 290
blossoms, 212, 262, 270, 276, 278, 279
blow, 39, 101, 111, 199, 223, 264, 285, 286, 326
blowing, 168, 250, 265
blows, 37, 139, 229, 270
blue, 84, 245, 262, 271, 275, 278, 279, 281, 285, 287, 290
bodies, 12, 14, 15, 26, 32, 61, 84, 109, 115–117, 119, 122, 123, 126, 129, 134, 138, 150, 151, 155, 158, 160, 161, 166, 171, 177, 189, 190, 192, 202, 222, 224, 225, 230, 235, 277, 293, 299, 321
bodily, 122, 130, 133, 139, 194, 202
bohem, 260, 269, 275
boiled, 168, 296
bolon, 306, 309
bond, 115, 122, 154
bonds, 30, 81, 94, 96, 97, 227, 231

bones, 47, 94, 95, 141, 155, 217, 285, 299
book, 35, 36, 60, 65, 322
bor, 217, 220
borders, 60, 94, 96, 199, 200, 225, 226
bore, 12, 14, 15, 22, 87–92, 94, 96, 102–104, 192, 228, 239, 293, 309, 314, 317
bored, 188
borne, 123, 131, 225
bosom, 26, 30, 69, 189, 239
bottom, 21, 200, 207, 208, 262, 279, 282–284, 302, 303
boughs, 74, 221, 235, 251
bound, 21, 33, 94, 96, 98, 115, 122, 123, 148, 208, 228, 303, 309, 325
boundary, 140, 141, 153, 158, 201, 208
boundless, 33, 34, 81, 86, 88, 97, 101, 111, 135, 235, 236, 316
bouquet, 309
bow, 17, 20, 22, 23, 29, 30, 264, 265
bowl, 148, 199, 206, 207, 284
boy, 103, 176, 179, 218, 259–261
boys, 107, 280, 293
brahmá, 178–182
brahma, 174, 176–180
brahman, 167, 174, 178, 181, 182, 184, 185
brahmana, 174–176
brahmanas, 174–177
brain, 155, 251, 252
brains, 220, 252, 309
branch, 99, 208, 228, 231, 252
branches, 178, 203, 222, 226, 229, 235, 247, 250, 261–263

brands, 189, 190, 260, 261
brave, 139, 224, 237, 252
brazen, 81, 98, 317
bread, 28, 48, 80, 81, 94, 226, 251, 263, 296, 309, 321
breadth, 62, 145, 147, 215, 309
break, 241, 269, 277, 281, 285, 287, 295
breast, 12, 15, 19, 177, 203, 225, 230, 235, 237, 309
breasts, 168, 252, 280
breath, 38, 39, 46, 51, 52, 78, 167, 171, 173, 184, 196, 235, 240, 264, 322
breathed, 46, 85, 90, 116, 163, 213, 281
breeze, 23, 33, 250
briareos, 87, 100
brick, 31, 55, 172
bricks, 21, 55, 74, 172
bridge, 145, 201, 202, 223
bridges, 145, 146
bright, 22, 26, 81, 85, 97, 126, 213, 218–220, 229, 230, 233, 279, 282, 317
bring, 15, 17, 25, 41, 51, 58, 69, 80, 84, 93, 99, 101, 102, 112, 127, 128, 149, 167, 189, 190, 192, 205, 231, 247, 257, 259, 261, 263, 264, 268–270, 273, 274, 279, 284, 299, 302, 307, 309, 316
bringing, 58, 80, 83, 104, 115, 127, 136, 143, 202
brings, 78, 90, 92, 203, 219, 231, 250
brink, 218, 315
broad, 99, 218, 220, 290, 309, 317
broke, 29, 30, 34, 44, 58, 111, 217, 218, 273, 287, 299, 321
broken, 74, 124, 197, 217, 227, 233, 237, 274
bronze, 81, 98–100
brood, 227, 228, 235
brothers, 41, 54, 58, 74, 94, 229, 230, 234–239, 260, 264, 265, 272–275, 293, 296, 303, 305, 318
bruise, 27, 47
brush, 285, 289–291, 294
build, 17, 55, 57, 62, 261, 285, 302
building, 31, 56, 74, 144, 146, 262, 263, 302
buildings, 142, 145, 146
built, 31, 49, 53, 55, 62, 64, 66, 74, 75, 142, 144, 146, 220, 221, 223, 249, 261, 263, 265, 271, 287, 293, 295, 298, 318
bull, 39, 100, 148, 173, 184, 194, 199, 206, 289
bulls, 61, 148, 177, 199, 206, 207
burden, 82, 149, 210, 222, 248, 302, 309
buried, 75, 98, 274, 280, 303, 306
burn, 55, 95, 125, 170, 267, 300
burned, 29, 40, 100, 227, 260, 261, 283, 286, 294, 317
burner, 311
burning, 17, 39, 97, 154, 171, 203, 212, 224, 259–261, 264, 272, 284, 298, 299
burnt, 53, 108, 148, 298, 318
burst, 39, 44, 136, 215, 219, 229, 243, 247, 273
bushes, 270, 279, 309, 325
business, 92, 108, 141, 212
buzzard, 276, 282
buzzards, 277, 282, 290

byblus, 74, 75, 77

C
cañari, 296
cañaris, 296
cabrakan, 300–305
cadmus, 81, 102
cain, 48, 49, 319
cake, 168, 169
call, 33, 46, 49, 65, 88, 89, 108, 112, 119, 120, 124, 125, 128–130, 144, 157, 174, 191, 194–196, 198, 199, 206, 230, 239, 255, 263, 269, 276, 277, 282, 295, 297, 302, 314, 316
calling, 73, 112, 203, 264
calls, 92, 240, 317
calm, 135, 241, 243, 250, 266, 315–317
calyx, 309
camel, 210
canaan, 54, 56, 66, 69, 70
canal, 144, 146, 147
canals, 147
cannot, 12, 25–28, 39, 57, 82, 96, 112–115, 119, 121, 124, 128, 131, 133, 138, 139, 157, 167, 170, 178, 184, 223, 259, 264, 267, 271, 273, 274, 277, 302, 305, 320, 321
captive, 19, 26, 204
cardinal, 174, 175, 281
care, 60, 83, 85, 136, 137, 142, 196, 217–219, 223, 237, 279, 293, 301
carried, 33, 57, 59, 79, 82, 98, 101, 109, 118, 123, 131, 134, 145–147, 218, 225, 257, 259, 260, 268, 270, 272, 284, 285, 297, 298
carry, 17, 19, 20, 28, 30, 98, 110, 173, 199, 209, 224, 225, 258, 259, 267, 270, 279, 302
carrying, 93, 125, 126, 148, 172, 221, 267, 303
case, 114, 135, 141, 157, 184, 237
cast, 28, 29, 75, 88, 92, 101, 131, 148, 201, 220, 226, 251, 302, 303, 314
catch, 74, 92, 236, 264, 268, 272–275, 288, 290
cattle, 38, 41, 93, 141, 146, 168, 189–191, 196, 208–210, 318
caught, 18, 30, 104, 123, 148, 220, 236, 252, 259, 264, 268, 271, 273, 274, 279, 281, 320, 323
cauldron, 215, 217, 220, 222
cause, 21, 32, 41, 51, 58, 79, 96, 113, 116, 119, 127, 133, 150, 151, 157, 159, 161, 162, 166, 167, 176, 178, 179, 182, 192, 195, 204, 213, 221, 222, 238, 239, 241, 243, 278, 300, 301
caused, 23, 29, 30, 32, 39, 46, 50, 59, 80, 111, 123, 193, 218, 288, 289, 299, 300
causes, 86, 108, 113, 126, 136, 150, 159, 167, 171, 179, 182, 314
cease, 53, 82, 88, 123, 217, 230, 240
ceased, 58, 64, 94, 134, 135, 215, 216, 317
ceasing, 84, 118
celestial, 21, 43, 65, 78, 189, 193,

196, 202, 204, 220, 221
center, 30, 116–118, 125, 143, 145–147, 150, 152, 153, 208, 278, 306, 309, 311
central, 145, 261, 269, 273, 304
certain, 33, 40, 65, 76, 108, 118, 120, 121, 129, 130, 132, 134, 162, 201, 203, 294, 295, 300
certainly, 22, 39, 107, 122, 130, 134, 138, 305
ceto, 89, 91
chains, 21, 94, 98, 119, 123, 225
chaldeans, 65
chameleon, 326
chance, 64, 73, 79, 117, 126, 167, 302
change, 28, 129, 134–136, 150, 152, 154–160, 221, 277, 293, 301
changed, 14–16, 26, 123, 125, 136, 156, 161, 211, 241, 252, 294, 295, 317
changes, 133, 134, 137, 141, 159, 161, 224, 250
changing, 129, 137, 156, 196
channel, 146, 241–246, 248
channels, 30, 145, 314
chant, 78, 85, 164, 172
chaos, 9, 25, 26, 33, 34, 44, 87, 97, 100, 136, 163, 234, 315
character, 135, 142, 181, 211
charge, 91, 97, 135, 158, 297, 309
chariot, 18, 29, 108, 122, 145, 171, 218, 223, 322
chariots, 148, 218, 219
charming, 89, 91, 114
charms, 74, 230
cheeks, 90, 134, 264
cherokee, 282

chief, 29, 43, 111, 152, 166, 174, 177, 179–181, 210, 217, 221, 240, 252, 253, 255, 256, 275, 278, 279, 299
chiefs, 140, 175, 246, 309
child, 42, 49, 75, 81, 92, 93, 100, 103, 129, 134, 142, 167, 223, 238, 243, 250–252, 256, 259, 279, 283
chorus, 241, 313–315
chose, 38, 110
chosen, 15, 21, 26, 193
christ, 309, 319, 322
chrysaor, 89, 90, 103
circle, 116–119, 121, 128, 152, 158, 278
circles, 118, 124, 146, 152
circuit, 62, 145, 158, 197, 207, 208
circular, 116, 117, 147, 158
citadel, 145, 146, 223
cities, 20, 31, 60, 62, 109, 110, 140, 146, 149, 316
citizens, 108–112, 138, 140, 142, 148
city, 31, 40, 49, 55–57, 62–65, 75, 77, 82–84, 107–112, 139, 141, 144, 146–148, 220, 221, 315, 319–321
clad, 26, 29, 223, 224
clamor, 100, 196, 204, 217, 219
class, 110, 124, 133, 140, 142
classes, 110, 128, 130, 140, 173, 210
clay, 58, 79, 141, 190, 213, 280, 285, 286, 293
clean, 51, 53, 259, 266, 320
clear, 21, 22, 32, 89, 91, 101, 155–157, 207, 211, 239, 266
cliff, 293, 316

cliffs, 222, 229, 235
climb, 64, 225, 284, 300
climbed, 251, 269, 284, 285
close, 29, 96, 102, 131, 132, 141, 164, 178, 181, 234, 259, 284, 287, 291, 294
closed, 35, 46, 125, 153, 268, 295, 300
closely, 164, 247, 265, 273, 301
clothed, 12, 14, 15, 48, 79, 80, 83, 95
cloud, 54, 58, 98, 128, 199, 206, 207, 212, 220, 239, 260, 272–275, 309
clouds, 33, 36, 37, 79, 80, 82, 95, 98, 200, 235, 273–275, 285–287, 290, 311
clover, 270, 271, 288, 290
clustered, 29, 30, 59
coated, 62, 145
cock, 222, 228, 306, 318
cold, 53, 99, 115, 143, 146, 159–161, 187, 207, 215, 222, 274, 283, 284, 287, 314
collect, 60, 199, 237, 294
collected, 12, 14, 16, 128, 150, 201, 256
color, 145, 159, 179, 181, 211, 249, 262, 297, 302
combat, 28, 29, 204, 223, 237
combined, 61, 151, 152, 154, 164, 181
comes, 39, 60, 83, 92, 98, 99, 103, 109, 125, 126, 128, 138, 155, 163, 168, 172, 175–177, 194, 197, 198, 203, 219, 220, 222, 226, 229, 230, 250, 258, 259, 270, 275, 276, 284, 316

coming, 42, 87, 141, 146, 196, 200, 203, 204, 207, 208, 220, 259, 260, 263, 265–270, 273, 275, 276, 279, 283, 286, 298, 302
command, 12, 15, 17, 26, 28, 39, 41, 42, 57, 58, 125, 148, 167, 206, 297, 314, 317
commanded, 28, 30, 41, 47, 51, 52, 61, 63, 66, 110, 139, 148, 190, 264, 321, 322
commands, 14, 16, 26–28, 30, 63, 77, 148, 297
committed, 123, 194, 225
common, 44, 109, 132, 139, 140, 142, 144, 148, 149, 160, 161, 235, 238, 319
company, 11, 12, 14–16, 20, 38, 41, 42, 82, 103, 104, 203, 309
compelled, 77, 108, 111, 126, 138
complete, 74, 75, 115, 133, 153, 158, 171, 175, 191, 205, 212, 301
completed, 21, 34, 99, 108, 120, 135, 198, 208, 240, 241, 306
composed, 118, 151, 153, 154, 181, 182, 238
compound, 117
compounds, 128, 130, 166
concealed, 44, 93, 163, 235, 236
conceived, 15, 69, 75, 87, 90, 92, 102, 113, 116, 150, 240, 314
condensed, 33, 128, 158
condition, 136, 179
conduct, 223, 300, 307
conflict, 75, 192, 195, 198, 199
confound, 25–27
confusion, 25, 58, 64, 135, 193, 195,

204, 236
connected, 22, 180, 191, 199, 202, 207
conquer, 15, 124, 159, 166
conquered, 98, 100, 123, 124
consented, 58, 234
consider, 112, 127, 130, 133, 138, 158, 179, 311
consists, 162, 170, 178, 212
consulted, 10, 148, 233–235
contact, 123, 124, 126, 132
contain, 122, 151
contained, 58, 60, 136, 157, 158, 162, 167
contest, 105, 192, 198, 206, 208, 209, 211, 239
continent, 110, 111, 140, 141
continue, 121, 153, 168, 205
continued, 144, 168, 183, 233, 237, 239, 285, 298
contrived, 18, 77, 79, 125, 303
control, 25, 30, 77, 135, 148, 175–177, 207
converse, 116, 187
conveyed, 62, 146, 147
cooked, 236, 268, 304, 305
cool, 47, 149, 226
copy, 113, 114, 118
cord, 265, 281
corn, 131, 209, 280, 313
corporeal, 115, 118, 160, 178
corrupted, 156–161
costly, 12, 14
cottus, 87, 96, 98, 100
council, 14, 27, 28, 57, 226, 227, 229, 230, 279, 283, 284
counsel, 10, 13, 20, 23, 26, 44, 57–59, 78, 97, 98, 217, 221, 223, 299, 320
counselor, 24–26, 28, 31, 57, 79, 84

count, 69, 218, 265, 307, 311
country, 39, 58, 60, 63, 65, 67, 76, 77, 108, 109, 111, 140–144, 147, 255, 267–269, 275, 277, 282, 296, 297, 306
courage, 19, 87, 111, 237
course, 40, 91, 118, 124, 132, 134, 135, 137, 142, 153, 157, 159, 169, 172, 309
courses, 120, 123–125, 127, 133, 218, 220
court, 112, 221
courts, 74, 79, 317
covenant, 53, 54, 70, 191, 319, 320
cover, 87, 141, 176, 247, 262, 280
covered, 35, 37, 52, 54, 58, 94, 96, 141, 145, 163, 181, 224, 261, 262, 265, 267, 270, 278, 285, 296, 298, 302, 318
covering, 53, 94, 155, 250, 262, 294
cow, 31, 184, 216
cows, 166, 184, 318
crafted, 12, 14, 15
crafts, 89, 102, 110, 314
crafty, 79, 84, 93, 303
create, 20, 23, 27, 124, 169, 175–177, 181, 213, 240, 297, 309
creates, 169, 182, 317
creation, 33, 44, 46, 112–115, 119, 126, 127, 135, 155, 163, 177–182, 184, 191, 192, 194–197, 202, 204, 205, 208, 212, 243, 294–296, 298, 306, 307, 313–315
creations, 113, 122, 194, 198, 202
creator, 23, 26, 35, 36, 39, 113–116, 118, 120, 122, 123, 132,

133, 136, 152, 164, 173,
174, 178, 182, 200,
294–296, 299, 317,
320–322
creature, 31, 45, 46, 54, 90, 114,
118, 123, 132, 135, 137,
202, 279–281
creek, 266, 286, 289
creeks, 269, 287–289
creeping, 35–37, 41, 45, 50–53, 153,
247, 320
creeps, 45, 51–53, 248
cried, 28, 29, 37, 38, 42, 58, 82,
197, 236, 257, 260, 266,
277, 279, 287, 303–305,
314
cries, 10, 18, 30, 41, 42, 48, 234,
298, 301, 309
critias, 107, 108, 111, 112, 137, 138
cronos, 78–81, 83–87, 92–97, 100,
103, 121, 132, 134, 135
cronus, 33, 61, 63–65, 75–77, 104
crooked, 78, 82, 83
cross, 220, 225, 252, 309, 315, 320
crossed, 90, 224, 284
crown, 30, 42, 84, 95, 174, 315
crowned, 18, 79, 103
cruel, 12, 14, 15, 78–80, 83, 94,
96–99, 101
crushed, 190, 220, 306
cry, 38, 39, 82, 97, 98, 164, 197,
204, 323
crying, 204, 260, 287, 301, 323
cunning, 10, 30, 39, 94, 95, 101,
221
cup, 31, 122, 149, 207, 240, 309
curds, 169
curse, 10, 26, 53, 66, 213
cursed, 47, 48, 50, 54, 295, 324
curses, 10, 29, 148

cush, 54
custom, 63, 92, 107, 121, 140
cut, 30, 54, 61, 76, 88, 89, 94, 99,
117, 125, 141, 145, 147,
148, 171, 237, 278, 281,
286, 299, 302
cutting, 49, 147
cycle, 132–136, 155
cytherea, 88

D

dâitya, 189
dagger, 187, 188
dagon, 75–77
dagr, 219, 226
daily, 38, 299, 302, 303
damascus, 65, 68
dance, 84, 121, 173, 255, 256, 259,
260, 287, 314, 315, 317
dances, 84, 173, 313
dancing, 256, 285, 302
danger, 111, 136, 283
dank, 81, 98, 99, 315
dark, 33, 58, 78, 85, 86, 91, 99,
100, 176, 191, 193, 195,
196, 198, 203, 204, 216,
217, 219–222, 225, 228,
230, 233, 235, 245, 247,
249–251, 279, 282, 283,
285, 295, 314, 316
darkness, 34, 39, 41, 44, 45, 58, 60,
61, 149, 153, 159, 163,
165, 180, 181, 191–193,
196, 200–205, 212, 215,
216, 218, 226, 233, 234,
240, 241, 243, 245–247,
249, 278, 295, 315–317
dart, 29, 38, 89, 276, 300
darting, 39, 207, 220, 264, 284
daughter, 31, 56, 62, 76–78, 83, 84,
90, 92, 93, 95, 99, 100,

102–104, 143, 202, 216, 219, 270, 280
daughters, 49, 50, 56, 76, 85, 86, 89, 91, 217, 294
david, 319, 320, 322
dawn, 42, 58, 91, 93, 218, 219, 226, 240, 247, 263, 314, 317
dawned, 215, 307, 309
daybreak, 149, 268, 280
daylight, 258, 259, 263
dead, 23, 29, 30, 39, 74, 96, 100, 134, 199, 204, 209, 211, 213, 217, 218, 220, 222–225, 229, 230, 276, 277, 302, 304, 305, 323, 324
deadly, 38, 89, 90, 94–96
deal, 79, 83, 138, 259, 262
dear, 82, 87, 92, 93, 95, 102, 107, 183, 185
dearer, 184
death, 42, 61, 65, 74, 77, 81, 98, 99, 105, 122, 149, 155, 163, 164, 166, 171, 173, 176, 177, 179, 187, 196, 204, 205, 213, 217, 222, 225, 230, 237, 240, 302, 310, 317, 321
deathless, 78, 81–83, 85–87, 89–93, 95–100, 102, 103
decay, 129, 157, 173, 179, 222, 223
deceitful, 79, 205
deceived, 47, 79, 101, 237, 280
decide, 28, 279, 283
decked, 12, 14, 15, 175
declare, 40, 86, 118, 121, 163, 311
declared, 31, 40, 86, 92, 107, 122, 168, 191, 193, 197, 200, 201, 203, 206, 208–210, 307, 319

declares, 118, 185
decrease, 59, 151, 156, 176, 207
decree, 15, 27–29, 31, 204
decreed, 12, 17, 28, 30, 37, 59, 319
decrees, 15, 18, 22, 23, 83, 221, 223
dedicated, 145, 146, 149
deed, 59, 88, 324
deeds, 11, 12, 15, 16, 23, 28, 33, 80, 81, 83, 86, 98, 109, 110, 114, 173, 175, 195, 224, 225, 314
deep, 25, 26, 30–32, 44, 46, 57–60, 62, 75, 81, 84, 87, 90, 91, 93, 97, 125, 141, 181, 189, 216, 221, 222, 226, 228, 230, 245, 247, 249, 251, 265, 269, 279, 285, 317
deer, 222, 256, 257, 271, 280, 288–290
defeated, 12, 105, 111
degree, 112, 122, 138, 197
deities, 25, 59, 121, 134, 135, 164, 167, 168
deity, 34, 61–63, 108, 114, 150–155, 174, 177, 180, 181, 185
delight, 47, 85, 88, 102, 145, 184, 192, 302
delighted, 27, 164, 165, 195
delights, 78, 79, 84, 102
delivered, 28, 53, 68, 75, 77, 94, 155, 212
deluge, 32, 57–59, 61, 63–65, 108, 109, 217, 296, 309
demarous, 75, 76
demons, 181, 192, 193, 195, 196, 198, 199, 203, 222, 301
depart, 28, 192, 296, 303
departed, 27, 35, 66, 75, 299, 306
departs, 125, 129, 186
dependent, 139, 152, 178

deprived, 75, 125–127, 136, 177
depth, 33, 87, 115, 145, 147, 163, 207, 215, 241, 245, 249
depths, 17, 19, 102, 111, 226, 237, 240
derive, 74, 156, 158
derived, 127, 130, 137, 155
descend, 213, 218, 223, 282, 302, 309, 316
descended, 27, 33, 74, 76, 104, 109, 147, 205, 216, 217, 220, 294–296, 299, 300, 306, 307, 309, 310
descent, 65, 309, 315
describe, 113, 139, 143, 147, 179
described, 61, 90, 112, 121, 140, 147, 149
desert, 41, 314, 315
deserted, 224, 237, 238
deserts, 223, 225, 315
design, 33, 64, 116, 126
desire, 21, 27, 28, 31, 38, 47, 48, 59, 75, 85, 88, 135, 155, 163, 173, 175, 178, 191, 217, 220, 235, 239, 321
desired, 47, 114, 123, 172, 211, 235, 318
desires, 25, 26, 28, 30, 186
desirous, 151, 168, 175, 178, 192
destinies, 9, 12, 15, 88
destiny, 122, 228, 314, 315
destitute, 33, 60, 109
destroy, 10, 21, 25, 39, 50, 51, 59, 82, 169, 171, 174, 176, 192, 195, 201, 205, 206, 223, 236, 238, 281, 304, 305, 316
destroyed, 18, 23, 28, 32, 38, 52, 58, 59, 61, 62, 81, 90, 108, 151, 157, 176, 220, 294, 296, 300, 320
destroyer, 17, 24, 104, 174, 176–179, 182, 192, 194, 196, 198, 208
destroys, 83, 92, 182, 222
detained, 76, 123, 129
determine, 30, 128, 131, 135, 233
devas, 164, 167, 185
devised, 30, 76
devoid, 114, 130, 159, 179
devoted, 167, 174–176
devour, 83, 84, 219
devoured, 94, 181, 238, 299, 305
die, 40, 47, 171, 211, 224, 225, 263, 277, 280, 281, 296, 323–326
died, 49, 50, 52, 54, 56, 61, 75, 80, 82, 109, 134, 136, 143, 206, 237, 280, 301, 323, 324
dies, 90, 170, 171, 202, 325
different, 62, 77, 78, 129–133, 138, 139, 145, 150, 152, 153, 155, 159, 162, 164, 175, 178, 211, 238, 252, 261, 275, 276, 280, 282, 283, 288–290, 297
difficult, 10, 99, 128, 137, 152, 154
diffused, 116, 195, 196, 201, 202
dim, 87, 90, 97, 100, 219, 239, 305
diminish, 41, 157
dione, 76, 77, 84, 91
dionysus, 103, 105
directed, 140, 149, 302
direction, 64, 116, 118, 119, 124, 125, 131–133, 135, 140, 144, 147, 181, 198, 204, 266, 267, 282
dirt, 248, 279
discourse, 111, 112, 127, 128, 130,

136, 138, 139
discrete, 178–180
disease, 115, 116, 124, 187, 196, 209
diseases, 39, 80, 115, 204, 209
dises, 223, 224
disorder, 102, 114, 136
dispersed, 91, 118, 128
disposer, 12, 14, 16
dissolved, 119, 122, 136, 156–158
distance, 143, 152, 203, 215, 258, 270, 272, 275, 287
distinct, 110, 130, 201, 202
distress, 23, 30, 58, 195
district, 108, 140
ditch, 147, 302
diverse, 117, 118, 120, 124, 143, 173
diversity, 64, 166
divided, 30, 44, 54, 55, 61, 79, 86, 94, 101, 117, 118, 122, 145, 152, 178, 194, 210, 212, 266, 317
divine, 27, 34, 38–40, 42, 57, 61, 62, 79, 85, 89, 91, 100, 101, 104, 110, 118, 120–122, 125, 133, 135, 138, 140, 149, 166, 173, 174, 221, 295
divinity, 152, 311
divisible, 117, 150
division, 65, 92, 128, 148, 162, 233
divisions, 181, 221, 222, 225, 233
docks, 144–146
doer, 59, 104, 201
dog, 12, 14, 210, 225, 250, 252, 284, 285, 288–291
dogs, 61, 74, 188–190, 272, 295, 299, 323
doing, 87, 88, 264, 295, 303, 318

dokos, 276, 277
domain, 40, 57, 159
dominion, 39, 45, 117, 118, 316
done, 20, 25, 36–38, 46–48, 53, 54, 59, 186, 224, 257, 258, 277, 281, 296, 297, 304
door, 48, 51, 58, 80, 98, 172, 190, 230, 263, 268, 275, 295, 301
doris, 89, 91
double, 38, 117, 145, 152, 153
doubt, 121, 132, 138, 139, 165, 301
doubtless, 168, 171
dove, 52, 58, 282
dragon, 28–30, 90, 100, 222, 225, 230
dragons, 12, 15, 26
drank, 54, 135, 149, 216, 289
draw, 98, 108, 200, 218
drawn, 74, 155, 206, 217
dread, 26, 53, 64, 81, 86, 88, 97, 314
dreaded, 29, 216, 219, 222, 225
dreadful, 97, 100, 234, 258, 300
dream, 59, 131, 278, 279, 316
dreamed, 278
dreams, 88, 126, 219, 223, 230
drew, 18, 26, 29, 42, 88, 148, 269
drink, 28, 175, 224, 228, 230, 288–291, 305, 309, 321
drinking, 149, 264, 296
drinks, 32, 144
drive, 93, 102, 108, 218, 219, 272–274
driven, 40, 48, 64, 83, 126, 206, 220, 225
drops, 88, 199, 206, 207, 216, 228, 239
drove, 29, 42, 48, 75, 90, 94, 199, 207, 217, 272, 319

drowned, 217, 225, 284, 285, 287, 294–296
drunk, 28, 54, 309
dry, 52, 109, 144, 155, 159–161, 209, 236, 239, 266, 282, 296, 304, 322
duck, 279
due, 62, 78, 92, 118, 133, 153, 164, 179, 213, 218, 220
dug, 144, 238, 247, 249, 261, 267, 278, 302
duration, 157, 182
during, 22, 111, 123, 133, 141, 153, 171, 195, 201, 204, 208, 239, 263, 271, 307, 309
dust, 38, 46–48, 98, 101, 270, 304
dwarfs, 218, 221, 226, 229
dwell, 21, 31, 54, 59, 81, 83, 86, 87, 89–91, 96, 101, 102, 109, 111, 123, 177, 221, 222, 230, 235, 250, 300, 319
dwelling, 11, 32, 40, 55, 78, 80, 91, 100, 125, 143, 189, 190, 218, 220, 227, 293, 301, 302
dwellings, 142, 210, 226
dwells, 78, 93, 102, 219, 222
dwelt, 73, 74, 80, 109, 110, 135, 139, 140, 142, 143, 221, 239, 240, 249, 251
dying, 103, 219, 323–325

E

ea, 11–13, 15, 20, 21, 23–28, 30–32, 57, 59
eagle, 94, 222, 229, 276, 293
ear, 78, 173, 181, 184, 257, 280, 295
early, 79, 142, 217, 218, 240, 268, 272, 273, 315

ears, 97, 99, 116, 174, 264, 280, 294, 316
ease, 21, 27, 28, 80, 86, 251
easiest, 152, 154, 250
easily, 78, 79, 82, 84, 89, 92, 152, 238, 247, 298, 301, 303
eastern, 152, 218, 230, 261, 269, 270, 272, 273
easy, 84, 135, 138, 139
eat, 28, 47, 48, 53, 80, 94, 96, 203, 211, 248, 250, 275–277, 281, 282, 288–290, 295, 304, 321, 324
eaten, 47, 51, 68, 135, 250, 256, 289, 290
eating, 90, 144, 210, 238, 256, 279, 295, 296, 326
eats, 90, 167, 211, 309
eber, 55, 56
echidna, 90
eden, 46, 48
edge, 219, 223, 225, 226, 247, 253, 267, 289, 293, 314–316
education, 109, 112, 124, 137, 140, 293
effort, 166, 234, 305, 311
efforts, 176, 234, 302, 303
egg, 33, 34, 181, 241
eggs, 246, 247, 249
egotism, 181
egypt, 77, 108, 110, 111, 144
egyptian, 69, 108, 112, 140
egyptians, 74, 104, 142
elam, 55, 68
elapsed, 111, 135, 139, 141
elder, 58, 78, 116, 143, 238, 272, 273, 276, 280, 281, 296
eldest, 41, 91, 99, 121, 143, 144, 252
element, 75, 87, 125, 128, 152, 154,

161, 169, 181
elements, 33, 34, 58, 77, 110, 115, 117, 122, 123, 128–132, 136, 152, 153, 160, 167, 178, 180–182, 305
elf, 219, 223, 226
elk, 211, 271, 288
elves, 221, 225, 226, 229
embrace, 33, 79, 184
embraced, 10, 35, 184
emitted, 35–37, 126
empire, 111, 144, 314
empty, 12, 15, 40, 44, 191, 202, 215, 227, 240
enclosed, 125, 142, 143, 146, 169
ended, 202, 237, 252, 306
endless, 100, 191, 201, 317
endlessly, 152, 191
endowed, 10, 36, 114, 126, 133, 179, 181, 216
ends, 41, 81, 98, 146, 267
endued, 44, 151, 174, 177
endure, 23, 41, 137, 158, 170
enduring, 118, 224, 240
enemies, 23, 28–30, 37, 42, 68, 139, 217, 219
enemy, 15, 17, 24, 28, 41, 202, 204, 205, 223, 238, 302
energies, 181, 182
energy, 34, 163, 173–175
engaged, 173, 181, 302
enlil, 21, 22, 30, 59
enmity, 73, 217
enoch, 49, 50
enormous, 262, 265, 279
enosh, 49
enough, 79, 114, 121, 126, 128, 136, 139, 140, 146, 147, 152, 263, 266, 274, 275, 277, 279, 314

enter, 19, 58, 124, 129, 134, 170, 172, 175, 183, 218, 225, 226, 241–248, 282, 295
entered, 29, 38, 58, 59, 66, 164, 168, 180, 183, 184, 195, 206, 295, 298
entering, 85, 167, 171, 172
entire, 28, 116, 117, 145, 146, 162, 169, 177, 181, 220, 307, 311
entirely, 130, 133, 152, 169, 238
entrusted, 12, 14, 209
enveloped, 30, 44, 181, 216
envoy, 15, 18
envy, 82, 175, 252, 309, 314
eos, 84, 91
equal, 18, 25, 29, 81, 87, 101, 117–119, 122, 145, 148, 151, 153, 154, 158, 178, 197, 198, 238, 250
equally, 61, 81, 112, 120, 130, 131, 182, 205, 206
erebus, 33, 34, 87, 94, 97
erech, 31
erected, 31, 62, 142, 240
eros, 33, 34, 76, 78, 87, 88
escape, 13, 17, 26, 29, 30, 38, 76, 80, 236, 260, 274, 284, 301, 303, 318
escaped, 59, 96, 171, 236, 260, 261, 274, 296
essence, 34, 42, 43, 117–119, 130, 158, 174, 178–182, 209
establish, 53, 70, 140, 171, 189, 309, 319
esteemed, 38, 63, 65, 105
eternal, 25, 85, 86, 99, 101, 113, 116, 118–121, 130, 131, 150, 152, 153, 174, 177–179, 222, 224, 225,

eternity, 33, 40, 118, 119, 153, 191, 206
ether, 33, 43, 44, 78, 181, 182
euphrates, 31, 46, 57, 60
europe, 110, 111, 142
eve, 48, 249, 317
evening, 30, 40, 41, 44, 45, 171, 172, 226, 280, 287, 317
events, 75, 108, 132, 140, 178, 303
ever, 28, 31, 44, 59, 83, 85–87, 95, 108, 109, 115, 119, 121, 124, 127, 131–133, 137, 144, 151, 162, 174, 179, 191, 199, 201, 217–220, 222–224, 227, 230, 233, 236, 238, 239, 256, 257, 261, 263, 272, 283, 284, 315, 316
evils, 80, 82, 123, 176
exact, 110, 114, 131
exactly, 109, 124, 152
exalted, 10, 12, 15, 18, 24, 26–29, 31, 78
example, 129, 295
exceeds, 97, 110, 117
excelled, 102, 110
excellent, 57, 75, 85, 86, 89, 94, 112, 114, 116, 178, 181, 189, 202
exception, 120, 127, 145, 154, 155, 234, 320
exist, 34–37, 39, 43, 98, 109, 130, 131, 142, 147, 150, 153, 155, 159, 162, 166, 168, 179, 248, 296
existed, 32, 34–36, 44, 60, 131, 134, 139, 141, 150, 156, 162, 163, 167, 179, 181, 211, 233, 240

existence, 25, 31, 37, 113, 123, 129, 131, 151, 156, 157, 159, 176, 178, 191–194, 200–202, 221, 234, 294, 313
existent, 130, 157, 165, 178
existing, 33, 34, 43, 112, 150, 170, 182, 240
exists, 38, 39, 114, 119, 131, 140, 155, 157–159, 179, 180, 184, 191, 201, 233
explain, 112, 129, 180
explained, 44, 60, 127
express, 113, 128, 138, 302
extend, 146, 171, 263
extended, 25, 55, 121, 125, 138, 140, 141, 151, 163
extending, 110, 141, 147, 240
extends, 133, 158, 164, 203
extent, 19, 130, 139, 143, 147, 178, 181, 204, 298
external, 118, 123–126, 133, 152, 157, 158, 164
extremity, 109, 111, 143
eye, 35–37, 39, 40, 78, 87, 125, 126, 138, 145, 149, 163, 164, 181, 184, 203, 207, 217, 220, 228
eyes, 29, 38–40, 47, 50, 69, 70, 77, 78, 90, 93, 97, 100, 101, 116, 125, 126, 173, 174, 177, 196, 203, 212, 219, 222, 228, 240, 261, 266, 271, 283–286, 299, 301, 303–305, 309, 313, 315–317, 323

F
face, 18, 26, 36, 37, 39, 41, 48, 58, 70, 78, 79, 82, 97, 109, 125, 126, 203, 228, 263,

faces, 54, 61, 154, 247, 306, 309, 275, 278, 297, 306, 309, 316, 318, 319, 321–323
faces, 54, 61, 154, 247, 306, 309
fact, 107, 109, 112, 124, 133, 141
fail, 14–16, 177
failed, 64, 95, 123, 137
fain, 231
fair, 78, 84, 90, 91, 101, 102, 104, 113, 126, 132, 140, 144, 187–190, 218–221, 223, 228–230, 235, 238, 249, 313, 314, 316
fairest, 87, 109, 113–115, 121, 132, 143, 149
fall, 12, 15, 37, 40, 88, 184, 189, 206, 213, 216, 227, 229, 258, 260, 275, 290, 306, 325
fallen, 48, 82, 136, 141, 257, 263
falling, 30, 76, 98, 136, 147, 155, 267, 295, 304
falls, 99, 125, 219, 226, 229, 268, 278
false, 82, 85, 89, 124, 162, 179, 252, 278, 299, 320
families, 53–55, 66, 139, 176, 178, 223, 247, 248
family, 58, 121, 144, 145, 217, 219, 269, 277, 279, 285, 303
famine, 59, 83, 89
famous, 22, 79, 94, 95, 99, 102, 104, 107, 108, 110, 228, 249, 301
fang, 12, 14, 15, 38
fares, 229
farewell, 314
fashion, 31, 79, 107, 114, 120, 204, 218, 279
fashioned, 21, 22, 38, 39, 59, 121, 130, 132, 147, 213, 226,

238
fast, 58, 82, 94, 97, 99, 124, 206, 225, 229, 241, 257, 260, 261, 264, 279, 280, 282, 283, 290, 291, 307
fastened, 12, 15, 19, 119, 164, 282, 284
fat, 48, 94, 95, 287, 288
fate, 15–17, 22, 26–30, 34, 89, 122, 135, 155, 217, 222, 227, 229, 236, 303, 316
fates, 25, 28, 80, 88, 101, 159, 223, 227
fathers, 15, 17, 18, 20, 21, 24, 29, 30, 163, 164, 171, 319
favor, 50, 82, 92, 95, 138, 139, 178
fear, 23, 26, 27, 29, 41, 53, 80, 82, 102, 123, 164, 174, 175, 183, 193, 195, 202, 220, 229, 243, 322
feared, 27, 183, 224, 303, 319
fearful, 81, 88, 90, 97, 99, 100, 250, 298
fearing, 28, 136, 234
fears, 167, 183, 203, 205
fearsome, 217, 219
feast, 14, 112, 225
feather, 264, 271, 276, 278
feathers, 42, 264, 265, 271, 278, 283, 304, 305
fed, 96, 216, 299
feeds, 211, 219
feel, 125, 247, 260, 288, 299, 305, 317, 323, 324
feeling, 112, 300, 301, 318
feet, 15, 19, 30, 37, 41, 60–63, 84, 86, 88, 97, 100, 116, 124, 145, 147, 174, 175, 181, 203, 206, 216, 224, 234, 258, 280, 288, 297, 300,

304, 309, 313, 318, 320, 321
fell, 30, 36–38, 48, 58, 64, 70, 73, 111, 143, 148, 193, 196, 202, 203, 212, 216, 229, 237, 257, 260, 262, 267, 268, 270, 273, 278–280, 284, 287, 298, 300, 305, 322
fellow, 112, 137, 280, 304
fellows, 83, 162, 304
felt, 23, 38, 40, 137, 176, 184, 240, 300, 322, 324
female, 33, 45, 49, 51, 52, 61, 69, 78, 97, 140, 150, 169, 184, 191, 203, 210, 211, 241, 250
fence, 98, 142, 273, 274, 318
fertile, 60, 143
festival, 21, 41, 107, 112
fetters, 229
field, 9, 31, 32, 46–48, 58, 60, 227, 314
fields, 58, 79, 83, 101, 109, 189, 226–228, 230, 316
fiend, 41, 194, 201, 204, 211, 212
fierce, 25, 26, 90, 98, 136, 173, 176, 189, 217, 219, 220, 225, 229, 234, 235, 237
fiery, 33, 235
fight, 15, 18, 22, 92, 97, 148, 193, 229, 237, 238, 270, 277
fighting, 96, 98, 270
figure, 89, 116, 121, 140, 158, 203, 309
figures, 61, 116, 121, 129, 130
filled, 11–17, 26, 28, 29, 39, 51, 59, 65, 97, 117, 148, 177, 181, 184, 216, 218, 227, 240, 243, 250, 263, 267, 269, 272, 293, 318
filling, 29, 101, 220, 243
final, 178, 198, 305
finally, 159, 181, 299, 300, 309
find, 10, 22, 110–112, 125, 127, 145, 147, 156, 169, 184, 223, 226, 227, 230, 255, 259, 260, 266, 279, 282, 296, 301
finding, 48, 62, 63, 113, 114, 138
finds, 103, 184, 222
fine, 212, 218, 221, 249, 259, 267, 280, 293
finest, 154, 189, 190
finished, 21, 46, 103, 104, 116, 240, 262–264, 268, 269, 272, 285–287, 295
fires, 126, 170, 171, 188–190, 212, 286
firm, 27, 38, 213, 282
firmament, 30, 174, 175, 177, 240
firmly, 40, 42, 171, 234, 262, 268, 310
firs, 288, 289
firstborn, 48, 170, 173
fish, 26, 30, 38, 41, 45, 53, 58, 60, 194, 210, 229, 234–236, 238, 243–245, 247, 268, 269, 275, 276, 283, 285, 287–290, 294, 295, 303
fish-hawk, 279
fish-man, 12, 14, 15
fishes, 57, 61, 84, 295
fit, 60, 125, 147, 275
fitted, 152, 184, 279
fitting, 96, 107, 117, 238, 314
fixed, 17, 18, 20, 30, 97, 98, 121, 140, 153, 157, 162, 164, 218, 268, 307
flame, 17, 40, 97, 100, 154, 175,

220, 229, 260, 261, 317
flames, 231, 260, 261, 263, 272, 298, 318
flaming, 29, 48, 58, 213, 223, 226
flashed, 100, 145, 260
flat, 249, 273, 282, 290
fled, 58, 70, 105, 192, 199, 235–237, 326
flesh, 30, 38, 42, 47, 50–54, 88, 90, 94, 155, 217, 220, 221, 274, 281, 294, 299, 304, 305, 319, 324
flew, 42, 58, 59, 77, 90, 97, 172, 210, 246, 247, 251, 261, 265, 266, 280–283, 317
flies, 59, 171, 222, 229, 235, 246
flight, 29, 30, 60, 76, 219, 220, 222, 241–248, 317
flinch, 14, 16, 316
flint, 87–89, 257–260, 272, 277, 280, 294
float, 57, 265, 288
flocks, 67, 74, 80, 81, 90, 93, 139, 188–190, 246
flood, 42, 51, 54, 55, 58, 59, 62, 63, 123, 124, 164, 207, 267, 294–296, 299, 300, 320
floods, 39, 111, 189, 236, 314
floor, 98, 145, 217
flow, 40, 86, 91, 125, 189, 190, 200, 207, 208, 215, 288
flowed, 76, 101, 199, 200, 269, 313
flower, 103, 144, 270, 294, 309
flowering, 101, 169, 170
flowers, 79, 89, 95, 262, 263, 270, 276, 286, 293, 309
flowing, 124, 128, 146, 155, 220, 290
flows, 38, 46, 85, 86, 99, 141, 155, 217

fly, 45, 80, 195, 221, 236, 237, 246, 247, 276, 280, 283
flying, 77, 82, 210, 230, 235, 246, 265, 266
foam, 88, 219, 288, 299
fog, 285–287
fold, 31, 189, 190
follow, 120–122, 137, 150, 214, 229, 264
followed, 18, 25, 29, 88, 123, 143, 147, 217, 294, 318
following, 38, 60, 117, 136, 144, 148, 149, 152, 157, 159, 180, 240, 256, 265, 311
follows, 43, 83, 99, 125, 129, 134, 142, 150, 156, 168, 169, 210, 235, 238, 311, 317
fond, 89, 172, 279
food, 40, 41, 45–47, 51, 53, 60, 62, 73, 83, 116, 122, 137, 140, 141, 143, 144, 147, 168, 183, 184, 189, 190, 211, 212, 216, 224, 234, 236, 238, 247, 248, 253, 256, 277, 281, 288, 290, 296, 303, 304, 309, 320
foolish, 124, 176
foot, 52, 148, 262, 269, 288, 289, 303, 305, 310, 316
force, 15, 75, 91, 93, 101, 117, 139, 150, 173, 192, 237, 302
forces, 11, 14, 15, 27, 29, 39, 115, 152, 163
foremost, 176, 177
forest, 31, 74, 208, 219, 226, 237, 241–249, 251, 302, 317
forests, 31, 220, 234–236, 238
forever, 23, 34, 48, 50, 162, 191–194, 198, 217, 223–225, 237, 263, 277,

281, 314–316
forgotten, 23, 95, 111, 142, 309
formed, 9, 14, 22, 25, 31, 33, 36, 44, 46, 61, 94, 95, 116, 118, 125, 129, 145, 146, 163, 164, 181, 192, 196, 201, 207, 212, 215–217, 235, 286, 294–296, 298, 313
former, 75, 92, 99, 109, 117, 127, 128, 132, 134, 150, 162, 168, 169
formerly, 109, 168, 323, 324
formless, 44, 130, 150, 159, 163, 176, 216
forms, 36, 39, 43, 82, 87, 119, 129–131, 135, 151, 154, 155, 159, 160, 169, 175, 176, 179, 180, 183, 199, 203, 206, 212, 215, 252
formula, 172, 201, 202
fortune, 149, 176, 223
forum, 221, 223, 224
forward, 94, 112, 121, 125, 151, 189, 190, 194, 201, 202, 213, 230, 257, 264, 265
fought, 81, 96, 98, 139, 228, 237
foulness, 181, 225
found, 17, 35–38, 42, 46, 50, 52, 55, 59, 60, 62, 70, 73, 74, 76, 108, 113, 114, 118, 135, 142–144, 158, 198, 205, 216, 221, 227, 233, 234, 237, 238, 245, 261, 266, 268, 269, 280–282, 294, 296, 298, 314, 315, 318
founded, 30, 64, 75, 110, 306
founder, 23, 108
fountain, 43, 70, 142, 182, 199, 215, 222, 223
fountains, 51, 52, 76, 141, 146, 199, 206, 207, 222, 297, 320
frôbak, 212
fragments, 32, 217
fragrant, 95, 144, 262, 309
frame, 78, 115, 137, 217
framed, 113, 114, 118, 119, 121, 217
free, 20, 21, 80, 85, 94, 114, 115, 130, 133, 163, 179, 196, 229, 303
freed, 164, 171, 175, 294
freely, 144, 279
fresh, 133, 138, 249
friend, 107, 138, 183, 277
friends, 58, 62, 142, 201, 221, 224, 249, 257
fright, 12, 14, 15, 199
frighten, 273, 281
front, 17, 26, 46, 58, 98, 99, 110, 125, 138, 168, 198, 202, 204, 207, 219, 247, 249, 259, 264, 288, 305
frost, 109, 189, 216, 223, 285
fruit, 45, 47, 48, 80, 81, 83, 88, 144, 158, 189, 190, 196, 230, 243, 251, 300, 320, 321
fruitful, 45, 53, 61, 70, 80, 81, 239, 316
fruits, 60, 135, 140, 144, 145, 147, 158, 212, 300
fulfilled, 30, 95, 104, 319
full, 15, 19, 29, 39, 79–81, 88, 92, 94, 96, 99, 131, 135, 136, 140, 141, 146, 149, 154, 171, 174, 175, 188, 224, 225, 228, 229, 241, 243, 252, 259, 267, 282, 287, 300
fullest, 30, 189, 190
fullness, 23, 118, 124, 135

fully, 30, 92, 96, 205, 210
fuming, 14, 15, 26, 27
furious, 14, 15, 26, 252
furnish, 123, 144, 147, 148, 303
furnished, 61, 125, 144, 221
furrow, 208, 269
further, 65, 114, 130, 138, 142, 147, 158, 161
fury, 58, 97, 100, 219, 239
future, 119, 121, 123, 137, 148, 167, 173, 178, 186, 191, 193, 194, 221, 223, 236, 269

G

gûsnasp, 207, 212
gaga, 14, 15, 28
game, 221, 255, 257, 299, 318
gap, 226, 273
garden, 46–48, 142, 293, 294, 319
garm, 228, 229
garment, 17, 28, 54
gate, 220, 321
gates, 30, 41, 98–100, 145, 225, 226
gather, 27, 29, 42, 51, 133, 213, 304
gathered, 26, 27, 36, 37, 44, 57, 66, 111, 147, 148, 216, 241, 262, 271, 298
ge, 75
general, 112, 124, 152, 157, 295
generated, 33, 61, 128, 129, 153, 156, 159, 161, 162, 169
gentle, 86, 89, 125, 287, 314
genus, 73, 162
germ, 163, 240
geryones, 90, 103
getting, 264, 290, 291, 301
giant, 14, 15, 26, 217, 219–222, 226, 228, 229, 300–305
giants, 33, 64, 85, 88, 105, 216, 217, 219–221, 223, 226–228, 231, 236, 294, 295, 300, 305
gift, 17, 80, 86, 279, 316
gifts, 19, 30, 86, 92, 137, 149, 175, 298, 316
gigantic, 215, 216, 219, 235
girl, 104, 218, 279
given, 20, 21, 29, 30, 41, 45, 49, 53, 64, 68, 95, 112, 123, 126, 127, 131, 137, 142, 144, 146, 149, 157, 173, 202, 211, 219, 224–227, 283, 293, 313, 314
giver, 173, 182, 321
givers, 80, 85, 86, 96
gives, 39, 84, 92, 110, 200, 219, 222, 235
giving, 100, 148, 149, 273, 278, 305, 309
glad, 14, 27, 65, 79, 85, 202, 228, 256, 257, 265, 268, 273, 274, 318, 322
gleaming, 25, 86, 88
glens, 87, 94, 100, 101, 104
gloom, 97, 98, 200–204, 212, 216, 240, 299
gloomy, 44, 86, 98, 100, 192, 193, 216, 219, 222, 235
glorious, 12, 15, 33, 80, 85, 86, 88–92, 94, 96, 99, 100, 102, 103, 121, 149, 212, 322
glory, 25, 79, 81, 92, 94, 136, 146, 171, 173, 177, 178, 182, 184, 192, 205, 211, 212, 220, 309, 319, 320
glowing, 86, 94, 99, 101, 235, 240
goat, 69, 90, 210, 211
goats, 61, 93, 184, 211
goddess, 15, 25, 35, 38, 77, 79, 88,

90–92, 95, 101, 102, 104,
107, 109, 110, 112, 140,
217, 222, 237
goddesses, 79, 85, 86, 88, 89, 91,
103, 112, 138, 221, 230
goes, 11, 12, 15, 16, 95, 99, 103,
124, 167, 171, 197, 198,
201, 207, 229, 270, 282,
325
going, 39, 66, 70, 99, 112, 125, 131,
137, 139, 189, 194, 207,
212, 220, 255, 256, 258,
260, 263, 267, 270–272,
275, 280, 281, 284,
303–305, 318
gold, 57, 66, 79, 84, 91, 95, 129,
142, 144–146, 149, 155,
162, 187, 211, 218, 221,
223, 226, 228, 230, 300
golden, 34, 78–81, 84, 88, 90, 99,
100, 102–104, 132, 148,
149, 187, 188, 190, 219,
221, 230
gomorrah, 55, 67, 68
gone, 107, 171, 226, 230, 250, 256,
266, 268, 270, 274, 275,
279, 306, 316
goodness, 84, 181, 191, 202, 309
goods, 57, 79, 149
governed, 63, 109, 120, 139, 158,
162, 175
governor, 40, 41, 57
gracious, 86, 89, 146, 227
gradually, 58, 169, 175, 181
grain, 79, 209, 210
grandson, 178, 256, 262, 263, 266,
270, 271, 274, 275, 317
grant, 92, 137, 138, 192
granted, 127, 131, 176, 177, 213,
296

grass, 31, 45, 88, 135, 189, 223,
226, 230, 271, 276,
284–286, 290
grasses, 270
gratified, 174, 176
grave, 224, 230, 280
graves, 224
gray, 82, 87, 89, 92, 136, 275, 285,
313
grazing, 210
greater, 33, 43, 45, 79, 84, 94, 107,
109, 120, 122, 123, 126,
127, 137, 139, 153,
156–158, 162, 170, 192,
218, 239, 313
greatest, 12, 14, 16, 60, 74, 76, 101,
108, 126, 127, 133, 153,
189, 190, 197, 204, 208,
283
greatness, 27, 110, 144, 146, 295,
318, 319
greed, 307
greek, 44, 61, 162
greeks, 73, 74, 104
green, 23, 31, 53, 221–224, 226,
227, 229, 271, 276, 283,
306, 309
grew, 26, 29, 37, 42, 58, 81, 88, 89,
94, 100, 134–137, 142,
144, 149, 200, 208, 209,
215, 223, 235, 241–249,
253, 265, 270, 279, 280,
283, 287, 288, 304, 309,
316
grief, 26, 27, 42, 80, 86, 93, 96, 225
grievous, 97, 103, 104, 199
grim, 12, 14, 15, 81, 90, 97, 219,
313
grizzlies, 287, 289, 290
grizzly, 277, 287, 290

groaned, 87, 97, 100
grow, 46, 80, 82, 98, 122, 129, 136,
    183, 209, 227, 230, 238,
    253, 261, 263, 265, 279,
    280, 282, 287–289, 317
growing, 97, 137, 141, 146, 208,
    212, 223, 226, 270, 288,
    290
growled, 299, 304
grown, 81, 100, 136, 200, 208, 209,
    220, 228, 260, 288–291
grows, 78, 90, 220, 221, 228, 229,
    240, 281
growth, 124, 173, 208, 222, 243
guard, 48, 88, 90, 223, 271
guarded, 241–248, 314
guardian, 121, 194, 197, 198,
    205–207, 317
guardians, 80, 140, 142, 213, 223
guards, 91, 99, 146, 205, 225
guide, 41, 42, 79, 139, 148, 282,
    314
guiding, 122, 124, 139
gulf, 81, 98, 207, 215, 216, 218,
    221, 225
gushed, 61, 88, 217
gyes, 87, 96, 98, 100

H

hades, 81, 90, 93, 99, 100
haha, 246, 251
hair, 82, 184, 198, 205, 216, 219,
    220, 228, 231, 249, 250,
    268, 283, 284, 302
half, 30, 61, 79, 90, 117, 145, 153,
    154, 176, 184, 197, 198,
    249, 265, 309
hall, 27, 221, 223, 225–228, 230
halls, 142
haloa, 253
ham, 50, 52, 54, 55, 67

hamingjes, 223, 224
hand, 11, 12, 15–18, 29, 35–38, 41,
    42, 48, 53, 59, 67, 68, 70,
    75, 88, 92, 97, 109, 115,
    122, 133, 135, 149, 151,
    153, 172, 197, 198, 202,
    205, 226, 257, 258, 261,
    262, 264, 265, 271, 305,
    309, 310, 314, 321
handed, 108, 142, 148, 236, 305,
    313
hands, 13, 23, 37, 50, 70, 73, 76,
    80, 81, 88, 90, 93, 95, 97,
    98, 100, 102, 103, 116,
    122, 125, 181, 184, 190,
    228, 231, 234, 258,
    262–264, 266, 274, 277,
    297, 298, 311, 322, 323
handsome, 91, 175, 218
hang, 274, 275
happen, 93, 132, 138, 178, 258,
    259, 279, 287, 298, 301
happened, 28, 38, 61, 77, 100, 108,
    109, 132, 140, 200, 296,
    310
happens, 96, 126, 193, 211
happily, 177, 230, 293
happiness, 149, 164, 176, 182, 225,
    230
happy, 81, 86, 92, 103, 110, 122,
    155, 174, 175, 189, 224,
    314, 317
haran, 56, 66
harbor, 110, 145, 146
hard, 80, 81, 84, 91, 94, 96, 97,
    100, 144, 229
hardly, 120, 131, 304
hare, 210, 323–326
hari, 177, 178, 180–182
harm, 80, 193, 197, 276

harmful, 80, 228, 281
harmony, 118, 127
hate, 29, 57, 277
hated, 87, 97, 225, 320
hateful, 89, 95, 99
hati, 219
hau, 257, 258
haumea, 252
havilah, 54, 55
hawaii, 240
hawk, 82, 222, 246, 275
head, 13, 18, 27, 29, 38, 39, 41, 47, 60, 61, 76–79, 89, 94, 95, 98, 102, 108, 121, 124, 125, 146, 155, 171, 174, 195, 198, 205, 216, 223, 229, 234, 249, 252, 257, 262–266, 268, 269, 271, 272, 276, 277, 280, 284, 285, 301, 306, 317, 325
heads, 61, 87, 90, 97, 100, 112, 199, 207, 272, 282, 286, 295, 299
hear, 49, 57, 62, 97, 100, 109, 132, 134, 138, 142, 164, 178, 223–225, 265, 269, 275, 297, 301, 302, 313, 315, 316, 321
heard, 12, 26–29, 47, 57, 62, 93, 97, 107, 108, 111, 116, 123, 132, 139, 142, 211, 217, 228, 229, 252, 258, 260, 264, 269, 277, 281, 285, 301, 313, 322
hearing, 18, 107, 127, 184, 218, 302, 304
hearts, 26, 31, 57, 85, 237, 305, 306, 314, 316, 319, 321
heat, 33, 40, 53, 97, 100, 115, 126, 157, 159–161, 167, 216, 218, 227, 251, 260, 283, 284, 286, 304
heavenly, 28, 33, 86, 120, 121, 133, 138, 172, 193, 196, 200, 218, 300, 319
heavens, 33, 38, 39, 46, 57, 58, 60, 61, 64, 109, 146, 150, 153, 162, 213, 215, 217–220, 234, 240, 241, 251, 252, 293–295, 297, 310, 311, 322
heavy, 80, 96, 97, 99, 131, 148, 210, 216, 220, 258–260, 274, 302
hecate, 33, 92
heed, 83, 229, 278
heel, 190
height, 41, 42, 57, 73, 145, 146, 199, 203, 282, 298
heimdal, 223
heimdall, 227, 229
hel, 228–230
hela, 222–226
held, 19, 58, 65, 74, 75, 90, 136, 144, 146, 226, 227, 229, 230, 243, 257–259, 264, 265, 283, 284, 320
helicon, 84, 85
helios, 103, 108
helius, 84
hell, 196, 201, 203, 230, 309, 310
hellenes, 108, 111, 139, 142
helm, 135, 136, 229
help, 48, 82, 100–102, 113, 116, 120, 123, 126, 127, 131, 148, 210, 262, 264, 267, 296, 301
helpless, 35, 42, 136, 192, 251, 314
hen, 35, 37, 246
hera, 84, 90, 93, 102, 103

heracles, 76, 90, 94, 103, 110, 111, 139, 143
herb, 31, 45, 46, 53
herbs, 41, 45, 74, 95, 209, 291, 293
herds, 67, 93, 134, 188
herdsmen, 67, 109
herit, 263–267
hermes, 43, 74, 75, 79, 93, 119
heroes, 81, 225, 228
hessiha, 270, 271
hid, 39, 40, 47, 79, 88, 93, 236, 252, 257, 296
hidden, 28, 30, 39, 40, 48, 57, 94, 98, 102, 167, 218, 223, 227, 228, 237, 239, 302, 315, 318
higher, 52, 126, 174, 263, 280, 282
highest, 28, 74, 84, 121, 163, 173, 175, 177, 182, 184, 189, 204, 222, 223, 255, 282
hilit, 258
hill, 141–143, 228, 243, 249, 256, 298
hills, 58, 87, 90, 141, 211, 267, 268, 272, 297, 313–316, 318
histories, 60, 110, 178, 315
history, 46, 50, 56, 60–62, 64, 65, 105, 139, 162, 178, 306
hit, 266, 323
hlihli, 270
hold, 23, 41, 78, 86, 93, 95, 99–101, 125, 198, 202, 230, 262, 279
holding, 86, 88, 97, 118, 124, 135, 139
holds, 82, 85, 92, 98, 99, 102–104, 151, 212, 309
hole, 203, 251, 274, 279, 284, 286, 318
holes, 199, 210, 241, 267

hollow, 79, 90, 95, 250, 255, 266, 283, 295
hollows, 141, 235, 316
holy, 10, 22, 31, 34, 38–41, 46, 76, 81, 84–86, 88, 90, 91, 93, 99, 102, 104, 145, 150, 177, 178, 186, 187, 190, 191, 220, 222, 223, 226, 227, 309, 319, 321, 322
homage, 15, 17, 23, 40, 316
home, 21, 40, 80, 81, 96, 98, 108, 111, 131, 174, 175, 215, 218, 220, 226–228, 241, 256–259, 261, 266, 271, 272, 274, 280, 281, 283, 284, 291, 313, 315, 317, 318
homes, 83, 85, 221, 229, 316, 317
honey, 155, 157, 167, 309, 310, 318
honor, 62, 74, 78, 81, 86, 88, 92, 101, 108, 109, 128, 141, 148, 317
honorable, 125, 144, 149, 158, 224
honored, 28, 83, 92–94
honors, 86, 92, 93, 101, 148
hope, 80, 132, 138, 202, 206, 230, 316, 319
horizon, 39, 41, 152, 219
horn, 211, 224, 227, 229, 285
horned, 12, 14, 15, 279, 283
horns, 21, 61, 78, 207, 223, 279, 285
horror, 12, 14, 15, 216
horse, 61, 89, 199, 206, 210
horses, 18, 61, 145, 146, 148, 166, 198, 199, 205, 206, 210, 223
horus, 40, 42
host, 82, 169, 227, 319, 322
hostile, 10, 26, 28, 29, 237

hosts, 12, 14, 16, 26, 98, 164, 225
hot, 97, 129, 146, 159–161, 183, 187, 229, 260, 282–284, 287
hoth, 228, 230, 231
hound, 90, 99, 230
hours, 39, 79, 219, 302, 313, 317
houses, 31, 39, 74, 81, 83, 141, 142, 146, 236, 256, 300
howls, 228, 229
hue, 176, 221, 227
huge, 90, 94, 97, 98, 100, 216, 226, 302, 303
human, 59–61, 79, 110, 122, 123, 133, 137, 138, 146, 149, 174, 176, 216, 220, 221, 234, 235, 239, 279, 285, 287, 289, 293, 294, 324
hun-apu, 300–305
hung, 17, 29, 96, 202, 225, 237, 262, 269, 286, 300, 315, 316, 325
hunger, 192, 196, 216, 296
hungry, 304, 316
hunt, 74, 256, 257, 281, 318
hunter, 55, 318
hunting, 74, 256, 318
hurakan, 299
hurled, 97, 100, 196, 206, 264, 266, 269, 300, 302
hurried, 15, 18, 123, 259, 267
hurry, 15, 27, 28, 264, 271
hurt, 82, 229, 277
husband, 18, 26, 47, 69, 184, 219, 243, 252, 256, 261, 280, 309
hut, 57, 296

I
iapetus, 79, 84, 87, 94–96, 98

iblīs, 213
ice, 155, 160, 215, 216, 219, 220, 320
igigi, 28
ignorance, 137, 165, 193, 240
ignorant, 137, 139, 176
ika-tere, 235, 236
ill, 27, 85, 196, 197, 203, 204, 228
ilus, 33, 75, 76
image, 40, 45, 49, 53, 114, 118, 119, 131, 140, 154, 155, 280, 319
images, 30, 126, 146, 299, 317, 321
imagine, 124, 128, 133, 135
imitate, 120, 127, 137, 138
imitating, 122, 125, 136
imitation, 123, 128, 137
immobile, 176, 177
immortal, 78, 79, 85, 88, 94, 103, 122, 123, 136, 163, 171, 192, 194
immortals, 33, 34, 81, 85, 86, 94, 100, 184
immovable, 43, 100, 113, 166, 213
immutable, 118, 158, 180
imparted, 110, 137, 179
imparts, 118, 157, 224
implanted, 122, 130, 139
impotent, 189, 190, 193
incapable, 126, 176, 177
incense, 59, 293
included, 115, 133, 141
including, 46, 52, 53, 145
increase, 53, 77, 93, 151, 156, 176, 187, 207, 234, 239, 240, 247, 250, 252, 277, 290
increased, 25, 52, 65, 93, 149, 233, 235, 239, 252, 283, 290, 291, 296
increases, 23, 93, 201

indeed, 84, 113, 133, 151, 152, 156, 161, 162, 168, 169, 172, 177, 184, 202, 211, 214, 223, 224, 304
inferior, 134, 135, 170
infinite, 114, 115, 120, 133, 136, 144, 158, 169, 176, 182, 191, 307
inflamed, 128, 130, 131
influence, 33, 127, 153
informed, 62, 109, 129, 135, 178
inhabit, 20, 34, 86, 234, 236, 238, 325
inhabited, 60, 62, 73, 140
inherent, 132, 136, 153, 157, 182
injured, 195, 204, 224
inland, 147, 236, 250
inner, 94, 117, 118, 145, 206
inquiry, 113, 124, 128, 140
inscribed, 148, 149
insect, 235, 241, 325
insects, 234, 236, 238
inside, 51, 171, 184, 195, 205, 221, 250, 262, 263, 270, 271
insignia, 28, 306
instead, 12, 14, 15, 26, 28, 49, 112
intellect, 34, 126, 164, 175, 178, 180, 181
intending, 114, 142, 180, 298
intention, 14, 15, 112, 115, 156
interior, 121, 145, 146, 155
internal, 126, 155, 203
interval, 62, 109, 117
intervals, 109, 117, 118, 146, 147, 151, 156, 157
invented, 73, 74, 76, 125, 127, 310
inventor, 65, 73, 77
invested, 179, 181
invisible, 44, 118, 126, 130, 131, 293, 315, 322

invoke, 37, 112, 138, 218
inward, 18, 29, 102, 126, 152
io, 246, 247
iris, 99
iron, 49, 74, 75, 81, 82, 99, 100, 211, 219, 225, 317, 318, 321
ishtar, 58, 59
isis, 36–40, 42
island, 76, 110, 111, 139, 143–149, 220, 225, 281–284, 297
islands, 54, 81, 104, 110, 141, 143, 146, 318
issue, 15, 18, 22, 35, 73, 75, 96, 207, 221
ivalde, 218, 222
ix, 309, 310

J

jagged, 88, 314
janardana, 174, 177
japheth, 50, 52, 54, 55
jar, 80, 199, 296
jared, 49, 50
jealous, 75, 78, 96, 252, 297, 314
jealousy, 114, 189, 190, 252
join, 47, 82, 99, 269
joined, 11, 14, 15, 67, 90, 117, 118, 164, 211, 260, 285, 298, 311
joktan, 55
journey, 137, 256, 297, 298
journeyed, 38, 62, 315
joy, 13, 92, 118, 175, 224, 225, 227, 229, 240, 315, 323, 324
joyfully, 27
judge, 32, 63, 69, 79, 148, 314
judged, 62, 223, 224
judgment, 79, 83, 92, 107, 113, 138, 148, 149, 160, 213, 221, 225

judgments, 78, 80, 83, 86
jump, 280, 287
just, 38, 74, 76, 82, 83, 89, 92, 109, 111, 114, 128, 130, 135, 137, 139, 153, 193–195, 200, 201, 208, 224, 256–260, 263, 264, 266, 268, 269, 272, 279–283, 304, 318
justice, 65, 83, 84, 101, 122

K

kála, 179, 180
ka, 40, 246, 274
kahit, 263–266, 271
kaisus, 256, 257
kan, 309
kane, 241, 250–252
kar, 275
karili, 259
katun, 306, 307, 309
kau, 41, 275, 276
keb, 41, 42
keen, 75, 223, 272
keep, 29, 51, 70, 80, 81, 83, 125, 142, 146, 193, 203–205, 250, 257, 258, 271, 274, 275, 283
keeper, 48, 104
keeping, 91, 144, 201, 206, 209, 218, 296
keeps, 37, 82–84, 90, 99, 206, 207, 226, 284
kenan, 49
kept, 93, 98, 125, 146, 189, 190, 204, 207, 210, 243, 257, 258, 260, 264, 265, 274, 278, 279, 295, 296, 319
kesava, 174
khepera, 35–37, 40
kicked, 287, 288, 321

kiemila, 255, 258, 263, 265, 270, 275
kii, 250–252
kill, 75, 206, 255, 257, 276, 277, 279, 281, 288, 298
killed, 48, 49, 75, 90, 103, 199, 256, 257, 277, 289, 302, 318, 324
kind, 11, 12, 14, 16, 36, 39, 41, 45, 51, 52, 57, 60, 79, 80, 89, 92, 96, 99–101, 103, 117, 121, 122, 128, 131, 133, 145, 147, 150, 154, 156, 189, 190, 202, 206, 209, 210, 223, 225, 238, 243, 261, 271, 272, 279, 287, 320
kinds, 26, 117, 122, 126, 129, 131, 133, 144, 152, 153, 164, 168, 173, 182, 189, 190, 201, 203, 204, 211–213, 238, 262, 265, 270, 275, 279, 280, 287–291
king, 9, 17, 24, 28, 32, 38, 40, 43, 63, 65, 67, 68, 76, 78, 93, 100–104, 108, 132, 136, 143, 144, 149, 166, 174, 177, 179, 187, 221, 313, 314, 317–319
kingdom, 33, 75, 77, 144, 146, 234, 316, 319, 320
kings, 60, 63, 67, 68, 70, 92, 105, 139, 144, 146–149, 178
kingu, 12, 14–16, 18, 21, 26, 27, 29, 30
kinsmen, 149, 218, 221
kiriu, 263, 275
kissed, 15, 27, 28, 195
klabus, 260, 261, 266–269, 272
klak, 276, 277

knees, 93, 193, 298, 305
knew, 33, 42, 47, 49, 53, 54, 93, 96,
    108, 127, 137, 140, 184,
    191–193, 218, 226, 230,
    233, 255, 264, 268, 278,
    283, 285, 302, 305, 313,
    324
knowing, 35, 36, 47, 48, 82, 138,
    139, 152, 170, 172, 174
knowledge, 27, 38, 40, 46, 59–61,
    110, 118, 126, 130, 135,
    137, 138, 150, 160,
    164–166, 175, 178, 185,
    192, 213, 221, 226, 293
known, 57, 62, 65, 121, 173, 175,
    179, 180, 186, 193, 198,
    213, 221, 222, 224, 227,
    240, 255, 258, 279, 315,
    322
knows, 23, 26, 47, 59, 84, 163–165,
    167, 171, 176, 184, 272,
    323
kolea, 246, 247
krishna, 174, 177
kshatriya, 175
kuntihle, 264, 265, 268, 269

L

labor, 82, 121, 196, 217, 314
labors, 104, 147, 217
lachamu, 25, 26, 28
lachmu, 25, 28
lacking, 123
lady, 25, 40, 58
laid, 10, 13, 21, 26, 28, 30, 31, 35,
    37, 54, 75, 76, 79, 141,
    173, 216, 217, 224, 225,
    230, 236, 249, 281, 286,
    293, 320
lakes, 60, 144, 147, 206, 297
lakhamu, 12, 14, 15, 22

lame, 79, 124
lamech, 49, 50
lands, 31, 38–42, 54, 55, 80, 200,
    227, 230, 236, 252, 316
language, 44, 54–56, 60, 61, 64,
    114, 128, 142, 143, 298,
    309
lapse, 107, 108, 132, 139
large, 64, 143, 177, 184, 207, 239,
    243, 245, 258, 259, 262,
    263, 266, 267, 269, 281,
    283, 285, 286, 288–290,
    295, 298, 302–304, 306
larger, 110, 120, 143, 146, 217, 279
largest, 141, 143–146, 189, 190,
    210, 263
last, 62, 63, 81, 85, 94, 115, 134,
    136–138, 141, 156, 179,
    193, 194, 205, 222, 223,
    231, 233, 234, 237–239,
    250–252, 256–258, 263,
    268, 274, 278–280, 282,
    284, 285, 289, 305, 318
lasted, 149, 221, 255
later, 123, 124, 152, 163, 298
latter, 140, 162, 170, 180
laurel, 85, 283, 309
law, 21, 84, 110, 112, 119, 148, 149,
    178, 187, 191, 309,
    319–321
laws, 60, 85, 89, 110, 122, 123, 140,
    148, 149, 227, 230
lay, 60, 80, 82, 87–89, 95, 102, 103,
    135, 202, 216, 260, 263,
    265, 285, 303, 313, 315
layer, 215, 285
lead, 155, 211, 297, 302, 305, 314
leader, 12, 14, 16, 18, 26, 111, 139,
    147
leads, 17, 84, 91, 214

leagues, 206, 210, 223, 296–298, 315
leapt, 29, 30, 58, 216, 217
learn, 83, 179, 183, 282
learned, 44, 93, 119, 156, 180, 318
learning, 120, 127, 135
least, 96, 133, 153, 302, 304
leave, 47, 57, 130, 132, 145, 213, 256, 298, 314, 323, 324
leaves, 47, 109, 177, 222, 237, 238, 246, 251, 253, 271
leaving, 109, 115, 117, 145, 146, 152, 237, 258, 260, 273, 297, 304
led, 59, 64, 92, 146, 148, 158, 195, 198
left, 15, 30, 38, 52, 66, 67, 81, 82, 84, 88, 90, 93, 111, 118, 123, 124, 126, 133, 136, 140–142, 148, 151, 161, 169, 172, 197, 203, 204, 216, 227, 235, 237, 238, 250, 257–259, 265, 266, 279, 281, 282, 286, 301, 303, 315, 318
leg, 281, 286, 287
legend, 107, 132, 134, 294
legs, 37, 61, 80, 116, 125, 226, 258, 286
leisure, 110, 119, 135, 140
length, 29, 57, 58, 62, 83, 125, 142, 145–147, 156, 176, 215, 217, 223, 234, 237
less, 81, 92, 93, 113, 136, 138, 156, 157, 162, 196, 197, 203, 211
lesser, 33, 45, 108, 109, 120, 127, 146, 153
lest, 47, 48, 55, 68, 296
letters, 60, 74, 77, 109, 128, 166

level, 141, 147, 226, 267, 272, 293, 309
liable, 109, 116, 122
libation, 59, 99, 148, 172
libations, 75, 171, 172
libya, 110, 111, 139
lie, 25, 26, 85, 234, 277, 325
lies, 79, 84, 89, 99, 225, 230, 233, 260, 314, 324
lift, 17, 195, 241, 302, 305
lifted, 13, 20, 26, 39, 41, 48, 52, 68, 226, 241, 302, 317
lighted, 120, 236, 280, 307
lightning, 17, 29, 86, 90, 97, 98, 100, 105, 220, 283
lights, 45, 126, 190, 197, 198, 202, 307
likeness, 45, 49, 79, 95, 113–115, 120, 121, 138, 199, 226, 239, 295, 319
limbs, 29, 39, 61, 79, 81, 87, 97, 101, 125, 148, 229, 234, 317
limit, 140, 151, 179
limits, 20, 30, 116, 202
line, 98, 125, 140, 147, 153, 159, 163, 246, 260, 298, 315
lion, 59, 90, 100, 174, 194, 287, 288
lips, 19, 38, 58, 64, 85, 86, 218, 304, 315
list, 227, 228
listen, 12, 13, 49, 59, 79, 84, 107, 122, 132, 320
listened, 11, 69, 111, 278
listens, 221, 223, 235
live, 23, 39, 40, 48, 62, 67, 81, 85, 86, 91, 92, 95, 96, 98–100, 109, 123, 134, 144, 167, 189, 191, 230, 234, 248, 250, 268–270, 274–276,

279, 281, 286, 289, 295, 303, 317, 318, 323, 325
lives, 28, 39, 53, 60, 84, 96, 99, 103, 184, 221, 223, 224, 227, 263, 264, 270, 272, 286, 315, 325
livestock, 45–47, 51–53, 66, 67
living, 31, 38, 45, 46, 51–54, 57, 81, 95, 102, 114, 116, 118, 119, 122, 132, 133, 137, 151, 152, 155, 165, 167–170, 174, 181–183, 195, 205, 209, 240, 255, 277, 316, 323, 324
loathsome, 98, 99, 235, 314
lofty, 12, 14, 15, 26, 64, 109, 147, 208, 220, 228, 235
log, 220, 266, 295
loimis, 263–266, 270, 271, 276, 277
loki, 228, 229, 231
lonely, 183, 184, 316
longer, 57, 125, 126, 136, 237, 277
longing, 79, 210, 317
look, 39, 54, 58, 69, 86, 134, 171, 235, 258, 260, 263–266, 268, 272, 276, 280, 281, 284, 285, 287, 289–291, 304, 318, 323
looked, 12–15, 18, 20, 58, 97, 113, 147, 198, 256, 258, 261, 263, 265, 266, 268–270, 272, 273, 279, 280, 285, 287–289, 303, 304, 321
looking, 18, 62, 143, 169, 170, 240, 256, 258, 264–266, 268, 272, 276, 279, 280, 283, 285, 288, 295
looks, 99, 113, 151, 221, 263, 284
loon, 275, 279
loose, 18, 58, 131, 225, 229, 231, 314, 316
lords, 42, 79, 252
lore, 313, 314, 316
losing, 122, 141, 149
lost, 18, 132, 138, 149, 184, 223, 224, 271, 294, 301, 305, 314, 315
lot, 56, 66, 67, 94, 96, 134, 143, 147
lots, 147
lotus, 173, 174, 177
loud, 18, 80, 97, 228, 229, 258, 266, 297
love, 39, 41, 78, 79, 86–88, 90–92, 100–104, 122, 135, 139, 143, 185, 239, 280
loved, 80, 81, 104, 223, 224, 316
lovely, 34, 79, 84–89, 91, 95, 101, 102
lover, 110, 126, 228
loves, 29, 78, 219, 321
low, 78, 196, 220, 226, 282
lower, 29, 99, 126, 135, 136, 170, 222, 226, 267, 275, 296
luminous, 165, 188, 215
lutchi, 264, 265, 267, 276
lying, 38, 83, 89, 134, 189, 190, 235, 250, 273, 280, 314, 323, 325

M

madhu, 173, 174
magic, 39, 65, 75, 218, 224, 227, 228, 230, 293, 315, 316
magnified, 15
magnify, 23
mahalalel, 49
maiden, 88, 94, 95, 101, 143, 219
maidens, 88, 227, 228, 231
maids, 217, 221, 223, 225
maintain, 128, 170

maintains, 131, 170, 205
majesty, 38, 40, 41, 322
maker, 39, 113, 187, 190, 191, 281, 298, 319, 322
makes, 10, 14, 23, 40, 41, 78, 83, 93, 103, 104, 115, 126, 138, 168, 172, 316, 320–322
making, 11, 14, 15, 17, 21, 26, 39, 41, 116, 123, 129, 130, 139, 143–145, 151, 153, 154, 212, 266, 268, 269, 279, 289, 306, 325
male, 33, 45, 49, 51, 52, 61, 78, 97, 140, 143, 150, 173, 184, 210, 211, 241, 250
malicious, 176, 192, 195, 258
mani, 218
manifest, 113, 196, 199, 206, 212, 234
manifold, 33, 37, 40, 41, 165, 178
mankind, 21, 23, 25, 31, 32, 58–60, 62, 82, 84, 107–111, 120, 127, 181, 192, 193, 196, 201, 202, 205, 237, 278, 294
manner, 44, 60, 76, 77, 111, 112, 116, 117, 120–124, 126–129, 131, 135–137, 140, 142, 144, 146, 148, 151, 155, 156, 158, 168, 169, 180, 192, 197, 199, 205, 208, 211, 216, 234, 237, 262, 296, 309, 324, 325
mannikins, 299, 300
marduk, 13, 15, 17–22, 27–30, 32, 58
mark, 45, 76, 83, 84, 134, 177, 317, 322

married, 56, 76, 105, 249, 252, 296
marrow, 155, 209
marsh, 9, 25, 31, 316, 317
marshes, 31, 58, 144
marten, 210, 211
maruts, 169
marvelous, 85, 100, 107
mass, 36, 181, 216, 270, 305, 306, 313, 314
master, 12, 14, 173, 174, 178, 212
mat, 262, 307, 309
mate, 102, 228
material, 44, 60, 117, 187, 189–191, 201, 212
matter, 34, 36, 38, 86, 113, 119, 128, 130, 135, 136, 150, 151, 153, 159, 179, 180, 192, 210
matters, 108, 127, 137, 138, 149
maya, 176, 305, 306
mead, 218, 222, 223, 228, 230
meal, 21, 82, 270, 299
mean, 108, 115, 117, 127, 132, 162, 176, 272, 305, 322
meaning, 129, 134, 137, 138, 142, 278, 295, 297, 311
meanness, 142, 189, 190
means, 36, 37, 42, 115, 117, 125, 135, 152, 168, 169, 175, 192, 194, 196, 199, 201, 202, 204, 213, 237, 295, 320, 322
meanwhile, 40, 138, 144, 279
measure, 30, 81, 90, 120, 132, 199, 203, 208
measured, 30, 120, 153, 176
medicine, 110, 283
meet, 28, 41, 73, 101, 121, 126, 188, 192, 206, 224, 230, 279, 280, 303

meeting, 98, 126, 146, 147, 159, 189, 191, 199, 200
melted, 100, 101, 128
mem, 263–266, 269, 271, 275, 276, 278
member, 209
members, 36–39, 42, 88, 124, 125, 209, 211
memory, 135, 166, 177, 217, 222, 224
mentioned, 40, 65, 138, 140, 198, 295
merciful, 27, 59
merciless, 12, 14, 15, 97
mercy, 23, 224
merry, 27, 28, 30, 80, 302
meru, 165, 175, 181
message, 28, 99, 264, 325, 326
messenger, 57, 80, 256, 315, 317
met, 33, 97, 123, 226, 230, 260, 267, 280, 300, 303
method, 73, 74, 128
metis, 44, 78, 91, 102
middle, 24, 44, 46, 47, 76, 77, 90, 94, 142, 148, 151, 153, 154, 165, 166, 189, 190, 194–197, 200, 203, 208, 211, 220, 221, 235, 256, 260, 261, 263, 269, 271, 273, 278, 285, 311
midgard, 220–223, 225, 226
midst, 58, 83, 87, 98, 215, 220, 225, 235, 310
mild, 92, 135, 219
military, 110, 111, 140, 147, 148
milk, 168, 169, 211, 216, 264
mill, 217
millions, 38, 40
mimer, 216, 217, 219, 221, 222, 224, 226

min, 269–271
mind, 64, 77–79, 85, 87, 94, 96, 101, 108, 111, 113, 116, 119, 120, 126, 127, 130, 131, 134, 150–152, 165, 175, 180–182, 184, 217, 220, 230, 314, 315
minds, 139, 165, 227, 303
mingled, 9, 34, 82, 117, 122, 196, 199, 204
minister, 31, 125, 155
mirror, 126, 314
mirth, 313, 314, 317
mischief, 78–80, 83, 94, 95, 101, 198, 302
misery, 80, 164, 299
mist, 46, 80, 83, 84, 128, 216, 220, 239, 286
mistress, 38, 40, 69, 70, 117
mists, 216, 239, 317
misty, 89, 97–99, 101, 215, 316
mix, 61, 79
mixed, 34, 61, 77, 127, 155, 160, 196, 199, 206, 209, 222, 224
mixture, 33, 117, 122, 152
mobile, 176, 177
mode, 126, 129, 136, 138, 156, 234
moisture, 61, 153, 160, 161, 216
mold, 21, 150, 217, 220, 221, 226
molded, 79, 213, 280, 295
moment, 18, 29, 36, 111, 138, 256, 257, 260, 303, 304, 319, 321
money, 318
monster, 90, 100, 247
monsters, 11, 12, 14, 16, 26, 30, 223, 224
monstrous, 12, 14, 15, 61, 216
month, 30, 35, 51–53, 62, 63, 120,

152, 195, 198, 203, 206, 250, 252, 295
months, 20, 30, 85, 119, 127, 166, 252, 316
moon, 30, 33, 36, 44, 61, 65, 78, 91, 118–120, 123, 152, 155, 157, 159, 162, 164, 174, 190, 193, 196, 197, 202, 203, 207–209, 218–220, 226, 240, 287, 295, 297, 307, 310, 316, 317, 322–325
morning, 40, 44, 45, 119, 171, 172, 178, 222, 226, 256, 257, 260, 263, 265–268, 271–273, 275, 300, 304, 305, 316
mortal, 73, 78, 80–83, 89–91, 94–96, 101–103, 114, 122–124, 127, 134, 138, 139, 143, 149, 152, 155, 158, 184, 187, 220
mortals, 34, 80, 94, 100, 164, 189, 190, 221, 222
moses, 44, 57, 320, 322
mostly, 125, 135, 252
mother, 9, 15, 25–27, 39, 41, 47, 75, 87, 90, 101, 102, 129, 130, 143, 150, 167, 169, 174, 177, 179, 219, 220, 231, 234–239, 261, 264, 268, 280, 299, 309, 321, 323, 324
motion, 18, 117–121, 123, 125, 131–133, 135, 136, 152, 153, 158, 159, 162, 181, 196, 197, 200, 202, 212, 218, 227, 245, 247, 309
motions, 65, 116, 119, 121, 123–127, 133

mount, 67, 75, 84, 93, 100, 197, 200, 303, 319
mountain, 26, 57–59, 62, 66, 101, 143, 181, 200, 208, 210–212, 218, 222, 223, 257, 258, 263, 268, 269, 282, 285, 289, 290, 294, 296, 297, 303–305
mounted, 205, 300, 304
mourning, 25, 309, 315
mouth, 10–12, 15–20, 23, 25, 27–29, 32, 35–40, 42, 53, 57, 59, 86, 146, 173–175, 177, 184, 211, 235, 265, 266, 280, 286, 300, 301, 309, 322, 323, 326
mouths, 13, 29, 39, 40, 59, 304, 313
move, 84, 116, 118, 125, 126, 133, 138, 175, 215, 216, 229, 237, 245, 250, 264, 280, 295, 304
moved, 33, 76, 88, 120, 123, 124, 126, 131, 154, 159, 162, 175, 176, 217, 227, 250, 251, 265, 270, 298, 307, 311, 317
movement, 25, 116, 121, 124, 133, 136, 151, 152, 154, 155, 206
movements, 121, 155
moves, 45, 53, 133, 241
moving, 53, 109, 114, 116, 118–120, 131, 133, 166, 176, 202, 240, 241, 303
mud, 33, 62, 63, 111, 139, 213, 246, 248, 270, 271, 280–282, 304, 305
multiply, 45, 47, 53, 70, 182, 239, 283, 297
multitude, 36–38, 65, 70, 147, 234,

mummu, 10, 12, 25–27
muni, 166, 176, 178
murderers, 224, 225, 228
murky, 88, 97
muses, 85, 86, 102, 103, 127, 138
musk, 210, 211
mutation, 156, 158, 159, 161
mutations, 156, 158–160, 162
mutual, 148, 160, 181, 197, 200–202, 206, 239

N

nagaitcho, 285–287
nahor, 56
naked, 47, 135, 250, 251, 266
nakedness, 54, 251
named, 25, 49, 50, 60, 61, 64, 74–76, 143, 179, 215–217, 220, 222, 223, 226, 227, 240, 293, 295, 296
namely, 125, 154, 162, 238
names, 22, 24, 31, 38–40, 44, 46, 63, 73, 74, 91, 124, 139, 140, 142, 150, 183, 184, 194, 217, 226, 235, 238, 239, 265, 297, 303, 320
narayana, 174, 176
narrative, 111, 112, 140, 142
narrow, 110, 225, 245, 250, 262, 273
nat, 219, 226
nations, 54, 55, 60, 70, 109, 139, 297
native, 123, 145, 162, 318
natives, 295, 296, 298
natural, 112, 116, 124, 125, 127, 129, 141, 145, 181
naturally, 133, 136, 139, 157–159
natures, 118, 122, 127, 129, 159, 162

near, 17, 18, 26, 58, 59, 83, 84, 88, 90, 98, 99, 142, 143, 146, 167, 222, 225, 256–258, 260, 265, 266, 270–273, 276, 281, 282, 284–286, 288, 296, 298, 303
nearer, 146, 184, 272, 294
nearest, 119, 134, 152, 154, 167
nearly, 107, 111, 120, 147, 281, 283, 284, 289
necessary, 62, 116, 119, 122, 140, 157, 159–161, 192, 194, 293, 301, 305
necessity, 96, 113, 115, 122, 126, 127, 131, 132, 134, 136, 137, 150, 151, 159, 167
neck, 59, 82, 217, 219, 271, 272, 276, 285
nectar, 96, 99
need, 113, 114, 116, 138, 154, 221, 228, 268
needed, 142, 144, 275
neighbor, 78
nereus, 76, 89
net, 17, 18, 20, 29, 30, 267, 268, 287
never, 15, 16, 23, 28, 38, 41, 42, 53, 54, 59, 80, 82, 83, 88, 98, 99, 108, 113, 114, 116, 118, 126, 128, 129, 131, 137, 138, 141, 144, 147, 151, 157, 162, 174, 185, 216, 222, 223, 229, 233, 251, 256, 259, 262, 263, 284, 296, 321
new, 128, 135, 174, 176, 225, 265, 266, 274, 277, 280, 296, 302, 307, 309, 314, 320
nidhog, 222, 225
nifel-hel, 224–226

nights, 51, 58, 85, 98, 119, 164, 196, 199, 206, 207, 239, 252, 267, 268, 283, 295
ninip, 57–59
noah, 50–55, 65, 319, 320
noble, 41, 65, 79, 81, 90, 95, 109, 141, 216, 217, 223, 249, 309, 314
noblest, 107, 109
noise, 33, 83, 100, 199, 208, 243, 251, 258, 264–266
noises, 241–248
northern, 41, 207, 220, 261
northward, 215, 216, 228, 259, 260, 273
nose, 181, 209, 286, 325
nostrils, 41, 46, 52, 304
nourish, 93, 185, 187, 197
nowhere, 226, 317
nu, 35, 37, 41
number, 32, 63, 115, 117, 119, 120, 122, 127, 132, 135, 141, 142, 144, 146–148, 208, 226, 266, 299, 302
numbers, 109, 115, 119, 146, 152, 157, 200, 251, 289–291, 296
numerous, 126, 144, 154, 175, 211, 235, 237, 250, 289, 291
nurse, 83, 93, 121, 128, 131, 150
nurture, 82, 124, 136, 140
nut, 36, 41
nuumea, 252

O

oak, 66, 83, 85, 261, 262, 264, 270
oaks, 261, 262, 289, 290
oannes, 60, 63
oath, 40, 82, 83, 89, 92, 99, 148
obedient, 27, 41, 123, 149

obey, 148, 236, 297
obeyed, 62, 93, 297, 314
object, 125, 126, 154, 160, 181, 182, 185, 279, 297
objects, 167, 176, 179
oblation, 168, 169
oblations, 167, 169
obscure, 78, 84, 140
observe, 110, 138, 295, 300, 322
obtain, 57, 69, 172, 174, 175, 238
obtained, 62, 139, 143, 175, 176, 196, 204, 237
oc, 311
occupy, 36, 64, 131
occur, 133, 161, 178, 202, 306
occurred, 111, 132, 134, 141, 306, 310, 311
ocean, 21, 34, 81, 88–92, 94, 99, 102, 103, 110, 139, 143, 166, 175, 181, 199, 200, 206–209, 217, 220, 225, 226, 235–237, 282, 287–289, 317, 318
oceans, 178, 181, 287
oceanus, 85, 87, 99, 121
odúm'la, 315
odúwa, 314, 316
odin, 217, 218, 221, 223, 225
odor, 262, 304
odudúwa, 315–317
offer, 169, 192, 298
offered, 53, 62, 75, 77, 137, 148, 169, 172, 236, 282–284, 287, 298
offering, 48, 59, 145, 169, 170, 293
offerings, 30, 41, 146, 169, 175, 224, 316
offers, 92, 169–172
office, 92, 93, 155
often, 75, 83, 111, 132, 134, 149,

274, 278
ojúmu, 316, 317
olókun, 315–317
olóssa, 316, 317
older, 117, 119, 134, 150, 274, 306
olelpanti, 255, 256, 261, 263,
    265–268, 270, 271, 273,
    275, 276, 278
olympian, 80, 83, 85, 92, 94, 101
olympus, 80, 81, 83, 85–87, 92, 96,
    97, 99, 100, 102, 103
ones, 23, 26, 41, 81, 85, 86, 97, 102,
    103, 108–110, 166, 173,
    174, 176, 201, 224, 226,
    227, 230, 250, 269, 275,
    278, 302, 306, 315
open, 26–28, 37, 45, 135, 144, 146,
    188, 200, 202, 217, 220,
    264, 273, 287, 309
opened, 10, 15, 18–20, 25, 29, 30,
    32, 38, 39, 41, 47, 52,
    57–59, 207, 313, 320
opening, 12, 15, 62, 145, 251, 268,
    273, 286, 295
opinion, 108, 113, 126, 128, 130,
    131, 138, 150, 156, 192,
    194, 319
oppose, 12, 15, 27, 160
opposite, 30, 110, 117–119, 123,
    124, 129, 130, 132–136,
    141, 150, 202, 262
orísha, 314–317
oranyan, 317, 318
orbit, 119, 120
orbits, 118–120
ordained, 9, 62, 84, 136, 176, 194,
    320
order, 12, 25, 37, 43, 61, 78, 81,
    101, 109, 110, 112,
    114–116, 119, 121, 122,
    125, 126, 132, 134,
    136–139, 148, 151, 152,
    157, 159, 162, 164, 169,
    199, 204, 206, 217, 218,
    220, 221, 236, 294, 297,
    306, 307, 311
ordered, 33, 150, 151, 252, 279,
    295, 297, 299, 304
orders, 157, 178, 230, 297
organs, 61, 116, 125, 130, 152, 155,
    181
origin, 74, 114, 117, 121, 125, 130,
    132, 142, 152, 163–165,
    173, 181, 200, 204, 280
original, 113, 114, 117, 118, 120,
    142, 191, 194, 197, 202
orthus, 90
osiris, 36, 37, 40, 42
othin, 227–231
ought, 108, 113, 114, 120, 122, 126,
    129, 130, 137, 142, 156,
    272
ouranus, 75–77
outer, 117, 145, 146, 205, 225, 283,
    314, 317
outside, 40, 54, 69, 115, 116, 139,
    141, 145, 146, 155, 157,
    172, 205, 258, 259,
    261–263, 265, 269–272,
    274, 284
overcame, 90, 123
overcome, 12, 14, 15, 26–28, 75, 80,
    86, 90, 93, 123, 131, 194,
    223, 238
overtaken, 119, 120, 325
overthrow, 29, 37, 41, 149, 303, 304
owing, 146, 195–197, 199, 201, 202,
    295, 298
owl, 283, 290
ox, 79, 94, 195–197, 203, 204, 209,

210, 212
oxen, 74, 90, 103, 189, 190, 210

P

pûshan, 168
paid, 15, 17, 23, 62, 164, 178, 249
pain, 38, 47, 82, 123, 167, 176, 196, 281, 295, 299–301
painful, 64, 88, 155, 222
pair, 143, 148, 169, 210, 233
pairs, 51, 143, 184
palace, 144–147
palaces, 144–146, 293
pallas, 79, 91, 95, 102
palm, 60, 258, 309
papa, 233–236, 239, 243, 252
parent, 109, 178, 235, 246, 250, 253
parents, 75, 82, 83, 92, 93, 107, 234, 235, 237
partake, 61, 116, 133, 216
partakes, 118, 130, 150
parted, 33, 46, 75, 145, 280
particles, 131, 154, 155
parts, 18, 29, 60, 64, 76, 77, 90, 94, 100, 102, 111, 114, 115, 117–119, 134–136, 141, 144–146, 153, 157, 158, 162, 193, 200, 208, 240, 286, 295, 300, 304
party, 236, 237, 257, 296, 301
pass, 15, 17, 40, 52, 60, 84, 98, 110, 123, 125, 145, 168, 172, 178, 200, 218, 224–226, 273, 293, 302
passage, 145, 198, 200, 203, 205, 208
passages, 107, 147, 180
passed, 35, 48, 60, 66, 81, 85, 107, 134, 136, 145, 148, 167–169, 183, 187, 188,
196, 197, 200, 204, 208, 209, 211, 258, 278, 294, 296, 297, 299, 304, 313, 315, 316
passes, 86, 120, 128, 154, 171, 213
passing, 39, 63, 89, 98, 146, 305, 316
past, 25, 58, 59, 100, 113, 119, 135, 140, 167, 173, 216, 221, 223, 230, 250, 273, 313
path, 17, 24, 27, 28, 83, 84, 91, 108, 164, 208, 225, 226, 245, 249, 250
pattern, 113, 119, 120, 128, 150, 151, 153
pay, 23, 62, 78, 83, 257
peace, 10, 19, 26, 28, 65, 80, 83, 101, 135, 175, 192, 206, 226, 300, 316
peaks, 85, 87, 99, 104, 285
peculiar, 153, 154, 158, 160, 181, 238
pegasus, 90
perceive, 95, 100, 130, 151, 156, 323
perceived, 18, 131, 150, 151, 167, 193, 201, 307
perched, 222, 281
perfect, 41, 42, 79, 89, 103, 112–116, 120, 122, 124, 133, 137, 151, 152, 155, 157, 194, 206, 213, 296
performed, 92, 109, 164, 175, 178, 194, 320, 321
perhaps, 57, 119, 142, 163, 258, 266
period, 60, 120, 134, 176, 177, 179, 181, 182, 192, 194, 196, 201, 202, 240, 309
periods, 35, 37, 38, 120, 153, 157,

178, 182, 201
perish, 83, 185, 186, 189, 191, 194, 325
perished, 58, 135, 159, 294, 303, 305, 320
permanent, 41, 113, 129, 157, 160
perpetual, 123, 157, 162, 215
perses, 78, 91, 92
person, 40, 61, 124, 127, 129, 138, 167, 202, 236, 251, 255, 263, 264, 266, 267, 269, 272, 276, 278, 279, 286, 315, 323
persons, 142, 146, 176, 256, 260, 276
petals, 173, 174, 309
pharaoh, 66
phoenicia, 65, 73–75
phoreys, 89, 91
piece, 271, 286, 294, 297, 309, 324, 325
pieces, 73, 124, 136, 225, 237, 277, 287, 295, 318, 321, 323
pierced, 82, 195, 196, 204, 294, 306
piety, 62, 65, 178
pig, 249
pillar, 148, 261, 269, 306
pillars, 74, 99, 110, 111, 139, 143–145
pilot, 62, 123, 135, 136
piltec, 307
pines, 288, 289
placed, 30, 37, 39, 48, 57, 84, 115, 117, 119, 122, 145, 146, 150, 162, 218, 221, 224, 263, 276, 277, 285, 288–290, 303, 306, 315, 318, 320
places, 21, 28, 30, 33, 43, 91, 93, 109, 118, 119, 125, 132, 134, 139, 141, 146, 151, 155, 189, 190, 194, 208, 210, 212, 248, 250, 265, 275–277, 285, 294, 297, 315
placing, 117, 145, 288, 289, 304
plague, 77, 79, 80, 83, 90, 94
plain, 25, 55, 143, 147, 210, 223, 298, 314
plains, 58, 141, 143, 144, 222–224, 297, 315, 316
plan, 10, 13, 18, 30, 87, 92, 93, 116, 129, 146, 319
planets, 61, 119, 152, 155, 157, 162, 178, 181, 196, 197, 203, 204
planned, 10, 11, 20, 79, 84, 155, 237
plans, 24, 26, 90, 234, 235
plant, 46, 78, 209, 211, 253, 261, 262, 265, 273, 319
planted, 46, 135, 146, 234, 262, 289
plants, 23, 37, 137, 157, 158, 162, 171, 193, 195, 201, 202, 208, 209, 212, 236, 238, 262, 270, 282, 283, 290, 293, 294
plate, 307, 309
pleasant, 46, 144, 185, 259, 323
please, 67, 69, 82, 107, 140, 145
pleasure, 122, 127, 139, 144, 167, 247, 319, 320
plenty, 57, 79, 83, 146, 189, 267, 285
plots, 15
plucked, 53, 264, 276, 278
plus, 294
poems, 107
poets, 107, 108, 218
poharamas, 259–261

pohila, 259–261, 268
point, 117, 128, 134, 138, 148, 196, 203, 223, 255, 259, 269, 296
pointed, 65, 269, 294, 300, 304
points, 129, 174, 175, 281
poison, 26, 38, 40, 199, 201, 206, 211, 305
polalouli, 249
pole, 121, 218, 264, 269
pom, 261, 263, 264
pond, 268, 269
pontus, 76, 77, 87
portion, 68, 88, 92, 117, 139, 148, 149, 153, 155, 164, 208, 239, 322
portions, 86, 94, 95, 114, 117, 123, 143, 145, 152, 153, 155, 182, 208
poseidon, 76, 77, 84, 98, 143, 145, 146, 148
position, 17, 124, 126, 153
possess, 39, 57, 126, 157, 208, 249, 323
possessed, 18, 29, 57, 136, 144, 149, 164, 173, 175, 202, 207, 209, 216, 293
possible, 38, 115, 119, 120, 124, 126, 130, 132, 133, 156, 160, 192, 201
potsherds, 168, 169
potter, 78, 190
poured, 13, 35, 58, 59, 74, 122, 206, 305, 317, 320
pouring, 109, 148, 198, 199, 215
pours, 99, 227, 228
powerful, 10, 25, 26, 28, 29, 33, 115, 152, 166, 216, 278, 288
powers, 30, 39, 44, 75, 118, 131, 139, 151, 155, 157, 159–161, 164
practice, 140, 175, 192, 212
pradhána, 179, 180
pragâpati, 167–170, 172
praise, 22, 41, 78, 82, 107, 184, 192, 206, 212, 263, 319
praised, 20, 40, 219
praises, 40, 41, 76, 138, 221, 319
praising, 84, 168, 173
pray, 92, 112, 137, 283, 321
prayer, 62, 137, 148, 169, 196, 294, 321
prayers, 92, 148, 234, 236, 238, 239, 294
preacher, 187
precept, 295
precious, 144, 149, 218, 222, 223, 305
precipice, 249, 314, 315
precisely, 114, 130, 136
prepare, 15, 279
prepared, 27–29, 62, 130, 194, 205, 212
present, 114, 119, 124, 128–130, 134–136, 149, 152, 159, 161, 173, 175, 180, 184, 194, 221, 223, 255, 279
preserve, 57, 119, 142
preserved, 57, 60, 61, 108, 109, 111, 132, 139, 140, 157, 158, 169, 182, 296, 319
preserver, 178, 182
preserves, 109, 157, 181, 182
pressed, 101, 154, 188, 240, 316
prevail, 13, 15, 96, 127, 237
prevailed, 136, 217, 314
prevent, 25, 29, 30, 109
previous, 109, 127, 130, 134, 136, 298

prey, 225, 283, 314
pride, 94, 175, 176, 295, 300, 304, 314, 319, 320
priest, 109, 112, 212, 309, 315, 316
priests, 77, 108–110, 139, 140, 166, 169, 313, 315
prime, 81, 126, 134
primeval, 36, 78, 99, 143, 196, 197, 204, 209, 222, 293
primitive, 141, 233
prince, 21, 28, 38, 41, 78
princes, 83, 86, 143, 145
principle, 34, 43, 61, 122, 123, 125, 128–130, 150, 154, 155, 160, 162, 179–181, 209
prior, 43, 117, 127, 140, 159, 179
private, 146
probable, 114, 121, 128, 140, 156
proceed, 112, 114, 118, 126, 139, 181, 301
proceeded, 22, 38, 117, 120, 136, 178, 179, 181, 302, 318
proceeds, 156, 181, 193, 209
process, 76, 113, 129
proclaim, 15, 23, 27
produce, 32, 45, 110, 126, 140, 154, 197, 211, 212, 238, 300
produced, 33, 34, 36–38, 44, 60, 61, 64, 123, 136, 150, 151, 153, 154, 160, 164, 168, 170, 179, 181, 183, 184, 192, 193, 199, 201, 202, 208–213, 217, 240, 243
produces, 128, 154, 161, 170
producing, 73, 151, 153, 158, 198, 212, 302
profound, 126, 175, 178
progeny, 166, 168, 182, 235, 237, 239, 240, 300
progress, 120, 136, 139, 193

proper, 31, 33, 75, 135, 139, 159, 162, 197, 201, 238, 276
properly, 119, 126, 139, 286
property, 140, 149, 162, 181, 202
prophets, 77, 319, 322
propped, 99, 241, 264, 267
proud, 78, 89, 93, 96, 100, 249, 303
proves, 84, 140, 141
providing, 116, 141, 213
provision, 144, 296
pui, 259, 260, 263, 264, 269–271, 275, 276
pulled, 238, 261, 276, 278, 279, 286
punish, 59, 87, 88, 148, 218, 277
pure, 23, 26, 27, 31, 80, 122, 125, 179, 181, 198, 201, 207, 211, 321
purified, 148, 209, 214
purity, 207, 212, 321
purpose, 25–28, 57, 97, 111, 112, 126, 127, 136, 142, 157, 159, 205, 221, 305, 313
purposes, 116, 133, 142, 175
pursued, 213, 219
pursuits, 110, 140
purusha, 167, 179, 180
pushed, 259, 279, 280, 286
puts, 39, 171, 172, 222
putting, 155, 170, 269, 288, 296
puyuk, 260, 269, 275

Q

qualities, 41, 149, 151, 159, 164, 166, 167, 178–182, 210, 212
quality, 159–161, 181, 209, 212
quarrel, 86, 99, 132, 134
quarters, 61, 168, 194, 235, 284
queen, 102, 217, 315, 316
queenly, 79, 84, 91

quench, 12, 15
question, 113, 130, 284
questions, 128, 179, 303
quick, 89, 100, 138, 256, 258, 304
quickly, 80, 82, 93, 134, 260, 264, 267, 268, 273, 279, 280, 287, 290, 301, 302, 318

R

ra, 35–41
race, 34, 58, 65, 74, 80–83, 85, 86, 95, 105, 109, 110, 120, 122, 133–135, 146, 149, 162, 168, 170, 173, 177, 196, 203, 213, 217, 219–222, 226, 228, 233, 236, 251, 294, 295, 300, 303, 314, 318
races, 210, 219, 236
raft, 284, 285
rage, 18, 77, 219, 227, 238
raged, 15, 58, 100
raging, 14, 15, 18, 26, 86, 87, 89, 90, 101, 199
rain, 46, 51, 52, 57, 58, 63, 74, 131, 141, 198, 199, 206–209, 213, 230, 239, 267, 274, 275, 284–287, 290, 299
rained, 209, 285, 287, 295, 300
rains, 147, 183, 287, 290
raise, 28, 64, 79, 128, 169, 226
raised, 12, 14, 17, 18, 25, 26, 28, 30, 35, 37, 98, 100, 128, 138, 140, 145, 164, 175, 203, 213, 218, 220, 240, 249, 260, 264, 265, 268, 280, 282, 293, 298, 300, 304, 307
ram, 69, 184, 211, 320
ran, 146, 216, 257, 259–261, 268, 270, 272, 273, 280, 281, 300, 305, 325
rangi, 233–235, 238, 239
rank, 41, 42, 152, 159, 160, 251
ranks, 97, 102, 154, 160, 228
rational, 61, 118, 124, 155
raven, 52, 59, 283
ravening, 12, 14
raw, 90, 289, 304
rays, 39, 126, 171
reach, 21, 39, 48, 64, 80, 84, 98, 125, 172, 201, 219, 223, 239, 282
reached, 21, 38, 84, 88, 97, 98, 143, 207, 230, 257, 259, 260, 264, 266, 267, 269, 272, 282, 283, 298, 303, 325
reaches, 40, 55, 96, 221–223, 226
ready, 17, 18, 26, 28, 29, 84, 93, 111, 112, 138, 146, 228, 256, 257, 259, 263–266, 277, 279, 282, 304, 319
real, 110, 113, 129–131, 136, 295
reality, 112, 131, 165, 301
realm, 215, 222, 224, 225, 235, 313, 314
realms, 65, 222–226
reasons, 115, 116, 119, 120, 128, 137, 149, 159, 224
receded, 52, 120
receive, 112, 116, 122, 130, 140, 151, 156, 159, 186
received, 12, 15, 19, 73, 80, 88, 92, 93, 102, 108, 120–122, 124, 132, 136, 139, 147, 149, 156, 211, 216, 225
receives, 92, 129, 130, 133, 138, 150, 151, 156, 222
receiving, 110, 123, 129, 131, 141, 143, 150, 151, 158, 159

recited, 10, 42, 107, 173, 193, 203
record, 112, 132, 306
recorded, 9, 110, 140, 236
recovered, 111, 112, 134, 142, 300, 318
red, 145, 176, 188–190, 210, 219, 222, 223, 228, 235, 246, 249, 250, 262, 266, 270–272, 274, 278–280, 282–284, 307, 309, 317
reduced, 33, 61, 304
redwoods, 288–290
reed, 31, 286
reeds, 31, 59, 73, 279, 285
refuge, 174, 177, 217, 302, 321
regard, 10, 62, 149, 168
regarded, 94, 127, 130, 140
regarding, 27, 57, 168, 192
regards, 150, 159, 171, 184, 234
region, 65, 109, 111, 140, 143, 159, 161, 162, 191, 198, 208, 216, 224, 314
regions, 77, 159, 162, 164, 168, 174, 175, 197, 198, 208, 212, 225, 226, 314
reign, 76, 93, 100, 101, 132, 134, 212, 249, 307, 309
reigned, 61, 63, 76, 105, 179, 313, 317
reigns, 63, 92, 94, 250, 313
rejoice, 10, 42, 278
rejoiced, 17, 28, 36, 87, 118, 320
relate, 65, 113, 179, 193, 226, 322
related, 57, 108, 111, 118, 125, 151, 160, 179, 296, 299
relations, 62, 148, 249, 298
relative, 107, 120, 129, 153, 177
release, 171
religion, 62, 191, 193, 202, 305
religious, 122, 233, 236

remain, 15, 27, 37, 57, 122, 126, 130, 133, 141, 160, 161, 213, 300, 315
remained, 25, 58, 62, 74, 80, 102, 120, 123, 145, 168, 172, 192, 193, 196, 199, 200, 203, 204, 217, 239, 249, 261, 276, 291, 294, 295, 298, 301–303, 306
remaining, 43, 116, 118, 133, 141, 151, 155, 298
remains, 21, 22, 53, 57, 62, 63, 77, 122, 155, 156, 234, 282
remarked, 111, 120, 143
remember, 54, 59, 97, 107, 109, 111, 114, 132, 138, 226, 319
remnant, 109, 140
remove, 170, 301, 319
removed, 53, 65, 172, 201, 301, 322
renown, 11, 12, 15, 16, 50, 189
repeat, 28, 111
repeated, 10, 63, 107, 132, 179
replied, 108, 170, 187, 301, 303–305
repose, 25, 26, 28
reproduce, 170
reptiles, 38, 61, 168, 203, 206, 234–236
request, 111, 137, 138
require, 53, 128, 157, 303
required, 116, 138, 142, 144, 147
resisted, 12, 14, 16, 237
resolved, 27, 118, 158, 178, 179, 299–301, 303
resorting, 168
resounded, 30, 86, 100, 230
respect, 48, 60, 63, 77, 114, 130, 149, 155, 157, 160, 162
rest, 10, 13, 25, 26, 41, 42, 52, 62,

63, 77, 80, 82, 85, 94, 107, 110–112, 114, 125–127, 129, 137, 141–143, 147, 148, 151, 152, 154, 167, 178, 180–182, 205, 211, 219, 226, 235, 248, 267, 273, 282
rested, 30, 46, 52, 77, 80, 233, 241, 249, 267, 293
resting, 15, 23, 59, 181, 209, 279
restored, 36, 123, 136, 210, 294
rests, 32, 119, 207, 208, 218, 234, 314
result, 33, 131, 133, 136, 153, 157, 279
retreat, 39, 317
return, 13, 48, 62, 70, 108, 112, 121, 123, 124, 127, 134, 158, 172, 192, 197, 215, 223, 236, 296, 297, 302, 315, 316, 323, 324
returned, 30, 52, 59, 62, 63, 67, 75, 123, 172, 216, 300, 316, 318, 323–325
returns, 118, 124, 282
revealed, 27, 28, 44, 57, 88, 128, 137, 138, 183, 191, 311
revenge, 237, 238, 302
reverence, 23, 65, 82, 86, 178
reversal, 133, 134
reverse, 121, 124, 133, 138
reversed, 126, 132, 134, 135
revolves, 78, 119, 132, 152
revolving, 116, 119–121, 154, 171, 204
reward, 171, 175, 176, 192, 201, 202, 301
rhea, 76, 77, 87, 93, 96, 121
rich, 57, 66, 68, 78, 80, 88, 92, 93, 103, 141, 318, 320

ride, 228
ridge, 212, 271–273, 285
right, 17, 29, 30, 41, 42, 67, 80–82, 84, 86, 88, 112, 114, 118, 123, 124, 126, 128, 132, 137, 138, 140, 153, 192, 197, 203, 226, 235, 252, 256, 259, 268, 275, 276, 282, 286, 304, 309, 319, 321
righteous, 32, 50, 81, 84, 173, 195, 198, 203, 205, 206, 212, 230, 319, 321
rightly, 115, 139, 305
rights, 92, 230
rik, 168, 172, 175
rind, 144, 181
ring, 17, 187, 188, 190
rings, 228, 230, 284
ripe, 64, 280, 290
rise, 40–42, 73, 85, 134, 152, 190, 195, 220, 229, 239, 288, 325
rises, 152, 167, 171, 234, 235, 325
rishi, 168, 174, 176, 177
rishis, 164, 166, 171, 173, 174, 176
rising, 58, 153, 156, 171, 205, 250, 261, 285, 296
river, 32, 46, 59, 89, 102, 108, 123, 140, 189, 200, 207, 212, 220, 224, 225, 228, 266, 269, 275, 284, 303, 314
rivers, 58, 59, 76, 86, 91, 109, 138, 141, 144, 147, 199, 200, 206, 207, 215, 223, 225, 228, 265, 269, 275, 276
road, 38, 39, 84, 144, 223, 230, 250, 286, 297, 321
roam, 80, 83, 314, 317
roar, 229, 260, 315

roaring, 26, 215, 217, 220, 222, 260, 264
robes, 82, 149, 175, 177
rock, 90, 99, 141, 145, 241, 260, 266, 268, 271, 277, 281, 286, 287, 297
rocks, 97–99, 217, 221, 222, 225, 227, 229, 240, 260, 261, 264, 266, 267, 285, 286, 288–290, 297, 306, 310, 311
rode, 228, 230
rods, 74, 225, 320
roll, 41, 132, 252, 258, 263
roof, 145, 146, 221
roofs, 141, 145, 300
room, 145, 188, 282
root, 43, 78, 153, 155, 168, 178, 200, 203, 208, 222, 238, 240, 269
rooted, 158, 209, 307
roots, 60, 78, 98, 100, 144, 200, 221, 222, 226, 238, 251, 261–263, 278
rose, 28, 38, 48, 52, 64, 65, 86, 97, 132, 134, 135, 163, 195, 227, 228, 230, 241, 251, 260, 265, 285, 293, 297, 316
rough, 84, 216, 280
round, 42, 78, 85, 88, 97–100, 116, 118, 133, 135, 145, 147, 171, 217, 220, 263, 265, 267, 268, 286, 300, 302, 317, 318
royal, 24, 77, 78, 80, 101, 144, 146, 148, 149, 187, 246
rubbed, 74, 154, 258
rubbing, 73, 184, 258, 274, 284, 295, 304

rudiment, 181
rudra, 181, 182
ruin, 89, 98, 136, 197
rule, 21, 26, 30, 37, 45, 47, 48, 101, 111, 123, 134–136, 143, 151, 164, 175, 187, 196, 221, 230, 307, 316, 320
ruled, 36, 65, 104, 116, 134, 151, 311
ruler, 117, 148, 152, 179, 180, 191, 217, 221, 230, 307, 309
rulers, 24, 57, 143, 230, 309, 311
rules, 81, 92, 94, 100, 135, 149, 164, 230
ruling, 93, 127, 305, 311
run, 79, 111, 152, 203, 229, 250, 256, 257, 268, 272, 277, 280, 284, 289, 309, 318
runner, 257, 325
runs, 98, 222, 272
rush, 31, 100, 101, 194, 198, 203, 220, 257, 260, 306
rushed, 192, 195, 196, 198, 200, 201, 206, 236, 237, 259, 260, 264, 265, 273, 305
rushing, 29, 78, 151, 260

S

sacred, 38, 77, 110, 112, 119, 125, 141, 144, 148, 152, 163, 169, 178, 200, 240, 249, 250, 252, 253, 297, 315
sacrifice, 21, 76, 77, 81, 149, 164, 168, 170–172, 174, 184, 250, 293
sad, 296, 316, 319
safety, 155, 169, 235–237
sagastân, 208
sage, 166, 178, 181
sages, 107, 163, 164, 166, 167, 174, 178, 179

sails, 172, 231
sake, 48, 53, 81, 103, 109, 127, 155, 170, 299, 320
salmon, 276, 287, 289
salt, 67, 74, 155, 159, 207, 216, 244, 245, 288
saluted, 178, 264
salvation, 319–321
sameness, 118, 152, 153, 155
sand, 34, 217, 226, 227, 288, 314, 316, 317
sands, 240, 247, 306
sank, 58, 111, 136, 278, 287, 301, 305
sarai, 56, 66, 69, 70
sari, 61, 63
sas, 270
sat, 11, 13, 28, 57, 58, 173, 228, 243, 251, 256, 266, 275–277, 281, 307, 309
satisfied, 129, 138, 149, 165, 216, 301
save, 27, 57, 59, 180, 217, 223, 224, 236, 282, 321
saved, 57, 64, 194, 284, 320
savitri, 168
sayings, 200, 233, 234
says, 37, 44, 104, 107, 134, 276
scattered, 55, 56, 64, 80, 131, 209, 220, 235, 270, 318
science, 108, 178
scorched, 100, 282–284
scorching, 100, 203, 213, 218
seal, 19, 30, 51, 190, 287
searched, 13, 40, 58, 163
seas, 45, 101, 175, 181, 199, 207, 235
season, 60, 101, 145, 166, 176, 180, 181, 197, 218, 316
seasons, 41, 42, 85, 88, 110, 135, 153, 166, 182, 219, 220, 282, 283
seated, 26, 136, 221
seats, 22, 41, 219, 221, 223
seaweed, 250
secret, 29, 87, 90, 91, 93, 166, 198, 316
sedit, 270, 271
seed, 33–35, 37, 45, 51, 53, 57, 109, 110, 122, 149, 155, 158, 163, 166, 168, 169, 181, 184, 209, 211, 212, 240
seeds, 45, 57, 60, 137, 158, 189, 190, 216, 270, 306
seeing, 61, 120, 136, 151, 152, 176, 184, 239, 296, 300, 305
seek, 112, 139, 166, 177, 219, 220, 223, 225, 230, 231, 236, 315, 318
seem, 124, 137, 189, 305
seemed, 97, 149, 192, 195, 228, 243, 272, 282, 298, 302, 314
seems, 128, 133, 177, 190, 194
seen, 9, 25, 38, 41, 51, 61, 93, 116, 126, 128, 134, 141, 152, 167, 173, 175–177, 184, 186, 189, 190, 192, 200, 201, 205, 218, 251, 267, 268, 272, 297, 298, 322
sees, 23, 41, 125, 203, 221
seized, 29, 30, 79, 81, 93, 97, 99, 100, 102, 104, 199, 207–209, 218, 225, 300, 303, 304, 306
self, 151, 165–167, 183–186, 202
send, 33, 57, 58, 80, 172, 213, 255, 256, 258, 270, 275–277, 299
sends, 99, 203, 204, 235, 249, 314, 316

sensation, 33, 113, 122, 150
sense, 113, 114, 118, 127, 128, 130, 131, 137, 151, 160, 181, 199, 227
senses, 77, 157, 164, 165, 174–177, 179, 182, 305
sensible, 113, 118, 119, 130, 154
sent, 15, 18, 27, 32, 35, 48, 52, 57–59, 62, 63, 76, 80, 93, 94, 172, 183, 201, 216, 218, 219, 224, 250, 255, 256, 266, 269, 270, 276, 278, 279, 282, 283, 305, 315–317, 321, 325, 326
separate, 30, 67, 123, 135, 146, 159, 208
separated, 33, 61, 76, 110, 131, 155, 180, 212, 236, 239
serpent, 38, 39, 47, 181, 202, 211, 229, 230, 319
serpents, 12, 14, 15, 26, 61, 166, 222, 228
servant, 54, 57, 69, 70, 86, 314
servants, 54, 58, 125, 214, 297–299
serve, 81, 91, 236, 238, 295, 296, 302
sesame, 28, 60, 209
seth, 49
settle, 20, 79, 128, 131, 135, 189, 288, 297
settled, 110, 143, 149, 168, 190, 208, 294
shadow, 35, 131, 226, 251
shaken, 93, 97, 131, 135
shakes, 84, 162, 220, 229, 325
shaking, 100, 124, 200, 325
shame, 73, 82
shape, 33, 61, 89, 125, 130, 147, 151, 153, 211, 213, 216, 221, 238, 280

shaped, 87, 217, 218, 220, 221, 280
shapes, 130, 151, 252, 298
share, 79, 92, 131, 135, 151, 162, 169, 224, 317
sharp, 14, 15, 26, 225
sheep, 48, 83, 93, 184, 189, 190, 195, 203, 210, 211
shell, 176, 184, 240, 241, 282, 317
shelter, 163, 174, 189
sheltered, 147, 235, 236
shem, 50, 54, 55
shepherd, 63, 104, 134, 187, 189
shepherds, 109, 110, 134, 139, 152
shield, 148, 228–230
shinar, 55, 68
shine, 40, 43, 152, 218
shining, 41, 94, 100, 216, 219, 221, 230
ship, 51–53, 57–59, 74, 104, 172, 225, 321
ships, 75, 81, 83, 101, 143, 145, 147, 148
shone, 33, 95, 111, 229, 300, 313
shook, 29, 38, 64, 131, 200, 276, 294, 302, 305
shoot, 85, 247, 257, 303, 304
shoots, 169, 170, 247, 256, 306, 317
shore, 81, 141, 207, 215, 237, 288, 303, 315, 316
shores, 207, 217, 220, 236, 316
short, 60, 61, 65, 157, 249, 250, 270, 300, 304
shortly, 108, 223, 301, 309
shot, 38, 39, 100, 246, 251, 257, 279, 301
shoulders, 54, 77, 81, 87, 97, 100, 218, 285
shouted, 9, 97, 192, 195, 236, 265
shouting, 260, 265, 285
show, 96, 137, 138, 237, 259, 304,

showed, 60, 97, 122, 177, 202, 258, 267, 317, 322
shown, 76, 98, 122, 137, 201, 210, 224, 237, 306, 323
shrines, 22, 226, 313, 315
shu, 35–37
shurippak, 57
shut, 13, 58, 323
sickle, 87, 88
sickness, 80, 99, 252, 278
siddim, 67, 68
sides, 97, 141, 151, 153, 154, 158, 172, 194, 199, 206, 260, 265, 299
sidon, 55, 76
sight, 18, 39, 46, 121, 125–127, 141, 151–154, 177, 223, 272, 298, 302, 315, 316, 318
sign, 48, 54, 94, 163, 197, 198, 252, 285, 297, 306
signifies, 65, 73, 75, 109, 218, 238
signs, 45, 157, 158, 213, 251, 320
silence, 58, 118, 159, 166, 240, 250, 266
silent, 166, 215, 221, 224, 278, 323
silver, 57, 66, 81, 91, 99, 142, 145, 155, 162, 211, 221, 223, 300
similar, 60, 63, 90, 124, 129, 131, 132, 136, 151, 155, 158, 279
similarly, 40, 125, 151, 157, 158
sin, 21, 48, 176, 201, 202, 295, 298, 309, 319, 321
sinful, 29, 225
sing, 85, 103, 104, 173
singing, 22, 76, 173, 271, 275, 302
single, 38, 109, 111, 115, 118, 133, 141, 142, 145, 152, 155, 170, 178, 194, 198, 199, 202, 203, 294, 295
sink, 229, 230, 281
sins, 59, 83, 84, 164, 175, 225, 296, 321
sippara, 62, 63
sire, 87, 174, 219, 313, 317
sisithrus, 63
sister, 42, 49, 75, 139, 217, 226, 256, 259, 272, 276, 283, 306
sisters, 76, 223, 229, 277
sit, 12, 14, 164, 172, 221, 225, 228, 256, 263, 279, 280, 306
sits, 78, 83, 92, 102, 220–222, 227, 263, 307, 309
sitting, 149, 266, 271
situated, 57, 60, 65, 76, 110, 145, 148, 155, 297
situation, 61, 138, 178
size, 64, 96, 133, 141, 144, 146, 147, 153, 206, 249, 263, 295
skies, 64, 234, 235
skill, 65, 111, 137
skilled, 18, 42, 89, 102, 178, 293
skin, 90, 175, 181, 219, 249, 251, 271, 273–275, 285
skins, 48, 73, 218, 275, 278
skuld, 223, 227, 228
skull, 30, 218
slain, 29, 49, 105, 174, 176, 225, 228, 229
slay, 28, 90, 229, 233, 234, 237
slayer, 79, 174, 229, 231
sleep, 46, 77, 80, 88, 98, 125, 126, 131, 176, 204, 219, 222, 226, 250, 274, 283, 324
slept, 46, 77, 173, 250, 287, 314, 324
sling, 265, 266, 269

slit, 37, 217, 325, 326
slope, 272, 273
sloping, 261, 262
slowly, 120, 234, 264, 326
small, 23, 109, 112, 123, 127, 136, 141, 142, 148, 166, 168, 179, 194, 196, 199, 207, 209, 210, 215, 239, 250, 258, 267, 268, 271, 276, 284, 287–291, 296, 299, 302, 306, 310, 324
smaller, 134, 143, 269, 303, 304
smallest, 133, 179, 189, 190, 210
smell, 41, 181, 189, 190
smiling, 95, 108, 314–316
smite, 27–29, 201
smitten, 38, 100, 227, 230
smoke, 79, 196, 204, 260, 261, 263, 268, 272, 283, 284, 293, 295
smooth, 84, 116, 125, 126, 130, 134, 147, 152, 259, 274
snake, 90, 91, 100, 195, 196, 203, 229, 276, 279, 284, 293
snakes, 166, 168, 284, 289, 291, 293
snare, 29, 273
snarled, 25, 26, 29
snow, 155, 230, 274, 275, 285, 290
socrates, 107, 111–114, 132–135, 137, 138
sodom, 55, 67, 68
soft, 84, 89, 91, 130, 135, 219, 239, 282, 315
soil, 139, 141, 143, 146, 316, 318
solid, 115, 123, 144, 151, 154, 279, 281, 293, 299
solon, 107–109, 111, 112, 139, 140, 142, 147
soma, 164, 168, 172–174, 184
sometimes, 109, 266, 274

song, 84–86, 102, 173, 313, 315
soon, 79, 86–88, 93, 111, 138, 168, 170, 217, 228, 229, 235, 238, 249, 256–261, 263, 267, 270, 272, 273, 275, 279, 280, 284, 285, 295, 303, 304
sore, 23, 82, 88, 99, 228
sorrow, 11, 25, 27, 79–82, 85, 86, 219, 224, 314, 316, 317
sorry, 50, 262, 277
sort, 51, 84, 110, 125, 135, 138, 140, 144, 191, 286
sorts, 124, 144, 146, 147, 189, 290, 299
sosini, 264, 265
sotchet, 264, 266
sought, 118, 170, 174, 225–228, 234, 236–238, 252, 298, 303, 309, 311, 317
soul, 40, 44, 46, 86, 114, 116–118, 122–127, 135, 151, 152, 155, 158, 167, 173–177, 179–181, 197, 204, 227, 315
souls, 39, 122, 127, 139, 142, 155, 175, 176, 195, 218, 222, 223, 320
sound, 33, 64, 85, 86, 97, 100, 127, 138, 146, 159, 179, 181, 209, 240, 252, 269, 285, 297, 305
sounding, 213
sounds, 100, 317
source, 46, 80, 126, 127, 129, 145, 164, 170, 174, 176, 207, 215, 218, 233, 241
sources, 155, 199, 206, 207
south, 17, 66, 77, 147, 172, 194, 198, 200, 207, 208, 215,

218, 226, 229, 235,
260–262, 264–266, 268,
270–272, 274, 275, 285,
286, 288, 290, 297, 298,
306, 307
southeast, 259, 261, 262, 270
southern, 41, 142, 207, 223, 268
southward, 215, 216, 269
southwest, 255, 259, 260, 268
sown, 122, 123, 135
space, 61, 63, 131, 150, 162, 174,
188, 191, 200, 202, 215,
216, 219, 233, 240, 259
spark, 220, 268
sparks, 216, 261, 317
spawned, 14, 15
speak, 12, 17, 25, 27, 28, 84, 85,
97, 108, 111, 112, 124,
126–129, 137, 199, 224,
230, 263, 285, 309
speaking, 82, 86, 108, 111, 113,
116, 117, 121, 129, 138,
141, 143, 165, 181, 184
speaks, 173, 313, 315
spear, 17, 75, 198, 205, 227
spears, 88, 110, 225, 227, 236
special, 112, 135, 143, 149, 209,
280
species, 61, 119, 120, 134, 209, 210,
246
speckled, 82, 90, 250
speech, 49, 56, 80, 86, 127, 172,
173, 184, 224, 228, 279,
298, 309, 320, 322
speedily, 28, 177, 301, 305
spell, 12, 14, 18, 29, 37
spenta, 188
sphere, 114, 118, 120, 151–154,
193, 196, 202, 204
spherical, 116, 125

spider, 248, 284
spirit, 10, 12, 14, 25, 34, 44, 50, 52,
76, 81, 85, 95–99, 101,
104, 115, 163, 178–182,
187, 191–193, 195–201,
205–207, 213, 217, 280,
281, 319, 322
spirits, 26, 28, 32, 38, 58, 59, 80,
81, 83, 149, 174, 191, 194,
198, 201, 205, 206, 239,
313, 314, 316
spiritual, 162, 178, 192, 194, 212,
221, 326
splendid, 33, 41, 92, 103, 112, 303
splendor, 12, 14, 15, 21, 26, 32, 36,
41, 152, 159, 171, 191,
263, 318, 319
split, 20, 30, 204, 259, 286, 287
spoken, 26, 64, 119, 126, 128, 137,
150, 173, 324
spot, 110, 116, 121, 145, 260
spouse, 15, 25, 239, 300
sprang, 34, 36, 37, 80, 87–89, 91,
96, 97, 121, 134, 139, 164,
175, 185, 195, 198, 210,
220, 233, 240, 250, 309
sprayed, 216, 218
spread, 18, 29, 36, 88, 95, 160, 210,
220, 221, 240, 243, 246,
247, 249, 250, 265, 267,
274, 277, 282, 285, 287,
305, 309, 318
spring, 23, 79, 84, 89, 129, 143,
175, 176, 197, 218, 250,
257, 275, 276, 288, 289,
321, 323
springs, 90, 143, 220, 222, 234, 282,
283, 288, 290, 294, 325
sprout, 246, 247, 253
sprung, 31, 33, 34, 46, 81, 85, 96,

173, 290, 318
square, 115, 147, 154, 189, 190
stable, 41, 158, 179
stadia, 62, 143, 145–147
stadium, 145–147
stage, 114, 124, 134
stand, 10, 12, 18, 27, 30, 35, 37, 92, 111, 228, 230, 234, 235, 250, 263, 272, 280, 287, 289, 322
standing, 11, 94, 145, 171, 202, 216, 243, 285, 302
stands, 64, 98, 207, 212, 217, 220, 228–230, 271
star, 30, 76, 91, 119, 122, 123, 152, 197, 198, 202–204, 208, 217
starry, 30, 78, 86, 87, 92, 93, 97–99, 101, 241
stars, 20, 30, 33, 41, 42, 44, 61, 69, 78, 86, 119–122, 126, 132, 134, 152, 153, 157, 162, 175, 190, 193, 194, 197, 202, 218, 219, 226, 229, 261, 294, 295, 297, 302, 307, 313
start, 177, 256, 259, 264
started, 195, 260, 264, 267, 268, 290, 325
state, 35, 37, 110, 113, 123, 127, 130, 131, 136, 141, 149, 150, 154, 186, 192, 204, 318
station, 20, 30, 197, 202, 203, 208
stations, 30, 226
statue, 74, 298
stature, 12, 14, 15, 26, 136, 211, 298
stay, 96, 176, 189, 190, 256, 257, 266, 267, 271, 274, 275,
304
stayed, 203, 251, 256, 257, 267, 268, 270, 276, 278
stays, 98, 263, 272
steadfast, 58, 104, 316
steal, 228, 231
steam, 229, 272
steed, 211, 219, 223
steeds, 29, 108, 218, 225
steep, 84, 235, 314
stench, 199, 209, 212, 225, 243
stepped, 287, 321
stick, 172, 255, 325
sticks, 221, 259, 304
stirred, 9, 15, 97, 118, 129, 220
stole, 79, 95, 172, 272, 315, 316
stolen, 79, 172, 259
stone, 29, 55, 85, 93, 94, 128, 145, 229, 252, 265, 266, 269, 297, 298, 303, 306, 309, 321
stones, 76, 128, 145, 217, 226, 288, 289, 291, 295, 298, 305, 321
stood, 15, 21, 27, 29, 59, 97, 136, 148, 195, 197, 199, 202, 203, 215, 216, 228, 237, 240, 250, 251, 256–258, 263, 265, 266, 268, 273, 278, 286–289, 293, 304
stop, 10, 262, 266, 272, 273, 277, 288
stopped, 52, 56, 80, 124, 256, 270, 285, 287, 304
stories, 132, 135, 142
storm, 29, 58, 98, 136
storms, 74, 219, 228, 234–238
story, 11, 57, 107, 108, 132, 134, 162, 324
stout, 90, 97, 103

straight, 12, 78, 83, 147, 214, 259, 261, 265, 268
straits, 110, 111, 136
strange, 107, 128, 131, 145, 220, 279, 281, 305, 314, 316, 317
stranger, 65, 132–135, 234
stream, 91, 99, 103, 109, 124–126, 189, 227, 289, 305
streams, 18, 97, 99, 100, 141, 142, 147, 200, 216, 282, 289, 290, 313, 317
streets, 189, 190
strength, 12, 26, 38, 42, 44, 48, 64, 79, 81, 82, 87, 90–92, 96–98, 100–102, 111, 194, 198–200, 203, 204, 209, 216, 219, 224, 228, 237, 251, 257, 299, 303
stretch, 188, 240, 286
stretched, 73, 88, 215, 216, 274, 286, 309, 322
stricken, 27, 29, 217
strife, 13, 21, 67, 78, 89, 96–100, 102, 159, 200–202, 216, 222, 231, 247, 252
strike, 53, 282
stripped, 251, 273, 274, 300
strong, 10, 15, 26, 28, 36, 78, 81, 85, 87, 88, 90, 93, 96–100, 103, 104, 181, 202, 204, 218, 258, 259, 265, 266, 272, 273, 280, 283, 286, 298
stronger, 40, 82, 102, 198, 205, 258, 266, 274, 277
struck, 67, 94, 100, 207, 252, 260, 261, 266, 269, 282, 283, 285, 300, 304, 325
struggle, 101, 196, 201

struggles, 204, 212, 234
stuck, 261, 269, 285
styx, 91, 92, 99
subdued, 30, 175, 241
subject, 43, 90, 103, 104, 112, 117, 119, 121, 124, 133, 137, 155, 158–160, 182, 314
sublime, 40, 212
submerged, 239, 294, 311
subsist, 156, 159, 162, 169
substance, 36, 40, 60, 122, 125, 130, 152, 154, 160, 178–180, 200, 202, 208, 212, 216
subtle, 34, 178, 179
succeed, 39, 180, 211
succeeded, 63, 75, 301
sucked, 217, 228, 309, 316
sudden, 135, 162, 306
suddenly, 102, 220, 223, 302
suffer, 20, 122, 218, 258, 309
suffered, 83, 89, 116, 203, 205, 224
suffers, 82, 83, 99
suitable, 111, 112, 116, 119, 123, 127, 140, 142, 146, 155, 210, 211
suited, 96, 112, 116, 132, 238
sula, 265, 275
summer, 53, 109, 142, 147, 197, 219, 228, 256, 270, 275, 283, 286
summit, 21, 57, 142, 220, 293, 300
sundered, 229, 314
sung, 33, 41, 78
sunk, 139, 141, 174, 175
sunlight, 58, 316
sunrise, 152, 171, 259, 260, 272, 313
superior, 65, 122, 151, 152, 173, 174

supply, 79, 140–142
support, 125, 140, 162, 175, 179, 240, 251, 261
suppose, 112, 114, 128, 129, 132, 135, 139
supposed, 73, 114, 133
supreme, 24, 31, 32, 44, 85, 121, 135, 173, 174, 177–182, 191, 205
sure, 86, 87, 111, 118, 174, 303, 314
surface, 44–46, 48, 50–52, 55, 56, 62, 115, 116, 126, 130, 154, 215, 279, 282, 302, 318
surprised, 111, 114, 142, 300
surt, 229
survivors, 109, 133, 139
sutunut, 264
swallow, 59, 102, 219, 236
swam, 210, 243, 244, 265, 284
sway, 101, 136, 144, 146, 187
sweat, 39, 48, 84, 174, 196, 203, 216, 257–259, 261–267, 269, 270, 275, 276, 278, 305
sweet, 59, 79, 82, 85–88, 157, 159, 203, 219, 223, 238, 262, 289, 309
swept, 58, 88, 199, 215, 236, 259
swift, 18, 34, 80, 104, 223, 225, 256
swiftly, 15, 82, 88, 93, 219, 260, 265, 272, 304
swiftness, 118–120, 157, 243
swim, 264, 265, 283, 289
swimming, 210, 237, 265, 266
sword, 48, 75, 90, 223, 226, 229
sycamore, 283, 284
sydyc, 74, 76, 77
symbol, 77, 306

T

taaroa, 240
taautus, 74, 77
tablet, 12, 15, 32, 149
tablets, 26, 30, 221
tail, 60, 99, 248, 249, 264, 266, 279, 288
tails, 61, 197, 207, 211
taitai, 269–271
take, 17, 21, 48, 51, 61, 62, 68, 80, 82, 83, 116, 125, 129, 130, 135, 138, 149, 162, 173, 176, 204, 219, 223, 237, 247, 256–259, 262, 264, 265, 268, 269, 271, 275, 277, 279, 297, 301, 309, 318, 323, 324
taken, 19, 26, 36, 40, 47, 48, 74, 75, 114, 116, 139, 141, 164, 177, 185, 204, 209, 257, 269, 278, 290, 297, 302, 306
takes, 38, 92, 96, 129, 133, 169–171, 182
taking, 26, 62, 116, 155, 293, 297
tale, 107, 108, 111, 112, 114, 132, 134–136, 142, 227
tales, 109, 201, 224, 226
talk, 230, 259, 262, 263, 269, 286, 309, 324
talked, 70, 234, 255, 257, 270, 277
talking, 255, 259, 271, 275
tall, 196, 203, 206, 246, 250, 253, 265, 286, 288
tane, 234, 236–238
tangaroa, 234–238
tangible, 113, 115, 160
tanned, 274
tanning, 274, 275
tartarus, 34, 87, 97–101

task, 112, 119, 128, 155, 314, 316, 317
taste, 99, 157, 159, 181
taught, 60, 65, 73, 74, 85, 110, 187, 238, 313, 315, 317, 320
teach, 79, 111, 187, 299, 314
tear, 17, 57, 233, 234, 323
tears, 36, 37, 58, 234, 239
tede, 265, 266, 268
teeth, 27, 29, 88, 211, 217, 223, 276, 277, 288, 299–301, 309
tefnut, 35–37
tell, 14, 28, 39, 78, 86, 91, 107, 108, 110, 112–114, 121, 127, 134, 136, 142, 164, 167, 174, 227, 255, 263, 264, 267, 269–272, 281, 304, 305, 315, 324–326
telling, 85, 87, 107, 271
tells, 83, 109, 132, 149, 313
tempest, 17, 18, 26, 58, 123, 216
tempests, 25, 26, 29, 217
temple, 21, 61, 74, 75, 145, 146, 148, 149
temples, 40, 60, 62, 82, 109, 142–144, 146, 149, 224, 226
temu, 39, 40
tend, 60, 74, 83, 96, 139, 155, 157, 315
tender, 84, 103, 136, 222
tent, 54, 66
tents, 54, 67
terah, 56, 321
term, 63, 115, 125, 154, 171
termed, 130, 133, 141, 178, 180–182, 233
terms, 115, 117, 151, 152, 154
terrible, 81, 87, 98–100, 102, 192, 219, 225, 230, 258, 260, 263, 265, 300
terribly, 97, 100, 258
territory, 143, 201, 297, 298
terror, 12, 14, 15, 26, 27, 29, 32, 40, 41, 206, 220, 228, 317
testimony, 114, 132, 140, 309
tethys, 87, 91, 102
thallus, 104, 105
thankful, 137, 314, 316
thaumas, 89, 99
thick, 33, 58, 84, 94, 97, 189, 220, 235, 240, 258, 287, 299
think, 26, 80, 84, 116, 121, 133, 157, 164, 171, 185, 201, 257, 258, 270, 275, 278, 301, 304, 314, 316
thinking, 95, 111, 149, 165, 184, 185, 233, 259, 264
thor, 219, 223, 227
thorns, 218, 224, 318
thought, 75, 80, 87, 88, 95, 107, 111, 119, 120, 126, 146, 163, 167, 168, 183, 184, 193, 196, 234, 237, 239, 264, 270, 279–281, 283, 296, 309, 316, 324
thoughts, 50, 83, 89, 103, 121, 131, 164, 178, 195, 234, 235
threshold, 98, 100, 252
threw, 75, 255, 260, 265–267, 269–271, 276, 278, 279, 287, 289, 297, 300, 304, 317
thrived, 144, 251, 253
throne, 17, 28, 38, 40, 41, 221, 307, 309, 321
throng, 229
throw, 132, 248, 265, 269, 277, 284, 318

thrown, 37, 217, 240, 245, 249, 267, 287, 299, 306
thunder, 29, 33, 58, 79, 87, 90, 93, 94, 97, 98, 100, 223, 285–287, 316
thundered, 58, 100, 286
tiamat, 9–16, 18, 21, 22, 25–30
tichelis, 259, 260
tidings, 202, 322
tied, 169, 265, 268, 318
tilikus, 256, 259–261, 268
tilitchi, 268, 269, 276
timaeus, 112, 114, 137, 138, 150
timber, 141
times, 41, 49, 60, 73, 74, 108, 109, 117, 132, 135, 140, 141, 154, 170, 174–176, 219, 227, 233, 238, 239, 251, 294, 298, 300, 306
tip, 271, 309
titan, 64, 65, 92, 96–98, 104, 105
titans, 74, 88, 92, 96–98, 100, 101, 104, 105
toil, 50, 78, 80, 96, 104
toko, 265, 266, 275
told, 20, 54, 62, 66, 79, 85, 87, 93, 107, 111, 112, 132, 135, 142, 147, 177, 227, 256, 257, 259, 262, 267, 272, 274, 278, 280–283, 286–289, 291, 298, 299, 301, 316, 323–326
tongue, 42, 86, 108, 181, 309
tongues, 64, 100, 220, 224, 294
tooth, 14, 15, 26, 189, 190
top, 21, 55, 64, 83, 84, 141, 148, 200, 208, 236, 256, 259, 260, 262, 263, 265, 269, 271, 283–285, 288, 300, 320

tops, 52, 189, 246, 299, 300
torches, 58, 260, 261, 317
tore, 29, 228, 234, 299, 314
torihas, 255–260, 272, 275
torn, 136, 208, 224, 225, 233–235, 237
torture, 222, 224–226
total, 43, 147, 148
touch, 47, 151, 154, 159, 160, 179, 181, 261, 265, 276
touched, 146, 240, 276, 315, 317
touches, 125, 260, 261, 267
toward, 55, 66, 69, 259–266, 270, 272–274, 276, 288, 294, 304, 305, 309
tower, 21, 55, 64
town, 40, 296, 309, 310, 317
tradition, 108, 109, 132, 134, 137, 139, 149, 326
trained, 18, 29, 202
tranquil, 237, 294, 295
travel, 83, 223, 224, 230, 264, 272, 274, 275, 287
traveled, 38, 55, 66, 224, 285, 290
traveling, 70, 76, 299
treasures, 201, 202, 213
trembled, 18, 26, 38, 100
triangle, 129, 153, 154
tribe, 64, 88, 95, 107, 221, 249, 251
tribes, 90, 95, 114, 122, 178, 223, 297
tried, 108, 170, 172, 237, 283, 288, 296, 300
tries, 82
triple, 65, 98, 152, 153
triumph, 19, 30, 193, 198, 202, 217, 225
troops, 12, 14, 16, 18
trouble, 82, 83, 95, 99, 119, 259, 263, 284, 318

troubled, 9, 18, 25, 29, 197, 220
troubles, 25, 89, 108
trout, 275, 287, 289, 290
true, 78, 79, 83, 85, 86, 107, 110,
    113, 121, 124, 130, 131,
    133, 140, 141, 149, 151,
    162, 179, 182, 186, 202,
    305, 309
trust, 26, 28, 62, 137, 322
truth, 41, 42, 113, 118, 119, 124,
    127, 128, 131, 141, 164,
    173, 175, 230, 285, 313,
    319
try, 128, 133, 237, 268, 280, 287,
    289, 290, 305
trying, 94, 260, 273, 279, 284
tsaroki, 256, 260, 261
tsurat, 269, 270, 278
tubal, 49, 54
tun, 309
turn, 86, 112, 120, 138, 151, 154,
    171, 219, 225, 237, 243,
    263, 264, 272, 273, 275,
    299, 300, 305, 314, 315
turned, 13, 15, 27–29, 38, 48, 58,
    126, 134, 136, 143, 173,
    199, 217, 241, 257, 258,
    262, 264, 266, 271, 273,
    274, 280, 282, 289, 295,
    299, 300, 303, 316, 322
turning, 118, 135, 264, 267, 268,
    277, 301
turns, 132, 133, 151, 197, 229
turtle, 247, 279, 280
tutu, 23, 24, 57
twilight, 215, 216, 226, 280
twin, 143, 150, 280
twins, 143, 251, 300
twisted, 124, 237, 265
typhoeus, 100

tyre, 73, 74, 76

U

ugly, 280, 281, 288
uinal, 311
unable, 30, 58, 131, 149, 170, 321
unborn, 179, 223, 315
unchanged, 27, 133, 179
uncle, 259, 263, 266, 267
under, 18, 19, 30, 36, 41, 44, 51, 52,
    58, 60, 65, 70, 74, 77, 80,
    82, 85, 90, 93, 94, 96–100,
    109, 117, 134–136, 141,
    153, 155, 160, 175–177,
    187, 189, 216–218, 224,
    226, 227, 234, 260,
    267–270, 279, 282, 285,
    295, 303, 318–320, 325
undivided, 118, 152
undying, 88–90, 97
unequal, 118, 153, 181
unfolded, 309
union, 33, 35, 37, 85, 87, 96, 102,
    115, 126, 167–169, 280
united, 61, 78, 118, 124, 139, 151,
    155, 181, 194, 302
unity, 43, 119, 181
universal, 78, 115, 122, 129,
    135–137, 158–160, 176,
    178, 180, 182
unknown, 65, 109, 230, 245
unlike, 116, 120, 125, 132
unlimited, 191
unmoving, 166, 192, 202
unrivaled, 14, 17, 191
untiring, 94, 98, 100, 102
unwilling, 230, 231, 259
unworthy, 114, 220, 224, 225
upper, 97, 126, 149, 200, 255, 282,
    296

upright, 169, 170, 224, 285, 322
upside, 124, 126
urd, 217, 222–226
utter, 81, 84, 85, 137, 205, 315
uttered, 10, 12, 14, 18, 26, 28, 29, 39, 100, 127, 168, 193
uttering, 30, 39, 42, 85, 86
utterly, 205, 206, 220, 302, 316, 322

V

vásudeva, 177–179
vîvanghat, 187–190
vâk, 172, 173
vaêgô, 189
vain, 121, 127, 173, 234, 236, 287, 322
vaisyas, 174, 175
vales, 228, 314, 315
valkyries, 225, 228
valley, 67, 68, 224, 225, 282, 285, 289, 290, 309, 315
valleys, 239, 268, 287, 289–291, 297, 311
vanished, 17, 28, 301, 315
vapor, 97, 100, 128, 215, 216
vara, 189–191
varied, 79, 148, 177, 290, 298
variety, 60, 120, 130, 131, 140, 143, 209
vast, 34, 61, 73, 78, 87, 93, 97, 111, 123, 133, 140, 147, 149, 176, 181, 215, 217, 233, 235, 238, 239
vedas, 165, 173, 175, 178, 180
vegetable, 209, 236
vengeance, 48, 88, 231, 258, 297, 302
venom, 12, 14, 15, 29, 39, 40, 199, 205, 215, 224, 225, 227, 228

venture, 74, 284
vessel, 57, 58, 62, 63, 124, 125, 131, 139
vessels, 59, 145, 146, 293, 317
vexed, 75, 87, 95, 195
victory, 91, 92, 96, 166, 177, 204, 205, 217, 219
view, 113, 116, 127, 130, 135
vigor, 206, 208, 309
vigorous, 37, 84, 199, 201, 206
village, 65, 258, 278
villages, 74, 147
violence, 51, 81, 82, 84, 104, 134, 192, 198, 217
vipers, 12, 15, 26
viracocha, 295–299
virgin, 75, 76, 83
virtue, 110, 111, 125, 139, 140, 149, 175, 176, 309
virtues, 138, 140, 142
vishn, 178–182
visible, 44, 52, 113–115, 118, 120, 121, 123, 126, 128, 130, 152, 179, 267, 322
vision, 61, 125, 126
vital, 119, 171
voice, 47–49, 60, 62, 69, 79, 84–86, 127, 164, 181, 280, 297, 311, 314, 315
void, 163, 184, 191, 216, 251, 314

W

wage, 27, 235
waged, 26, 198, 217, 236
waiolola, 241, 242, 244–246, 248, 250
waiololi, 241, 242, 244–246, 248, 250
wait, 27, 247, 266, 304, 315
waited, 52, 273, 302

waiting, 174, 302, 314
wakea, 252, 253
wakes, 176, 177, 228
wakpohas, 261, 263, 272
walk, 89, 212, 281, 290, 309
walked, 50, 172, 197, 210, 224, 250, 263, 274, 279, 280, 285, 286, 289, 290, 309, 320, 326
walking, 47, 116, 200, 202, 210, 220, 280, 291
walks, 84, 124, 172
wall, 40, 75, 98, 145, 146, 220, 227
walls, 74, 83, 145, 228, 288
wandering, 123, 218, 280, 281, 303
want, 130, 138, 168, 196, 256, 257, 259–263, 267, 271, 276, 277, 285, 317, 323
wanted, 50, 139, 195, 258, 274, 280, 318
wants, 140, 152, 201, 277
war, 11, 14, 15, 26–29, 64, 65, 67, 75, 76, 78, 81, 83, 96–98, 102, 104, 105, 109, 110, 134, 139, 140, 148, 149, 198, 227, 235–237, 314, 315
ward, 37, 220, 223
warfare, 202, 217
warlike, 90, 111, 142, 194, 227
warm, 143, 146, 239, 274, 290, 317
warmth, 163, 215, 216, 222
warned, 61, 188, 236
warrior, 12, 57, 59, 140, 142, 205, 212, 219, 249
warriors, 110, 198, 205, 224, 225
washed, 84, 141, 175, 215, 217, 228, 236, 247, 266, 285
waste, 79, 115, 116, 158, 215, 314, 315

watch, 80, 83, 99, 146, 187, 198, 204, 205, 226, 247, 268, 272, 273, 283, 315, 317
watched, 93, 268, 272, 273, 280, 313, 317
watches, 212, 223, 272
watching, 77, 256, 264, 265, 268, 272, 273, 281, 296, 304
waters, 9, 25, 30, 32, 33, 39, 41, 44, 45, 51–54, 58–60, 62, 76, 91, 123, 146, 173–175, 181, 189, 190, 200, 206, 215, 217, 220, 222, 243, 245, 246, 250, 285, 287, 293, 296, 299, 311, 315, 316
watery, 33, 34, 36, 120, 206
waves, 89, 100, 223, 226, 229, 235, 236, 260, 261, 265, 285, 304, 314–316
ways, 10, 20, 86, 124, 127, 131, 224
weak, 29, 317
wealth, 78, 80, 86, 92, 95, 103, 144, 149, 165, 178, 184, 238, 318
weapon, 12, 14, 15, 17, 18, 28, 29, 32, 102, 257
weapons, 12, 14, 15, 18, 26, 29, 30, 110, 148, 166, 202, 224, 298
wear, 212, 271
weary, 79, 137, 219, 224
weeping, 58, 83, 307, 317
wept, 36, 307
west, 17, 66, 132, 152, 153, 194, 197–199, 218, 235, 260–263, 265–267, 269–274, 276, 282, 286, 306, 307
western, 152, 219, 226, 262, 273

wet, 227, 228, 247, 271, 282
whirling, 58, 97, 217, 220
whirlwind, 12, 14, 17, 29, 64
whistle, 264, 265
white, 40, 42, 82, 88, 94–96, 129, 134, 145, 159, 176, 199, 203, 209–211, 216, 220, 222, 225, 227, 261, 262, 264, 265, 272, 274–276, 278, 279, 284, 289, 290, 301, 306, 307, 309
wholly, 78, 124, 134, 165, 194, 325
wicked, 18, 82, 83, 175, 195, 203, 205, 217, 222, 224, 225, 277
wide, 19, 29, 58, 83, 85, 86, 91, 93, 94, 97–101, 103, 220, 258, 263, 309, 314, 316, 318
width, 51, 145–147
wife, 35, 47–49, 51, 52, 56, 59, 62, 66, 69, 73, 74, 90, 92, 96, 102–104, 143, 184, 217, 219, 243, 247, 249, 252, 295, 300, 301
wild, 31, 74, 75, 136, 144, 147, 210, 228, 229, 238, 273, 298
wildly, 235
willing, 122, 129, 140, 142, 259, 277, 279, 323, 324
wills, 78, 84, 92, 93, 193
wima, 276, 277
win, 219, 231, 314
wind, 17–19, 29, 33, 41, 52, 58, 73, 74, 162, 168, 173, 175, 181, 187, 198–200, 206–208, 213, 219, 220, 228, 266, 272, 278, 284–286, 293, 299, 313, 316, 317
window, 52, 58, 190

winds, 17, 18, 28, 29, 33, 41, 64, 89, 98–100, 213, 220, 234, 235, 238, 287, 317
wine, 28, 54, 148, 209, 296, 313, 317
wings, 34, 42, 61, 77, 220, 222, 230, 264, 265, 282, 317
wini, 269, 275, 276
winter, 53, 109, 142, 146, 147, 189, 198, 219, 241, 270, 275, 283
winters, 187–189, 204
wisdom, 65, 91, 95, 97, 110, 135, 139, 149, 155, 179, 182, 194, 201, 213, 222, 227, 228, 231, 314, 315
wise, 25, 27, 31, 47, 57, 80, 85–87, 90, 93, 94, 101, 114, 165, 179, 217, 222, 227, 228, 240, 301, 316, 317
wisest, 101, 107, 110, 123, 314
wish, 122, 130, 151, 178, 188, 195, 249, 258, 259, 261, 266, 272, 277, 304, 321
wished, 39, 184, 188, 190, 198, 235, 262, 277, 301
wishes, 171, 173
wishing, 108, 137, 164
wit, 92, 94, 269, 270
withstand, 11, 12, 14, 15, 82
wiu, 266, 268
wives, 49–51, 56, 75, 146, 228, 317
wokwuk, 266, 271
wolf, 195, 203, 225, 228, 229
women, 36, 37, 73, 83, 95, 96, 104, 135, 140, 142, 146, 172, 173, 189, 190, 223, 224, 227, 255, 256, 261–263, 265, 267, 269–272, 274–277, 287, 296

wonder, 95, 177, 220, 221, 255, 287, 314, 321
wonderful, 91, 95, 100, 110, 111, 129, 132, 146, 173, 177, 200, 224, 257, 263, 297, 298, 300, 304, 314
wondrous, 144, 177
wood, 51, 59, 63, 73, 97, 141, 144, 147, 220, 227, 238, 261, 273, 295, 299, 304, 306, 309, 320, 321, 325
woods, 138, 144, 228, 300, 317, 320
word, 15, 17, 18, 22, 36, 42, 69, 85, 87, 97, 109, 121, 123, 129, 157, 239, 309, 311, 317, 321, 322
words, 12, 15–18, 26–29, 35–40, 59, 62, 64, 74, 75, 79, 82, 86, 89, 101, 109, 111–113, 122, 126, 128–130, 137, 140, 147, 159, 166, 193, 201, 205, 227, 269, 277, 315, 316, 322, 325
work, 20, 21, 25, 27, 35, 46, 50, 64, 78, 79, 95, 97, 101, 113, 114, 122, 127, 144, 145, 147, 155, 169, 182, 186, 196, 199, 231, 237, 241, 261, 267, 268, 273, 279, 281, 283, 296, 297
worked, 21, 35–37, 40, 79, 95, 221, 320
workers, 58, 126, 228
working, 79, 155, 274, 298
works, 20, 39, 81, 87, 101, 103, 118, 122, 127, 171, 196, 201, 202, 204, 212
worlds, 115, 164, 168, 173, 174, 176, 187, 221, 226, 228
worn, 233, 281, 285

worse, 38, 155–158
worship, 64, 164, 165, 175, 176, 184–186, 227, 297, 298, 305, 314, 321, 322
worshiped, 74, 176, 224, 305
worships, 185, 186
worthy, 82, 107, 122, 169
woven, 212, 236, 262
wrapped, 82, 83, 93, 98, 262, 299, 306
wrath, 15, 27, 32, 59, 94–96, 175, 217, 224, 235, 237
writing, 74, 139, 142, 148
writings, 60, 62, 63
written, 60, 109, 156, 202, 210, 306
wrong, 69, 83, 92, 130, 137, 192, 213, 214, 258
wrote, 32, 60, 149, 322
wrought, 75, 135, 145, 219, 226, 320

X

xbalanque, 300–305
xisuthrus, 61, 62

Y

yahweh, 46–48, 50, 51, 53–56, 66, 68–70
yama, 166, 174
yawning, 221, 226, 315
year, 20, 30, 51, 53, 60, 67, 76, 79, 81, 85, 98, 99, 120, 147, 148, 152, 153, 164, 172, 190, 197, 198, 206, 275, 283, 294
yellow, 159, 176, 177, 210, 250, 288, 289, 300, 306, 307, 309
ygdrasil, 221, 222, 224
yield, 40, 48, 252, 314, 315
yielded, 45, 140, 237, 317
yilahl, 267–269, 272

yima, 187–191
ymer, 216–218, 220
yoga, 165, 173, 174
yoholmit, 264–266
yonot, 256, 259–261, 268
young, 31, 49, 57, 68, 69, 93, 103, 108, 132–135, 195, 211, 236, 247, 261, 279–281, 283, 301, 302, 313, 314, 317, 318
younger, 116, 119, 123, 143, 150, 162, 250, 252, 273, 280, 281, 314
youngest, 54, 76, 87, 93, 100, 252, 317
youth, 53, 103, 107, 134, 218, 313
youths, 74, 91, 134, 302

Z

zeboiim, 55, 67, 68
zillah, 49
zion, 319–321
zipacna, 300–303
zone, 145, 146
zones, 143–146

You May Also Like...

ISBN: 978-1-7343000-2-4

THANK YOU FOR READING.

*"A reader lives a thousand lives before he dies...
The man who never reads lives only one."*
– George R.R. Martin

www.ingramcontent.com/pod-product-compliance
Lightning Source LLC
Chambersburg PA
CBHW051032160426
43193CB00010B/919